Rekindling the Flame

Published in cooperation with the Judah L. Magnes Museum—Berkeley.

Rekindling the Flame

 American Jewish Chaplains and the Survivors of European Jewry, 1944-1948

Alex Grobman

WAYNE STATE UNIVERSITY PRESS   Detroit

Copyright © 1993 by Wayne State University Press,
Detroit, Michigan 48202. All rights are reserved.
No part of this book may be reproduced without formal permission.
Manufactured in the United States of America.

99 98 97 96 95 94 93   5 4 3 2 1

Library of Congress Cataloging-in-Publication Data

Grobman, Alex.
    Rekindling the flame : American Jewish chaplains and the survivors of European Jewry, 1944–1948 / Alex Grobman.
      p.   cm.
    Includes bibliographical references and index.
    ISBN 0-8143-2413-4 (alk. paper)
    1. World War, 1939–1945—Chaplains—United States. 2. Rabbis--United States. 3. Holocaust survivors. I. Title.
D810.C36U47 1993
940.54'78—dc20   92-28678

Designer: Joanne Elkin Kinney
Cover art: Babenhausen, October 1946. Photo courtesy of the Mintzer Collection, Magnes Museum.
Special Acknowledgment: Photographs in this book from the Mintzer Collection of the Blumenthal Library, Judah L. Magnes Museum.

*In loving gratitude
to my parents—*

*my father, Frank,
of blessed memory
and my mother, Reba,
may her light continue to shine.*

Acknowledgments

A BOOK LIKE THIS is not written without the help of a number of people and institutions. Many colleagues, mentors, friends and family all have had a part in this book. Professor Moshe Davis of the Hebrew University suggested the topic for this study and arranged with Rabbi Aryeh Lev for me to gain access to the archives of the National Jewish Welfare Board and its Commission on Jewish Chaplaincy (CJC). Having visited the chaplains in Europe several years before becoming director of the CJC, Rabbi Lev knew first-hand of their struggles and what they had accomplished, and wanted their story to be told. His openness and insight proved invaluable in my research.

My profound thanks to Professor Yehuda Bauer who guided this work in its early stages, but who should not be held accountable for any of its shortcomings. My years of graduate study at Hebrew University were greatly enriched by having had him as my mentor.

The Memorial Foundation for Jewish Culture, Yad VaShem and the Leonard Davis Foundation at Hebrew University provided financial assistance for the research of this study which was conducted at the institutions listed in the introduction. My sincere gratitude to these foundations and to the personnel in these libraries and centers who helped me in my research. My thanks also to the Simon Wiesenthal Center and Dean Rabbi Marvin Hier, my friend and colleague, for publishing two articles, early versions of some parts of this book.

A grant from the Oscar A. Mintzer Endowment for Holocaust Studies at the Judah L. Magnes Museum assisted in the publication of this book. As the American Jewish Joint Distribution Committee (JDC) Legal Advisor for the United States zone of Germany, Mr. Mintzer played a pivotal role in bringing the legal problems of the *Shearit Hapletah* (the surviving remnants of the European Jewish community) to the attention of the American Army and to the leadership of the American Jewish community. I am indebted to Mrs. Minna Mintzer and her family for having chosen to perpetuate the memory of Oscar Mintzer in this manner.

It has been a unique experience to work with Mr. Seymour Fromer, Director of the Judah L. Magnes Museum, and his superb staff, including Ms. Paula Friedman, Director of Public Relations, and Ms. Jane Levy, Head of the Blumenthal Library. My appreciation to the Magnes Museum, and to Rabbi Yoseph Miller, for the photographs in this book. My thanks also to Ms. Julie Goodman for having introduced me to Mr. Fromer and his outstanding institution.

The Wayne State University Press has been unflaggingly supportive and encouraging throughout this project. I would especially like to thank Mr. Arthur Evans, Director; Ms. Lynn Trease, my editor; Mr. Patrick Callahan, Assistant Director of Marketing; and Ms. Ann Schwartz, Promotion Manager.

The chaplains, their assistants and all those who shared their experiences, personal correspondence and documents with me deserve a special thank you. Their help was crucial to reconstructing the history of this period.

A number of other people also need be acknowledged: the physical preparation of this book would not have been possible without the help of Mr. Vedas Sorreda; Rabbi Yale Butler, Mr. Abraham Hyman, and Mr. Harvey Lutske for their suggestions and insights; Rabbi Herschel Schacter for his ongoing support.

None of this would have been possible without the tremendous support, love and encouragement of my family: my wife Marlene, my sons Elon, Ranan and Ari, and Joseph and Belle Weisblum, my beloved in-laws. Hopefully the lessons learned from this study will serve as a legacy to them, as it is written: "Do not let this memory leave your hearts all the days of your lives. Teach your children and children's children" (Deuteronomy 4:9).

Abbreviations

AH (Advisor on Jewish Affairs Archives, property of) Abraham Hyman, Jerusalem
AJA American Jewish Archives, Cincinnati, Ohio
AJC American Jewish Committee, New York
AJYB *American Jewish Year Book*
BACHAD Brit Chaluzim Dateyim
CAD Civil Affairs Department
CAH The Central Archives for the History of the Jewish People, Jerusalem
CANRA Committee on Army Navy Religious Activities
CCAR Central Conference of American Rabbis (Reform)
CCNY City College of New York
CHS Center for Holocaust Studies, Brooklyn, New York
CJC Commission on Jewish Chaplaincy (Archives, New York)
DA U.S Army Military History Research Collection, Carlisle Barracks, Pennsylvania
DJHS Delaware Jewish Historical Society, Wilmington
DPX Displaced Persons Executive
HTC Hebrew Theological College (Orthodox)
HUC Hebrew Union College (Reform)
IZL National Military Organization (Irgun Zvai Leumi)
IRO International Refugee Organization
JA *Jewish Advocate*, Boston
JDC (American Jewish) Joint Distribution Committee
JE *Jewish Exponent*
JF *Jewish Frontier*

JIR Jewish Institute of Religion (Reform)
JTA *Jewish Telegraphic Agency Daily News Bulletin*
JTS Jewish Theological Seminary of America (Conservative)
JWB Jewish Welfare Board (Archives, New York)
NA National Archives
SM Suitland, Maryland
DC Washington, D.C.
NYT *New York Times*
OH Oral History (Division of the Institute of Contemporary Jewry), Hebrew University, Jerusalem
ORT Organization for Rehabilitation through Training
OSE Oeuvre de Secours aux Enfants
PM The author's private files
RAA Rabbinical Assembly of America (Conservative)
RCA Rabbinical Council of America (Orthodox)
SHAEF Supreme Headquarters, Allied Expeditionary Forces
UJA United Jewish Appeal
UNRRA United Nations Relief and Rehabilitation Agency
UNSCOP United Nations Special Committee on Palestine
USFET United States Forces, European Theater
WJC World Jewish Congress
  NY New York
  GA Geneva
  IJA Institute of Jewish Affairs, London
WRB War Refugee Board
YIVO Yiddish Scientific Institute (Yiddishes Wissenshaftliches Institut), New York
YMHA Young Men's Hebrew Association

INTRODUCTION

ALTHOUGH JEWISH CHAPLAINS served in the American military since the Civil War, World War II and its aftermath provided them with difficult challenges of a new magnitude. Jewish chaplains were assigned to officiate at religious rites, advise commanders on problems of morale, inspire their men to perform with greater effectiveness, aid in combating delinquencies, encourage character development, visit the sick, counsel individual soldiers, and "provide an effective unofficial channel for redress of grievances."[1]

In 1943 the chaplains faced a new civilian dimension to their responsibilities. In that year, Chaplain David Rubin reported finding many Lithuanian and Polish Jews in a refugee camp in Teheran; he also indicated that he had been assisting them.[2] Other early reports from North Africa and later from Italy foreshadowed the problems American Jewish chaplains would encounter when large numbers of Jewish survivors in France, Germany, Holland, Belgium, and Austria requested their assistance.[3]

The existing literature about American Jewish chaplains and the Jewish survivors in Europe has been largely autobiographical.[4] Few, if any, have attempted to discuss the major issues involved or tried to place the role of the chaplains in historical perspective. Some activities of the chaplains have been discussed in passing in early historical works of postwar resettlement and Jewish survivors.[5]

The present study is a historical analysis of the European Jewish survivors' impact on American Jewish chaplains and indirectly on

American Jewry. A central question is the American Jewish community's response to the survivors in the American zone of occupation in Germany and Austria from 1944 through 1948. I focus on the interaction between the chaplains and survivors, with particular attention to their efforts to keep American Jews informed about conditions in Europe; the response of the American Jewish community; the chaplains' attempts to persuade the American Army to recognize Jewish displaced persons (DPs) and survivors as a separate entity requiring special consideration; their contributions to the political organization of the displaced persons; and their influence on American Jewish soldiers.

The chaplains were among the first liberators to meet the survivors; and their accounts of the situation in Italy, France, Holland, Belgium, Austria, and Germany were among the first reports sent to American Jews. This information, supplemented by reports from American soldiers and journalists, helped shape American Jewish response to the former victims.

At the end of the war, the United States was in a position to ameliorate conditions in the displaced persons camps under its control and to play a key role in formulating permanent solutions to these problems. The United States, as we know, influenced the United Nations' decision to partition Palestine in November 1947; and it was, in part, the presence of survivors in displaced persons camps that motivated this action.[6]

The American Army had responsibility for the overall welfare of the survivors. Unfortunately, the army did not always understand the problems of Jewish survivors and the chaplains mediated these needs with official military bodies in occupied Germany and Austria. The displaced persons and (to a lesser degree) American Jewish soldiers also participated in this process. Neither the army nor the American Jewish community had anticipated Jewish chaplains mediating with the military on behalf of the survivors or becoming involved in their daily welfare. Often, this was a spontaneous response to the suffering of their fellow Jews. Since chaplains who chose to assist the survivors were not acting as official representatives of the American rabbinate or any other institution, they had to decide the extent of their own involvement.

The chaplains and the soldiers were not the only groups assisting Holocaust survivors. Various official and nonofficial organizations were also directly involved. Among these were the American Jewish Joint Distribution Committee (JDC), a nonpolitical American social aid agency founded in November 1914 that played a primary role in the rescue, relief, and rehabilitation of European Jewry; the United Nations Relief and Rehabilitation Agency (UNRRA), established in 1943 by the United Nations to provide relief to areas and

Introduction

people stricken by war; the representatives of the Yishuv (the Jewish settlement in Palestine); the advisor on Jewish Affairs, a position created in August 1945 to keep the commanding general in the European theater of operations apprised of problems affecting Jewish displaced persons; and the World Jewish Congress (WJC), an international "voluntary association" of representative Jewish bodies, institutions, and communities organized to defend the interests of Jews and Jewish communities throughout the world. The relations that existed between these groups and the chaplains will add another important element to this study.

It should be noted that the JDC and WJC continually quarreled over who should administer aid to the Jews. The differences stemmed from the congress's belief in the unity of Jews throughout the world and its attempt to establish a political entity to represent world Jewry. The JDC rejected this view of Jewish nationalism and was disturbed that the congress competed with it for funds to aid the survivors.[7]

This work is based on three types of sources. First, chaplains' monthly reports and other records were located in the archives of the National Jewish Welfare Board (JWB) and its Commission on Jewish Chaplaincy (CJC) in New York. Founded in 1917 as a "single all-embracing organization" through which the American Jewish community provided for the specialized religious, cultural, and recreational needs of the Jewish military personnel, the JWB had also been authorized by the American government to recruit and grant ecclesiastical endorsement to Jewish chaplains for the military. To procure rabbis for the chaplaincy, the JWB established the JWB Committee on Chaplains which was later reorganized to become the Committee on Army Navy Religious Activities (CANRA). These committees, in cooperation with the three rabbinical associations—the Conservative Rabbinical Assembly of America (RAA), the Reform Central Conference of American Rabbis (CCAR), and the Orthodox Rabbinical Council of America (RCA)—set qualifications (in addition that is, to those established by the military authorities) for rabbis entering the chaplaincy, as well as their own method of enlistment. Endorsement was an ongoing process. Aside from the initial certification, re-endorsement was required on an annual basis. Withdrawal of endorsement by the JWB could be made at any time under emergency powers authorized by the military. To keep the JWB apprised of the chaplains' activities, the chaplains were required to send monthly reports to JWB headquarters in New York on the number of religious services, marriages, circumcisions, funerals, hospital and guard house visits, pastoral and condolence letters, and other relevant activities.[8] Not all chaplains wrote such reports; moreover, many reports and documents were lost or discarded when the JWB moved to its present location. The chaplains involved in displaced persons work neither had the time to write contemporaneous accounts of their activities nor appreciated the historical importance of their actions. Furthermore, they were reluctant to write reports that were subject to censorship, since they did not know whether the JWB would support the activities considered illegal by the army.

Second, to supplement fragmentary archival documentation, I conducted systematic oral interviews with chaplains. To supplement and verify the data, I held extensive interviews with chaplains' assistants, JDC personnel, Palestinian Jews, American soldiers, Holocaust survivors, and several of the advisors on Jewish Affairs and their assistants. Supplementary data found in interviews with American Jewish soldiers conducted by the Center for Holocaust Studies (CHS) in New York were useful, as was my correspondence with Jewish chaplains serving in the British Army. Chaplains' assistants were a particularly useful source of information. Each chaplain had his own clerk, (generally a corporal) with clerical experience, cantorial skills, or some other special talent. The clerks (or "chaplains' assistants," as they became known) worked closely with the chaplains, often having extensive involvement with the survivors.[9] Holocaust survivors who had been helped by the chaplains were the most difficult to find. Advertisements in the Israeli press, mailings to members of Holocaust survivors' organizations in Jerusalem, and discussions with the Buchenwald survivors' organization in the United States yielded several interviewees. The chaplains also supplied names of a number of survivors who were subsequently interviewed for this study.

Third, I consulted letters, diaries, and personal correspondence of chaplains to their wives. This material corroborated the chaplains' oral testimonies and provided additional details about these activities. Other material was found in the American Jewish Archives (AJA) in Cincinnati; the Central Archives for History of the Jewish People (CAH) in Jerusalem; the Oral History Division of the Institute of Contemporary Jewry (OH) in Jerusalem; the Yiddish Scientific Institute (YIVO) in New York; Yad Vashem in Jerusalem; the CHS in New York; the United States Army Military History Research Collection in Carlisle Barracks, Pennsylvania (DA); the Delaware Jewish Historical Society (DJHS) in Wilmington; the WJC archives in Geneva (WJC–GA) and New York (WJC–NY) and in the Institute of Jewish Affairs (WJC–IJA) London; the archives of the American Jewish Committee in New York; the archives of the JDC in New York; the National Archives in Washington, D.C. (NA–DC) and Suitland, Maryland (NA–SM); the Truman Library in Independence, Missouri; the Abraham Hyman (AH) Archives in Jerusalem, and the Zionist archives in Jerusalem and New York.[10] (These and all other abbreviations are cataloged on pages xi and xii.)

I consulted periodicals such as the *New York Times, Jewish Telegraphic Agency Daily News Bulletin, American Jewish Year Book, Contemporary Jewish Record, American Jewish Conference Record,* and *Jewish Chaplain,* as well as a representative sample of the Anglo–Jewish press, the displaced persons press, and the Yiddish newspapers including *Der Tog, Forward,* and the *Yiddisher Kempfer.* These papers and periodicals published the chaplains' reports and provided what the American press reported about conditions in Europe. I shall attempt not only to determine the adequacy of the American Armed Forces and the U. S. government's response to the survivors but also to provide some understanding of the American Jewish response to the Holocaust and liberation. The chaplains' work with the remnants of European Jewry raised a number of problems for the JWB and the American Jewish community.

1

FIRST ENCOUNTERS WITH SURVIVORS

The Call to Serve

When the United States entered World War II on December 8, 1941, there were fewer than thirty Jewish chaplains serving in the armed forces. To meet the demand for more chaplains, chief of chaplains of the army, General William R. Arnold, asked the JWB on December 9 for "a goodly number" of their best rabbis.[1]

Since 1917, the JWB had been the official Jewish agency authorized by the U. S. Congress to recruit and grant ecclesiastical endorsements to Jewish chaplains for the military. In that year, the JWB became responsible for caring for the religious, cultural, and recreational needs of the Jewish military personnel. Additionally, the JWB served as coordinator for the Jewish community centers and Young Men's Hebrew Association throughout America.[2] Until 1940, the JWB handled the recruitment and endorsement of chaplains through the JWB Committee on Chaplains with a minimum of interference from the three rabbinical associations: the Conservative RA, the Reform CCAR, and the RCA. From World War I to his death in 1940, Cyrus Adler, president of the Jewish Theological Seminary, the educational and spiritual center of the Conservative movement, consulted with the rabbinical associations; but in his capacity as chairman of the JWB Committee on Chaplains and an officer of the JWB, he alone made the final decisions regarding the recruitment and procurement of the chaplains. Adler maintained his control over the committee in part because of his preeminence in the American Jewish community and in part because the chaplaincy involved a limited number of rabbis. During World War I there were only twenty-six Jewish chaplains commissioned for the military, and after the war they returned to civilian life. Between the wars, the JWB cared for the needs of the Jewish personnel serving in the army and navy.[3] When David de Sola Pool, a leading Orthodox rabbi and communal leader, became Chairman in June 1940, changed conditions precluded the concentration of authority either in his hands or in those of the JWB.[4]

The rapid increase of the American military forces, and especially the entrance of the United States into the war, enlarged the war function of the JWB and the role and the number of the Jewish chaplains. The rabbinical associations, which in the period between the wars had become better organized and more articulate and influential, demanded a decisive voice in determining policy regarding the chaplains.[5]

The JWB responded to these demands and reorganized the committee in January 1942 and again in November of the same year to reflect the equal status and increased influence of the rabbinical associations. CANRA was established with six representatives from each of the three rabbinical associations. Rabbi David de Sola Pool continued as chairman; Barnett Brickner, a Reform rabbi, became administrative chairman; and Philip S. Bernstein, also a Reform rabbi, became executive director. Louis Levitsky, a Conservative rabbi, became chairman of the newly established executive committee.[6]

This recognition meant that CANRA, which had become the representative agency of the American rabbinate, remained within the framework of the JWB and operated without restraint with regard to the chaplaincy and religious policy and practice. CANRA became a functional arm of the JWB and of the rabbinical associations. Through CANRA, the JWB could discharge its responsibilities to the Jewish military personnel in areas of religious welfare. As an arm of the rabbinical bodies, CANRA had only limited powers, which were delegated by the rabbinical associations. CANRA's authority was limited to the needs of wartime and it did not decide religious policy and practice affecting civilians. Even the task of assisting demobilized chaplains to secure pulpits remained with the rabbinical associations.[7]

By limiting CANRA's role to wartime needs, each rabbinical association maintained its independence, its unique code of ritual practice, and its distinct concept of Judaism. Each group remained an equal partner in CANRA with no decisions being forced upon anyone. For the sake of unity, however, denominational differences were submerged, enabling a common religious program for the military to be developed.[8]

As to the recruitment of chaplains, each rabbinical association had its own approach to procurement. The (Reform) CCAR informed its members of what was needed and expected them to act to meet those needs. Individuals who refused to enter the chaplaincy ran the risk of losing the conference's endorsement; without this approval, a Reform civilian congregation would most probably not hire him. The CCAR went so far as to try to censure and block the advancement of any rabbi who tried to jeopardize the position of the chaplains. The conference also established a policy of providing supplementary income for chaplains, with their home congregations paying the differential between their peacetime salary and what they earned as military officers. In general, members of the CCAR "responded beyond expectations."[9]

The rabbis in the Conservative movement followed many of the same procedures adopted by the CCAR except that they had a voluntary draft agreement. This meant that the rabbis allowed the Rabbinical Availability Committee of the RAA assembly to "summon them in categories by lot"[10] to fill specific needs. Unlike the Reform movement, the RAA did not screen potential candidates before they appeared before CANRA. Conservative rabbis who were drafted appeared as soon as they were invited. The Orthodox rabbinate presented a different problem, since no one organization existed to which all rabbis belonged. The largest Orthodox group, the RCA, assumed the responsibility for securing Orthodox chaplains.

To qualify for the chaplaincy, CANRA required that all candidates be graduates of a recognized theological seminary and hold at least a bachelors-of-arts degree. The War Department, on the other hand, was satisfied with the rabbinical degree and the *equivalent* of a bachelor-of-arts degree. CANRA interviewed each candidate to assess appearance, speech, psychological and religious views.

In response to the request of William R. Arnold (the army chief of chaplains) for more Jewish chaplains, the heads of the theological seminaries, rabbinical associations, congregational associations and the officers of the JWB sent a joint appeal to rabbis and congregations throughout the United States, asking that congregations grant a leave of absence to their rabbis for the duration of the war. More than half the rabbis in the country volunteered for the chaplaincy in response to this appeal, either through their own rabbinical organization or through CANRA.[11] One thousand forty-five rabbis applied for ecclesiastical endorsement from CANRA, 495 were interviewed, 422 were endorsed, and 311 received commissions as officers in the armed forces. Many other rabbis applied directly to their own rabbinic organizations but were rejected for not meeting the requirements. Every Jewish chaplain entered the military with the rank of first lieutenant in the army and lieutenant (junior grade) in the navy.

The number of Jewish chaplains in the army was established by the War Department at 2 percent of the total Chaplain Corps. The quota was based on the number of Jews serving in the army during 1928 and did not accurately represent the needs of those serving in World War II. By January 1945, the quota had been raised to 3 percent to reflect the larger number of Jews in the army;[12] in May it became 3.7 percent. Jewish chaplains were usually assigned to the headquarters of a division or some similar installation or unit, rather than with a regiment, because there were not enough Jews in these groups to justify the assignment.[13] In many cases, Jewish chaplains were in charge of distributing religious supplies.

The 311 Jewish chaplains actually selected were a representative cross section of the American rabbinate: 147 were Reform, 96 Conservative, and 86 Orthodox.[14] Over 90 chaplains had contact with the Jewish displaced persons. Of these 90, close to 60 were married, and more than 50 were born in the United States. Their average age was approximately 33.[15] Two hundred sixty-seven chaplains served in the army, 43 in the navy, and 1 in the maritime service.[16] Nothing in their education, persona, and religious background gave any indication how they would respond to the survivors.

To prepare the Christian and Jewish chaplains for their military duties, the War Department sent them to Chaplains' School, which was run by the military. Locations of the school varied; but the purpose remained the same, namely, "to instruct chaplains in the fundamentals of military policy, training, administration, regulations, and customs of the service, especially as such apply to their professional duties, and to acquaint them with the best methods of serving the commands to which they might be assigned."[17]

To acquaint the Jewish chaplains with CANRA's policies, each class of chaplains received a visit from either Rabbi David de Sola Pool or Aryeh Lev, a Reform rabbi. Lev was assigned to the Office of the Chief of Chaplains in Washington, D.C., where his primary responsibility involved "planning and training" the Chaplains Corps. He also acted as advisor to the Jewish chaplains and worked closely with CANRA and the JWB.

These special seminars at the Chaplains' School focused on the issues and problems chaplains would face in administering to a minority group found in varying numbers in thousands of military installations in the field around the world. Discussions were held on the proper procedures for officiating at religious services, marriages, divorces, funerals, and circumcisions; the problems of maintaining the Sabbath, holidays, *Kashrut* (keeping kosher); and the difficulties of personal adjustment in a non-Jewish milieu.[18]

The one area that CANRA did not discuss sufficiently or at all with the chaplains was that of establishing guidelines for dealing with

Jewish Chaplain School, Harvard University, November 1942. (Photo courtesy of the Mintzer Collection, Magnes Museum.)

civilian Jewish survivors in Europe. Aryeh Lev, who lectured at the special sessions at the Chaplains' School, maintained that nothing was mentioned at these meetings about the Holocaust and the displaced persons because no one knew what to expect.[19] Philip Bernstein, executive director of CANRA, agreed that while there were no formal sessions at the school about the survivors, "whenever chaplains were accessible, we transmitted to them information and resources that were available. There was a constant and reasonably prompt correspondence between the chaplains and ourselves. When we knew of their destination in advance, . . . we were able to meet with them and share whatever we knew. And we incorporated items of information and inspiration [in the *Jewish Chaplain*]." The *Jewish Chaplain* was a CANRA publication published about eight times a year, containing the latest accounts of the activities of individual chaplains, CANRA, and the JWB. "That we missed out in many situations, there is no doubt," Bernstein concluded; "but we were in the midst of a dynamic, fluid, and explosive war."[20]

Though CANRA did brief individual chaplains regarding conditions in Europe, the majority received no specific orientation either at the Chaplains' School or elsewhere. Articles written by chaplains describing their efforts appeared in the *Jewish Chaplain;* but they were written by the very chaplains who had gone to Europe in 1943, 1944, and 1945 without any prior orientation. Moreover, these articles did not contain suggestions on how to handle refugee problems.

A number of chaplains commented on the absence of guidelines. Herschel Schacter, an Orthodox rabbi in his late twenties, who had been inducted into the army in November 1942 and was the first chaplain to aid the Jews in the Buchenwald concentration camp, declared that neither he nor any other Jewish chaplain had been told what to expect.[21]

Eugene Lipman, a Reform rabbi in his middle twenties, who entered the army in August 1944, argued that the possibility of meeting Jews had not been discussed at all: "Not in our interviews with Jewish Welfare Board people when we entered [the] chaplaincy and went through Chaplains' School; not in interviews we had in New York before we left for Europe." Moreover, Lipman observed, "it hadn't occurred to any of us as an active possibility that we might have to face Jewish survivors."[22] Schacter and Lipman were among those chaplains who became most involved with the survivors.

Initial Meetings with Survivors

The first contact of chaplains with Jewish survivors occurred in March 1943, about two months before the last Axis army force in Africa capitulated. In his monthly report to CANRA, Chaplain David

Rubin, an Orthodox rabbi in his late thirties who had been in the army since April 1942, told of finding many Lithuanian and Polish Jews in a refugee camp in Teheran and indicated that he was assisting them. This group included some of the Jewish civilians—among them close to a thousand children—who managed to leave the Soviet Union with the Polish armed forces under General Wladyslaw Anders.

They and hundreds of thousands of other Jews fled to Russia to escape the Nazi invasion of the eastern areas of Poland annexed and under Soviet control. Many thousands more were taken by force to Russian concentration camps. Exactly how many is not known. There were approximately 1.8 million Polish civilians in Russia in 1941. In July of that year, the Russians signed an agreement with the Polish government-in-exile resulting in the release of Polish citizens in Russian camps. Further agreements with the Poles, Soviets, and British enabled two groups of Polish soldiers to leave Russia in April and August 1942, each with a number of civilians, including this group of Polish and Lithuanian Jews. Iran, which had been conquered by Anglo–Soviet forces in 1941, became a haven for these Jews and a gateway to Russia for Jewish relief organizations.[23]

Jewish chaplains in North Africa helped the Jews they met and aided in the local reorganization of Jewish communal life. Unfortunately, not much more information is known about the work of the chaplains in Teheran or North Africa.[24]

From North Africa, the Allies quickly moved to capitalize on their victory by invading Sicily on July 10, 1943. Thirty-nine days later, on August 17, the Allies occupied all of Sicily. By late 1943, three Reform chaplains—Edward Ellenbogen, Earl Stone, and Samuel Teitelbaum—sent reports about their contacts with the Jews they met in Palermo, Sicily, which had been captured by General George Patton and the Seventh Army in July 1943. Stone and Teitelbaum found a number of survivors. With the aid of the Jewish Brigade personnel (Palestinian Jews serving in an all-Jewish unit within the British Army), they were able to provide them with money, canned goods, and other necessities.[25]

Stone realized in October 1943, that what he experienced in Palermo would happen to other Jewish chaplains when they would meet large numbers of Jews in France, Germany, and Austria in need of financial assistance. Stone alerted Philip Bernstein, executive director of CANRA, to the problem in a letter on October 10. Stone pointed out that the chaplains had very little money at their disposal except for their small discretionary funds and that in any event, JWB money could not be used by civilians. Even while some soldiers voluntarily donated money to help, army regulations forbade chaplains from directly soliciting those funds. To do so would be to risk a reprimand, which, depending upon the offense, ranged in severity from a scolding to a court martial.

Stone believed that the responsibility for this relief work lay with the JDC, but he knew that they would not be allowed to enter Italy until the armistice had been signed. The army did not want civilian relief agencies who were not directly under its control interfering with military occupation and civilian relief work. Stone suggested, therefore, that the JDC supply the chaplains with money until its workers arrived.[26]

As a result of Stone's and perhaps others' communications, CANRA alerted the JDC to the problems facing the chaplains and asked the JDC to channel some funds through them. After several months, the JDC agreed to send money to Jewish chaplains in Italy and on a smaller scale, to those in Iran. The JWB raised an additional fifteen hundred dollars, which Rabbi Barnett R. Brickner, administrative chairman of CANRA, distributed to the chaplains when he visited them in late 1943. This overseas mission and others undertaken by CANRA, as well as by the leadership of the Protestant and Catholic clergy, enabled them "to observe the work of the chaplains, present recommendations to the military authorities, and report back to the denominational endorsing agency."[27]

Although Rabbi Brickner's mission and the JDC's funneling of money solved the immediate need of providing some aid to the Jewish survivors, CANRA adopted no overall position on the subject. On November 30, 1943, Philip Bernstein wrote in a memorandum to Louis Kraft, executive director of the JWB, "that conscientious chaplains will, as predicted long ago, increasingly encounter problems and needs of this kind and will need guidance and help." It is not clear what Bernstein meant by "long ago" when little or no mention of the displaced persons was made at the Chaplains' School. Yet Bernstein understood the problems the chaplains were facing and asked Louis Kraft that Stone's request for financial aid be considered as a "question of policy."[28]

The JWB responded by advising the chaplains to use those discretionary funds already in their possession. At this point, apparently, no one had envisioned the additional forms of assistance—such as food, clothing, and shelter—that the chaplains would be called upon to provide.[29]

Two additional factors must be taken into account to explain CANRA and the JWB's response. As already noted, CANRA and the chaplains had a mandate from the American government and the American Jewish community to provide assistance to the Jewish personnel in the military. CANRA's responsibilities were clearly defined and limited. It did not have the funds, the personnel, or the desire to become involved in relief work. CANRA never saw itself as an extension of the JDC or any other relief agency and did not want to conflict or interfere with such agencies. Information about the survivors, was transmitted to the JDC. Thus, the chaplains became involved in relief work when no one else was available or when the situation mandated their involvement.

Moreover, CANRA intentionally did not formulate policy for assisting survivors in order to preserve its status as the official agency for aiding Jewish military personnel. CANRA could not officially encourage the chaplains to assume responsibilities beyond those prescribed by the military without jeopardizing its own position.[30] The issue was also complicated by the military command's lack of preparation or understanding for the needs of the Jewish survivors. Since the military did not anticipate Jewish chaplains' being involved in relief work, the chaplains required special permission from their superior officers to help the survivors or undertook this work at their own risk.[31] To worsen matters, in Germany and Austria, a policy of nonfraternization with the indigenous population had been invoked by the military government. This, of course, included Jews and added still another obstacle to their being given any real assistance.

And what about the chaplains themselves? While CANRA did not provide guidelines to assist chaplains vis-à-vis the survivors, it is also important to explore whether the chaplains had asked for such directives. As leaders in the American Jewish community, it was not unreasonable to expect that the chaplains should have anticipated some of the conditions they found.

From the beginning of the war, the Jewish Telegraphic Agency and the Yiddish press provided almost daily accounts of Jewish suffering. Information also appeared regularly in the Anglo–Jewish[32] and the American press.[33] Though fragmentary and exaggerated at times, enough information existed to form a general picture of the devastation in Europe.

As early as 1942, information reached the West about the mass extermination of European Jewry.[34] The American Jewish community reacted with protests, memorial services, a day of fasting, and periods of silence for the dead. On December 17, 1942, the Allies officially acknowledged the Nazi extermination policies and condemned it.[35] By then, most of the Jews of Europe were dead.

Yet with all the protests and demonstrations, it was not until late 1943 and early 1944 that the tragedy became accepted as fact. Until then, it was "not fully grasped, not really understood, but accepted as a kind of verdict from which one would have to restart life."[36] Even then, there were still Jews who were unable to internalize this information until after the war when they saw the newsreels and pictures in the press. For the chaplains, a realization of the enormity of the tragedy often occurred after meeting the survivors face to face. Directives from CANRA were not requested by the chaplains before they left for Europe because few, if any, of them had given much thought to finding Jews there.

Chaplain Abraham J. Klausner, a thirty-year-old Reform rabbi who entered the army in June 1944, believed that there would be nothing for him to do in Europe when the war ended, so he volunteered for duty in the Far East. At least there, he reasoned, he would be of some service to Jewish soldiers. The army rejected Klausner's request and assigned him to Europe instead. There he became a legend among the displaced persons for his relentless efforts on their behalf.[37]

Even a Jewish chaplain who had fled from Europe had difficulty in comprehending the extent of the destruction. Chaplain George Vida, a Conservative rabbi who had fled Hungary in 1939 at the age of 33, observed: "In 1943, before I entered the Chaplaincy, I attended a meeting in Camden, New Jersey, where the speaker described the mass extermination of the Jews in Europe. These were big words. They did not mean much." When Vida arrived in Europe as a chaplain, he asserted: "I was totally unprepared for what I found. I had heard of the brutal beatings and inhuman treatment of prisoners in the concentration camps but they were only stories to me." Only after Vida discovered a Jewish family in Verviers, France, did the picture of what happened to these Jews begin to form in his mind,[38] he declared.

That the chaplains themselves had not anticipated the possibility of meeting Jewish survivors is an example of the insulation and isolation of American Jews—many of them, ironically, also refugees from fascist oppression. An incident involving Supreme Court Justice Felix Frankfurter illustrates the problem American Jews, as well as other Americans had in transforming information into knowledge. In late 1942, Jan Karski, the Polish underground's emissary to the West, arrived in the United States to inform the American government and the American Jewish leadership about the systematic mass extermination of European Jewry. Karski had visited the Warsaw Ghetto in October 1942 and then, disguised as an Estonian guard, had entered the Belzec extermination camp, where he witnessed the slaughter of the Jews.[39] After hearing Karski's report, Frankfurter told him that he did not believe him. Jan Ciechanowski, the Polish ambassador who had accompanied Karski to the meeting and Frankfurter's friend, immediately protested. Frankfurter replied that he did not say that Karski had lied but that he was unable to believe him, which was different.[40]

Marie Syrkin, a Zionist leader and an editor of the Labor Zionist monthly *Jewish Frontier*, added further insight into the "psychological unreadiness" of American Jews to believe the truth about Hitler's Final Solution. Sometime toward the end of August 1942, Syrkin and a group of Jewish journalists and writers were invited to a small private meeting by Leon Kubowitski of the WJC. Kubowitski, a Belgian Jew and former chairman of the Brussels Jewish community, told them of a report from the WJC office in Geneva about the Nazi plans to exterminate the Jews of Europe—a plan already being implemented. These individuals, who since 1933 had been actively involved in the fight against Nazi persecution through meetings, political pressure, and writings, listened to the news "in numb disbelief." "All the words we had written about Nazi atrocities had not prepared us for this horrifying revelation," Syrkin declared. For this reason it was not until the November 1942 issue of *Jewish Frontier*, which appeared in black borders, that the editors had accepted the facts. They informed their readership of the Nazi "policy of systematic murder of innocent civilians which in its ferocity, its dimensions and its organization is unique in the history of mankind."

Syrkin observed: "Today when genocide, gas-chamber, and mass-extermination are the small coin of language, it is hard to reconstruct the more innocent state of mind when American Jews, like the Jews in Europe's ghettos, could not immediately grasp that the ascending series of Nazi persecutions had reached this apex." Further, she asked: "If such was the psychological unreadiness of sophisticated publicists whose overriding concerns since the advent of Hitler had been to expose each new phase of the Nazi terror, what could be expected from a less informed general public?"[41]

The Liberation of Italy and Western Europe

Allied forces landed in southern Italy on September 3, 1943; Rome was liberated by June 4, 1944; and Florence on August 4. Though the American Fifth Army and the British Eighth Army continued their attack to the north, they were halted at the Gothic line (the German line of defense extending across most of northern Italy) until September. At the end of 1944, there were approximately 22,000 Jews in Italy, 5,000 of whom were refugees but not Italian. When the Germans invaded Italy in September 1943, there were about 45,000 Jews in Italy—8,000 of whom were killed between 1943 and the end of the war.[42]

Nearly all twenty American chaplains serving in Italy during this period had some contact with Jewish survivors but for the most part did not play a major role in relief work. Those who served in frontline units or in isolated areas claimed they had little opportunity to meet Jews. If chance encounters did occur, the chaplains were unable to assist them in any substantial way. Other chaplains who were in an area for a few days or weeks usually visited the local synagogue, where they met survivors. These visits created much excitement even though the chaplains could do little more than offer encouragement. Survivors appreciated any visible concern for their plight and were proud of seeing American Jewish chaplains openly wearing the Star of David and the Ten Commandments on their lapels—the standard insignias worn by Jewish chaplains. Under the Nazis and their allies, these same Jewish symbols were used as badges of shame.[43]

On June 9, Chaplain Morris Kertzer, a thirty-four-year-old Conservative rabbi, addressed four thousand Jews at *Tempio Israelita*, the synagogue of the chief rabbi of Rome. After he spoke, Kertzer was mobbed by those wanting to touch him or kiss the Jewish insignias on his lapels. Some pressed their children into his arms to be blessed. Wherever the chaplains went, they were greeted as saviors. Kertzer and Chaplain Aaron Paperman, a thirty-one-year-old Orthodox rabbi, sent the first report to the United States about the remaining Jews of Rome.[44]

Jews from Palestine serving in the British Army were the first to aid the survivors. In 1939 the Jewish Agency for Palestine appealed to the Jews in Palestine to volunteer for national service. When over twenty-five thousand Jews volunteered to join the British Army the Jewish Agency proposed that a Jewish army be formed composed of volunteers from Palestine and neutral countries. Although the British initially rejected the idea, fearing demands for political concessions if they succeeded, the British agreed in 1940 to accept some Jews for service in the British Army. By 1945, over twenty-five thousand were involved in transportation, engineering, and fighting units. Most were in all-Jewish units with Jewish officers, serving in Egypt, Greece, Crete, Italy, and France.[45]

The Palestinian Jews began working with refugees in late 1943. They were instrumental in setting up communal kitchens and hospitals; helping the local communities organize; preparing people for immigration to Palestine; initiating vocational training programs and workshops; offering courses in Hebrew language, Zionism, and other subjects; and removing Jewish children from convents in southern Italy. Many survivors lived in private homes or displaced persons camps. Others lived in transit hostels, schools, orphanages, old age homes, and *hachsharot* (schools or camps that prepared them for immigration to Palestine) established by the Palestinian Jews.[46]

In September 1944 the British announced the creation of the Jewish Brigade. In October 1944, the brigade trained in southern Italy. Not all of the Palestinians serving in Italy were absorbed into the brigade, but they did join them in coordinating aid and Zionist educational activities. This coordinating group, established on October 29, 1944, became known as *Merkaz Lagolah* (Center for the Diaspora).[47]

Funds for these projects were provided by the JDC and the Jewish Agency. Additional monies were donated by UNRRA and Palestinian Jews who contributed one day's food ration each week. The JDC arrived in April 1944 and during June and July established offices in Rome and Bari.[48] For some time, the JDC worked under the aegis of the Intergovernmental Committee on Refugees.[49]

At times the Palestinians came to the chaplains for help in negotiating with the army. A few weeks after the liberation of Rome, a group of Palestinian Jews asked Chaplain Selwyn Ruslander, a thirty-three-year-old Reform rabbi assigned to Advance Amphibious Base at Salerno, to accompany them to a conference with Colonel Charles Poeletti of the U. S. Fifth Army, Allied regional commander in Rome. As a result of this meeting, the army recognized the Jewish community's relief agency as being in the same category as the Vatican relief agencies, according it preferential treatment. Free elections in the Jewish community were promised as soon as stability could be achieved; access to Captain Maurice Neufeld (Colonel Poeletti's adjutant) was assured; gasoline was disbursed so that they could buy supplies outside the city; and Captain Neufeld agreed to find out why the JDC representative could not obtain permission to enter Rome.[50]

Aside from requesting help in negotiations with the military, the Palestinian Jews also asked the chaplains for food, clothing, and anything else they needed. Generally, the amount of aid the chaplains were able to supply was minimal, since they had no direct access to supplies. To obtain even modest amounts of food or clothing required inventiveness. Chaplains who asked the army for help met with various degrees of success. The army had geared itself for war and its fighting units were not adequately equipped for civilian needs. Moreover, UNRRA had been assigned this responsibility once peace was secured.

Whether an army officer chose to respond favorably to a chaplain's request for aid depended on the individual's willingness to bend regulations. Army supplies were only for use by military personnel; but some soldiers, recognizing the dire plight of the Jewish refugees, gave what they could.

Other chaplains bypassed the official route and used their Jewish and non-Jewish personal contacts in the commissary, post exchange (PX, where soldiers purchased goods at a discount), and elsewhere. Often, this was faster and less complicated. Naturally, there was a limit to the quantity of goods that could be acquired in this manner.[51]

Chaplain Samuel Teitelbaum, a forty-three-year-old Reform rabbi attached to the Peninsula Base Section, recognized the inadequacy of this random and limited assistance. He had arrived in Naples in January 1944 and remained the only Jewish chaplain in that city for many months. After he and his assistant, Corporal Irving Fishman, visited a refugee camp at Campagna in February 1944, he began a relief program for the seventy old men living there with the help of a local civilian committee and a Palestinian Jewish chaplain. He also approached Jewish soldiers who came to services and other gatherings for their assistance. They responded generously with money and other items. Teitelbaum realized, however, that more reliable and permanent sources of funds were needed. Periodically he could request GI support; but regulations prohibited conducting organized campaigns for money, and he had no wish to violate this rule.[52]

A week after making this initial contact, Teitelbaum wrote to Philip Bernstein about this new development. In this first detailed account from the Italian front, Teitelbaum urged that the United Jewish Appeal and the JDC immediately send their representatives to Italy. Teitelbaum had "neither the time nor the facilities to engage in this essential project." Nevertheless, he asked that one thousand dollars be transferred to him at once to supplement the aid already being given to the refugees.[53]

Bernstein explained to Teitelbaum in a subsequent letter that the JDC had not yet received permission from the State Department to enter Italy but that negotiations were in progress. Bernstein encouraged Teitelbaum to continue his work and suggested that the discretionary funds already supplied by CANRA be used in this emergency. Bernstein wanted to be kept informed about the refugees and asked Teitelbaum what further steps should be taken to help them. In keeping with CANRA's policy of working within military guidelines, Bernstein informed Teitelbaum that they would send him whatever he needed so long as his commanding officer approved.[54]

While Bernstein passed along to the JDC information about the refugees he received from Teitelbaum and other chaplains, the WJC sent letters to chaplains in Italy, asking for news about the Jews there. It wanted accurate statistics on how many Jews survived, how many escaped, and how many were deported. The congress hoped to devise its own program of relief, but this could not be implemented until it obtained permission from the military to send its representatives to Europe.[55]

The chaplains informed the WJC about conditions in Italy in the hope that it would pressure the American government to allow Jewish relief agencies to enter the country as soon as possible. That the congress valued this information can be seen by its frequent praise of the chaplains' efforts and by its use of this information to help formulate its own policies.[56]

One example of how the congress used this information can be seen in an incident involving Chaplain Teitelbaum. In a letter to the WJC, Teitelbaum urged that chaplains be empowered by the congress or some other relief agency to act in a semiofficial capacity until its own representatives arrived. On May 9, 1944, the congress sent this proposal to Major General John H. Hilldring, director of the Civil Affairs Department (CAD) of the War Department.[57] The CAD had been established on March 1, 1943, and was charged with the responsibility for improving the conditions in Europe and training military government officers.[58] It was therefore the appropriate agency to consider Teitelbaum's proposal. A few weeks later, however, the adjutant general's office replied that chaplains were so occupied by their official responsibilities that to use them in private relief work would be impractical. Moreover, the army believed the refugees were receiving adequate care and hoped improvement would be apparent in the near future.[59] The WJC dropped the idea of using chaplains in relief work after this correspondence and after consulting Patrick Malin, of the Intergovernmental Committee on Refugees.[60]

Simultaneously with Teitelbaum's question about temporarily empowering the chaplains to act on behalf of a relief agency, a misunderstanding arose about whether a number of other chaplains had asked to become involved in JDC work. The JDC responded by informing the chaplains that it could not use them while they were still in the army. It also ruled out the possibility of assigning chaplains as area organizers, because these assignments had to be made before the end of the war in Europe. The JDC did express interest in individuals with backgrounds in community organization, psychiatric social work, or similar fields. Chaplains who possessed the proper credentials would be considered for positions after being demobilized but could not be guaranteed such positions even if qualified.[61]

On November 13, armed with information gleaned from the chaplains, the press, and its own sources, the WJC approached Hilldring again to ask that the American Army provide special treatment and consideration for the remnants of European Jewry. In particular, the WJC requested that "Jewish displaced persons, regardless of their formal nationality" be considered "as friendly elements" by the military authorities and be "treated accordingly"; that during the transitional period (between their repatriation and the time that their final fate would be decided upon) the Jews not be placed "in the same camp with Nazis or with other enemy nationals, at whose hands, only yesterday, they suffered most cruelly"; and that the Allies should not assume that the Jews would want to be repatriated. "On the contrary," declared the WJC, "it is very likely that Jewish deported persons from such countries as Rumania, Austria, Hungary and perhaps even Poland, will in many, probably even in the majority of cases, be most reluctant to go back to countries, in which they had been so terribly persecuted and in which they may still be surrounded by a hostile atmosphere."[62]

The WJC did not realize that it had only a remote chance of influencing American policy through CAD. When Hilldring assumed command in April 1943, Henry L. Stimson, secretary of the War Department, informed him that he did not want the army involved in making policy about the military government. General George C. Marshall, army chief of staff, reiterated this point when he told Hilldring that he should "start planning from the day you go into business, how you're going to get out of it as fast as possible," since governing was never regarded as part of the proper duty of the military.

Before the war ended, CAD had little to say about what the policies would be regarding the occupation of Germany "because Washington provided only arguments about theories." Hilldring pointed out the difficulty of formulating policy when he complained that "there wasn't even a clear and lasting decision as to what civilian departments and agencies of the government should participate in the making of policy. . . . This very bitter and troublesome controversy was never resolved."[63]

Unfortunately, the WJC did not share its concerns about the need for separate Jewish camps and the question of repatriation with the chaplains. If the WJC had done so, it would have helped the chaplains in Europe and those about to leave for overseas duty place the problems of the survivors in perspective. The JDC did not keep the chaplains apprised of these problems, either; and this caused friction between them.

Arthur Greenleigh, a JDC worker in Rome, reported that in the fall of 1944 he met with all the chaplains in the southern part of Italy. At this meeting, Greenleigh explained what the JDC had found, what it hoped to accomplish, and how the chaplains could help. "They were fascinated," Greenleigh observed, "and it really seemed to us that they were hearing most of this for the first time. It was interesting to watch the change in the attitude of most of the men during the meeting. It was evident that most of them came to the conference with a 'chip on the shoulder' because we entered this country so late and because they thought we were doing so little. It was a revelation to even the most skeptical and we made friends and converts of everyone present."[64]

Despite this activity, chaplains continued to become involved in situations when they were called upon by the survivors and circumstances to perform relief work. The overwhelming magnitude of the situation confronting them and the delay of the JDC in beginning this work caused frustration for the chaplains and the survivors. Wherever chaplains went in liberated Europe, they were asked about the JDC. European Jewry had become accustomed to expecting the JDC's help; and when it did not appear immediately after the American Army arrived, they were very disappointed. Since few of the chaplains were aware of the obstacles placed in the JDC's path by the American military, they, too, became critical of this delay.[65]

Sometimes the chaplains' efforts caused the JDC embarrassment and raised policy questions for CANRA. A particularly annoying incident involving the JDC took place in France. The Allied invasion of France began on June 6, 1944; and within one hundred days most of France, Belgium, and Luxembourg were liberated. At the same time, the Allies established a bridgehead in Holland; and in early 1945 they made significant advances into Germany.[66] Chaplain Robert Marcus, a thirty-five-year-old Orthodox rabbi attached to Headquarters Ninth Tactical Air Corps, became so disturbed by the poor conditions he saw in France during the middle of 1944 that he appealed to a number of Jews in Long Island, New York, for funds to improve this situation. Also, he suggested to CANRA that American Jews launch a national campaign to send food packages to the chaplains stationed in Europe. When the leadership of the JDC learned of Marcus's direct plea for money, they were disturbed and embarrassed; for it raised many questions about the effectiveness of their own programs.[67]

The JDC had been trying to gain admission to Italy and Western Europe as quickly as the army would permit it. It was eager to establish its presence there and review the problems it faced in conjunction with other relief agencies with similar tasks.

Joseph C. Hyman, executive vice-chairman of the JDC, made this point clear in a letter to Louis Kraft of the JWB in response to Marcus's attempt to launch a package program: "The problem . . . is not one of getting women in the United States to organize a package program at this time, but rather to find out how soon circumstances will permit the Joint Distribution Committee, through its European Chairman, Dr. [Joseph] Schwartz, . . . to get directly into France, to effect contact with the reorganized committees which are beginning to function openly, to work out a concrete program and to give us the details. . . . I believe that the whole question of food package relief in France must be reviewed, not alone on the basis of Jewish need, but with a number of organizations which are interested in the same problem."[68]

To prevent further direct solicitation, Philip Bernstein sent a letter to the chaplains instructing them not to send any more direct appeals to individuals or organizations in the United States. Requests for assistance were to be directed instead to the JDC office that had just opened in Paris. The JDC began to function in late 1944 and early 1945 and had earlier assisted French Jews with financial credits during the Occupation.[69]

Bernstein realized there would be a gap between the time the chaplains encountered Jews in need of help and the time the JDC would be allowed to begin its work. At the chaplains' request, Bernstein arranged for JDC funds to be made available through Chaplain Judah Nadich, a thirty-two-year-old Conservative rabbi who served at the Office of the Theater Chaplain in Paris. While Bernstein seemed personally pleased that the chaplains were assisting Jews in distress, these activities raised some basic questions for CANRA.

Since civilian relief work went beyond the chaplains' formal responsibilities, Bernstein expressed concern about the army's response to their activities. The lack of knowledge of what the chaplains were doing further complicated the problem. In a letter of November 14, 1944, to members of the JWB board, Bernstein discussed these issues and suggested a way to handle them. He pointed out that CANRA had already tried to protect "the status" of the JWB and the chaplains by making it clear to each chaplain that they must conduct these relief efforts "always within the framework of military procedure and with the knowledge and consent of your Commanding Officer."[70] A letter to this effect had been sent out on June 22, 1944.[71]

Another issue for the JWB was whether it should formally approach the army to assess its position on the chaplains' involvement in civilian problems. "To the best of our knowledge," Bernstein declared from CANRA's headquarters in New York, "this humanitarian assistance has not been subject to any criticism." Therefore, he saw "no reason" for the JWB "to raise from this side of the ocean any questions with military authorities about the appropriateness of this conduct. Our chaplains are in the heart of the military process. What they are doing is obviously known not only because it is done by themselves and others—but because some of it actually has been publicized in the press. If any problem should arise, we will be prepared to deal with it." "But at present," Bernstein observed, "there are no problems or issues before us."

Bernstein further asserted, "It is not only unnecessary but decidedly unwise [for the JWB] to address any inquiries or communications at this time, which, however intended, might lead to the impression that JWB is discouraging or placing obstacles in the way of such assistance as the chaplains are called upon to render." "I know these chaplains well," he declared, "and I also think I sense the mood of the American Jewish community. There would be intense resentment against anything but a helpful, humanitarian attitude. One ill-advised communication of this kind which might fall into the hands of the Jewish press would undo a large measure of the good will that JWB and the chaplains have built up during the war."[72]

As a result of this letter, the JWB adopted the policy "that there must be no written communications of any kind on the entire subject [of chaplains' relief activities] and that whatever is done should be done wholly on the [personal] initiative of Army chaplains."[73]

While Bernstein feared the chaplains' involvement with the survivors might strain the relationship of the JWB and the chaplaincy with the army, a number of chaplains did not let this interfere with the need to find immediate solutions to the problems confronting them. This was particularly true of men like Chaplain Abraham Haselkorn, a thirty-nine-year-old Reform rabbi attached to Headquarters Loire Section, who was among the first to help Jewish children.

A number of Jewish children who were hidden in farms around Bonnetable, France, a village not far from Le Mans, had been found by Chaplain David Max Eichhorn, a thirty-eight-year-old Reform rabbi attached to the Fifteenth Corps Headquarters on August 14, 1944. Since his unit would shortly be leaving the area, Eichhorn placed the children with Chaplain S. Appelbaum, the head of the Civilian Affairs detachment of Le Mans.[74] On August 18 Chaplain Abraham Haselkorn arrived in Le Mans and learned from a Jew named Trachtenberg that other Jewish children were still in the vicinity. Trachtenberg, a Paris antiquary, had hidden in the Loire region and worked with the French resistance. Shortly after the liberation, he discovered the presence of these orphans.

Many of the children had been placed in the area through the efforts of Father Devaux of Notre Dame de Sion in Paris. The deportations of July 1942, in which thousands of Jews were rounded up in France, convinced many Jews that they must save their children. By temporarily turning them over to the church, many had hoped to protect them from the Nazi terror. Every month, the farmers received a prescribed amount of money for each child they hid. These funds were provided by Oeuvre de Secours aux Enfants (OSE), a Jewish health and childcare society, which organized the major rescue operation of Jewish children in France. The OSE received its funding from the JDC.[75]

Trachtenberg, Haselkorn, and Haselkorn's assistant Milton Teicher found over three dozen children in two weeks. Many were sick or in poor health. They lacked proper food, clothing, and housing.

Chaplain Abraham Haselkorn at his desk. (Photo courtesy of Mintzer Collection, Magnes Museum.)

Speaking as an "unofficial" army representative, Trachtenberg persuaded some of the farmers to hand over the children to him. The presence of Haselkorn in his army uniform with a car and driver contributed to the air of authority they sought to create.[76] If this ploy failed, they resorted to threats. Some of the farmers were intimidated and agreed to release the children if Haselkorn compensated them for the loss of their child labor. Since money had not been appropriated for such purposes, Haselkorn had to draw it from his own reserves.[77]

A third group of farmers were unwilling to free their charges unless they received permission from Father Devaux. Many of these children were still being hidden, and Haselkorn wanted to find them.

In October he went to Paris and confronted the priest. In the name of the Jewish community, Haselkorn demanded a complete list of names and the location of each child. Devaux refused, claiming the children could not be returned without the consent of their families. Of course, he knew full well that most families had been killed in the extermination camps.[78]

Later, the priest complained to Chaplain Judah Nadich about Haselkorn. While Father Devaux succeeded in temporarily halting the return of these children, eventually hundreds were returned.[79] The children (ranging in age from three to sixteen) were placed in nursing homes or in French hospitals; but as their numbers increased, Trachtenberg and Haselkorn decided to establish a separate children's home for them. The mayor of Le Mans suggested using Chateau Mehancourt, an empty house at the end of the town. At a special tea held by Haselkorn, the French mayor agreed to handle all the arrangements for maintaining the institution if Haselkorn would provide from fifteen hundred to two thousand dollars per month to cover the expenses and guarantee to subsidize the orphanage for at least three months.[80]

Haselkorn accepted the terms of the agreement and appealed to the Jewish soldiers at High Holiday services for their financial support. Five-thousand-dollars' worth of French francs were collected from fifteen hundred GIs as well as pledges for large quantities of chocolate, candy, chewing gum, and army rations.

The need for clothing for these children prompted Haselkorn to seek assistance from his own family and friends in the United States. He also informed Bernstein about these Jewish children and asked for the JDC or some other relief agency to assume responsibility for their care.[81] In response to Haselkorn's request for clothing, his wife asked Philip Bernstein to have CANRA send to France whatever garments she could collect. Bernstein rejected the idea because CANRA did not have permission from the military to ship any articles for civilian use. In a letter to Haselkorn on November 2, 1944, Bernstein declared: "It is a frightful thing to be impotent in such matters when one knows of the terrible need. However, we are absolutely prohibited from sending anything but military religious supplies and we cannot overcome this limitation at present. However, as you know, JDC has a world of experience in such matters and they possess vast resources. I am certain that they will achieve results as rapidly as possible." The "reluctance of some religious authorities to return Jewish children to their Jewish families, is obviously a very delicate and very serious problem," Bernstein observed. He assured Haselkorn that Joseph Schwartz, European director of the JDC, had been told of the problem and that "he will undoubtedly investigate and act upon it as circumstances require."

Chateau Mehancourt. (Photo courtesy of the Mintzer Collection, Magnes Museum.)

Bernstein closed by affirming his support to Haselkorn: "My best wishes are with you at this time. I realize that you are being called upon to serve far beyond the line of duty. The heartbreaking problems that you encounter undoubtedly impose a tremendous strain on you. However, there are undoubtedly such satisfactions in the service that you render as you would not normally encounter in a life in the civilian rabbinate in this country. My blessing and best wishes and readiness to help are always with you."[82]

Haselkorn could not wait until the JDC arrived or until a way had been found to send clothing to France from the United States. When he heard that a chaplains' conference would be held in England, he convinced Judah Nadich to let him go. In London, Chaplain Samuel Rosen (an American rabbi who had toured the Chateau) introduced Haselkorn to many Jewish women who helped secure enough clothing for the approximately sixty children under his care.

In December the army transferred Haselkorn from Le Mans. At that point, the orphanage was well established and served as a model for other similar institutions in France. Under Trachtenberg's supervision, a woman managed the Chateau, with American Jewish soldiers' continuing to provide the required support. Many GIs spent their spare time finding and fixing toys, building benches, and playing with the youngsters. They even had their families in the

Le Capitaine A. HASELKORN
Aumonier de l'Armée Américaine

vous prie de bien vouloir honorer de votre présence le Vin d'honneur qui sera servi à la Colonie de vacances au Château de Méhoncourt, route de l'Eventail, Le Mans, le Vendredi 24 Novembre 1944, à 15 heures.

M.

Invitation to special tea at the Chateau hosted by Chaplain Araham Haselkorn to raise money for the children's home. (Photo courtesy of the Mintzer Collection, Magnes Museum.)

United States send clothes and other items for the children. Morton Shanok, a cantor by profession and Haselkorn's unofficial assistant, remained to look after the children and continued to teach classes in Yiddish, Hebrew, and Judaism. Ultimately, most of the children went to Palestine.[83]

Meyer Levin, the noted author and journalist for the Jewish Telegraphic Agency, reported on the project for the agency; and at least one major Jewish newspaper, the *Jewish Advocate* of Boston,[84] gave prominent coverage to the story. Although it is not certain what impact this article had on the American Jewish community, *Der Tog* (a Yiddish daily) used an article on the same subject to persuade its readers to donate funds for Jewish orphans in France. On November 2, 1944, *Der Tog* reprinted a letter written by an American soldier to his family about Haselkorn's orphanage. The soldier had attended a High Holiday service where Haselkorn told about the children's home and appealed for their financial support.[85]

Haskelkorn's accomplishments impressed the chief of chaplains so much that he printed the story of the orphanage in a circular sent to all chaplains in the military.[86] Apparently, he did not realize that Haselkorn had violated a number of army regulations by threatening local French farmers, confronting Father Devaux as a

First Encounters with Survivors 29

representative of the American and French Jewish community, and flying to England specifically to collect clothes for the children instead of attending the chaplains' conference. In general, the army did not object to chaplains' working with civilians as long as it did not interfere with official military duties. Individual officers, however, did prohibit chaplains from engaging in relief work because they did not view this as being the responsibility of chaplains.[87]

In other areas of France, chaplains were busy with different types of problems. As only a fraction of the French rabbinate survived Nazi persecution, many small Jewish communities were without spiritual leadership. In Rheims, for example, the Jewish community asked Chaplain Isaac Klein, a thirty-nine-year-old Conservative rabbi of the Ninth Bomber Command, to serve as their rabbi. During the six to eight months he remained there, Klein organized a religious school and a youth group; reclaimed Jewish homes; had Hebrew textbooks and Yiddish newspapers, magazines, and books sent from the United States; and established a free loan society with money from Jewish soldiers and his congregation in Springfield, Massachusetts. When Chaplain Herschel Livazer, a forty-year-old Orthodox rabbi, came into the area, they alternated in conducting religious services at the Rheims synagogue.

Before coming to Rheims, Klein had been in Chartres, where he found twelve families who had been hidden in the vicinity. Throughout the war, they had used assumed names and were unaware of the identity of other Jews in the region. When Klein heard about them, he had his helmet painted with the Jewish chaplains' insignia and took a Yiddish newspaper to the city's main square. Within half an hour all the Jews appeared. Most of these Jews were self-sufficient and did not require Klein's assistance. They greeted him with affection; people touched his clothes and crowded around him. At every opportunity, they introduced him with great pride to the townspeople as the "Jewish Chaplain of the American Forces." Recognizing that the Jews would not have survived without the cooperation of the French, he made a point of personally visiting every family who had helped. In the name of American Jewry he thanked them for their sacrifices and presented them with gifts. But whenever he offered money, they refused to take it.[88]

Another chaplain involved in re-establishing a Jewish community was Morris Dembowitz, a twenty-nine-year-old Conservative rabbi assigned to the 179th General Hospital. He had been the first rabbi to arrive in Rouen after liberation. Although he stayed for a short time, he helped reorganize the Jewish community and provided clothes, food, and other commodities that could be purchased at the PX.[89]

The Jewish children who lived at the Chateau. (Photos courtesy of the Mintzer Collection, Magnes Museum.)

Many of the religious institutions that chaplains discovered in France were desecrated and vandalized and in need of repair. As a result of efforts by Chaplains David M. Eichhorn, Emanuel Schnek (a thirty-six-year-old Reform rabbi), Herman Dicker (a thirty-year-old Orthodox rabbi), Herbert Eskin (a twenty-one-year-old Orthodox rabbi), and Aaron J. Toifeld (a thirty-two-year-old Conservative rabbi), synagogues were cleansed and rededicated, *siffrei Torah* (Torah scrolls containing the five books of Moses) were found and returned, and at least one Jewish cemetery was restored. On several occasions, German prisoners of war were used as laborers in these renovations.[90]

Chaplain Jacob Segal, a thirty-one-year-old Conservative rabbi, established and taught a Hebrew class for the few remaining Jewish children in Chalon in between visits to twelve army hospitals and various units in the area. Chaplain Aaron Decter, a thirty-two-year-old Conservative rabbi at Headquarters Normandy Base Section, spent much of his time traveling from one military post to another but managed to raise money from American Jewish soldiers for a soup kitchen in Paris. Additional funds were distributed to individuals in need of relief or on their way home to Paris.[91]

The thirty-six chaplains who served in France at various times immediately following liberation were only peripherally involved in relief activities; French Jews did most of the work themselves with funds provided by the JDC. Despite these few examples, many of the chaplains were on the move, and there were few opportunities for them to become more than minimally active.

Perhaps one of the most important contributions the chaplains made before the JDC entered France was to circulate information about the condition of the French Jews. Through their monthly reports and personal communications, they channeled very useful data to CANRA, the JDC, the WJC, and prominent individuals in the Jewish world. This information alerted American Jews to the situation facing French Jews: the problem of arranging the return of Jewish children placed in convents or other places of refuge and caring for those whose parents were killed; the need for relief for a fair proportion of the entire Jewish population to sustain them through the winter months; the need to solve the legal questions concerning the repossession of confiscated property and the status of foreign Jews in the country; and the problems of trying to reunite families.

Some of the correspondence sent to the United States contained the names of many surviving French Jews who wished to locate relatives there. In Paris, Judah Nadich acted as a conduit for some of this news and he succeeded in establishing contact between several families. By virtue of his position, Nadich also became an unofficial spokesman on Jewish affairs to the foreign correspondents of the American press in the area. He provided Meyer Levin with names and locations of chaplains he should see and met with correspondents like Fred Graham of the *New York Times* and Morris Davis of the *New York Herald Tribune*. French Jewish leaders also sought his help in dealing with the American military authorities.[92]

The chaplains' work did not end when the JDC began to function in late 1944 and early 1945. Projects already under way frequently required continued attention, as did new problems that arose. The Rheims Jewish community, for example, continued to be supported by Chaplain Isaac Klein for some time after the JDC arrived. The JDC simply did not have the staff or the resources to cope with the massive difficulties they encountered in Europe.

In Holland and Belgium, American Jewish chaplains also reported finding conditions similar to those in France: desecrated synagogues in need of repair, a need for immediate financial assistance for returning survivors, Jewish children still in Christian care, and Jewish cultural life waiting to be rebuilt. For the most part, however, the chaplains were only able to provide temporary relief. In Maastricht, Holland, Chaplain Robert Marcus restored the community synagogue, supplied monetary aid to its eighty-three survivors, and requested additional help from the JDC. When Chaplain Meyer Goldman, a forty-four-year-old Orthodox rabbi assigned to the Ninth Air Division, took over after Marcus left, he learned that four Jewish children had been found in a nearby town. They had managed to support themselves during the war and wanted Goldman to introduce them to other Jews and suggest a way to lead a Jewish life.[93]

Chaplain Morris Sandhaus, a thirty-three-year-old Conservative rabbi assigned to Headquarters Channel Base Section, also became involved with Jewish orphans when Leo Friedman, a Jewish soldier, returned from Brussels and told of finding fifty-six Jewish children living in a Jewish home there. Eleven of the children had been released through the efforts of Friedman's childhood friend, and they were now in need of assistance. At a special meeting called to discuss this problem, the Jewish personnel at the headquarters signed two months' pay over to Chaplain Sandhaus so that he could take care of them.

In November 1944 Friedman wrote to the WJC about the children and pointed out that thousands of other Jewish children in Belgium were still in Christian homes. Some priests had agreed to turn over more children if Friedman's friend could prove that sufficient funds were available to take care of them. Friedman urged that everything be done to alert American Jewry to this problem so that it could be resolved quickly.[94]

The WJC welcomed such information, since it eagerly sought news about the condition of Jews in liberated Europe. A month before, Leon Kubowitzki had written to Marcus thanking him for his great interest in the Brussels Jewish community and for donating fifty thousand francs to aid the Jewish orphans. At that point, he noted that he and WJC were "paralyzed by our total ignorance of the present situation and by existing regulations." Kubowitzki asked Marcus to keep him informed, urging him to convince the Brussels Jewish community to compile a list of surviving Jews and requested that all data on the deportation of Jews be forwarded to him.[95]

The desire to re-establish cultural and religious ties with the American Jewish community was very strong among the liberated Jews of Europe. In Italy Chaplain Jacob Hochman, a thirty-two-year-old Conservative rabbi of the Rome Allied Area Council who helped coordinate relief activities for Jews in the city, attempted to restore the library of the Rome Jewish community. At the same time Robert Marcus endeavored to rebuild Jewish libraries in Paris and Brussels. In a letter of October 18, 1944, Marcus asked the Jewish Publication Society of America to send as many magazines, periodicals, pamphlets, books, and newspapers as could be spared. These resources, he believed, were extremely important in assisting survivors to break out of their cultural and spiritual isolation. Until adequate transportation could be found, however, none of this material could be sent to Europe. Louis Kraft, executive director of the JWB, suggested that in the meantime, the chaplains should donate the books and periodicals they had with them. This was, again, a stopgap measure.[96]

During the first few months of 1945, the Allies made important military progress in Germany; but there were few encounters with European Jewish survivors. When Chaplain Manuel Poliakoff, an Orthodox rabbi attached to the Ninth Army Twenty-Ninth Division, reached Munchen-Gladbach in early March 1945, he found two young Jewish girls (ages fourteen and sixteen) who had survived by posing as Polish Christians. He and the Jewish soldiers in his unit were able to provide whatever clothing and food they required; but when informed that the Twenty-Ninth Division would shortly be crossing the Rhine, Poliakoff decided to take them to Brussels. They remained there with a Jewish couple whom he had met on a previous visit.[97]

On March 22, 1945, Chaplains Robert Marcus and W. Gunther Plaut, a thirty-three-year-old Reform rabbi assigned to Headquarters 104th Infantry Division, conducted a service for the surviving Jews of Cologne. There were approximately 20,000 Jews in the city in 1933; only 11,000 by 1941; and only 275 when Marcus conducted his own survey in March. The local clergy had hidden some; others had been sheltered by non-Jewish friends and neighbors. Marcus sent these findings as well as a list of the survivors to the WJC. The *Congress Weekly* (a publication of the American Jewish Congress) published this report in its April 20, 1945 issue.[98]

Shortly after the Ninth Infantry Division established its headquarters in Bitterfeld, Germany in April, a group of eight or nine Hungarian Jewish teenagers approached Chaplain Max Wall, a thirty-year-old Conservative rabbi, for help. The children, who had just been released from a nearby slave labor camp where they survived by passing as non-Jews, were in need of food, clothing, and temporary shelter. Wall obtained clothing for them from the division's warehouse and food from a nearby German military storehouse. He then appropriated three houses for the children, who now numbered fifteen.

In appreciation for his help and kindness, they invited Wall to celebrate their first Sabbath together with them. He remembered this as being a highly emotional event: "We cried, and we ate and we danced and we talked." As with many chaplains in their initial meetings with the survivors in Germany, Wall believed these children were all that remained of the Jewish people in the country. "This was all that was left as far as I was concerned," he declared. "I hadn't seen anybody . . . you know I hadn't been reading the *New York Times.*"[99]

A few days later, the group said goodbye to Wall as they left for Hungary in what turned out to be a dangerous and often fatal search for their families. Several were killed by anti-Semites along the way, two were beaten to death when they arrived in their former towns, one or two disappeared, and a couple ultimately reached Palestine.

Wall had no trouble obtaining supplies or housing for the children even when German families had to be evicted from their homes in the process. Many of the men in his division had been fighting the Germans since the North African campaign and had just seen the Nordhausen concentration camp.[100]

The experience of the chaplains in North Africa, Italy, and Western Europe was a preface to problems that would confront them in Germany and Austria. It presented a dilemma not only for the chaplains but for CANRA as well. CANRA was unsure how to deal with the chaplains' unexpected involvement with Jewish survivors because it lacked sufficient knowledge about the conditions in Europe, the extent of the chaplains' activities, and the army's response to them. Until satisfactory answers could be obtained, CANRA chose not to intervene. In this way, it hoped to preserve its good relations with the army and within the American Jewish community. As difficult as the chaplains and CANRA found this period, the greatest challenges awaited them in Germany and Austria.

2

ISSUES AND PROBLEMS AFTER THE LIBERATION OF THE CAMPS: APRIL–JUNE 1945

American Military Government and Its Policy Toward Jewish Survivors

With the breakthrough of the Siegfried Line in March 1945, the American Army moved rapidly into southern and central Germany, reaching as far as the Alps and the Elbe River. As the war came to an end in May, the military government assumed responsibility for implementing American policy in the American zone of occupation. According to an agreement reached by the Allies, Germany was divided into four zones: French, Soviet, British, and American. The French occupied the Rhineland and the Saar Valley; the Soviets occupied eastern Germany; and the British were in northwestern Germany. The American zone included the southern states of Bavaria, Hesse, and North Württemberg-Baden; Bremen and Bremerhaven were in the British zone; and a portion of Berlin was under the joint authority of the Four Powers.[1] Austria was treated as a separate entity, also under Four Power occupation.[2]

By the latter part of June 1945, the American Army and the bureaucracy of the military government were established in Frankfurt. Supreme Headquarters, Allied Expeditionary Forces (SHAEF), which had been in Paris, was replaced by United States Forces, European Theater (USFET) and moved to Frankfurt. The army implemented a general demobilization after the war, but the Third and Seventh Armies were maintained for occupation duties. The Third Army was stationed in Bavaria, and the Seventh in Württemberg and Hesse.[3]

American actions and policies were governed by a broad range of goals, including the denazification and demilitarization of Germany; the rapid economic rehabilitation of Germany and Europe to ensure the continuation of free enterprise; and the halting of the growth of communism, or at least the containment of the Soviet Union in Central Europe. These goals, some of which were stated in directives, assumed a vital role in American policy and practice in Germany.[4]

Nevertheless, these objectives had to yield to more immediate problems of preventing mass starvation and homelessness created by the devastation of war, problems exacerbated by the presence of over ten million displaced persons in Germany, including concentration camp inmates, prisoners of war, slave laborers, voluntary workers, and foreign volunteers who had been transported to the Third Reich during the last months of the war.[5]

The Allied armies had expected to find millions of displaced persons; but estimates ranged from nine to thirty million. UNRRA had been established in 1943 to help the Western armies repatriate and resettle the vast number of uprooted people, since the Allies recognized that the task could not be accomplished by the military alone. While UNRRA was to provide medical, welfare, and administrative workers to aid the displaced persons, they could not operate in the liberated areas without consent of the military authorities. The Soviet Army was the only army not to use UNRRA. Instead, it repatriated the displaced persons as quickly as they were able to travel.[6]

To bring some order to the processing and care of the displaced persons, the army established a special displaced persons executive (DPX) at SHAEF. SHAEF incorrectly assumed, however, that many of these people had left their homeland unwillingly and were eager to return and that their governments and fellow citizens would welcome them back. While millions of non-Jews did return to their former homes, those who had collaborated with, or worked for, the German Army or industry were unwilling to return. They feared prosecution for their involvement with the Nazis. Many who had left Soviet territory also refused to go home because they wanted to live in freedom.[7]

Of all the displaced persons, the Jewish survivors presented the Allied armies with especially difficult problems. The majority of Jews who had survived were found in concentration camps.[8] The consequences of many years of maltreatment included malnutrition and severe medical problems. When the American and British armies entered the concentration camps in Germany and Austria in April and May, they found rampant epidemics—above all, widespread typhoid. In Buchenwald and other camps the American Medical Corps worked to save everyone they could, but large numbers of former inmates died.[9]

The chaplains were among the first American Jews to enter the camps; most were there for short periods, since their units were on the move. At Dachau, about twelve miles northwest of Munich, Chaplains Eli A. Bohnen, Max Braude, and David M. Eichhorn arrived at the camp within three days after it was liberated on April 29.[10]

On April 30 Eli Bohnen, a thirty-six-year-old Conservative rabbi attached to the Forty-Second Infantry Division, which had participated in the liberation of Dachau, and his assistant Eli Heimberg met with the inmates, listened to their stories, and wrote a number of letters to their relatives in the United States. The Jews found it difficult to believe they were free and in the presence of an American rabbi. Bohnen and Heimberg remained in the area for several days and then left when their unit was transferred to Kitzbuhel, the famous ski resort. After a short time, the Forty-Second moved on to Salzburg.[11] Chaplain Max Braude, a thirty-two-year-old Orthodox rabbi attached to the Seventh Army Headquarters, also arrived at Dachau on April 30. He visited the survivors; and when the army decided to quarantine a segment of the camp, he was included.[12]

The next day, Chaplain David M. Eichhorn entered Dachau and spent one week involved in relief activities there and at Allach, a satellite camp about five miles away. He supervised the gathering of lists of survivors and became a liaison between the Jews, the army, and Dachau's International Prisoners Committee. At Allach, Eichhorn presented the Jews with a *sefer Torah* at a special ceremony. En route to Munich, Eichhorn's unit passed through the city of Treuchtlingen, where he received the scroll from a local official who had hidden it in the town hall on *Kristallnacht* (the Night of Broken Glass, November 9–10, 1938), when the Nazis burned the local synagogue and killed the Jews in the city or chased them into the woods. After the service, Eichhorn was mobbed by hundreds of people trying to kiss his hand and ask for his autograph. The camp was administered by a Lieutenant Schreiber, a non-Jewish American officer, who, along with a small group of American soldiers and a well-organized group of inmates, worked very hard to save as many as they could. On Friday afternoon, May 4, Eichhorn held a service at the women's barracks at Dachau. A campwide service had been planned for the next day at the main square; but when the Polish inmates threatened to use force if a Jewish service was held there, the survivors had it moved indoors.

At the May 4 service, Lieutenant Colonel George Stevens, a Hollywood film director and head of the Signal Corps unit taking official army pictures of Dachau, heard of the threats against the Jews and immediately went to the camp commander to complain. The next day, under the protection of an American military honor guard, the service was held in the square with Stevens's unit filming the proceedings.

Before Eichhorn left Dachau on May 7, he called Seventh Army Headquarters to request that a chaplain be sent to the camp as soon as possible.[13] Within a couple of weeks Chaplain Abraham Klausner arrived at Dachau. Braude, who reported having helped expedite Klausner's transfer, wrote to Judah Nadich to ask that a JDC worker be assigned to the Munich area, where there were thousands of Jews in need of assistance within a fifty-mile radius of the city.[14]

While waiting for help to arrive, Braude began his own relief effort with the aid of a number of American Jewish soldiers. "We beg, we borrow, we steal, we cajole, we cuss, and we get the stuff that is needed," Braude wrote to his wife. He saw the task as enormous, but not hopeless: "Slowly we keep things going until this transition period is passed and adequate and thorough coverage will replace the necessary hits and misses."[15]

When Klausner learned of his assignment to the 116th Evacuation Hospital Unit, he was disturbed. Now that the war had ended in Europe, he had asked to serve in the Far East where he could be of more use to the soldiers still in combat. Instead, at the Chief of Chaplains' Headquarters in Paris, he was told that thousands of American Jewish soldiers were in a camp in Germany in need of a Jewish chaplain. This possibility seemed remote to Klausner, since Jews were not assigned in the American Army in this way. Reluctantly, Klausner set out to find the 116th but took his time. He reached Dachau during the third week in May.[16]

At Buchenwald, near the city of Weimar, Chaplain Emanuel Schenk arrived at the camp on April 11, 1945, with the Fourth Armoured Division, which had liberated the camp. After dropping off a company of men to stand guard, his unit continued in "hot pursuit" of the Germans leaving no opportunity for Schenk to offer assistance to the survivors.[17]

The following day, Chaplain Herschel Schacter arrived with the Third Army's Eighth Corps. Schacter remembered going from barracks to barracks declaring in Yiddish, *Shalom alecheim Yidden, ihr zint frei* (Hello Jews, you are free). Many seemed unaware of what had transpired. He explained that the war had ended and that he was an American rabbi who had come to help them. Soon, he was surrounded by people eager to hear him and talk to him. After Schacter received permission from the military commander in charge of Buchenwald to hold a religious service the following evening, he repeated his earlier statements over the camp's public address system. Hundreds of people attended this Friday night service conducted in a large auditorium on the camp grounds.[18]

After procuring an office in what had been the medical building, Schacter established a *chevrah kadisha* (Jewish burial society) and acquired a plot from the military for use as a Jewish cemetery. He also organized a group of Jews to compile lists of their fellow survivors in Buchenwald, including many women who drifted into the camp from surrounding areas. The information was passed on to the Bergen Belsen concentration camp in the British zone of Occupation resulting in a number of reunions. Lists were also forwarded to Judah Nadich who sent them to JDC headquarters in New York.

Many survivors wanted to communicate directly with their relatives and friends throughout the world, but no mail service existed at that point and civilians were prohibited from using the army postal system. To circumvent these regulations, Schacter sent survivors' correspondence under his own name and return address. To prevent the army from curtailing this project, each letter was placed in a military envelope and readdressed by a committee of Jewish soldiers.[19]

Chaplain Robert Marcus, who arrived in Buchenwald more than three weeks after Schacter, also handled survivors' mail, which he sent to the WJC in New York. Many of the letters he sent could not be delivered to the survivors' home towns because of misspellings and insufficient information. A large number were addressed to Christians, probably friends and neighbors, indicating that few believed their fellow Jews were alive. When a visiting American Jewish journalist informed them that approximately forty thousand Jews were still in Poland, they refused to believe him. They were convinced that none had survived.[20]

Many of the letters, written on scraps of paper, began with the same theme: "I cannot describe my sufferings to you. It is sufficient to tell you that I am all alone in the world; all of my relatives have been killed by the Nazis. I wonder how and why I have survived. I do not know what to do with myself. I would be very grateful to you if you were to facilitate my immigration to Palestine or to the United States."[21]

Marcus, who prior to the war had worked for the American Jewish Congress (an affiliate of the WJC), kept the WJC informed of his activities and sent them lists of Jewish survivors in Buchenwald and Bergen Belsen. He also wrote about his experiences for the *Congress Weekly* and was the subject of at least two articles in the *World Telegram*, a New York daily paper.[22] Unlike Marcus, Schacter sent most of his information to the JWB and to his family. The Jewish Telegraphic Agency and the Yiddish press in the United States quoted him several times but he had no time to write articles.[23]

Of the approximately two hundred thousand Jews who were liberated from the camps, about three-quarters returned to their former homelands. Jews from Western Europe (France, Holland, Belgium, Denmark, Norway), Hungary (the largest group), Rumania, and Czechoslovakia wanted to be repatriated so they could search for their families, reclaim their possessions, and reestablish themselves. Most of the sixty-five thousand surviving Jews from Poland and Lithuania were reluctant to go back home.[24] Many wondered how they could return to streets and towns empty of Jews: "To wander in these lands, lonely, homeless, always with the tragedy before one's eyes . . . and meet, again a former Gentile neighbor who would open his eyes wide and smile, remarking with double meaning, 'What! Yankel! You're still alive!'"[25]

Some Jews (how many is not known) returned to Poland, Lithuania, and Latvia in search of families and friends. Wherever they went in Eastern Europe, they were greeted with surprise and disappointment that they had survived. Also, they were subjected to all sorts of harassment, including arrests for collaborating with the Nazis. Most found that their homes and property, if they were intact, were in the hands of new owners; the possibility of restitution of such property was nonexistent.[26] Those who demanded the return of their possessions did so at the risk of their lives. Many Jews were murdered, despite the Polish government's efforts to prevent such acts.[27]

Once they completed their search, these Jews returned to Germany. Except for the Russians, who refused to acknowledge that a displaced persons problem existed in their zone, the other Allies assumed responsibility for the displaced persons in their areas.[28] Some of the problems the Jews posed for the Allies included their legal status; their need for food, clothing, shelter, rehabilitation, and medical care; and their desire to reestablish contacts with relatives and friends. After years of systematic persecution and mass killings by the Nazis, the Jews assumed that the Allies would provide special treatment for them. In particular, they expected separate camps where they would not have to share facilities with their former guards and tormentors.[29]

It soon became clear the Allies would not treat the Jews any better than the other displaced persons. The British refused to do so out of fear that the Jews would use their special status as leverage to obtain visas to enter Palestine, which the British vehemently opposed.[30] The Americans also rejected the idea of special consideration, in part because it would "tend to perpetuate the distinction of Nazi racial theory,"[31] which they viewed as a real danger. Even some American Jewish soldiers accepted this logic.[32]

To ensure that persons who had been persecuted "because of their race, religion, or activities in favor of the United Nations" were accorded the same treatment granted to the United Nations displaced persons, the DPX issued administrative memoranda to its unit commanders on April 16, 1945. This and similar memoranda were not heeded by local commanders, which caused difficulties for Jewish survivors. Jews from Germany, Austria, and other Axis countries, for example, were not treated as United Nations displaced persons but, rather, as belonging to former enemy nations. Jews from nonenemy countries were often forced into displaced persons camps and installations with their former guards and killers. The April 16 DPX memorandum also stated that no person should be repatriated against his will except Soviet citizens and war criminals. Many local commanders failed to inform the Jews of this option and even bribed and threatened them to accept repatriation.[33]

In general, the survivors suffered from intolerable living conditions, inadequate food and clothing, and the lack of freedom to choose their own destinies. Abraham J. Klausner, who surveyed the plight of approximately 14,000 Jews in seventeen displaced persons camps in Bavaria during May and June 1945, sent a report to the leadership of American Jewish community about the conditions in Germany. At the Turkheim camp Klausner found 450 Jews still living behind double barbed wire fences that were electrically charged. The camp "is literally a cesspool," he noted: "By any standards," it should be "condemned." At Buchberg, a former powder factory, 1,000 Jews were crowded into "dilapidated structures." Everywhere, soap, linens, toothbrushes, and laundry facilities were unobtainable. Even at better camps, accommodations were overcrowded, people slept on the floors, and cellars were converted into dormitories. Plumbing, when available, was always inadequate.

Food was generally scarce in the immediate postwar period; some claimed they had received more in the concentration camps. The average intake per day at some camps was between nine hundred and one thousand calories. The clothing situation was no better, since the majority of Jews were still clothed in their striped prisoner uniforms. Although responsible for assisting the survivors, UNRRA was unable to do anything at first, while the Red Cross helped for only a short period at the end of the war. A limited number of Jews received clothes from the Dachau storehouse because of Klausner's intervention.

Another problem was the lack of any overall plan for the supervision or dissolution of the camps. One camp was under the control of the military government, another under the Dachau Command (of the American Army), and a third under the jurisdiction of still another military unit. American officers in charge of these camps had little or no training for the job. At two camps, the commanding officers operated under their own improvised rules. In Pensing, the commanding officer of the airport arbitrarily forced sixty Jews to leave an area requisitioned by the military government without the slightest concern about where they could go.

Several groups and missions "of varying hues" came to visit these Jews and offer "verbal balm for their wounds"; but for the most part, they only raised false hopes: "Here and there a Jew would speak up as a representative, but in most cases he turned out to be a false messiah on a picture taking tour or in search of an experience to give him the right to say—'I was in Dachau.'" Klausner summarized the predicament of the Jews: "Liberated but not free, that is the paradox of the Jew." The Jew "still waits only because he must. The guard at the gate, the blocked roads, the tattered garb, the endlessness of the road all say—wait! But it is with little faith and less hope." Klausner's criticism was in part a response to the indifference—and at times outright hostility of the United States military—to the Jewish survivors.[34]

The negative attitude of the American military toward the Jews had several causes. Many officers could not comprehend why Jews would not return to their former countries or why they wanted recognition as a separate nationality. Part of the problem was that the American Army failed to understand the unique situation of the Jews and informed its officers not to treat them differently than other displaced persons. As a result, the soldiers perceived the Jews as an added burden and did not want to be responsible for providing them with food (which had to be confiscated from the Germans) or other necessities. In some cases, the soldiers feared their careers would be damaged by adverse reaction from the military if they mishandled their involvement with displaced persons.

Furthermore, many officers were combat soldiers uncomfortable in their new role as civilian administrators; they resented anyone who disturbed the status quo. As one authority of the American occupation has noted, "Some Military Government detachments conceived themselves as perfectly free agents and a few even boasted that they had thrown away their *Handbooks* and read almost nothing which came to them" from the American Army. Some officers expressed surprise that Washington was interested in Germany's problems and that there was any place in field operations for policy decisions made in Washington.[35]

These attitudes are not surprising, since the military government personnel had been trained "to get communication and transport going again, behind a front line, not to govern." With rare exception, they knew "nothing about Germany." They did not speak the language; had to rely upon "unreliable interpreters"; and had not been taught German history, politics, or economics. Moreover, "they knew next to nothing about how to deal with the wreckage of human minds and spirits which was to constitute one of their major responsibilities in Germany."[36] It should be noted that there were many American officers and soldiers who were deeply moved by the plight of the Jewish displaced persons and tried to assist them. A few even helped Jews illegally to enter the American zone of Germany.

A large percentage of the "officers who had been trained went home in the first six months of the occupation because they had sufficient points to be discharged." Those who stayed were "disheartened by the chaotic conditions in which they had to work, by the absence of any clear idea of what they were supposed to do, and by the hopeless inadequacy of the 'teenage' replacements." Most commanders of tactical units and their troops did not understand the role of the military government and were reluctant to allow its personnel to function in territory under their control.[37]

These problems affected the survivors and were further exacerbated by UNRRA's inability to function effectively from the start. UNRRA workers were often chosen in haste and poorly trained; many were incompetent, inefficient, unable to adapt, and incapable of communicating with the displaced persons because they lacked knowledge of the requisite languages. Moreover, UNRRA policies were confused; its programs were uncoordinated and poorly administered; and, in general, the organization was on poor terms with the army.[38]

The JDC wanted to assist the survivors immediately after the cessation of hostilities. The army, at that point, however, would not permit the JDC to enter Germany because it did not want civilian relief agencies not directly under its control to interfere with its own occupation and relief efforts. Once the military was ready for the JDC, it would be allowed into Germany and Austria. If the JDC entered earlier, the army feared, Protestant and Catholic relief agencies would also demand the same right.[39]

The absence of any well-organized relief effort meant that the survivors had to rely heavily on American Jewish chaplains, members of the Jewish Brigade, and self-help. During April, May, and June approximately thirty chaplains passed through Germany. Some stayed, but most were in the country on temporary assignment.

In helping the displaced persons, the chaplains had comparatively few options. Although local commanders determined how displaced persons policies would be implemented in their areas, chaplains could try to influence how these policies were carried out, attempt to minimize the effects of a hostile or insensitive attitude, or (failing that) take the initiative—which sometimes meant jeopardizing their own careers by engaging in covert actions to ease at least the most immediate traumas and dilemmas of the survivors.

One of their first obstacles was how to circumvent the army's nonfraternization policy. Officially announced on September 13, 1944, the day after the Allied forces first entered Germany on the Western Front, this policy remained in effect without change until June 8, 1945 and further (with some changes) until October 1, 1945. The army defined *nonfraternization* as "the avoidance of mingling with Germans upon terms of friendliness, familiarity, or intimacy, whether individually or in groups, official or unofficial dealings." This meant that American soldiers were prohibited from "visiting German homes, drinking with Germans; shaking hands with them; playing games or sports with them; giving or accepting gifts; attending German dances or other social events; accompanying Germans on the street, in theaters, taverns, hotels, or elsewhere (except on official business); discussions and arguments with Germans, especially on politics or the future of Germany." At the same time, however, the soldiers were told that nonfraternization "does not demand rough, undignified or aggressive conduct, nor the insolent overbearance which characterized Nazi leadership."[40]

The army instituted this policy to ensure the success of the military occupation. The proponents of nonfraternization feared that the Allies would encounter large-scale resistance and a hostile civilian population. Moreover, they felt that once hostilities ended, the soldiers, particularly the Americans, would be susceptible to German propaganda. Prohibiting friendly relations between the Germans and the Allies would also "impress a people imbued with militarism and a respect for uniforms" and thus make the task of the military government that much easier. At the same time, it would also raise the morale of the American Army.[41]

It is difficult to determine the extent to which this policy inhibited the chaplains from working with the survivors. During this period of transition, their commanding officers were not always aware of how involved the chaplains were in displaced persons work or the degree to which army regulations were being violated. Some encouraged the chaplains to help, while others adamantly opposed this assistance.

It is equally difficult to determine the effect the nonfraternization policy had on the American Jewish soldiers. Many soldiers sent letters to the United States describing the plight of Jews in Germany, but the extent of their private activities is undocumented. One survivor in Buchenwald, however, complained to the WJC that this policy did create problems. "The American soldiers," he observed, "are not sure whether the law of nonfraternization must be employed on them [the soldiers], too, or not, therefore a lot of Americans—amongst them Jews!—avoid any contact with the Jews in Germany."[42]

Some of those who became involved with the survivors were dedicated. There were some who threatened physical violence against German officials reluctant to open up their food storehouses to feed Jewish displaced persons. In some cases, soldiers might have even killed Germans to get this food.[43] Other Jewish GIs helped by finding survivors employment in the army as butlers, tailors, bakers, and cooks. Food was sometimes supplied from the army mess hall (dining room) or donated by sympathetic army cooks. Lists of survivors were also passed on to Paris. Some soldiers worked with the displaced persons in their camps, but this was pitifully small in comparison to the massive aid that was needed.

It is to be doubted that the soldiers understood the magnitude of the problem during these early months. In June 1945, after visiting the concentration camp Dora near Nordhausen, one GI wrote to the JDC to inform them that its job was not really that difficult. He declared that most Jews in the area were dead; only small clusters of Jews remained. He advised them to send a Yiddish-speaking representative who would come to boost their morale and gather them into one or two camps. There they would be cared for until a permanent solution could be found. At about the same time, another soldier wrote to his fraternal organization in New York that he had rescued the only survivors from the Dachau concentration camp and that these seven men (ranging in age from eighteen to twenty-three) were now working in his battalion's kitchen. Once his unit would leave Germany they would have no place to go so he urged the organization to find some way to help them.[44] How the soldiers could have reached this conclusion is not clear. At Dachau twenty-seven hundred Jews were liberated on April 29 as were thousands more at Allach.[45]

"Liberated but Not Free"

The magnitude of the problems facing survivors and the uncertainty of how long chaplains would be in the area meant that they could alleviate only a few of the more pressing problems. The only exception was Chaplain Abraham Klausner, who spent all of his time on displaced persons work and tried to deal with the broader issues of army policy toward the displaced persons. Other chaplains were often able to influence the army in specific ways. Thus, chaplains were able to convince their commanders to give Jews special consideration, but this generally had little cumulative effect on policy.

Several weeks after Chaplain Abraham Haselkorn (formerly in Le Mans, France) arrived at the Mannheim-Heidelberg area, he learned that 249 survivors (Jews from Random, Poland) from the Vaihingen concentration camp near Stuttgart desperately needed his help. After being liberated they had been taken to a village in the French zone of occupation to be nursed back to health. When Haselkorn visited them in late May or early June, he found them in the care of a French Red Cross team and under the jurisdiction of the French military government. Only a hundred of them were well enough to meet with him; the rest were still bedridden with typhus.

At this meeting, Haselkorn learned that the French planned to send these Jews to a Polish displaced persons camp and that they all feared for their lives. Deeply concerned, he contacted Lieutenant Albert A. Hutler, an officer in charge of displaced persons in southwest Germany, to have the group transferred to the American zone. At first, Hutler appeared reluctant; the army was extremely strict about moving displaced persons from one zone to another, especially when this required feeding, clothing, and housing them for a lengthy period. Haselkorn, however, remained adamant; after Hutler himself had met with the survivors, he, too, agreed that they had to be transferred. The French officer in charge proved very sympathetic and willingly provided the beds, mattresses, and pillows the survivors needed. Hutler arranged for transportation and had the group temporarily housed at a camp in Bensheim until more permanent quarters could be found.

Hutler then surveyed the area and found a castle, Schloss Langenzell, about nine miles from Heidelberg. He proceeded to evict the few German families and non-German collaborators living there and moved the Jews in on June 18, 1945. Two workers from UNRRA under the direction of Lieutenant Cal Plessner of the Heidelberg *Landkreis* (rural counties) detachment ran the "camp" for this group of Jews. The army provided their basic needs; and many soldiers, both Jewish and non-Jewish, contributed clothing, food, and books. Within a short time, a camp committee was established, one of its many functions being to trace the survivors' families. Haselkorn spent much of his time with these survivors, serving as both counselor and friend.

Shortly after he had moved the Jews into Schloss Langenzell, Hutler informed his commanding officer, Lieutenant Charles Winning (a former professor at New York University), what he had done. Until then he had acted strictly on his own initiative, knowing full well that the penalty for such independent action could have been a court-martial. But instead of reprimanding him, Winning praised his work and requested to see "our Jews." Hutler then went to the camp to arrange for him to visit Meyer Guttman, chairman of the Jewish Survivors' Committee. When Winning arrived, he was satisfied with what he saw and expressed his desire to help in every way possible.[46]

Like Haselkorn, some chaplains found they could count on the good will of their superior officers. In Buchenwald, for example,

Chaplain Herschel Schacter convinced the colonel in charge of civilian affairs that the Jews deserved special consideration. Although it required many long hours of discussion, Schacter received permission for a group of young people from the camp to set up a kibbutz to prepare them for life in Palestine.[47]

On June 3, 1945, the first group left Buchenwald for their new home on a farm at Eggendorf. With this move they had hoped to demonstrate their abhorrence to living in the former camp, their dislike of being dependent on philanthropy and the good will of others, and their desire to channel reawakened energy that was seeking an outlet.[48] Most members of this new kibbutz, which they named Kibbutz Buchenwald, had been Zionists before the war (from such divergent groups as Agudat Yisrael and Hashomer Hazair), while the rest came to realize, as a result of their suffering, that the only place for Jews was *Eretz Yisrael* (The Land of Israel).

Within a few weeks, however, they were forced to move farther west, as the Russian Army advanced into their area. On June 24, 1945, the group arrived in Geringshof, outside the city of Fulda. Before the war, there had been a religious *hachshara* there and the members of Kibbutz Buchenwald persuaded the American military authorities to let them rebuild it. Chaplains Herschel Schacter and Robert Marcus visited the kibbutz whenever they could and brought food, clothing, and reading material. With the cooperation of the American military, Marcus provided furniture and household utensils and bought tools with money donated by Jewish soldiers in his unit. He was also instrumental in obtaining immigration certificates that the group had requested.[49]

As accommodating as some of the military officers could be, the chaplains recognized that they could not expect these officers to violate army regulations indefinitely; and in some cases, they had to strike out on their own. This was the experience of Chaplain Ernst Lorge, a twenty-nine-year-old Reform rabbi assigned to the Sixty-Ninth Division. During the period from April 26 to June 30, he assisted over one thousand Jewish women who had survived Auschwitz. He discovered that they were living in displaced persons camps east of Leipzig, in Wurzen, Grimma, and Torgau on a level close to starvation. He requested help from Major General Emil F. Reinhart, the commander of his division. Reinhart immediately ordered a 20 percent cut in the division's rations and had the surplus given to the Jews. Lorge organized a "mercy caravan" of five jeeps to distribute the food and also arranged to have medical supplies sent along.

Shortly before the Americans were to evacuate the region and allow the Russians to take over this zone, the Jews besieged Lorge with requests that they not be left behind. The army, in fact, provided special trains to transport many of the displaced persons who wished to go to the American zone; but it insisted that Jews travel together with Christian Poles. These Jews adamantly refused to board the train, and Lorge spent considerable time negotiating with the American military and German railroad authorities until the Jews were allowed to have their own train.

Lorge then had to decide what was to be done with the Jews who were still confined in the hospital in Grimma. They had vowed to commit suicide unless they were taken to the American zone, and Lorge believed many of them were prepared to carry out their threat. Rather than ask his commanding officer to violate the army rule strictly prohibiting the removal of hospital patients without authorization, Lorge chose to act in disregard of this rule. With the help of a Jewish major in the Ordinance Corps, he found two trucks and non-Jewish drivers, who transported about thirty of the patients from Grimma and began searching for a hospital in Bavaria. Two hospitals refused to admit them; but they were accepted in a third, a field hospital.[50]

Like Lorge, other chaplains ran the risk of jeopardizing their careers in order to assist survivors. For example, Herbert Eskin, an Orthodox rabbi attached to the Special Troops, 100th Infantry Division, won support for some of his requests concerning special rights and privileges for the German Jews and displaced persons in Stuttgart, where his unit was stationed. But when his other requests were denied, he resorted to a number of illegal activities.

He obtained assistance for the most immediate problem he encountered: how to find a home for the Jews who were wandering aimlessly through the city looking for aid. He asked the new mayor of Stuttgart to allow him to use a three-story, block-long building that had once belonged to a prominent Jewish family. The mayor agreed; and Eskin established a committee, the Israeliteische Kultusvereinigung of Stuttgart, to organize relief work. Subsequently, as a tribute to his efforts, the building became known as the Eskin House.

Each of the survivors who came to this center was able to find someone with whom he could discuss his problems. In addition, room, board, and clothing were provided for all those in need; and an effort was made to contact their relatives. The city administration also supplied these Jews with a daily ration of two thousand calories, the amount accorded physical laborers. Eskin was able to supplement this with food provided by two Jewish soldiers in the Quartermaster Corps.

For the first few weeks after the liberation, Eskin obtained meat from the local farmers and additional food from German groceries. Subsequently, however, he had to procure food through illegal means. At night, he and five or six Jewish soldiers would go off to different villages in the area and force the farmers at gunpoint to slaughter their cattle and prepare them for cooking. For these trips, Eskin "borrowed" a two-and-a-half ton army truck from the motor pool and followed behind in his jeep. On the way back, he and his men would raid a German grocery store and take whatever else they needed. By four o'clock they would return the truck and be ready for the six o'clock formation.

During this same time, Eskin learned that twenty Jewish girls were in a labor camp near the city of Heilbronn, where they were still being used as prostitutes. When Eskin arrived with three other Jewish soldiers, he closed off the rear exit of the building; and as the men came out the front, his soldiers struck them with their rifle butts. Eskin and his men liberated the girls, who were then taken to an army hospital and later to a convalescent home in Degerloch.

They were not the first group of Jews Eskin arranged to have transported to Degerloch. After learning that former residents of Stuttgart were still in Theresienstadt, he arranged to have them brought back to the city. He was forced to use charcoal-burning buses, because his request to the American and French military governments for gasoline had been denied. Actually, according to official regulations, he was prohibited from asking even for assistance with transportation.[51]

Another chaplain who took severe risks was Eugene Lipman, a Reform rabbi, assigned to Headquarters XII Corps. In the Cologne region he found displaced persons who desperately required his help—two hundred Jews from Buchenwald, Dachau, and Theresienstadt. To aid them, Lipman asked many Jewish soldiers scattered through the Ruhr (the region from below Cologne to Essen and Duisburg) to beg, borrow, or steal food packages from their mess units. In addition, together with a few Jewish soldiers, he would go out at night to army food dumps and steal huge amounts of rations. This project lasted only about a month; for on June 15, 1945, he was transferred to Pilsen, Czechoslovakia.[52]

For several reasons, most chaplains rarely encountered Jewish children. Very few children had managed to survive the war; and those who had were quickly removed from Germany by the army. A SHAEF cable of June 7, 1945, stated that all unaccompanied children under seventeen years of age were to be taken out of Germany and cared for temporarily in liberated areas.[53] To ensure that the children would be safely relocated, several Jewish organizations asked the French government to accept some of the orphans in late May. France agreed to admit five hundred of them in the first of two transports. At the time, the Jewish organizations that requested the move could not have foreseen the complications it would entail; nor could the Jewish chaplains who helped transport the children to France.

In addition to the 500 children permitted, others managed to board this transport, raising the number to 535. Most of them had been interned in Buchenwald, though ninety-two had been in the Bergen-Belsen concentration camp. Sylvia Neulander, a Jewish woman working for the American Red Cross, brought the latter group to Buchenwald, because she learned that Hillersleben, the area to which the liberated Belsen group had been assigned, was about to be turned over to the Russians. From Buchenwald she then went on to Paris to await the children's arrival there.[54]

Chaplain Robert Marcus, who had worked with many of these children in Buchenwald, accompanied them on this trip. Flags and banners decorated the train, some with the legend To Liberty and a New Life. From the moment the train pulled out of the station, Marcus was kept busy. Some of the children would pull the emergency cord every ten or fifteen minutes, causing the train to stop. Others rode on the outside of the train throwing stones at the Germans and shouting, "Nazi murderers, where are our parents?" During frequent stops along the way, they gathered fruit or vegetables from local fields, brooking no interference from the German owners. When a German threw a stone at the train, about fifty children jumped off while it was still moving and ran after the assailant. Failing to catch up with him, they attacked other Germans until Marcus separated them.

Despite such behavior, the children tried not to aggravate "Herr Rabbiner." The older youngsters were particularly helpful in distributing the food. Marcus was amazed that many of the fifteen- and sixteen-year-old boys, who had attended yeshivot in Poland and Hungary, were still able to discuss the Bible and Talmud. In some of the cars *minyanim* (religious services) were held three times a day. To occupy themselves, they sang Hebrew songs about Palestine and of their faith in the future; and for Marcus they held a concert of songs of the ghettos and concentration camps.

On June 7 the transport reached Thionville, a French border town, where it was met by representatives of SHAEF, the American Red Cross, and the French government. The children were then divided into two groups. A SHAEF representative took 427 of them to a chateau in Normandy belonging to the French branch of the OSE. According to an agreement announced on May 25, these children were to be cared for by the OSE and financially supported by the JDC. The other 108, including the 92 from Bergen-Belsen, went on the Paris with Marcus. He was determined to keep the Belsen survivors intact as a group in Paris, because they already had immigration certificates for Palestine.[55]

Nonetheless, when Marcus and his group arrived at the Gare de L'Est on June 8, an official of the French Ministry of Prisoners, Deportees, and Refugees informed him that "the children are in France now" and that the French government would decide their fate. Marcus reminded the man that the De Gaulle government was obliged to adhere to the agreement reached with SHAEF. The official refused to listen, and a heated debate ensued.[56]

Sylvia Neulander, who was at the station to greet the children, tried to help Marcus; but several French welfare workers brushed her aside, explaining that the affair was none of her business. She then appealed to Carl Levin, a correspondent for the *New York Herald Tribune*. After Levin arrived and witnessed the scene, he wrote a story that appeared on the paper's front page under the headline "Europe Vies for Orphaned Jews; Seeks Them To Build Population."

Marcus did not know how the French proposed to handle his charges; but until a satisfactory solution could be found, he consented to have them taken to the deportee center at the Hotel Lutetia. There he discovered that the French planned to send most of them to the Nonsectarian Committee of the Resistance, as wards of the French state. This disturbed Marcus deeply; and seeing nuns circulating among the children, he realized that the struggle for the children's souls had begun. France was not the only country vying for the custody of Jewish orphans, but this confrontation brought the problem into the open.[57]

Marcus had to return to his unit before the question could be decided, but Neulander stayed in Paris to continue the fight. She sent letters to Hadassah; to the Jewish Agency for Palestine; to Rabbi Stephen S. Wise, president of the American Jewish Congress and one of the most prominent leaders of American Jewry; and to anyone else she thought could help. What impact, if any, her correspondence had on these organizations and individuals cannot be determined.

In the meantime, the children were moved to a rest camp; but with the aid of a Jewish chaplain, she found them. This episode generated so much publicity that the French ambassador to the United States issued a statement reassuring all those concerned that his government would not interfere with any program sponsored by a Jewish organization to rehabilitate Jewish children. Shortly thereafter, the children were returned to the OSE.[58]

All these facts notwithstanding, it is equally true that Jews throughout the world owe an enormous debt of gratitude to the nuns of France, Belgium, and Italy, especially for giving refuge and care to thousands of Jewish children in the prewar and early war years. Had it not been for the nuns, these children doubtless would have perished.

Chaplain Herschel Schacter accompanied a second transport of children from Buchenwald to Switzerland on June 19. The Swiss government had stipulated that only 350 children under the age of sixteen would be allowed into the country. Schacter found only 250 in Buchenwald, but Chaplain Ernst Lorge sent along others. When the transport left, it included 279 children under the age of sixteen. When Schacter's help, another 171 stowaways of varying ages, some over the age of sixteen, also managed to get aboard the train.

While still at Thionville, Schacter obtained permission from the French government to allow 102 of his charges to remain in France, where they would be cared for by the OSE. The remaining 348 continued on to Switzerland with him. When the train reached Switzerland, armed troops surrounded it to ensure that only the prescribed number of children and only those under age sixteen would enter the country. After the troops discovered there were children over the age limit, they refused to admit the transport. Schacter contacted the Swiss Jewish community and the American consul to help with this impasse; and after some time, the Swiss agreed to admit all 348 children.[59]

Schacter also met in Switzerland with representatives of the Jewish Agency for Palestine, the WJC, the Hechalutz World Organization, the Committee for the War Stricken Jewish Population, and the Swiss representatives of the Palestine Office. The meeting took place in Geneva on June 27, 1945; and Schacter reported on the condition of Jewish refugees in Germany. At the end of the session, they urged him to inform his superior officers that the group wanted to send representatives to Germany as soon as possible. Having failed to gain the necessary permission on their own, they hoped that an American Jewish chaplain would be able to explain how essential it was for them to make contact with fellow Jews.[60]

When Schacter returned to Buchenwald in early July, the camp had already been transferred to the Russian zone of occupation. If Schacter discussed the issues raised at the Geneva meeting with his superior officers, the result was a foregone conclusion: they could not change army policy, even if they wished to do so.

Chaplains spent much time and energy working with the military leaders at the local level to try to change policies toward the Jews. When they failed, some complained to SHAEF (and later, to USFET) headquarters. Chaplain Harold Saperstein, for example, went to the offices of Lieutenant General Lucius B. Clay of the Civil Affairs Section (G-5) of SHAEF to protest how the Jews were being treated. Saperstein expected to see a major or colonel; instead, they took him to the office of Lieutenant General Clay, General Dwight D. Eisenhower's deputy in charge of the military occupation. In addition to Clay, another general and a corporal were present.

Saperstein recalled Clay as being "very friendly, receptive to my coming with no formalities about why are you bothering us." He was, however, "completely unaware of the significance of the problem that I was trying to present to him. In other words the Jewish problem which to us Jewish men was central to our concern in fighting the Nazis was not at all a factor in the minds of the military." When he asked Clay why the JDC was not permitted to enter Germany, Clay claimed that if the Jews were given permission, the Protestants and Catholics would also demand to be let in, which would only compound the confusion. Once the military had completed its initial work, the doors would be open to all. The fact that the Jews were the central target of the Nazis, that they had suffered more than any other group and thus required special treatment "never apparently entered his mind." "He was well meaning," Saperstein asserted. "It was not anti-Semitism. It was just . . . a lack of understanding."

Having failed to move General Clay, Saperstein, like other chaplains who were unable to effect a change in army policy, turned to American Jews for help. On June 22, 1945, Saperstein sent Stephen S. Wise a letter describing what had transpired at the meeting and suggested that the civilian agencies were in a better position to influence policy changes. After all, he said, a soldier in uniform cannot keep saying *but* to a three-star general. Saperstein also told Wise that he had assured hundreds of Jews that Wise would do something about their plight. "They had looked forward to the coming of the Americans as to the coming of the Messiah," Saperstein concluded. "They are understandably impatient—they have already waited so long."[61]

There is no record of Wise's answer to Saperstein's letter, but it is clear from similar communications sent to Wise by other chaplains that he was aware of these problems and felt frustrated by the WJC's inability to have its representatives sent to Europe. It is also clear that these letters to Wise had some impact, since he included information from them in a report on conditions in the camps that was distributed throughout the United States and quoted in the *Jewish Spectator*.

In addition, Arieh Tartakower of the WJC sent Chaplains Robert Marcus, Judah Nadich, and Joseph Shubow a letter on June 25 stating that he wanted "to express once more in the name of Dr. Stephen S. Wise, Dr. Nahum Goldmann and the entire Executive Committee of the World Jewish Congress, our thanks and our profound admiration for your relentless efforts on behalf on the unfortunate remnants of our people in the German concentration camps liberated by the Allies." Tartakower assured the chaplains that this information "enabled us to draw the attention of the proper authorities to the appalling conditions under which our people are still living and to ask for the alleviation of their situation." He concluded, however, that "what counts is not only the material help which you tried to organize for them, but even more the moral spirit—so badly needed by those who for six long years had to live under the most inhuman conditions."[62]

Tartakower's last point is particularly important because the chaplains offered more than just material aid. The survivors also needed spiritual assistance; and a number of chaplains reported that they were overwhelmed by the demand for GI prayer books, *mezzuzot,* and any religious articles available. Chaplain Sidney M. Lefkowitz, a thirty-seven-year-old Reform rabbi assigned to the Third Armored Division, reported that he "rarely witnessed such emotion" as when he gave *mezzuzot* to the survivors at the Nordhausen concentration camp.[63] Abraham Klausner reported that a "riot ensued" when only two hundred prayer books were available for the over a thousand survivors attending a religious service at which he officiated. He asked CANRA to send him large quantities of religious items immediately to meet the demand.[64]

Chaplain Herschel Schacter observed that these religious articles were in such great demand because "it reminded the people of their homes, of Jewish tradition, and of their renewed ties with the world Jewish community."[65]

More important, however, were the religious services conducted by the chaplains and displaced persons rabbis for the survivors. Services were held in Buchenwald, Dachau, Allach, Nordhausen, and elsewhere. These were generally the first religious services the survivors attended after the war and were charged with emotion. Jack Bretkopf, a survivor of Buchenwald, summed up the feeling of many who attended a seder conducted by Herschel Schacter when he recalled how they "crowded into the house that the Nazis had used and listened to Rabbi Schacter speak of freedom, of the meaning of Passover. What he did, no money can pay back for the love and warmth he gave us."[66]

Abraham Klausner

In dealing with the military most chaplains avoided confrontation, except for Abraham Klausner. He did everything possible to make the army acknowledge the uniqueness of the Jews' situation. He worked not only to improve immediate problems and needs but also to have Jewish survivors recognized as a separate nationality, to establish separate camps for them, and to create an organization that would represent their interests to the military. At the same time, he tried to alert American Jews to their plight.

Klausner arrived at Dachau during the third week in May to join the 116th Evacuation Hospital Unit. No one knew what functions Klausner was to perform aside from presiding over the burying of the dead and signing the death register. Klausner was surprised and relieved that the survivors did not vent on him the anger they felt toward American Jews for failing to save them. Instead of recriminations and bitterness, they expressed an eagerness to rebuild their lives and rejoin their families. He was embarrassed because he had nothing to offer except the little *mezzuzot* ordinarily distributed by chaplains to Jewish soldiers.

Shortly before his unit was ordered out of Dachau on June 2, 1945, he realized that he could do something to improve their lot. Many inmates questioned him about their relatives in the United States, among them a man so ill that he was still confined to his barracks. He told Klausner he had a brother who had emigrated to America and become an Orthodox rabbi. Fortunately, that very rabbi, Chaplain Abraham Spiro, had come to Europe with Klausner and had been assigned to the 17th Reinforcement Depot. After Klausner had brought the two brothers together, he realized how urgently survivors needed to be reunited with relatives, and he conceived of a plan to help facilitate such reunions.

His idea was to compile and publish volumes containing systematic, exhaustive lists of survivors and distribute these volumes throughout the world. Before he could implement his plan, however, his unit was ordered out of Dachau and sent to a resort over a hundred miles away to recover from battle fatigue. The soldiers had been in Europe since the battle of Anzio. Klausner accompanied the men; but once at the resort, he realized that he was needed back at Dachau. As the truck began its return trip, he jumped on board, being careful to disembark before it entered the camp, so as to forestall objections to his return. He then went to the 127th unit, which also had been working in Dachau, and informed the army staff that he had been reassigned. His papers, he assured them, would arrive later. After the 127th departed, Chaplain Max Braude arranged to have Klausner assigned to another unit to prevent his being court-martialed. Fortunately for Klausner, this period of postwar transition was utterly chaotic: either no one knew of his return or whoever knew did not report him.[67]

Once back at Dachau, Klausner set up a committee to compile lists of Jewish survivors. In Landsberg, where Adolf Hitler had written *Mein Kampf* over twenty years earlier, he found a print shop and bribed the printer to publish these lists. On June 21, 1945, the first volume appeared. Containing the names of thousands of Jewish survivors in Bavaria, the volume was sent to Jews throughout the world. Just how important it and the subsequent volumes were can be gauged by the enormous demand for copies. Requests for all six volumes came from Jewish relief agencies in the United States, England, France, Spain, and Palestine, as well as from other chaplains, UNRRA teams, and civil affairs officers.[68]

The first volume had particularly great significance for the survivors because it represented their first major attempt to communicate with Jews in the West. Klausner used this *Shearit Hapletah* volume not only to comfort and reassure the survivors but also to inform them of their rights. In his foreword he explained that for several reasons the volume could not provide a definitive account of all survivors in the area: former inmates of the camps and hospitals were constantly on the move and some camps were being closed; in addition, a number of Jews were returning to their former lands. Consequently, in some cases, a name listed merely signified that an individual had been at the camp indicated when the list was compiled. Klausner assured the survivors that he would do everything he could to reunite them with their families and friends and that more complete lists of all the Jews in Germany would be forthcoming within a few weeks.

Klausner also pledged in his foreword to do whatever he could to help the survivors until they were free to rebuild their lives where they chose. By this time, schools were being established at the larger displaced persons camps and initial efforts made to provide Jews with religious materials. The latter became available when the United States military government seized an enormous library that the Nazis had stolen in Warsaw and brought to Germany. Klausner acted quickly and had the collection distributed throughout Bavaria.

To enable survivors to know and understand their rights, Klausner also prefaced this volume with a special page entitled "Regarding Your Rights." Here he emphasized that Jews did not have to return to their former countries, that they were entitled to decide the question of repatriation freely, not under duress. He pointed out that those who wanted to be repatriated would be able to return home when regular transports began operating and that all other immigration problems would be resolved on an individual basis by the JDC as soon as it established its office in Germany.

Klausner also asserted that the Jews had a right to communicate with their families and friends throughout the world. Since no mail service existed at this point and civilians were forbidden to use the army postal system, Klausner urged Jewish displaced persons to give their mail to their camp leaders. The latter then forwarded the letters to Klausner, who sent them through the army mail under his own name and address. Much of this correspondence was sent to the JWB in New York. The JWB sorted the letters and then mailed them to all parts of the world.

Klausner concluded his foreword by asking for the survivors' indulgence: "It is difficult to beg of those who have so long and severely suffered to be patient. Yet we must constantly remind our unfortunate brethren that the tyrants destroyed our world in six years and as much as we would like to, we cannot repair it in six weeks."[69]

His next project involved placing the Jewish displaced persons in Bavaria in separate Jewish camps, and those in need of medical care in separate hospitals. At the end of the war, individuals released from concentration camps were allowed to enter any of the displaced persons camps established by the army. Although the army had learned from bitter experience in Italy "the necessity of segregating nationalities into separate camps or at least within separate parts of the same camp," it overlooked this lesson when dealing with the Jews in Germany.[70] To Klausner, the need for separate Jewish camps had become clear after his lengthy visits to seventeen displaced persons camps in Bavaria. Someday, he believed, an organization or group would come and lead the Jews out of Germany; and he wanted them to be ready. Until then, by consolidating them in Jewish camps, he could at least protect them from the frequent harassment and mistreatment they had suffered earlier at the hands of non-Jewish inmates.

There were also hundreds of Jewish survivors left in German hospitals, where they were being cared for by German physicians. Klausner understood how traumatic such an experience was for them; but before he could remove the Jews from these hospitals, he had to find suitable replacement quarters.[71]

The first turned out to be St. Ottilien, a Benedictine monastery located in the village of Schwabenhausen about thirty miles from Munich. During the war the Nazis used the monastery as a military hospital. When Klausner found St. Ottilien, it was still functioning as a hospital, caring for four hundred Jews, as well as a number of German and Hungarian soldiers. Most of the Jews there, former inmates of Dachau, had been removed from the camp by the Nazis just before it was liberated. Subsequently, they were freed by the U. S. Army in the village of Schwabenhausen. Captain Otto B. Raymond, one of the first American officers to arrive in the village, immediately placed Dr. Zalman Grinberg, a young physician from Kovno, in charge of the hospital. Grinberg had been among the Jewish survivors liberated at Schwabenhausen. Together with Captain Raymond, he had the wounded among the survivors driven by ambulance to St. Ottilien. Klausner then proceeded to have the Hungarian and German soldiers moved out, so that St. Ottilien became a displaced persons hospital strictly for Jewish survivors.

Klausner soon found a second hospital, Gauting, a tuberculosis sanatorium southwest of Munich, and informed the German in charge that he was taking over. Grinberg came down from St. Ottilien to help organize the hospital and ensure that it was staffed with competent Jewish physicians. Until the latter arrived, the German physicians were retained. Klausner tried to set up other medical centers for the Jews during this period, but the obstacles proved too great. Eventually, though, he did manage to establish a third Jewish hospital.[72]

Having satisfied the need for separate medical facilities, Klausner devoted his energy to setting up separate Jewish camps. He chose a camp called Feldafing, which previously had been an internment camp for prisoners of war and, at an earlier date, a training school for Hitler youth. Lieutenant Irving J. Smith, an American Jew serving with the United States military government, supervised the camp. Smith had arrived in the nearby village of Tutzing in early May 1945 and, together with other officers, had found many former concentration camp inmates in an abandoned train at the Tutzing railroad siding. These inmates had been in Muhldorf and Wald concentration camps; they had been brought to the railroad siding by a small group of SS guards. After Smith and his men had liberated these survivors, he placed the most seriously ill among them in local hospitals and transported the rest to the Feldafing camp.

In the surrounding areas, Smith found another large contingent of Jews whom he took back to the Feldafing camp. Thus, during the month of May, there were 3,500 Jewish displaced persons in the camp, including 800 women and 300 children. Smith also established a hospital and staffed it with refugee physicians. He had food procured from the local German villages and supplemented with Red Cross packages. Together with a group of American Jewish soldiers, Chaplain Max Braude also provided food for the people in Feldafing.[73]

Despite all these efforts, Feldafing had not yet become an exclusively Jewish camp. Braude, Klausner, and Smith were eager that it should; but before this could be accomplished, the Hungarian nationals had to be moved elsewhere and Jews brought in from another camp. Although this transfer of Hungarians and Jews ran counter to army regulations, Klausner had no difficulty in convincing the authorities of the wisdom of the move. An upsurge of nationalistic feeling in many camps throughout the region had resulted in fights and killings. By limiting the number of national groups in each camp, most of these episodes of violence could be prevented. Naturally, the army could not provide separate camps for all nationality groups; but it agreed to permit Feldafing to become predominantly Jewish. Some Jews were also sent to the Landsberg displaced persons camp; ultimately, through Klausner's efforts, it became a Jewish camp as well.

Klausner adroitly resolved the question of which Jews should be sent to Feldafing. As with the transfer of the Hungarians, he found a solution that coincided with the needs of the military. Dachau was then to become a processing center for captured Nazis, which meant that all the camp inmates had to be transferred elsewhere. Klausner offered to resettle them at St. Ottilien, Gauting, and Feldafing. With the official aid of Colonel Milton Richmond, who headed a special American military transport unit in Dachau, the transfer was arranged. Those who went to St. Ottilien and Gauting were transported in ambulances provided by the medical officer at Dachau. Klausner also used these ambulances to search for, and transport, Jews scattered throughout Bavaria. Dr. Sidney (Burke) Berkowitz, attached to the Tenth Army Hospital at Allach, accompanied Klausner on these trips and personally determined which Jews needed special care. By late June or early July, when they had completed their trips, Feldafing was predominantly Jewish. Although Lieutenant Irving J. Smith regarded this as an end in itself, Klausner intended the success of Feldafing merely as the first step toward a broader goal: the official recognition of the Jews by the army as a separate nationality.

To implement this goal, in mid-June 1945 Klausner went to the army headquarters in Munich to speak to Captain McDonald, the officer in charge of displaced persons affairs. While waiting for his interview, Klausner observed that McDonald was virtually besieged with endless demands for help from displaced persons of various nationalities. When Klausner's turn came, he used a different approach. Instead of adding to the lists of grievances, he offered to relieve the army of some of its responsibilities toward the Jews. He proposed to assemble the Jews of southern Germany and Austria into an organization that would represent them in all negotiations with the American authorities. McDonald was so impressed with the wisdom of Klausner's proposal that even before clearing it with his superior, he gave Klausner permission to proceed. Obviously, the scheme did not accord with army regulations; but McDonald was more intent on finding practical solutions than on pleasing the higher echelons of the military bureaucracy.

Having obtained approval for his plan, Klausner acquired part of the Deutsches Museum in Munich to house the organization; then he toured all the camps to build support for it. On June 24, 1945, he discussed his ideas with an enthusiastic group of camp representatives, who had come to the Flak-Kaserne (a displaced persons center in Munich) to greet the first men to arrive with the Jewish Brigade. Together with the camp representatives, Klausner decided to convene a special conference on July 1, 1945, at Feldafing to establish this organization, which subsequently became known as the Central Committee of Liberated Jews in Bavaria.

Just before the conference, which was to be attended by representatives of all displaced persons camps, McDonald's superior officer, a Colonel Elkins, called Klausner into his office and told him that army regulations prohibited the founding of such an organization. He advised Klausner to restrict himself to supplying information; as Klausner was leaving, he added, "But do a good job." Klausner thanked him and returned to Dachau.[74]

In the short time that Klausner had been in Bavaria, he had initiated many crucially important changes that inspired renewed faith and trust in many of the Jewish displaced persons. By establishing a unique relationship with the army, he had acquired the freedom to act exclusively on the Jews' behalf and significantly improved their lot.

Rabbi Klein and the Jews of Belgium

For the most part, chaplains reported meeting Jews in Berlin, Bonn, Frankfurt, Czechoslovakia, and Austria. Generally, these were brief personal encounters in which they provided little or no aid. They did, however, help in restoring synagogues, finding Jewish religious items, and holding services.[75] In Belgium, however, Chaplain Isaac Klein reported helping a number of Jews.

In Lesves, a village not far from Namur, Klein found a *hachshara* operated by Brit Chaluzim Dateyim (BACHAD, a religious Zionist youth group). It had fifteen boys and girls, ranging in age from fifteen to twenty-two who were in need of clothing. Before Klein could activate Jewish soldiers in the area to procure the clothing, he received word to report to the commanding officer of the 304th Base Group. The general knew that many of his Jewish GIs were involved in relief and rehabilitation activities and that this had cured their morale problem. Most soldiers suffered a letdown at the end of the war because they were eager to go home and were bored with being stationed in one place. The general felt that if the non-Jewish soldiers could be included in this work, the morale on the base would be improved.

Klein agreed, and they began a clothing drive. At the same time, he contacted an American theatrical troupe in the area that contributed enough clothes to outfit all the girls at the *hachshara*. To raise money, Klein held a luncheon in the main mess hall. The funds were placed in a trust fund in Brussels and used for scholarships for the orphans. Since Klein could not administer the fund himself, he turned it over to the JDC.

Klein became so concerned with the survivors that they became his personal responsibility. If someone needed psychiatric care or funds for professional training, he found the money needed. In Namur, Chaplain Klein found two hundred Jewish survivors who had hidden there during the war. Only two or three Jewish families had previously lived in the city. The man most responsible for saving these people was Vicar André. By converting his parish home into an orphanage, he had been able to keep Jewish children alive during the Nazi occupation.

Shortly after Klein arrived in Namur, during the second week in April, he began to reorganize the Jewish community. It had been established as a relief society, with the priest attending each meeting and practically dictating policy. At Klein's suggestion, they became a *Kultusgemeinde* (religious congregation), so that Vicar André could not participate.

Vicar André also tried to dictate policy with regard to the children. He did not want Klein to arrange religious instruction for them; and when Klein suggested the children be moved to a Jewish orphanage in Brussels, he adamantly refused. All types of excuses were given, but André clearly wanted to keep them under his control. Three children had already converted to Catholicism; another three were on the verge of doing so, and two others had shown an interest as well. While Klein was determined that these Jewish children would receive a Jewish education, it is not clear why he allowed them to remain under André's control. The children remained under the influence of the priest until one of the other chaplains took it upon himself to free them.[76]

British and American Cooperation

For the most part, the American chaplains in Germany had little contact with their counterparts in the British Army. Two American chaplains who reported having met their British counterparts were Joseph Shubow and Robert Marcus. During the latter part of April, while visiting Bergen-Belsen, Chaplain Joseph Shubow met the Reverend L. H. Hardman, a British Jewish chaplain at the camp. Hardman had six Lithuanian women who were very ill, and he was eager for them to be transferred to an American Army hospital. The Americans were much better equipped to handle such emergencies and Hardman urged Shubow to return with an ambulance truck filled with white bread. Shubow brought the ambulance with the bread and distributed it to the survivors. Then he loaded the women on the truck and took them to an American Army hospital.[77]

At the request of Nahum Goldmann, chairman of the Administrative Committee of the WJC, Marcus visited Bergen-Belsen on May 9. In a report to Rabbi Stephen S. Wise, he noted that the Jews in the camp were in need of food, medical supplies, and medical personnel. The next day he had a truck full of provisions sent to the camp, but he understood it was only a "drop in the bucket." Marcus praised the work of the Reverend Hardman, who did everything within his power to alleviate the problems at Belsen but criticized the senior British chaplain, the Reverend Isaac Levy, who he claimed was preoccupied with writing articles for the London *Jewish Chronicle*.[78]

Another meeting between the British and American Jewish chaplains took place in Paris with Judah Nadich, Aryeh Lev, and Chaplain Isaac Levy of the Second British Army. At this meeting, Chaplain Levy raised the issue of regular cooperation between the American Jewish chaplains and the British Jewish chaplains. The British Army had agreed to have a Jewish chaplain in each concentration camp until international organizations could take over, as well as to establish an experimental camp for all stateless people. Lev thought cooperation between the American and British chaplains was important and particularly wanted to coordinate these two groups' compilations of survivor lists. Nadich pointed out, however, that since the U. S. Army would not assign Jewish chaplains to concentration camps (as a matter of policy), there was little possibility of coordination between the respective chaplains. Lev suggested that instead, all inquiries be sent to the JDC representative in Paris who would check it against their lists, the most comprehensive of all.[79]

CANRA and the Displaced Persons

There is no question that by June CANRA knew of the extent of the chaplains' work with the survivors. While Philip Bernstein did not know that Chaplain Herbert Eskin had been stealing cattle from German farmers to feed the survivors or that Abraham Klausner occasionally carried a gun (in violation of army regulations) while searching for Jews in Bavaria, he did understand that the chaplains could be court-martialed for some of their activities. Nevertheless, he encouraged Klausner and others to continue their work and report on the condition of the Jews. This attitude seems to signify a change in CANRA policy, but no documents can be located to substantiate this hypothesis. All information about the plight of the Jews was passed on to the JDC. The JDC thanked Bernstein for this data, but there was no indication of what impact it had on JDC policy.

The chaplains were not the only source of information about the survivors received by the JDC. Many American Jewish soldiers were agitated by the way Jews were being treated and sent letters to friends, relatives, rabbis, and Jewish fraternal organizations. A number of these letters were highly critical of American Jews, and particularly of the JDC, for having failed to respond adequately to the emergency. These letters were often brought to the attention of the JDC for response. Since the JDC had been trying to get into

Europe without success, it felt it could do little else. These letters did, however, raise the question of the efficacy of its efforts on behalf of the survivors.[80]

Communication between the chaplains scattered throughout Europe during these early months was minimal, because there was neither the time nor the opportunity for a formal meeting. Many chaplains, as Aryeh Lev pointed out, thought that they alone were helping the Jewish survivors and that these Jews were all that remained in Germany. This disturbed Lev because he believed that although the JDC could not get into the camps at that time, it could have at least guided the chaplains' efforts through Judah Nadich. "Our chaplains are not informed as to what is going on in other camps—who is governing them—or if lists are being made available of the survivors. It is all one grand mess," he declared.[81]

Despite their deep commitment to helping European Jews, the chaplains were eager for the JDC and other Jewish relief organizations to assume this responsibility. After all, these organizations were equipped for this purpose, while the chaplains (except for Abraham Klausner) could only devote a portion of their time to relief work. Furthermore, few chaplains knew how long they would be in any particular area, and they wanted to be sure that someone would take over once they had left.

The risk of being court-martialed was another overriding reason for the chaplains to be relieved of their relief activities as quickly as possible. Herschel Schacter spent so much of his time with the survivors at Buchenwald that he did not always have the time to conduct religious services for the Jewish personnel in the Eighth Corps. When the chief of chaplains of the Eighth Corps discovered this, he reproached Schacter for failing to fulfill his military duties. Schacter believed that he lost a promotion because of this reprimand, but he still continued his work.[82] Neither Schacter nor the other chaplains who chose to help the survivors felt that the Jewish soldiers were being deprived of their services. Generally, they tried to strike a balance between their involvement with the survivors and their responsibilities to their men. They did not always succeed, since the needs of survivors were greater and more urgent than those of the Jewish soldiers. Some chaplains tried to include GIs in displaced persons work, and this met with varying degrees of success. The chaplains were divided in their opinions about the extent of soldiers' contributions.

By writing letters and reports to leaders of American Jewry, the chaplains hoped their appeals would hasten the arrival of the JDC and other Jewish relief organizations. Until these groups were able to assume responsibility for the welfare of the survivors, the chaplains in Germany and elsewhere had to continue this work on their own.

3
THE HARRISON REPORT

Chaplains' Attempts To Alert American Jewry

Most of the chaplains did not send detailed accounts of the problems facing the survivors back to the United States, for several reasons. Some claimed they were too busy working with the displaced persons to write; others did not realize the importance of alerting American Jews. Furthermore, many were on the move and had little contact with Jews. Even so, there were chaplains who managed to warn CANRA and American Jewry about the plight of their coreligionists.

Some of the most detailed information sent to CANRA during April, May, and June came from Abraham Klausner. In mid-June, Klausner wrote to Philip Bernstein:

> Six weeks ago they were liberated. They were taken to a series of camps in the uniform of the Concentration Camp and remained garbed in that infamous outfit. They are housed in dwellings that are unfit for human occupation and are fed in many cases less than they received at the Concentration Camps. I do not use words recklessly. I have travelled this entire area (Bavaria). I have visited with each of the camps. [I have] spoken with the leaders, observed their mode of life and I turned aside in the best situation and silently cried—for all of Israel's sufferings, this! There seems to be no policy, no responsibility, no plan for these . . . stateless Jews. At some camps they are kicked around by some smart second Lt. At others an UNRRA man with less power than a glow worm sits at his YMCA desk and at [best] one or two conditions are a bit better because a Jewish Officer is enraged.

> Twelve hours a day I tell my lies. "They will come," I say. "When will they come?" they ask me. UNRRA, JDC, Red Cross—can it be that they are not aware of the problem? It is impossible. The JDC representative did visit one of my camps. There he asked our people—"What can I do for you?" What can you do for a broken, hungry, spiritless people! RED CROSS has sent in a few packages here and there, but nothing more. Clothes? Only those we manage to steal.

His frustrations, the enormity of the problem, and the lack of outside assistance are clearly expressed in the conclusion:

> Of what use is all my complaining; I cannot stop their tears. America was their hope and all America has given them is a new camp with guards in Khaki. Freedom, hell no! They are behind walls without hope. Can not [sic] American Israel raise its voice? Can not the leaders of our people cry out demanding a new day for these who have hated the dawn of each day. There are so few left. Forgive my incoherence, calmness is not with me.[1]

To ensure that other American Jewish leaders received this information, Klausner prepared a report on what he witnessed in Bavaria and sent it to Stephen S. Wise, Abba Hillel Silver, Julius Morgenstern, Maurice Eisendrath, and Philip Bernstein. These were the prominent leaders in both the Reform and general Jewish community. In his report of June 24, 1945, entitled "A Detailed Report on the Liberated Jew As He Now Suffers His Period of Liberation Under the Discipline of the Armed Forces of the United States," Klausner described in detail the deplorable conditions of the camps, the lack of sufficient food and clothing, the desire of the Jews to be reunited with their families, their unwillingness to return to their former countries, and the failure of the American Army to recognize them as a separate nationality.[2]

I could not locate the responses of Silver, Morgenstern, and Eisendrath. On July 16, Wise replied: "I thank you with all my heart for the report which you sent me and your personal note. We are doing everything we can, though I know that everything we do, and it is not a little, is not enough. With most cordial appreciation."[3]

Wise dictated this letter before leaving for London to attend the Zionist Conference. Upon his return, he appears to have forgotten about the July 16 letter; for on July 25 he wrote to Klausner: "I hope that I have long before this replied to your letter calling my attention to a report which you enclosed. What you write is moving, but you must know that we of the World Jewish Congress have moved steadfastly forward in order to relieve those in need, and as far as possible to save them. True it is that none of the Jewish organizations, perhaps not even the Red Cross and UNRRA, were ready for the sudden and overwhelming collapse of Germany." Although Wise ended this second letter "with most affectionate greetings," the tone and content did not reflect these sentiments.[4] Nowhere in the letter did Wise thank Klausner for what he had done or offer him encouragement to continue this work. One possible explanation is that Wise and the WJC were under a great deal of pressure to bring relief to the Jews in Europe; and their inability to do so was frustrating, especially for Wise. He may have also felt that this reflected poorly on the WJC and himself. Wise continually received reports from chaplains that the survivors were counting on him to provide the help they so desperately needed; and the American Jewish press felt that not enough was being done to have Jewish relief workers sent abroad.

This pressure on Wise and the WJC can be seen in the following reports. On May 12, Chaplain Robert Marcus reported to the WJC after visiting Bergen-Belsen at the request of Nahum Goldmann:

> Despite the fact that these people were liberated by the British on April 15, they were still on May 9th living under the most unsanitary conditions imaginable. . . . There is a terrific scarcity of food, medical supplies and *no* personnel.
>
> Even when they do get their meager rations, there is no one available to feed the very sick who do not have the strength to walk to the kitchen. You can imagine how frightful the situation is that some of the wasted girls stated that it was worse than under the Germans. There has been tremendous psychological letdown and a feeling of helplessness about the future after the short lived joy of having been freed. Needless to say, many have died; and the lists I am sending you may not be accurate when they reach your hands because of the intervening casualties.[5]

Another chaplain, Joseph Shubow, wrote several letters to Wise in May complaining about some of the same conditions Marcus had found in the British zone, pointing out that the Jews were depending on Wise for help. "The sights I saw," he exclaimed, "I shall carry with me to the grave if I live to be the age of Methuselah [sic]." Like Marcus, he found there was not enough manpower, medical help, or food to care for the thousands of survivors. "I appeal frantically to you," he declared to Wise, "to make sure that as many Jewish physicians, nurses, and social workers be sent as soon as possible in order to help save some of the lives of the remnants of Israel." Shubow asserted:

> Another vital problem is the question of the future of those who are strong enough to return to their homes. Almost to a man and woman, the Jews of so-called Polish nationality refuse to return to Poland. Many of them have told me the Poles were worse than the Nazis and that the Poles begrudge their existence and were preparing crematoriums for them in Poland; this no doubt is absurdly extravagant but it is clear Polish Jews do not wish to return to their horror scenes.

> I have advised them to declare themselves as stateless—*Staatenlos*—and they will thus have the protection of the nations of the world and American Jewry. They want to go to America or Palestine or anywhere else in the world, but not to Poland. No doubt you and the World Jewish Congress are doing everything possible in their behalf. They all know your name and it has proved a magic charm, when I state to them that you have a personal interest in their welfare. I trust that representatives of the Congress will be here as soon as possible to give all these people the necessary advice.

With regard to his own plans after being discharged from the army, he said,

> I would be prepared myself to spend a little time in Europe in order to help rebuild the lives of these shattered human beings. I have been holding services for them and they have told me in weeping terms that these were the first Hebrew words they have heard in assembly in five or six years; on Saturday morning I called them to the *Torah* and they came up for the *Aliyoth* [going up the Torah to recite the blessings] with wonderful reverence and kissed the *Torah* lovingly and caressingly.[6]

Wise responded to the Marcus and Shubow communications by including parts of their observations and appeals for medical and social work personnel in a report on the conditions in the camps he published under the auspices of the WJC in June 1945. Key sections of this report were reprinted in the *Jewish Spectator* under the title "The Challenge of Suffering European Jewry." Although both chaplains were quoted in the article, there was no mention of them by name or that this information had come from chaplains. Shubow was referred to as "an identified and reliable informant."

Wise and the WJC also responded to these communications by sending telegrams and messages to government agencies in the United States and England asking that appropriate action be taken to improve these conditions. At the same time, they also requested that the WJC be permitted to send representatives to Europe. These requests were rejected. Moreover, Wise and the WJC were attacked by the *Jewish Spectator* for not doing more to bring immediate relief to the survivors. "This is not enough!" declared the magazine:

> It is high time for American Jewry to press at once for government permission to sent not tens but HUNDREDS of Jewish social workers to Europe to bring solace, comfort, and personal encouragement to the physical and psychological wrecks of Jewish men and women in the former concentration and UNRRA camps, to say nothing of those who wander about in the woods and fall by the roadsides.

The *Spectator* concluded:

> For the sake of those of our brethren who still can be saved, we must compel ourselves to visualize every minute of the day and in

the still house of the night, emaciated, sick, hungry, desperate, hopeless and homeless men and women who will perish unless we rescue them. This will inspire us with the unflagging determination and the courage to demand of our government to authorize us to send to Europe the kind of relief and the crew of social workers which can bring effective aid to the sufferers.[7]

While Wise's response to Klausner's report was defensive, Philip Bernstein's reaction was positive. In a letter to Klausner, Bernstein told him how much he appreciated "all that you have been doing to help displaced persons. I would like you to know also that we share your sense of indignant dissatisfaction with the help received from American Jewish agencies and we utilize letters from chaplains to put dynamite under the organizations that have these responsibilities. I think that the chaplains and we have some responsibility for the growing concern and more energetic activity that seems to be evident." Bernstein urged Klausner to "continue to bombard us with reports, complaints, and helpful materials. I would be humiliated if JWB did not do everything possible to help in this matter."[8]

What is particularly important about Bernstein's letter is that it followed a request by Chaplain Max Braude to prohibit chaplains from "writing anything pertaining to Jews or Jewry" which was "not cleared" through the JWB Public Relations Office. Braude was disturbed by Klausner's June 24 report, and he wanted Bernstein to issue a directive to stop this type of negative publicity. Braude was concerned that although this report contained "much that is factual," it also contained "many statements which are appraisals of the situation based on nothing." The most damaging part of the report, he maintained, was that Klausner had written that the authority to make his survey had been given through Braude's Seventh Army Headquarters.

Klausner had not received official permission to prepare this report. Braude feared that if it were publicized as an official document, "the repercussions could seriously impair our Chaplaincy program in the Theate," since it would "embarrass the Theater and Army Chaplain Office, and affect Judah [Nadich] and all men doing this vital work in Europe." Braude was particularly disturbed that Klausner was responsible for this situation. He pointed out, "I had Klausner ordered here for the purpose of doing [the] work he is doing—but in order to do so devious methods had to be used since Chaplains cannot be assigned to serve displaced persons. Klausner is actually working in Third Army territory—though officially he is assigned to this office (Seventh Army Headquarters)."

This incident highlighted a basic difference in approach taken by both men—in part, a result of their different positions and personalities. Klausner believed that no fundamental changes would occur unless the army was confronted publically, whereas Braude was willing to circumvent the rules but did not want to bring official attention to his actions. Braude also complained of having to spend "a great deal" of his time "in covering [Klausner's] tactless errors like sending the report." With all of these problems, however, Braude acknowledged that Klausner had "done an excellent job to date."[9]

Bernstein's strong endorsement of Klausner's activities (which were obviously illegal as far as the army was concerned) seemed to represent a change in CANRA's policy. No documents could be located to indicate such a change had indeed taken place. Previously, CANRA had been careful not to do anything that would strain its relationship with either the army or the American Jewish community. Partly, that was because CANRA was not sure what the chaplains were doing for the survivors.

Although Bernstein did not know all the details about the chaplains' work with the displaced persons, he understood that some of these activities were not sanctioned by the military. One important source of information for Bernstein was Chaplain Aryeh Lev, who accompanied General William P. Arnold, the chief of chaplains, on a fact-finding tour of Europe during May and June 1945. Lev took time out of his schedule to meet with as many Jewish chaplains as possible. In one of his reports Lev observed:

> Insofar as our chaplains are concerned, they have done a magnificent job. There were plenty of camps and enough displaced persons to keep each chaplain busy for the next ten years. Each one I have met thought that he was the only one doing such work and that he was saving all the remaining Jews in Germany. JWB has probably been receiving mail from each one telling of his work. They have all done enough to assure them and their posterity a place in heaven. They have done it all at the expense of personal sacrifice, court martial threats and deprivation—but they have done it. God bless them for it. Thousands of Jews are blessing them, too.[10]

The Harrison Report

The chaplains did not realize that their reports—alongside the letters and stories sent by soldiers, newspaper correspondents, displaced persons, and other observers in Europe—did have an impact. This information enabled American Jewish organizations to draw the attention of the American government, the Congress, and the army to the plight of European Jews.[11] At the urging of the American Jewish Conference,[12] for example, Congressmen Emanuel Celler (D-NY), Samuel Dickstein (D-NY), Herbert P. Koppelman (D-Conn.), Samuel A. Weiss (D-Penn), Leo Rayfial (D-NY), and Benjamen J. Rabkin (D-NY) sent a cable to General Eisenhower on May

10, 1945, asking him to "appoint special Jewish liaison officers under military assignment and control to act as consultants at Allied Military Headquarters and/or in the field, dealing with displaced persons and their repatriation and resettlement." These congressmen were disturbed about reports describing the "utter helplessness and bewilderment" the Jews experienced due to the "absence" of Jewish liaison officers who would have a "sympathetic awareness of their special needs, mentally, [and] language difficulties." Unless this special attention would be provided, the congressmen asserted, there would be a good possibility that the precarious position of the Jews would be further imperiled. To help Eisenhower select appropriate liaison people for these positions, the American Jewish Conference and the Board of Deputies of British Jews volunteered to prepare a list of qualified officers.[13]

On May 29, 1945, Major General J. A. Ulio, the adjutant general, sent Congressman Celler Eisenhower's answer. Eisenhower assured the congressmen that the plight of Jewish survivors had been brought to the attention of his headquarters and that UNRRA had arranged to present voluntary relief agencies to care for specific problems.[14]

The rejection did not deter the American Jewish Conference, for it made further representations to UNRRA and the War Department. In two detailed memoranda to the War Department, the conference outlined American Jewish concerns and pointed out that it would be in the interest of all parties involved if these liaison officers were appointed. In addition, the American Jewish Conference held a meeting to discuss this matter with former New York governor Herbert S. Lehman, then director general of UNRRA. Similar requests were made by the Board of Deputies of British Jews to their counterparts in London.[15]

Despite this pressure, liaison officers were not appointed. It did, however, prompt President Harry S. Truman to take limited action. In early June (probably June 3) he asked Anna M. Rosenberg, a manpower and industrial relations consultant, to report on the condition of French Jews. It is probable that this had not been her primary purpose since she in any case had planned to be in Europe for the U. S. War Department. On June 13, 1945, she and her aide, Lieutenant Commander Fischer, met in Paris with Chaplains Judah Nadich and Irwin Hyman, a thirty-six-year-old Conservative rabbi who later replaced Nadich in Paris. At this meeting, they discussed the problems of French Jews and decided that a memorandum would be prepared for her to take back to President Truman.

Later that day, Nadich met with David Shaltiel, and Ruth Kluger (Aliav) of the Jewish Agency, and Mark Jarblum, the Zionist leader, to prepare this document. Nadich delivered the memorandum to

Mrs. Rosenberg on June 22; but there is no way of determining what impact, if any, it had on Truman.[16]

This pressure from the chaplains and other observers in Europe resulted in a request from American Jewish leaders to Secretary of the Treasury, Henry W. Morgenthau, Jr., that he speak to the State Department about launching an investigation of conditions in Germany. At the same time, Rabbi Stephen S. Wise and Nahum Goldmann contacted George Warren, the State Department's advisor on refugees and displaced persons, to urge that his department give serious attention to the reports about the horrible conditions in the German displaced persons camps.

In May 1945 Morgenthau suggested to President Truman that he set up a cabinet-level committee to handle the displaced persons problem, since the army had been having difficulty in dealing with this group. After Truman rejected this idea, Morgenthau approached the State Department and urged Acting Secretary of State Joseph C. Grew to launch an immediate inquiry. Morgenthau proposed that Earl G. Harrison, former U. S. Commissioner of Immigration and United States representative on the Intergovernmental Committee on Refugees, be appointed to conduct the investigation. Grew agreed, and Truman's approval was also obtained.[17]

On June 22, 1945, Truman sent Harrison a letter endorsing the mission and asked that Harrison submit a report to him at its conclusion. Harrison's mandate was "to inquire into the needs of stateless and non-repatriable refugees among the displaced persons in Germany and to determine the extent to which those needs are now being met by military, governmental, and private organizations."[18]

To help him investigate conditions in Germany, Harrison had the State Department request the services of Joseph Schwartz, European director of the JDC. At various stages during the trip, he also had the assistance of Herbert Katzki, of the War Refugee Board (WRB) and Patrick M. Malin, deputy director of the Intergovernmental Committee on Refugees.[19] The Third Army planned an itinerary for Harrison structured so that he would have bypassed most displaced persons camps. Fortunately, Colonel Milton Richmond saw the schedule and suggested to Abraham Klausner that he intervene. Klausner went to Harrison's hotel in Munich; and after an all-night meeting, they changed the itinerary, with Klausner being asked to join the inspection tour.[20]

For almost two months, Harrison toured Germany and Austria, visiting the concentration camps and displaced persons centers. He interviewed many survivors as well as army and UNRRA personnel. At some installations where he had been told that no survivors remained, Harrison found hundreds living under deplorable conditions. Harrison submitted a preliminary report of his findings to President Truman before August 3, and on August 24 he handed the final report to the president at the White House. Truman released the report on September 29, and the next day it made front page news across the United States.[21]

Klausner's influence of this investigation went beyond directing Harrison to visit specific camps and centers. As he accompanied Harrison to these installations, Klausner pointed out the unique predicament facing the Jews, their need for special recognition by the American government and military, and their desire to leave immediately for Palestine.

One example of Klausner's impact can be seen in Harrison's sensitivity to the physical and psychological problems of Jewish survivors in Germany and Austria. He noted that Jews were still living behind barbed wire,

> amidst crowded, frequently unsanitary and generally grim conditions, in complete idleness, with no opportunity, except surreptitiously, to communicate with the outside world, waiting, hoping for some word of encouragement and action on their behalf." Furthermore, he reported that many were dying of malnutrition and emphasized that the refugees "had no clothing other than their concentration camp garb—a rather hideous striped pajama effect—while others, to their chagrin, were obliged to wear German SS uniforms. It is questionable which clothing they hate more.[22]

Klausner expressed his outrage more ironically: "the greater percentage of the liberated are still imprisoned in the striped uniform forced upon him by the oppressor."[23]

Klausner also helped shape Harrison's understanding of the uncertainty felt by the survivors. Harrison wrote, "They dwell upon their plight, the uncertainty of their future and, what is more unfortunate, draw comparisons between their treatment 'under the Germans', and 'in liberation'."[24] Klausner summed it up rhetorically, "Liberated for what?" and "Liberated but not free—that is the paradox of the Jew."[25] Harrison expressed similar sentiments when he noted, "They see or hear nothing in the way of plans for them and they wonder and frequently ask what 'liberation' means."[26]

Their need to be reunited with their families was also understood by Harrison. Klausner had emphasized that the survivor "wants to make sure that he has pursued every path that may lead to a limb of his once possessed family. His problem: Where Is My Family?"[27] Harrison's cooler language stressed that "the most absorbing worry of these Nazi and war victims concerns relatives, wives, husbands, parents, children. . . . They cannot understand why the liberators should not have undertaken immediately the organization effort to reunite family groups."[28] Harrison summarized the inadequate attempts to provide such information through military channels and noted the contribution "devoted rabbis" had made to provide information about families.

The section of Harrison's report headed "Needs of the Jews" revealed his understanding of the solutions required to solve the problems of survivors. In six paragraphs, he argued, "The first and plainest need of these people is a recognition of their actual status and by this I mean their status as Jews" and "Refusal to recognize the Jews as such has the effect, in this situation, of closing one's eyes to their former and more barbaric persecution, which has already made them a separate group with greater needs." Harrison emphasized "that it is not a case of singling out a particular group for special privileges. It is a matter of raising to a more normal level the position of a group which has been depressed to the lowest depths conceivable by years of organized and inhuman oppression."[29]

The failure to recognize Jews as a separate group created difficulties, Klausner asserted: "He is not recognized as a Jew even though of his original number a handful remain. He is counted among his persecutors. . . . Polish Jews (not a single Polish Jewish child under the age of fourteen has as yet been found alive in this area) are to date considered Polish nationals and are subject to all directives bearing upon that people." The Jew "does not want to return to his former home. He seeks a new place for the rebuilding of his new life. His problem is: Where Shall I Go?"[30]

The second greatest need after recognition of the unique status of the Jews, Harrison reported, was the development of a plan to assist their desire to leave Germany and Austria: "With respect to possible places of resettlement for those who may be stateless or who do not wish to return to their homes, Palestine is definitely and pre-eminently the first choice." He informed the president that "there is no acceptable or even decent solution for their future other than Palestine" although there were some few who considered the United States or other countries as options. Since most Jews wanted to emigrate to Palestine, Harrison recommended that the United States "express an interest in and support of a plan to settle Jews there."[31]

In particular, Harrison asserted that "some reasonable extension or modification of the British White Paper of 1939," which limited Jewish emigration to Palestine to seventy-five thousand over a five-year period beginning that year "ought to be possible without serious repercussions." In arguing for Palestine as the solution to the problems of Jewish statelessness, Harrison pointed out that "this is said on a purely humanitarian basis with no reference to ideological or political considerations so far as Palestine is concerned."[32]

A decision on this issue had to be made shortly, Harrison insisted, because certificates for immigration to Palestine were to be exhausted by August 1945. "To anyone who has visited the concentration camps and who has talked with the despairing survivors, it is nothing short of calamitous to contemplate that the gates of Palestine should be soon closed," he declared.[33]

He then noted that the "Jewish Agency for Palestine has submitted to the British Government a petition that 100,000 additional immigration certificates be made available. A memorandum accompanying the petition makes a persuasive showing with respect to the immediate absorptive capacity of Palestine and the current, actual manpower shortages there."[34] Harrison observed:

> While there may be room for difference of opinion as to the precise number of certificates which might under the circumstances be considered reasonable, there is no question but that the request thus made would, if granted, contribute much to the sound solution for the future of Jews still in Germany and Austria and even other displaced Jews, who do not wish either to remain there or to return to their countries of nationality. No matter is, therefore, so important from the viewpoint of Jews in Germany and Austria and those elsewhere who have known the horrors of the concentration camps as is the disposition of the Palestine question.[35]

He also proposed the United States "should, under existing immigration laws, permit reasonable numbers of such persons to come here, . . . particularly those who have family ties in this country." This should not be a major issue, he believed, since "the number who desire emigration to the United States is not large."[36]

Harrison declared that "the urgency of the situation should be recognized" because it was "inhuman to ask people to continue to live for any length of time under their present conditions." Harrison was also concerned about how American treatment of the Jews might be viewed by the German people. "As matters now stand," he charged, "we appear to be treating the Jews as the Nazis treated them, except that we do not exterminate them. They are in concentration camps in large numbers under our military guard, instead of the SS troups. One is led to wonder whether the German people, seeing this, are not supposing that we are following or at least condoning Nazi policy."[37]

Harrison had been careful to point out exceptions to this behavior and that the American Army had done a phenomenal job in repatriating more than four million displaced persons. He also remarked that there had been some improvement in the living conditions for those who remained.[38]

Harrison had obviously been persuaded by Klausner's arguments; the text to the president confirms this. Although Harrison did not use Klausner's terminology, the sentiments and the priorities expressed were identical. Moreover, while other non-Jewish observers like Harvey D. Gibson and Bryon Price, who visited Germany at a later date, saw conditions similar to those witnessed by Harrison, none showed the same empathy for the plight of the Jewish survivors.

Before making Harrison's report public, its findings were used by Truman to spur changes within the army. Although Truman did not release the entire text of the Harrison report to the military authorities in Frankfurt until early September, General George C. Marshall, chief of staff, sent a summary of Harrison's conclusions to General Dwight D. Eisenhower on August 3, 1945.

Even before Eisenhower had a chance to respond to this communication, Secretary of War Henry L. Stimson sent him another cable requesting that he verify the conclusions of the Harrison Report. The cable, which arrived on August 10, indicated that Stimson had conferred with Henry Morgenthau, Jr., and Joseph Grew and that they were very concerned about the implications of the report. Stimson asked that everything be done to improve the existing conditions.

At the same time, Stephen S. Wise went to London to attend the World Zionist Conference where he met a number of chaplains and JDC representatives who were working in Europe.[39] They discussed the need for someone to coordinate a relief effort for Jewish survivors, and on August 3, Chaplain Robert Marcus submitted the following cable to Wise: "There is urgent necessity to assign liaison officer to Headquarters G-5 for purpose of coordinating activity of Jewish displaced persons. Such officer would aid in establishment of all Jewish camps, including religious program for these people. Immediate action advisable in order to avoid suffering next winter and remedy deplorable conditions in some camps as reported by daily press. Respectfully submit that Captain Robert S. Marcus . . . be assigned said post."[40] On August 9 Eisenhower sent a cable to Wise rejecting his request for a liaison officer, maintaining that such an individual would not be necessary, since the interests of the Jewish displaced persons were already being looked after by Allied liaison officers. He also reported that Jewish survivors were being placed in special assembly centers staffed by JDC personnel. Eisenhower was referring to new orders he issued on August 5 recognizing the right of the Jews to live in separate camps and repeating previously issued regulations designed to ensure that they received adequate assistance.[41] (He was to repeat these orders on August 22.)

Stimson's cable of August 10 forced Eisenhower to reconsider his rejection. In his answer to Stimson on August 10, Eisenhower announced that a Jewish chaplain would be designated immediately as a special advisor on Jewish affairs[42] but suggested that a prominent civilian be appointed at a later time. A chaplain would be selected to take advantage of his presence in the theater and knowledge of both the problems and the army's modus operandi. Although Wise had recommended Robert Marcus for the post, the JDC and perhaps other American Jewish organizations blocked his nomination. Marcus had been affiliated with the WJC and it is most probable the JDC wanted someone less partisan.

Opposition to the Marcus appointment also came from members of the army. Jacob Trobe, director of the JDC mission in Germany, recalled that Lieutenant Colonel Charles I. Schottland, chief of the Procurement Division in the Combined DPX (successor to the DPX), was one of the leading opponents of the Marcus appointment. He and other army officers believed that Marcus was not suited for this position because of his abrasive approach in dealing with the military. They felt that whatever could be done to ameliorate the plight of the displaced persons would only be accomplished with the active cooperation of the USFET. Therefore, it was essential to have an individual who could work well within the army bureaucracy.[43]

As has already been noted, Marcus had been determined to improve the condition of survivors and had gone to great lengths to bring this about. One of several incidents that probably disturbed Schottland took place in early July, when the American Army evacuated Buchenwald. Virtually all the remaining Jews were moved to Wildflecken, a camp about twenty-four miles from Fulda. Marcus visited the camp on July 10 and found living conditions there intolerable. The daily food ration consisted of a liter of watery soup, a loaf of black bread shared between four persons, and a can of preserved meat shared by twenty-one individuals; they were also alloted three to five cigarettes per day. There were no medical supplies, and Marcus feared a typhus epidemic in the extremely overcrowded camp. In addition, the Jews were housed with approximately eleven thousand Poles, many of them anti-Semites.

Marcus found the camp commandant to be sympathetic and cooperative but unable to provide preferential treatment for the Jews. He bitterly complained to the army; and as a result of a letter he sent to Colonel Schottland, the Jews were moved to the Landsberg camp, which was in the process of being turned into an all-Jewish camp by Abraham Klausner.[44]

Not long before the advisor was to be chosen, Schottland asked Trobe to supply him with an alternative choice to Marcus. Since this was such an important decision, Trobe tried to contact the JDC office in Paris for instructions. Telephone service was slow and he could not reach them in time. On his own, he submitted the name of Judah Nadich. They had met the preceding weekend in Paris and Nadich had impressed him. Furthermore, Nadich was already serving at the office of theater chaplain.[45] This recommendation was passed along to Eisenhower and it "tipped the scales in favour" of Nadich.[46] On August 22, 1945, Nadich was transferred from Paris to USFET Headquarters in Frankfurt.

On August 27 Nadich began his first tour of duty as advisor by visiting the Zeilsheim displaced persons camp outside of Frankfurt. Two days later, he began an extended tour of the camps in the Third Army area (Bavaria). On both occasions, Joseph Schwartz, of the JDC, accompanied him. A second major tour of inspection on September 5 covered the area supervised by the Seventh Army around Heidelberg. Nadich also spent two days in Berlin (September 12-13). On his return to Frankfurt, he met with General Walter Bedell Smith, Eisenhower's chief of staff. Under normal circumstances, Nadich would have submitted his findings to General Stanley M. Micklesen, who was in charge of the displaced persons. Instead, Eisenhower asked that he report to Smith directly, so that problems could be corrected at once.

At this meeting, Smith told Nadich about President Truman's letter to Eisenhower of August 31, 1945.[47] Truman was very disturbed that Eisenhower's subordinate officers had failed to follow policies set forth by the Combined DPX and wanted this promptly corrected. In particular, Truman was upset that military government officers who had been "authorized and even directed" to requisition German homes for the Jewish displaced persons had not done so on "any wide scale." Truman observed:

> Apparently it is being taken for granted that all displaced persons, irrespective of their former persecution or the likelihood that their repatriation or resettlement will be delayed, must remain in the camps—many of which are overcrowded and heavily guarded. . . .
> The announced policy has been to give such persons preference over the German civilian population, in housing. But the practice seems to be quite another thing. We must intensify our efforts to get these people out of camps and into decent houses until they can be repatriated or evacuated.

By requisitioning houses from the German population, the United States would be implementing the Potsdam policy of showing the German people that they "cannot escape responsibility for what they have brought upon themselves."

President Truman also advised Eisenhower that appropriate military authorities should make frequent visits throughout the American zone of occupation "so that the humane policies which have been enunciated are not permitted to be ignored in the field. Most of the conditions now existing in displaced persons camps would quickly be remedied if through inspection tours they came to your attention or to the attention of your supervisory officers."

The president knew that Eisenhower agreed that the United States had a "particular responsibility" to the displaced persons in the American zone: "We must make clear to the German people that we thoroughly abhor Nazi policies of hatred and persecution. We have no better opportunity to demonstrate this than by the manner in which we ourselves actually treat the survivors remaining in Germany."

Truman asked Eisenhower to report to him "as soon as possible" the steps made to improve the conditions detailed in the Harrison Report. Truman closed by informing Eisenhower that he was communicating directly with the British government to have the gates of Palestine open to all those wishing to enter.[48]

Since Nadich had just completed his own tour of inspection, Smith wanted to hear his assessment and any recommendations that he could make. Smith was particularly displeased to hear that in the Third Army area (under General Patton), American soldiers stood guard at the gates of the Jewish displaced persons camps, that Jews living inside these camps had to obtain passes before they could leave, that only 10 percent of the camp population were allowed out at any one time, and that nearby towns and villages were "off limits" to all displaced persons. As a result of this discussion, Smith phoned a number of generals including Patton and, in the name of Eisenhower, demanded an immediate improvement of conditions. Smith also conveyed the contents of Nadich's verbal report to Eisenhower on September 15.

Eisenhower responded to Truman's letter by visiting Feldafing and Stuttgart on September 17.[49] Until then, Eisenhower had not shown much interest in displaced persons despite his role as military governor. He had not given much prior thought to the occupation. Soon after the war ended, he took a month-long vacation, leaving General Clay in charge of laying the foundation for the military government.[50] Although Eisenhower "had the theoretical authority to enforce an order compelling uniformity in military government policies throughout the ETO [European Theater of Operations] . . . he failed to carry through this coordination."[51] Eisenhower's failure to give adequate attention to the problems of the displaced persons raised questions in Washington about the effectiveness of his command, causing him embarrassment and placing him on the defensive.

Eisenhower toured Feldafing and Stuttgart not only in response to President Truman's suggestion to visit the displaced persons installations in the American zone but also to see for himself what was happening and show that he was in command of the situation. To ensure good coverage, the press corps was alerted and they accompanied Eisenhower on this visit. At Feldafing, Eisenhower received an enthusiastic welcome from the Jewish survivors and was a guest at their Yom Kippur service.[52] In an address delivered at the camp synagogue, he pointed out that the American Army was in Germany to help them and that they must be patient until they could leave the country. Later, he inspected the camp and received two memoranda prepared by the Zionist organization of Feldafing and by the camp leadership. The first described the life and problems of Jews in the camp, while the second urged that the gates of Palestine be opened and a Jewish state established.[53]

Three days after visiting Feldafing and Stuttgart, Eisenhower issued a memorandum to all his subordinate officers. In it, he stressed they could no longer plead ignorance of the directives sent from headquarters and had to be sure that these policies were being carried out. In order to relieve overcrowding in the camps, he reiterated that whatever was required should be requisitioned. The need for wholesome and sufficient food was also underscored, as well as the importance of providing work for the displaced persons. In the last paragraph, Eisenhower asked that all necessary guarding of the camps be done by the displaced persons themselves, on a voluntary basis and without arms. "Everything should be done," he concluded, "to encourage displaced persons to understand that they have been freed from tyranny and that the supervision exercised over them is merely that necessary for their own protection and well-being and to facilitate essential maintenance."[54] To ensure that these policies were executed, he urged that frequent inspections be made by all commanders and that all incompetent personnel, whether civil or military, be removed by the army commander.

While this was an important directive, there were certain problems in implementing it, as Nadich observed: "In too many cases, American officers were more sympathetic to the Germans than with the Jews and they searched for loopholes in this official document in order to justify their actions." Other officers "frequently misinterpreted and distorted" the policy established in Eisenhower's memorandum. For example, in Kassel, the major in charge of the city insisted that all Jews living there had to move to Jewish displaced persons camps. If they refused to be evacuated, he threatened to take away their extra rations. According to army regulations, no Jews were to be forcibly removed from German cities and towns and they were to receive preferential treatment wherever they resided. Nadich reported that he intervened, but he realized that even the best policy could become ineffective and even destructive if improperly put into practice in the field.[55]

Since the majority of Jews were in the Third Army area there could be no major improvement in the region as long as Patton remained in command. When Eisenhower visited Feldafing on September 17, Patton went along. During the tour, Eisenhower made it clear to Patton that he wanted an immediate change in conditions. He ordered Patton to seize German houses in the neighborhood to relieve congestion in the camp.[56] Several days later, arrangements were made to move twenty-two wealthy German families from their homes; and Patton asked that they be treated with as much consideration as possible. He wanted the army to provide transportation so they could take a large portion of their property with them.

Patton was quite disturbed that Germans had to be evicted from their homes and often complained about the way the Americans were handling the German people. In his area, American officers were luxuriously entertained by the Germans, and no one could be ousted from his home without the approval of Patton's chief of staff.[57]

Patton was also disturbed that too much fuss was being made about the army's efforts to weed former Nazis from public positions in the denazification program. On September 23 the *New York Times* quoted Patton as saying that too much was being made of "this Nazi thing," because "it's just like a Democratic–Republican election fight." One of the first lessons he learned from his experiences in Germany was that "the outs are coming around saying that the ins are Nazis. . . . More than half the German people were Nazis and you'd be in a hell of a fix if you tried to remove all Party members. . . . To get things going, we've got to compromise with the devil a little bit."[58]

Patton was not as understanding about the Jews. Although he removed the armed military guard from the displaced persons camps, he believed this was a serious mistake. He noted in his diary that if the Jews were "not kept under guard, they would spread over the county like locusts, and would eventually have to be rounded up after quite a few of them had been shot and quite a few Germans murdered and pillaged." To Patton, the Jewish displaced person was not a human being but something "lower than animals" and he often marveled "that beings alleged to be made in the form of God can look the way they do or act they way they act." The "only decent people left in Europe," he observed, "were the Germans."[59]

Six days after Patton's comments appeared in the *New York Times*, he received word that he was to be transferred to the Fifteenth Army. Apparently, Eisenhower realized that Patton's continued presence in the area would only cause further embarrassment. One day after Patton was notified of his transfer, the Harrison Report made the front pages of newspapers across the United States. Eisenhower's reaction to the report was fairly predictable. He accused Harrison of "failing to consider the difficulties they faced and failing to recognize that improvements had already been made." While admitting that "there is need for improvement," Eisenhower argued that "we are conscious of these problems" and "are working on them" with the "expert advice of UNRRA, of Jewish agencies and of our chaplains."

"Perfection never will be attained," he told the president; "but real and honest efforts are being made to provide suitable living conditions for these persecuted people until they can be permanently resettled in other areas." Moreover, since Harrison's visit in July, he asserted, "many changes have taken place with respect to the condition of Jewish and other displaced persons."

In his concluding statement, Eisenhower made it clear that Harrison had not taken into account all the problems facing the army. "Mr. Harrison's report," he declared, "gives little regard to the problems faced, the real success attained in saving the lives of thousands of Jewish and other concentration camp victims and repatriating those who could [be] and wished to be repatriated, and the progress made in two months to bring these unfortunates who remained under our jurisdiction from the depths of physical degeneration to a condition of health and essential comfort."[60]

To prove Eisenhower's contention that there had been significant changes, General Smith arranged to fly a group of American correspondents to the "worst-known camps" in the American zone. They arrived in Feldafing on October 1, 1945; and after touring the camp, a United Press reporter asserted that the Jews were "living better than many Americans in slum areas." He acknowledged that they "were unhappy and that conditions were not the best, but at least they were not being victimized."[61]

Feldafing was not known to be the worst displaced persons camp in Germany; and Rabbi Israel Goldstein, cochairman of the American Jewish Conference, tried to set the record straight. In a statement issued in early October, he charged that in comparison with other camps, Feldafing was a model institution. Furthermore, he pointed out that this visit by newspaper correspondents might be misconstrued as an effort to "whitewash" the shortcomings revealed in the Harrison Report.[62]

Harrison concurred with Goldstein's criticism of the Feldafing visit and suggested the correspondents should have been taken to see some more representative camps. Moreover, Harrison believed that they had missed the point by underlining the improvement in these "model centers." What should have been stressed was that in spite of Eisenhower's orders that Jews be given preference in housing, these directives were not being carried out.[63]

Jacob Trobe was also concerned about the emphasis on improvements in the camps, since he feared these stories would blind the American public to the vast unfinished agenda ahead. He asserted that with few exceptions, the Jews had nothing with which to occupy their time; that they were distressed over their future; that no long-term medical program had been initiated to deal with their very special physical and mental problems; and that while UNRRA was staffing its teams with higher-quality men and women than they had done earlier, they did not have a Jewish team (or even a Jewish administrator and Jewish welfare worker) for each camp. Trobe believed that this was essential.[64]

This controversy over conditions in Europe would continue for some time. In early October, Harvey D. Gibson, commissioner of the American Red Cross to Britain and Western Europe from August 1942 to May 1945, visited seven displaced persons camps at the request of General Eisenhower. They included Zeilsheim near Frankfurt, Ludwigshohe near Darmstadt, Mannheim, Stuttgart, Goppingen near Stuttgart, and Feldafing and Wolfratshausen, near Munich. At the end of this tour, Gibson stated the army was carrying out its duties in the camps "as well as could reasonably be expected and, generally speaking in a commendable way."

With regard to the Jewish camps he found that "there appeared to be every indication of considerate treatment" on the part of the American Army personnel. He added that the officers in charge of the camps worked fifteen to eighteen hours a day and deserve "something besides criticism for their efforts." Gibson's report was sent to Eisenhower and the general's headquarters regarded it as an answer to the Harrison Report.[65]

On November 28, 1945, President Truman released a memorandum that described the position of the Jewish displaced persons in the camps as adequate. The information was part of a report submitted to Truman on November 9 by Byron Price, former director of the Office of Censorship. Price had gone to Germany as special representative of the president to study the relationship between the German people and the United States occupation forces. He reported that although the Jews were not living under the best conditions, no one complained of physical suffering. At the request of General Eisenhower, he visited the Jewish camps at Stuttgart, Feldafing, Wolfratshausen, and Deggendorf. He found that there was no serious shortage of clothing, blankets, or medicine and that the Jews were receiving more calories than the average European family.[66]

While Gibson and Price were convinced that the position of the Jewish displaced persons was adequate, the *New York Times*, *PM* (a liberal New York daily), the American Jewish press, chaplains,

JDC representatives, and UNRRA workers were reporting that the situation had actually deteriorated.[67] At a news conference at the JWB headquarters in New York on November 21 called by the American Jewish Congress and the JWB, Chaplain Robert Marcus charged that the American military personnel responsible for administering the displaced persons camps were generally "incompetent and disinterested" and that they were not carrying out Eisenhower's directives. "Any improvement in the condition of the Jews," Marcus declared, was "the result largely of their desire to help themselves." After the publication of the Harrison Report, Marcus asserted, "conditions improved for a while, but they have deteriorated again." The situation at the camp at Wildflecken was cited by Marcus as an example of the problems confronting the Jews in Germany.[68]

The news conference was held shortly after Marcus returned to New York from two years in Europe. After his discharge from the military, Marcus became director of the World Jewish Affairs Department of the American Jewish Congress and lectured to Jewish groups throughout the country on the declining situation of the remnants of European Jews. He also wrote extensively about his experiences with the survivors for the *Congress Weekly*.[69]

The decline in Jewish morale that Marcus and other chaplains observed is also found in the popular saying that "it was better to be a conquered German than a liberated Jew."[70] Zalman Grinberg also expressed his frustration in an appeal to the United Nations: "Give us a chance to live, give us the right to live, give us Palestine: and if not, restore the crematories and gas chambers and exterminate us in the name of democratic justice."[71]

The morale problem resulted from several factors. Many Jews were unable to establish a family life, had little chance of finding gainful employment, and had difficulties in again becoming useful members of the community. Moreover, they were puzzled and frustrated that after so many months they were still regarded as refugees without a homeland.

Zalman Grinberg described their morale decline in this way: "The average inmate . . . is in a state of unfathomable despondence, because hovering over the hard cheerless present is the unanswered question of the future. A cruel and terrible yesterday, a hard and bitter today, and a uncertain tomorrow impart to our people the impression of broken men who lapse ever more into endless despair, so that cases of suicide are now daily occurrences in our camps. Such is the lot of the liberated Jews . . . "[72]

The situation was compounded by the strained relationship with the army personnel. A large portion of the GIs in Germany had not personally witnessed Nazi atrocities and were not properly prepared to deal with the displaced persons. In fact, according to one

JDC representative, American soldiers knew so little about the Nazi treatment of Jews that when they were taken to Dachau, a majority of them were positive that it had been staged for propaganda purposes.[73]

The average soldiers' attitudes toward the Jews were shaped by the Germans. Widespread fraternization existed between Germans and American military personnel despite regulations. Judeophobia also influenced the soldiers' attitude toward Jewish displaced persons. This led to an increase in anti-Jewish feeling, an unwillingness to carry out objectives, and a general attitude of irritation and impatience with the whole displaced persons problem.[74]

Impact of the Harrison Report

Although Eisenhower and other army personnel tried to discredit Harrison's findings by sending newspaper correspondents and other observers to visit selective displaced persons installations, the report had an important impact. First, it brought the problems of the displaced persons to the attention of the president, who in turn ordered the military to improve treatment of the Jews. The resulting publicity brought the report to the attention of the American public, both Jewish and non-Jewish, who also demanded that improvements be made immediately. It also brought about the appointment of an Advisor on Jewish Affairs.

In general, American Jews viewed Harrison's report as an objective and accurate account of the situation in Europe. "It is our belief," declared the Interim Committee of the American Jewish Conference in a letter to Harrison, "that you made an objective and dispassionate statement, accurately conveying the real facts of the situation in Europe and that your report may prove to be the impelling force precipitating the long-awaited constructive action of the United Nations to relieve the distress of the Jewish people."[75] The *Indiana Jewish Chronicle* observed that this report was "perhaps the greatest single service rendered by a non-Jew to the Jews in the past half decade."[76] The *Jewish Exponent* in Philadelphia went even further when it asserted that Harrison had "earned the lasting gratitude not only of world Jewry, but of the entire American people. By presenting the tragic facts as he did without frills or embellishment, but in their stark reality, he nipped in its early stages a shame and a disgrace that our country would not be able to wash away for many years to come."

American Jews believed that the army was responsible for conditions described in the Harrison Report, and the *Jewish Exponent* refused to accept the excuses that were being offered "on behalf of the military authorities." "To say that Mr. Harrison's findings are outmoded," the newspaper declared, "is only to admit that for three months at least, the dastardly conditions he describes did prevail. An admission that is damnable as it is damning. Who knows how many lives were lost during those earlier three months?"[77]

In view of the army's performance, the *Exponent* was not willing to accept assurances that conditions had actually improved. The newspaper noted that it was continuing to receive "reports describing conditions no less vile than those contained in the Harrison document." Moreover, it had serious reservations about the military personnel responsible for caring for the survivors: "Men who can be as criminally neglectful as those entrusted with the task of establishing the peace as we in America envisage it should not expect us to take them at their word. These men have demonstrated beyond the shadow of a doubt that while they may have been, and many of them doubtless were, fit to wage war, they are wholly unfit to establish the peace. This is only one of the major lessons taught by the Harrison report—a lesson that cannot be learned and applied too soon."[78]

It is interesting that American Jews did not hold General Eisenhower responsible for his subordinates' behavior, either because they did not believe him culpable or because they thought that personal attacks would be fruitless. On October 17 Israel Goldstein issued a public statement of gratitude to Eisenhower for his "energetic actions" to correct the conditions in Europe. At the same time, Goldstein acknowledged that Eisenhower's orders were not always followed. "It is undoubtedly true that General Eisenhower has acted with the best will in the world," Goldstein asserted, "and that he has secured improvements in the administration of the camps where displaced Jews are housed, but there have been times when his directives have not been carried out."[79]

The American public, sympathetic to Eisenhower's position, was nevertheless disturbed by conditions described in the Harrison Report. The *New York Times,* for example, declared that the transfer of General Patton from his Bavarian position should have only one meaning—"that General Eisenhower and the United States government will not tolerate in high positions in our part of occupied Germany any officers, however brave, however honest, who are inclined to be easy on known Nazis and indifferent or hard toward the surviving victims of Nazi terror."[80] The impact of this publicity in both the Jewish and non-Jewish press caused some military men to reexamine their relationships with the displaced persons.

The appointment of an advisor on Jewish Affairs was another positive result of the Harrison Report. For the first time, Jews were recognized as having special needs that had not been met. From late August 1945 until early October 1945, Judah Nadich held this position and was responsible for advising Eisenhower on all problems affecting Jewish displaced persons and German Jews. He was also the liaison between the army and UNRRA and Jewish voluntary agencies. In this capacity, Nadich had contact with the JDC, the American Jewish Congress, the Jewish Agency, the WJC, and other Jewish organizations in the United States, Great Britain, and Palestine.[81]

Eisenhower had been uncomfortable with this arrangement from the beginning and told this to the CANRA Executive Committee at a meeting at the Pentagon in Washington in December 1945. Eisenhower stated that "while having a chaplain as an advisor had been of some value to him, it was not sufficiently helpful." The arrangement was subject to criticism, he observed, since, as an officer on his staff, Nadich might have felt inhibited in offering criticism. Eisenhower therefore requested that a Jewish civilian be appointed in his place. A civilian, he maintained, "would have the freedom to investigate wherever and however necessary and to report without restraint to the American community."[82]

Nadich was replaced by Judge Simon H. Rifkind, United States district court judge of the Southern District of New York, who arrived in Frankfurt on October 20, 1945. Nadich stayed on for over three weeks as advisor until Rifkind became fully acquainted with his new position.[83] Nadich then returned to the United States, where he was discharged from the army.

In the wake of the Harrison Report, the American Jewish Conference succeeded in gaining permission to send its representatives to Europe to study the problems of Jewish displaced persons in the American zone. This visit was another positive result of the Harrison Report. In late 1945, three individuals were chosen for this mission: Samuel L. Sar of Yeshiva College in New York; Hans Lamm, assistant to the director of the American Zionist Emergency Council; and Major Alfred Fleishman, former chief of the Special Projects Branch, Office of the Air Surgeon, in Washington. After an extensive tour of the region, they concluded that while there had been a definite change for the good since the Harrison Report, "these improvements were in large measure . . . negated by the apparent absence of any long-range coordinated and effective planning or a sense of urgency of the immediate problems."

They found that many army directives designed to aid the Jewish displaced persons were not carried out; that the U. S. military government and UNRRA did not work closely together, so that the Jews were not receiving effective rehabilitation; that UNRRA personnel were unprepared for their responsibilities; and that Jews subconsciously compared the concentration camps and their present existence without finding many differences between the two.[84]

The impact of the Harrison Report can also be seen in Truman's effort to convince the British to permit a hundred thousand survivors to enter Palestine. On August 31 Truman sent a copy of Harrison's Report to Clement R. Attlee, the newly elected prime minister of Great Britain. In an accompanying cover letter, Truman stated that "no single matter is so important for those who have known the horrors of concentration camps for over a decade as is the future immigration possibilities into Palestine." He urged that the British government grant a hundred thousand entry certificates to the Jewish survivors and pointed out, "If it is to be effective, such action should not be long delayed."[85]

Although Attlee originally rejected Truman's request, the British decided to call for an Anglo–American Committee of Inquiry after Truman made his demands public on September 24, 1945. Foreign Secretary Ernest Bevin, who wanted the Jews to return to their previous homelands, hoped that the formation of the committee would enable the British to delay a resolution of the problem of what to do with the refugees and involve the United States in the process of finding a solution. In negotiations preceding the establishment of the committee, the United States found that deliberations about the future of Palestine and the question of the displaced persons were thoroughly intertwined. After some discussion, the Anglo–American committee was set up in November 1945.

4

THE STRUGGLE FOR FREEDOM: JULY–DECEMBER 1945

Waiting for the Liberation

During the first months after liberation, Zalman Grinberg observed that the Jews were "too weak to feel joy. They were too humiliated to exult on the graves of their brothers and sisters. Then they could not comprehend their liberation." After "having regained" their strength, the remnants of European Jewry began to understand what liberation meant. "We were saved from death," Grinberg concluded, "but we were not liberated."[1]

During the last six months of 1945, the survivors moved from a struggle for life itself to a struggle for their freedom. Abraham Klausner noted that in this second phase, "Life conquered Death and made many promises to the children of Israel. Day by Day we shed our garments of apathy and despair. Eyes no longer questioned and faces wore a new expression. A new faith was born! 'We shall live again!' we repeated in our hearts 'And that life will be of our own making'."[2]

The enthusiasm did not last long; for the Jews were forced to wait "day in and day out, for the fulfillment of" their liberation. Months after they were freed, Zalman Grinberg complained that "we still live in camps and in barracks, we are still hedged in by regulations, we are still separated from the remnants of our families and often we are still unaware of their fate, we are still in a land of the enemy."[3]

The Harrison Report, which "defined the problem of the displaced persons, specified the causes of that problem, and offered specific recommendations for its resolution,"[4] resulted in some immediate changes, but it did not alleviate the need for the continued involvement of the chaplains in displaced persons work. By providing better housing, food, and clothing, the chaplains sought to improve living conditions. By establishing a central committee, they helped survivors regain greater control over their future.

Many chaplains were convinced that Palestine was the only solution for most survivors. For this reason, some took risks in aiding the Palestinian Jews move survivors from Poland and elsewhere in Central Europe into the American zone and then on to Palestine, provided the Palestinians with material and logistical assistance, and agreed to smuggle arms for them to be used in Palestine.

Attempts To Improve Living Conditions

The need for better living conditions had been an ongoing problem a number of chaplains tried to solve. Only 60.5 percent of the homes in the American zone could be used. Of the 870,000 houses still standing, 32,000 were in need of major repair.[5] Chaplain Abraham Spiro, an Orthodox rabbi assigned to the Seventeenth Reinforcement Depot, arrived in Nuremberg at the end of June and by early July reported that he had been aiding eighty Jews living in a former SS barracks. The camp was managed by a number of tired, apathetic, and "hopelessly unqualified" army personnel, who kept the Jews under appalling living conditions in groups according to their countries of origin. They were thus at the mercy of Hungarian, Polish, Ukrainian, and Baltic anti-Semites and former SS guards.

Spiro asked the military to give the Jews special treatment by allowing them to leave the camps, but it denied his request. He then decided to move them elsewhere by himself. On one of his trips to Bayreuth, he inspected the city's housing facilities and found it could accommodate several hundred people. At that point, there were only seventeen Jewish displaced persons in the city. Before the Jews could be officially removed from Nuremberg, the army had to sanction their transfer, which it refused to do. Spiro complained to various officers, but they told him that displaced persons were the responsibility of the army and could not be permitted to care for themselves.

Realizing that further requests would be futile, Spiro began smuggling Jews out of the camp himself. Civilian cars were contracted for transport; and within a few days, the Jews were living in homes in Bayreuth. Several times each week, Spiro brought them supplies. Other communities in Schwabach, Fürth, Pottenstein, and Marburg were also established with Spiro's help. In September, after Eisenhower ordered that German homes be requisitioned for the Jews, Spiro's task was made easier. While housing Jews in the cities solved the immediate problem, Spiro recognized that they needed to be educated and given something to occupy their time. Since the majority of those that Spiro met wanted to emigrate to Palestine, he began preparing them for their new life there.

Spiro contacted Colonel C. J. Reilly, then head of Bayreuth's military government, to determine if there were any former Nazi farms in the area that could be used as kibbutzim. Reilly assured him that there were none. He viewed the Jews as an albatross and on previous occasions had threatened to expel them from Bayreuth. Spiro refused to believe Reilly, and with the aid of the *Landrat* (similar to a county commissioner in the United States) they found a farm. Reilly, still reluctant to allow the farm to be used by the Jews, relented after continued pressure from Spiro.

In the middle of November, a special ceremony was held to formally celebrate the opening of Kibbutz Geulim and Spiro arranged for Colonel Reilly and the commanding general of the 102d Division, Frank H. Keating, to be present. Jews from neighboring towns also attended. The publicity generated by this affair inspired other Jewish communities to establish their own kibbutzim. After the military government officers in the region heard about the kibbutz or read about it in the army newspaper *Stars and Stripes,* they were more willing to cooperate with Spiro.

Spiro continued to establish other kibbutzim with the help of Ann Liepah, a JDC worker, and provided them and other Jewish communities with various supplies. Most of these provisions came from soldiers who not only donated their own rations but also managed to secure food and clothing from a wide variety of sources, including packages from the United States.[6]

Chaplain Herbert Eskin also succeeded in securing shelter for the displaced persons but in the process received a reprimand from his superior officer. In mid-July, Albert Hutler received orders to evacuate the Jews from the Langenzell Castle and set up a camp for them in Stuttgart. He and his assistant went to Stuttgart and with the help of Chaplain Eskin found several blocks of apartment houses. Each one of the fifty-one apartments was equipped with a kitchen, a bathroom, and two or three bedrooms. The German occupants were ordered out and 150 Jews were moved into the complex on August 2. Life in the apartment camp then became as normal for the Jews as could be expected. There was no barbed wire, and passes were not required to leave the area.

Eskin's involvement was reported to Colonel William W. Dawson, director of the Regional Government Coordinating Office, who accused him of engaging in Nazi tactics. After a heated exchange, Eskin told the colonel that he could not turn his back on his people and walked out. Within a day, he was called before General Walter

Burris, the commanding general of the 100th Infantry Division. The general read a long list of charges against him and asked if they were accurate. Eskin told the general that he would pay the penalty for his actions but asked to be transferred to a rear-echelon unit because he would not stay and do nothing. General Burris, who had seen the concentration camps, told Eskin to continue his work.[7]

Chaplain Morris Dembowitz, who was assigned to the Sixth Corps Headquarters, also worked with Jews in the Stuttgart area. In an old isolated castle about thirty miles from Heidenheim, Dembowitz found over eighty former concentration camp survivors. The mayors of the nearby villages supplied them with food, and Dembowitz offered additional assistance. Since the building had not been winterized, Dembowitz and Saul Elgart, senior field representative of the JDC (one of the thirteen JDC representatives working in Germany by September 1945), approached the military government of Heidenheim and received permission from them to move the Jews to a modern old age home in the city. On October 9 they made the transfer under the supervision of the JDC representative.[8]

In Bremen, Chaplain Manuel Poliakoff reorganized the Jewish community, acted as their advisor, and effectively argued their case before the army. With the blessings of General Charles H. Gerhardt, military governor of the Bremen enclave, Poliakoff requisitioned a twenty-five-room palatial home on the Weser River, which he converted into a Jewish center. In this building, he set up a synagogue, a social hall, a large office for officials of the Jewish community, and living quarters for himself, his assistant, and two displaced persons that he hired through the army.[9]

In Northern Bavaria, Eugene Lipman found Jews in every town in Niederbayern and Oberpfalz. They were disorganized and in need of clothing and were looking for a means to contact their relatives. He helped establish *hachsharot*, which he and his assistant Simon Pava watched over and provided with supplies. Each day Lipman and Pava visited different camps and communities throughout the region, handling black market violations, medical and social cases, and legal problems, providing relief and assisting children's groups.

The enormity of the work became too much for one chaplain and his assistant, even when each community began functioning in an organized and democratic way (although erratically). In November, a Central Committee for Northern Bavaria was established, with headquarters in Regensburg. Joseph Levine, the first JDC worker to arrive in north Bavaria, gradually began assuming the tasks Lipman had been handling and established them on a legal and regular basis.[10]

In other areas of Germany, chaplains reported working with Jews in response to similar needs. Chaplain Isadore Breslau, a thirty-five-year-old Conservative rabbi—and, later, Chaplains George Vida and Irving Ganz—worked with the displaced persons in Frankfurt. Chaplain David Lefkowitz, Jr., a thirty-four-year-old Reform rabbi attached to the Ninth Air Force Headquarters, reported supplying food to Jews in the Zeilsheim displaced persons camp and helping rededicate a synagogue at Bad Neustadt. Chaplain Bert A. Klein, a forty-three-year-old rabbi attached to the Central Flying Command, helped Jews in southern Bavaria.[11]

At Fürstenfeldbruck, Chaplain Meyer Goldman organized a Jewish community and secured a building that later was converted into a synagogue and community center. In Bamberg, Chaplain Herman Dicker, a thirty-one-year-old Orthodox rabbi assigned to Headquarters First Medical Battalion, worked with the Jewish committee in the city and persuaded the military to provide them with an automobile. He also endeavored to reclaim German Jewish property.[12]

Most chaplains worked individually in their areas and tried not to provoke adverse reaction from the military. Abraham Klausner, however, directly challenged the army to change its policy regarding the treatment of displaced persons. The army, stunned by the Harrison Report, attempted to avoid confrontation. This can be seen in an incident involving a former German Army ammunition dump called Buchberg. During the war, slave laborers were housed in Buchberg's ramshackle houses. The Germans who supervised this operation lived in Wolfratshausen, a small complex of nearby brick buildings.

When he discovered that Jews were living in Buchberg and the *Volksdeutsch* (ethnic Germans) in Wolfratshausen, Klausner complained to the army. Rather than resolve the problem itself, the army decided to turn it over to UNRRA. Ultimately, Klausner succeeded in obtaining Wolfratshausen for the Jews, but only after initial opposition from UNRRA.[13]

Another example of the army's determination to avoid conflict can be seen in an incident involving Leo Srole, a professor of sociology and the principal UNRRA welfare officer at the Landsberg displaced persons camp. At the Landsberg camp, approximately sixty-two hundred Jews were living in substandard dwellings that normally accommodated forty-five hundred.[14] Jean Gafan, a field representative for the JDC, reported to JDC headquarters in New York that the camp was so overcrowded that two and three people were forced to sleep together in one bed and that the sanitation facilities were grossly inadequate.

The UNRRA director at Landsberg sent a number of reports to his headquarters, detailing the problems of the camp; but nothing had been done to alleviate the situation. Complaints were also lodged with Major Irving Heymont, the Commander of Landsberg; but he, too, had been unable to effect any changes. The UNRRA teams for the Jewish camps in Germany then sent a joint protest to their camp commanders. After this attempt failed, Srole decided drastic action had to be taken.

Srole was convinced that there was an immediate danger of a cholera epidemic. He feared that if the disease spread through Landsberg, it would decimate the inhabitants. This concern was also expressed by the doctors at the Fahrenwald displaced persons camp. They believed that while the general health of these Jews was not poor, their resistance to infectious diseases was very low.

Srole decided to tender his resignation to call attention to the appalling conditions at the camp. He thought that his views would be taken more seriously because he was an academic. Before submitting a letter of resignation, he showed it to Klausner, whom he had met in Germany. Klausner agreed and quietly had a copy of Srole's letter sent to the press corps in Nuremberg. Without press coverage, they reasoned, the protest would have very little significance.[15]

The army received Srole's letter of resignation on December 5, 1945; and within hours General Smith was on his way to the camp. Accompanying Smith at his request were General Albert Kenner, the surgeon general; General Lucian K. Truscott (Patton's replacement as commander of the Third Army); Judge Simon Rifkind; Major Irving Heymont, the former commander of Landsberg; officials of UNRRA and the JDC; and a horde of newspaper correspondents.[16] They arrived by train on the morning of December 6; and after a lengthy conference with the officials of the camp, they inspected the area.

Apparently, Smith decided before coming to Landsberg to use the visit to deflect criticism from the army to the Jews. At the conclusion of his visit, he claimed that though the sanitary conditions in the camp were intolerable, the Jewish inmates were at fault. The army could not be responsible for the human defecation found littering some of the rooms and he told the camp committee they were not doing enough to keep the place clean. Furthermore, Smith claimed that there was no real danger of epidemics unless they were brought on by continual disregard for hygienic discipline.

Smith acknowledged there was much overcrowding in the camp but attributed this to the unauthorized influx of Jews who began slipping into the American zone of occupation from the Russian and British zones beginning in the summer of 1945. This movement had been partly spontaneous and partly an organized effort to transfer Jews to staging points for emigration to Palestine. Smith told the inmates' committee that he would request additional housing but asserted that UNRRA had been partly to blame for the overcrowding, allegedly for failing to make the proper requisitions in writing.

General Kenner supported Smith's assessment, claiming that although the food was starchy and monotonous, there was an adequate supply. As evidence, he cited the absence of any cases of malnutrition in the camp. He also maintained there was enough warm clothing for everyone and that all the living quarters were sufficiently heated.[17]

Judge Rifkind, the newly appointed advisor on Jewish Affairs, agreed with this assessment and felt that the morale was superior to many of the other installations he had visited.[18] He was furious with Srole for having openly attacked the army.[19] A far more constructive approach, Rifkind believed, would have been to credit the military for their accomplishments while indicating what still remained to be done.[20]

Rifkind was also concerned that Srole's accusations and those of newspaper correspondents and chaplains[21] would give the American Jewish community the wrong impression about conditions in Europe. This misinformation would then be used to formulate their course of action. To warn American Jewry of this danger, Rifkind sent cables to Stephen Wise, Nahum Goldmann, and other Jewish leaders, assuring them that he had visited every Jewish displaced persons center in the American zone and that there was no cause for alarm.[22] If the situation was as scandalous as was portrayed, the representatives of the American Jewish Conference would have discussed it in their report, he noted.[23]

While the representatives of the American Jewish Conference did not specifically mention conditions at Landsberg, they did report that "cold, hungry, scantily clothed men, women, and children" who were coming from the British and Russian zones were in need of immediate housing and food. "A real emergency and pitiful conditions" existed in part of Bavaria, they concluded—and urged that these people not "be regarded as numbers or inanimate objects which may be set aside and dealt with at a later or more convenient date."[24]

The WJC was very disturbed with Rifkind for having sided with the army. The WJC recognized that General Smith had been trying to pass the blame for overcrowding on to UNRRA when it was the army's own responsibility. In September, Eisenhower had ordered that German homes be requisitioned for the Jews; and the WJC charged that the army had a moral obligation to care for these people regardless of what UNRRA did or did not do. The WJC knew that UNRRA officials tried to obtain whatever was needed from local military authorities but their requests were denied.

The WJC also found it difficult to accept that the Jews were responsible for the unsanitary conditions in the camp. Overcrowding in and of itself made for an unhealthy environment, and many Jews were not strong enough to care for themselves. Furthermore, what could be expected, it asked, when there was only one latrine for every one hundred persons? "If from the start, the army had shown a friendly helping hand," the WJC asserted, and "had engaged in psychological therapy instead of treating these people like vermin under their feet, there would be very little of a problem along these lines."[25]

Before General Smith left Landsberg, he asked Srole to withdraw his resignation. Srole had originally said that if conditions at the camp would improve, he would not leave his post. Smith knew that if Srole left Germany, it would cause the army a great deal of embarrassment. Srole realized the general would not publicly admit that the army had been at fault but would ensure that immediate improvements were initiated. He therefore agreed to remain. As he told Smith, he had come to Germany to help his fellow Jews and wanted to stay as long as possible. Some thirty members of Srole's family had been killed by the Nazis, and his parents were from the same area as many of those in Landsberg. Smith said he understood how Srole felt, since his mother was Jewish.[26]

As a result of Smith's visit, new centers were opened at Leipheim, Bamberg, Ainring, Schwandorf, Teuchenreuth, Pocking, and Ansbach. Two *hachsharot* were also established: one at Schongau, the other at Wallenberg. To further reduce overcrowding, General Truscott arranged to move a number of Jews out of Landsberg and Feldafing to other camps. At first, these transports created problems because the army had not properly prepared the Jews and failed to take into account that civilians could not be ordered around like soldiers. After years of living in the camps, the Jews were extremely apprehensive about unexpected changes. The thought of joining a transport brought back many traumatic memories of their recent past.[27]

On December 10, 1945, after having visited Landsberg, a group of seven American and Allied newspaper correspondents (including one from the Jewish Telegraph Agency) issued a signed declaration reiterating Srole's condemnation of the conditions there. They charged that the wooden barracks were unfit for human habitation; that people were living in damp basements that were full of smoke from green burning wood; that there were not enough clothes or blankets; that the food was inadequate and unpalatable; that there was only cold water to wash with; that the washroom was covered by a sheet of ice; and that the pipes were frozen and rusted so that there was only one toilet for every one hundred persons.

The correspondents further asserted, "Immediate and drastic action is imperative if these people . . . are not to continue living in indescribable misery and under the constant threat of disease and death." They knew that nothing would be done until the army officers took a more sympathetic approach and began carrying out Eisenhower's directives. The problem, they believed, was that some of the officers and enlisted men were anti-Semitic and would not exercise their authority unless forced to do so. The UNRRA workers, on the other hand, were eager to help but could not do anything on their own.[28]

While the chaplains in Germany had to take the initiative to improve living conditions, in Austria Chaplain Eli Bohnen reported that Major General Harry J. Collins, commanding general of the Forty-Second Division, had instructed him to rectify the horrible conditions the general saw in a displaced persons camp in the Salzburg area where the Forty-Second Division was stationed.[29] Austria, like Germany, had been divided into four zones: Russian, French, British, and American. The Russians controlled Lower Austria and Vienna, the British the southeast, and the French and the Americans Upper Austria. General Mark Clark was in command of the American forces in Austria and was virtually independent of Eisenhower and USFET Headquarters.[30]

Sometime in late July, General Collins called Chaplain Bohnen and two other Jewish officers in the Division into his office. One was the commander of the division's medical battalion and the other Collins's personal physician. Collins had just visited a displaced persons camp in the area and was shocked by the plight of these people. He ordered the officers to visit the camp and do whatever necessary to improve the situation.

Bohnen and his assistant Eli Heimberg went to the camp, where they found 450 Jewish men, women, and children living under intolerable conditions. The Jews were herded together in buildings that had been used as German cavalry stables, and they lived in constant fear of Yugoslav displaced persons in the same camp. Bohnen returned with a list of items needed to clean up the camp, which he presented to the general. When Collins gave the list to his supply officer, the officer claimed he could not fulfill the request because the Austrian economy had collapsed. The general refused to accept any excuse and demanded every item on the list.

Bohnen believed that Collins would have done more had not the lack of clear-cut army policy toward displaced persons made him more cautious. Collins was so concerned about this situation that he told Bohnen to come directly to him any time he had a question regarding Jewish displaced persons. This was a highly irregular arrangement, since meetings normally had to be cleared first by his chief of staff.[31]

By mid-August, Bohnen was helping about a thousand Jews, most of whom had been in concentration camps. As in Germany, their plight was horrible. "Except for having a fear of death removed from their consciousness," Bohnen noted, "their lot can be but little better that it was in these camps." "In many instances," they were "sleeping on the floor of empty buildings. Their food is terrible, though it probably measures up to the 2,000 calories they are supposed to get. They are in great need of clothing. They are not living as people should who have endured so much."[32]

As bad as conditions were in the Salzburg region, they were much worse in the area of Austria covered by the Twenty-Sixth Division. Colonel Epes, then in charge of displaced persons in the area, had very little sympathy for the Jews. On October 3, a number of displaced persons in the Linz area were to be transferred, without prior notification, to a German camp that was unfit for human habitation. The Jews refused to budge, but the army insisted that they would be forced at gunpoint if necessary. Before a solution could be worked out, James P. Rice, the JDC representative in the region, sent a cable to JDC headquarters in Paris suggesting that the situation in the whole of Upper Austria be given closer attention. The cable was sent on October 5 and at 3:00 A.M. on October 6, General Clark telephoned Rice and asked him to withhold the cable from the press. Clark felt that the cable might create the wrong impression; and after the Harrison Report and Truman's letter to Eisenhower, he did not want any adverse publicity. To ensure that incidents like this would not happen again, he dispatched his chief of staff, General Brann, to Linz. There Brann reprimanded General Rinehart, the commanding general of the Twenty-Sixth Division and his chief of staff for failing to carry out Clark's orders regarding the Jewish refugees.

The next day, October 7, Clark met with the generals under his command in Vienna and castigated them for disobeying his orders. He asked about the conditions of the camps in their areas, and only General Collins knew the answers. He had been briefed on the way to the meeting by Eli Bohnen and others involved with displaced persons. At the end of the conference, Clark appointed James P. Rice, Rabbi Bohnen, and General Hume of the Civilian Affairs Division to find suitable housing for the displaced persons.[33] Places were found in the resort area of Bad Gastein and at the Bindermichl apartment houses in Linz. Bindermichl became known as New Palestine, and General Collins placed Eli Heimberg on special duty there. Through Heimberg's efforts a kosher kitchen was installed, a school for children was established, a newspaper was started, and a piano was obtained. In addition, Heimberg published a primer, *Englisch für Jedermann,* to help the Jews learn English.[34]

By early December, the housing situation had greatly improved. The main problem was to get the Jews out of the country and into Palestine. All other solutions, Bohnen asserted, "were merely palliatives."[35]

Attempts To Obtain Basic Necessities

Aside from adequate housing, the survivors required other basic necessities, such as shoes and clothing. The situation had become so desperate that on September 28, 1945, Zalman Grinberg sent a public letter to the American Jewish community declaring: "The clothing situation is catastrophic. None of the many organizations—UNRRA, JDC—have helped us so far. Winter is approaching and our people are without proper clothes and footwear. Most of them have no overcoats, no pullovers, and no underwear, let alone shoes. . . . In short, I advise you that neither UNRRA or the JDC has so far been able to master the situation."[36]

In response to these conditions, Abraham Klausner met with seven or eight chaplains stationed in Germany in late August and urged them to start a package program with the help of American Jewish soldiers. The chaplains agreed and decided to make the appeals during the High Holidays because the maximum number of soldiers could be reached at that time.[37]

From letters reprinted in their hometown newspapers and from the tons of packages that began pouring into Germany in late 1945, it is clear these appeals had a profound impact on large numbers of soldiers. One soldier described the New Year's services he attended in Munich as providing "a negative sort of inspiration, an emotion embodying a sense of shock, futility, of need for action." It had been created by the presence of approximately fifty survivors from a nearby displaced persons camp and by the sermon delivered by Abraham Klausner. "The survivors' prayers were genuine," the soldier explained, "their weeping from the soul—but without tears. Their tears had long ago become dried from years of tragedy and sorrow." He could not "possibly reduplicate the atmosphere created by this group of circumstances" but wanted to pass along the facts, so that those reading his letter would not rest until they had "done something to alleviate the situation." The soldier told of Abraham Klausner's graphic description of the plight of the Jews in Germany and his attack on the Red Cross, the JDC, UNRRA, and the other relief agencies for failing to come to their aid. The soldier then urged that new clothing, soap, toothbrushes, toothpaste, Yiddish papers, modern Hebrew books, *talitot* (prayer shawls), *tefillin* (phylacteries), and *siddurim* (prayer books) be sent to Germany at once.[38]

According to Erich Maier, a representative of the WJC, who toured the displaced persons camps in Bavaria, Klausner's *Kol Nidrei* speech at the Opera House in Munich was even more impressive. The opera house was filled to capacity with American soldiers and a few Jewish civilians when Klausner took to the podium:

> Before him he had a table with something covered under a white cloth. He spoke about the suffering of our people, especially of those placed in the United States Army camps for displaced Jews. But then, Chaplain Klausner removed the cloth from the table and showed his audience the food the Jews in the camps have to eat. This was a moment of great dramatics and it could be seen how deeply the audience was impressed. Continuing in his speech, Chaplain Klausner assailed especially the Joint Distribution Committee who had failed to bring any relieve [sic] to our Jews. He also spoke of brutal treatment of Jews by our own United States Army, who fled from Poland toward Germany to escape the persecution by the Poles. The Jews, in one case numbering 500 were beaten and forced to enter freight cars to be returned to Poland. He introduced to the audience a Polish Jew who was one of the 500 and had escaped. The man described in all details the brutality committed by the soldiers of our own Army. Chaplain Klausner ended his speech with an appeal to all for help, before it was too late.[39]

The soldiers appealed to friends and families for aid; and soon, packages began arriving in Bavaria at the rate of three to five tons a day. Most were addressed to Chaplain Max Wall, who was actively involved with the survivors in the area. Klausner could not officially receive the packages because of his unique position in the army, so Wall agreed to have them sent to him, instead. Rather than distribute the packages himself, Wall brought them to a committee of survivors, who handled the operation. Klausner believed the survivors should be in control of their own affairs, since only they could change their status. He tried to help them to where they could care for themselves.

The tons of material that arrived each day provided only 1 percent of the survivors' needs. Many people sent old clothing, discarded eyeglasses, and worn-out shoes. Klausner stood "aghast" as he watched this spectacle of the American Jewish community "ignominiously dumping its closet rags on our proud remnant of a people." "Aside from the uselessness of the object," it created "an animosity on the part of our people for those people in whom they deposited that bit of hope which the concentration camps could not destroy."[40]

In a letter to the American Federation of Lithuanian Jews, Klausner pointed out, "More than once did I hear our Lithuanian brethren remark when they saw some of the rags that have been arriving—'in Lithuania we would be ashamed to give such articles to help our brethren'." "If nothing more," Klausner declared, "we owe our courageous brethren a respect due them for their unswerving faith that kept them alive and a zealous faith that drives them on to a new life. This respect must be demonstrated in the form of aid we offer."[41] To be sure, there were individuals and groups that sent new clothing and usable items; and Klausner graciously thanked them.

In Northern Bavaria, Eugene Lipman launched a package and mail service project. Between October 1945 and May 1946, Lipman received between 175 and 180 tons of packages. He requisitioned a warehouse near the Jewish community house, where the packages were processed under the direction of Simon Pava, his assistant. Vital foods were given to pregnant women, children, nursing mothers, and the aged. Within a short time, the project became a significant enterprise.

The postal system became one as well. Mailboxes were installed in each community. At its peak, 2,000–2,500 letters were mailed out of Germany, and 500–600 were received each week. Initially, each outgoing letter had to be readdressed with Lipman's address and military rank. The displaced persons were still not allowed to send mail on their own. When the volume of outgoing letters became overwhelming, Lipman contacted Jewish organizations in the United States, Canada, England and Australia and Chaplain Alvin Fine, a Reform rabbi, in Shanghai and sent the letters to them in bulk packages for remailing.

While the outgoing system worked well, the incoming letters presented a problem. Many arrived without a displaced persons address or identification. A typical cover letter read:

Dear Chaplain Lipman,
   It is good of you to forward my cousin's letter. Please give him this one in return.
   JLS

The letter to his cousin had no address, but only:

"Mein Lieber Jacob" (My Dear Jacob).

These letters had to be returned to the sender with a reminder that two envelopes had to be used—the outer one addressed to Lipman and an inner one addressed to the displaced persons addressee.

In late 1945 a package of mail sent to England broke open, scattering letters all over the plane. The European theater postal officer ordered an immediate investigation, and Lipman was called before the chief of staff of his division. The officer insisted that military channels were not to be used for displaced persons mail, but Lipman protested that the displaced persons could not wait six to twelve months for the army to rectify this problem. The officer appeared to agree; for, with a broad grin, he told Lipman, "Consider yourself reprimanded and get the hell out of here."

In early 1946 the JDC received permission from the military to take over the mail service legally.[42]

Supplies came not only from the United States but from the United Kingdom, as well. Chaplain Louis Milgrom, a thirty-six-year-old Conservative rabbi assigned to the Ninth Air Force, arranged to have large quantities of supplies sent from England. He had spent the previous year with the United States Eighth Air Force in Great Britain and had met civilian rabbis and chaplains serving in the British Army. When he asked for their support, they gathered canned goods, soap, warm winter clothing, old fur coats, milk, and kosher food provided by Chief Rabbi Hertz of Great Britain. So many packages arrived that Milgrom needed three assistants to help him distribute it. He also received packages from his congregation and friends in the United States. Any excess packages were sent to Munich.[43] In addition, supplies from England were sent to chaplains in all parts of Germany from Chaplain Paul Gorin, a thirty-four-year-old Reform rabbi stationed there.[44]

Germany was not the only country in which chaplains initiated package programs. While little is known about the actual implementation of the project in Italy, a number of chaplains did receive and distribute clothes. In Austria, Chaplain Eli Bohnen launched a package program in early September. At High Holiday services, he appealed to the soldiers in Salzburg to give up their PX rations and to have their families send them packages. He also urged them to write home about the survivors and ask that pressure be put on the United States government to open Palestine to Jewish settlement. Since the soldiers did not know when they would be leaving the area, packages were addressed to the Jewish chaplain of the Forty-Second Division.

Within a short time, Bohnen was swamped with parcels. Storerooms were set up near the division's post office to handle the deluge, and several displaced persons worked full-time opening and sorting the supplies. Each package had to be acknowledged by a letter, so that the people would know that their package had arrived and was appreciated. A portion of the contents of these packages was used to pay the people in New Palestine and Bad Gastein who worked as security guards, garbage collectors, kitchen help, and school teachers.

The army had been sympathetic to this project; but when Bohnen received two freight cars full of packages in one day, the inspector general of the army thought Bohnen might be involved in the black market. When he learned that General Collins knew about the program, nothing further was said.[45]

In Brussels, the commanding officer of Chaplain Benjamin Gorrelick, a thirty-nine-year-old Conservative rabbi assigned to the Chanor Base Section, was not so sympathetic. During the third week of June, Gorrelick found ten Jewish orphanages in and around Brussels in need of assistance. The JDC was already supporting these institutions, but it was not yet in a position to supply all that was required. The directors of the orphanages urged Gorrelick to have his wife organize their congregation in Albany, New York to send packages of food, clothing, soap, and other items. Within a short while, Gorrelick began receiving about one hundred packages a week. By the time he left in January 1946, he had provided the orphanages with at least two thousand packages. When the commanding general of the base section learned of the high volume of packages being sent to Gorrelick, he ordered him to his office for an explanation. The general sympathized with the goals of the project but ordered Gorrelick to stop because it violated army regulations. Gorrelick did not want to end the program, so he instructed his wife to send the packages to a dozen Jewish soldiers, who in turn gave them to him. Eventually, mail from the United States became more normal, and packages were sent directly to the orphanages.[46]

To prevent the army from interfering in his package program in France, Abraham Haselkorn asked his wife to have the packages sent as religious supplies. The army permitted each chaplain to receive seventy-pound packages containing "religious material" to be used "in their official capacity." Prior approval was not needed. Haselkorn's wife tried to enlist the support of thousands of women in Hadassah groups (the Women's Zionist Organization of America) throughout the United States; but Judith Epstein, the national president, refused to involve the organization because the project violated American law. Instead, Epstein directed Mrs. Haselkorn to a woman who undertook the project herself. Within two months she sent seventy wooden crates containing 106 wooden boxes full of food.[47]

Chaplain Herschel Livazer, a forty-one-year-old Orthodox rabbi working with the Jews in Rheims, France, also succeeded in thwarting the army from stopping his package program. So many packages began arriving in Rheims that the army complained it affected the delivery of military mail. An attempt to confiscate the packages failed when Livazer learned of an impending raid and moved the operation to a new location with the aid of Palestinian Jews.[48]

Most chaplains were eager to receive supplies from the United States, but at least one chaplain opposed the idea. Chaplain Herman Dicker suggested to the JWB that "the recent habit of using the names of the Jewish Chaplains as a channel of supplies for the displaced persons should be discouraged." Instead, he urged the JWB to refer those wishing to send packages to the JDC. Dicker was concerned that "the distribution of such relief supplies, while in themselves very useful and necessary, becomes a grave problem of additional travel, work and help. Very often three quarters of the mail for the whole unit are packages for the chaplain." If this practice continued, Dicker concluded, "the JWB was jeopardizing the overall effectiveness of the Chaplain in the field."[49]

While no response could be located to Dicker's letter, the package program raised a number of issues for the JWB. On October 9, 1945, Louis Kraft, executive director of the JWB, expressed the organization's dilemma when he stated: "We are in the uncomfortable and unclear position of not being able to say yes or no. First, we do not wish to do anything that may embarrass the chaplains as military officers. Secondly, we wish to avoid the impression that we are going into overseas relief as a program of the JWB or of the [JWB] Women's Division. Nevertheless, the needs are very pressing, and the people who receive the letters will not be satisfied with a non-committal reply from us."

Kraft assumed that the JDC's women's group would launch a clothing program, but he knew this would take some time. "In the meantime," he suggested, "urgent needs can be met at least in part through the chaplains." One solution would be to arrange for the army to approve chaplains' requests for packages. "This can be either in the form of a general approval or individual approval of each request by the appropriate superior officer in the chaplain's unit," Kraft explained. He believed that "as a temporary and interim measure until the JDC can work out its program, this ought to be acceptable to the army authorities in Europe."[50]

Chaplain Aryeh Lev advised Kraft against seeking army approval for shipping packages. Since the army was not responsible for supplying food and clothing to the survivors, it would not allow its shipping facilities for this use. He also feared that if the army was asked to provide help, it might investigate the package program and have it stopped. The question of how to respond to requests for chaplains' addresses in Europe was not a new problem, Lev assured Kraft. When contacted, CANRA provided individuals and organizations with chaplains' addresses. They were advised to write directly to the chaplains about what they intended to send and ask if there were any objections.[51]

Apparently, the JWB did not heed Lev's advice. In late October, Chaplain Edward Sandrow, a Conservative rabbi assigned to the Office of Port Chaplain in New York City, arranged for Jewish organizations to send packages through his office to chaplains in Europe. Individuals were advised to send their packages to the American Jewish Congress, which would include them as part of its bulk shipment. While most items were shipped by sea, Sandrow also had some packages sent by air.[52]

The package program continued throughout 1945, and the army did not try to stop the flow in most areas. That would come in the following year.

Additional Sources for Food and Clothing

Since the package program supplied only a small fraction of the food and clothing needs of the displaced persons, the chaplains sought additional aid from the soldiers. In Brussels, Chaplain Gorrelick had empty barrels placed near the PX and in the British-sponsored Jewish Soldiers Center in Brussels, frequented by hundreds of Jewish soldiers. They donated not only toys, food, shoes, and candy but also money. Many soldiers also became personally involved with the children and visited them regularly.

At one point, Haskell Hollander (Gorrelick's assistant) launched a drive among the Jewish and non-Jewish soldiers to collect uniforms, pants, shirts, underwear, and other articles of clothing for the large number of displaced persons arriving in Brussels. Hollander spoke to the non-Jewish quartermaster, who suggested that the men turn in all articles of clothing that were ripped or had any mark on them. In return, they would be issued new clothing. Instead of giving the displaced persons damaged clothes the soldiers insisted on giving them the new clothing. The GIs then went back and retrieved their old uniforms that they had just turned over to the quartermaster. The army reacted negatively to Gorrelick's involvement with displaced persons during working hours. His senior chaplain asked that these activities be carried on outside of his regular schedule.[53] Gorrelick complied, but this severely limited his efforts.

Abraham Haselkorn also called upon Jewish soldiers for support and found them eager to help. At services he conducted in Marseilles, Haselkorn would mention the need for a particular item, whereupon someone from the congregation would arrange for its procurement.

Perhaps the most ingenious plan devised by chaplains was to use rations of Jewish personnel who came to services on Yom Kippur, a fast day. This idea occurred to at least two chaplains in Germany: Eugene Lipman and Abraham Haselkorn.

Lipman ordered one thousand GI rations of vegetables, eggs, potatoes, and coffee and four thousand Red Cross doughnuts, ostensibly for soldiers who were to attend the breakfast at the end of the Yom Kippur service. Instead, he loaded this food and a barrel of salted herring Chaplain Paul Gorin had air-expressed to him onto a truck and gave it to the nearly a thousand Jews in Regensburg.[54] During the morning Yom Kippur Schacharit service, Abraham Haselkorn realized that nearly twelve hundred soldiers were entitled to food and that many were not eating. He dispatched Cy Caller, his assistant, to get their rations and take them to one of the *hachsharot.*

Shortly after the holiday ended, Caller received orders to appear at army headquarters in Paris. There he was ushered into the offices of a Colonel Marcus, who asked how he had disposed of the food. Caller pulled out his dog tags to show that it had an *H* for *Hebrew.* He told Marcus that he had given the food to the displaced persons and had not sold it on the black market, as Marcus had suspected. Marcus said he understood and tore up the report and dropped all charges against him. He also warned Caller to refrain from these activities in the future. Before leaving, Caller asked the colonel if he could continue to count on his help. Marcus said that he had already done the best he could.

The warning did not deter Caller. On a more regular basis, Caller obtained supplies with the help of Patrick Fay, a Catholic chaplain. Several times a week, Caller visited army depots in and around Marseilles to fill his truck with supplies, which were then distributed to a number of *hachsharot* in the area. At each stop, Caller presented a requisition form signed by Chaplain Fay, who was very sympathetic to Jewish displaced persons and extremely helpful to the Jewish chaplains under his command. According to an agreement reached between Haselkorn and Fay, a Catholic orphanage in the region received between 10 and 25 percent of each cargo.[55]

Some chaplains, like Jacob Kraft, assigned to the Fifteenth Air Force, were able to obtain food simply by approaching their superior officers. In one case, Kraft's superior officer permitted him to bring several truckloads of supplies to a displaced persons camp in southern Italy. The WJC had asked Kraft and Chaplain Bernard Ziskind, a forty-five-year-old Orthodox rabbi also stationed in southern Italy, to visit the camp and write a report detailing the spiritual and economic destitution of the Jews they found there.[56]

The Establishment of the Central Committee

While these chaplains worked to improve living conditions, Abraham Klausner recognized that the survivors needed some control over their daily lives and a role in choosing their future residence. The survivors had also reached this conclusion on their own. For that reason Klausner helped them establish a committee to determine priorities and long-range goals and to deal directly with the American military. In June 1945 Klausner obtained permission to house the central committee in part of the Deutsches Museum. He then began touring the displaced persons camps to build up the support for this committee to succeed. On July 1, 1945, about forty representatives from the displaced persons camps assembled in Feldafing to discuss the condition of the Jews in the camps and to debate the importance of setting up a displaced persons committee. Over twenty additional guests were present, including Chaplains Klausner and Braude.

Lieutenant Irving J. Smith, the commander of Feldafing, did not approve of this conference, viewing it as an excuse for demanding more rations. It is also possible that after being a dominant force in the camp, he feared a loss of power. In his address to the group, Smith said that if the Jews would keep their camps in order, they would be treated fairly and would receive Red Cross packages. Angered by this patronizing attitude, Zalman Grinberg and Klausner dissolved the meeting and resumed their deliberations in the camp kitchen without Smith.

At this session, Klausner described his efforts to publish the *Shearit Hapletah* volumes. He also pointed out there were 825,000 displaced persons in the American zone, including 15,000 Jews and stressed that anyone could legally refuse repatriation as long as he had not lived within the 1939 boundaries of the Soviet Union. Klausner urged that a representative body for the Jewish survivors be established, since he believed they had the power to effect a change in their lives.

After a short discussion, the group elected a provisional committee with Zalman Grinberg as its acting chairman. For the most part, the central committee represented not only the larger camps in Munich and its environs, but also the *Landsmannschaften* (groups formed according to countries of origin) in the area. Soon after joining the central committee, the Austrian camps pulled out to form their own group in Salzburg.

On July 11 the committee moved to their new headquarters at the Deutsches Museum. Departments for food, clothing, health, religion, education, culture, emigration, and tracing relatives were established; but their power was severely limited. The army had not officially recognized the committee, so most of the important work had to be channeled through Klausner. He was the only one in the group in a position to deal with the authorities. As a result, most of these departments did not become fully operational until much later.[57]

To continue the work begun at Feldafing, a general conference of Jewish survivors arranged by soldiers of the Jewish Brigade was held at St. Ottilien on July 25. Ninety-four delegates representing about forty thousand Jews from all parts of Germany and Austria were transported to the conference in brigade vehicles. Here rep-

First Conference of the Central Committee of Liberated Jews in Bavaria. Second from left, Rabbi Abraham Klausner; on his left, Dr. Zalman Grinberg. (Photo courtesy of the Mintzer Collection, Magnes Museum.)

resentatives from Bergen-Belsen, Frankfurt, Salzburg, Mauthausen, and elsewhere were able to meet with their counterparts in Bavaria for the first time. Also present were Eliyahu Dobkin, representative of the Jewish Agency; Hoter-Yishai, of the Jewish Brigade; and chaplains Robert Marcus and Abraham Klausner. They had come to encourage the establishment of a committee to represent the Jewish survivors in Germany and Austria.

In his address to the conference, Klausner pointed out that although every effort had been made to inform the Jewish organizations in the United States about problems facing the survivors, the representatives of these organizations had not been seen thus far. Until organized assistance arrived, the Jews alone would have to "care for themselves."[58]

This attempt to establish a united body did not succeed for several reasons. Occupation policies in liberated Austria in the autumn of 1945 and those in the American zone of Germany differed. Difficulties in obtaining permission to cross between the two countries led to isolation of the camps on both sides.[59] Moreover, the Bergen-Belsen Committee, which was already established and represented approximately the same number of displaced persons in all the camps in the United States zone combined, was reluctant to relinquish its autonomy to a general organization that might restrict its powers.

As a result of the Bergen-Belsen group's decision to remain autonomous, the central committee represented only Jews in the United States zone of Germany. The committee's official title became the Central Committee of Liberated Jews in Bavaria.

Although the St. Ottilien Conference failed to unite the survivors in Germany and Austria into one group, it did accomplish some of its other objectives. It provided a forum for the survivors to demand publicly that they be permitted to emigrate to Palestine. On the evening of July 26 they drove to the Munich Burgerbrau beer cellar (the birthplace of the Nazi movement), where they read their demands in the presence of foreign press correspondents. The delegates then recited the *kaddish* (prayer for those who had perished) and sang "Hatikva", which became the national anthem of the State of Israel.

The conference also initiated serious discussions about problems confronting the displaced persons in an estimated 30 camps throughout Germany and Austria. The Austrian representatives reported that the United States army had failed to provide them with adequate food, clothing, and accommodations. Furthermore, they resented being humiliated by the military authorities. Although food rations were fixed at twelve hundred calories a day, they received only seven hundred. When the Jews attempted to procure their own food in Wels, the army surrounded the camp and fired upon a few people inside. Elsewhere, when a request was made for better living quarters, the army directed them to vermin-infested camps. When the Jews refused to move, the army withheld their food. On another occasion, the army arrested thirty-five Jews for allegedly loitering in the streets past curfew and drove them to jail at gunpoint where they were imprisoned overnight. The Jews denied the charge but remained in jail until the next day.

While the American military's attitude toward Jews in Austria was not good, many Austrians were friendly and attempted to help them.

American Jews in the army also offered aid; but it was limited to money, which had very little value at that point. The Jews in Austria (about sixteen thousand, including both those in the camps and those living outside) felt abandoned by the American Jewish community, since they had not received any assistance or had any contact with them. The delegates recommended that a central assembly point be established, so that they could obtain assistance from the American military. Practically every Jew wanted to leave Austria immediately, since the situation was growing more oppressive each day. Most saw Palestine as their only hope.

The representatives from the American zone of Germany reported that the treatment by the American military varied from camp to camp because there was no definite policy regarding Jewish displaced persons. The representatives from Bergen-Belsen in the British zone stated that although the situation had been very serious after liberation, there had been much improvement since. They singled out Chaplain Joseph Shubow as having made an important contribution to their recovery.

At the end of the conference, the delegates adopted several resolutions, including a demand that war criminals be punished and that the surviving Jewish youth be taken into the Jewish Brigade. The delegates left the conference with no illusions about emigrating to Palestine in the immediate future. In his speech, Eliyahu Dobkin made it clear that Palestinian certificates necessary to enter the country could not be obtained and that an all-out struggle might be necessary to gain admittance. He urged them to prepare for *aliyah* (settlement in the land of Israel) by learning vocational skills and demanded that they move to a few central camps.[60]

5

FLIGHT AND RESCUE:
THE ATTEMPT TO REACH PALESTINE

Berihah

For some survivors, the struggle to enter Palestine had already begun. In the spring of 1944 small groups of survivors began organizing in the first areas liberated by the Red Army to discuss their future. They did not want to return to their former homes and concluded that emigration to Palestine was their only hope. They believed that anti-Semitism would continue to threaten world Jewry, that another Holocaust was inevitable, that Jews in the Diaspora had to be warned and properly prepared, and that Palestine had to be established as a refuge for the Jewish people. Plans for revenge against the Germans were also discussed but, under the pressure of events, never materialized.[1]

In December 1944 these liberated groups came to Lublin, where, in January 1945, they met with the former Warsaw ghetto fighters. Together they formed a secret organization called Berihah (Flight). This became part of a mass underground operation that smuggled Jews out of Rumania, Yugoslavia, Hungary, Czechoslovakia, the Baltic countries, and the Soviet Union between 1944 and 1948. They were taken to points on the Mediterranean coast, where they would be in a better position to reach Palestine.[2]

The Jewish Brigade was also involved in taking Jews out of Europe and into Palestine. Most of the members of the Brigade were members of the Haganah, the Jewish armed underground in Palestine. The Brigade worked independently of Berihah until they learned of each other. At the end of the war, members of the Brigade began searching throughout southern Germany and Austria for survivors. Everywhere they went, survivors greeted them as heroes.[3] The sight of self-assured Palestinian Jews in military uniforms had an uplifting effect on the survivors.[4] From the middle of June 1945 to mid-August, an estimated fifteen thousand Jews from Central Europe arrived in Italy. Many came on their own; others were brought by Palestinian Jews. In Italy, they were assisted by the Merkaz Lagolah.

Between six and seven thousand Jews were originally in displaced persons camps in Germany and Austria. When the influx became so great that there was no room for all of them in Italy, the Palestinians decided to divert as many as possible to the American zones of Germany and Austria. There they would remain until they could be taken to Palestine. They chose the United States zone because the refugees would view it as a temporary transit area and because they would be treated better there than in any other zone.[5] Moreover, in the British zone, no additional refugees with displaced persons status were being accepted.

Individual chaplains were recruited to work in Berihah by the Palestinians, who asked them to provide material and logistical support. During the latter half of June, Eugene Lipman arrived with his unit in Pilsen, Czechoslovakia, where Sylvia Neulander recruited him. Czechoslovakia had been divided by the Russian and American armies so that a control line ran northwest and southeast between Prague and Pilsen, with the border rigidly controlled.

Jews who were in hiding and those who left Poland and the Theresienstadt concentration camp came to Prague in search of relatives and to find a means of leaving Europe and a way to emigrate to Palestine. Instead they were kept in Prague by the Russians, who refused to let them leave the city. There were six thousand Jews starving in Prague with another sixteen thousand still in Theresienstadt (about sixty-five kilometers northwest of Prague in the Russian zone) when Neulander approached Lipman.

When Sylvia Neulander first heard of the problem, she asked the Jewish Brigade for help. If she could get the Jews to Salzburg, Austria, the Brigade promised to transport them to Italy. From there they would be taken by ship to Palestine. Neulander had been asked by Ruth Kluger of the Jewish Agency to organize this Berihah operation. After arranging a transfer to Pilsen as director of the GI Club for the Eighth Corps, Neulander began counseling Jews who were being repatriated from the British zone of Germany to Poland. They had been unaware of the anti-Semitism and oppressive conditions in Poland. After speaking with her, many Jews decided to stay in the city or go to displaced persons camps in the American zone.

When Neulander began planning the transport of Jews from Prague, she realized that additional help was needed. Lipman had not finished unpacking his bags when Neulander asked him to join her. "I was so staggered," he reported; "I wanted desperately to say no, to insist that my job was to assist Jewish GIs, to pray for troops, . . . but little (4'10") Sylvia looked tough, and somehow a negative answer was revolting, so I agreed to help."

There were three objectives to their plan: to transfer the Jews from Prague to Pilsen; to keep them in Pilsen until transportation was secured; and to transport them across the Danube to Salzburg without being apprehended by troop patrols, the military police, or counterintelligence agents. Neulander, who had been trained by the Haganah in Palestine, had a solution. The first phase of the operation required typing about five hundred copies of a letter authorizing the bearer, a United Nations displaced person, to enter the American zone to search for missing relatives. The document was signed by a nonexistent colonel and had a big red advertising stamp on it. Lipman and Neulander then took the letters to Berihah headquarters at the Jewish community center in Prague on 7 Josefovska Street. The documents were distributed, and soon Jews began boarding the regularly scheduled trains from Prague to Pilsen.

Upon arriving in Pilsen, they went directly to the GI Club but did not enter the premises until it closed at 10:00 P.M. They were met by Neulander and Lipman, who, after relieving them of their forged documents (so that they could be used again), took them to the Karlow displaced persons camp outside the city. According to an arrangement with Andrew Carnegie Dunn, a Scotsman from Pittsburgh, Pennsylvania, and his assistant Fay Green, a Texas social worker, up to three hundred Jews a week were allowed into the camp. They were not registered with the army but did receive food and lodging. At the end of the week, the group moved on to Austria. Trains would have been the fastest and easiest way to transfer Jews to Salzburg; but since the trains were under Third Army control, Lipman decided to use trucks instead. At first, the trucks were returned to the motor pool at the end of each day; but as they became needed on a regular basis, they were not returned. Gasoline was also appropriated from the army; but when a shortage developed, they were forced to purchase fuel on the black market. Lipman's senior chaplain, a Presbyterian minister from Kansas, knew of Lipman's work and authorized his use of the trucks. He even supplied Lipman with large amounts of scotch for the non-Jewish soldiers who drove the transports. The chaplain's support enabled Lipman to maintain this underground operation for some time. Regular transports began on July 10. In Salzburg, the Palestinian

Jews took the groups to a house along the river bank in a quiet part of the city. They arrived by day, and at night brigade trucks took them to an Italian displaced persons camp.

On July 26, the American military halted the operation when they caught Lipman leading one of the transports into Austria. By that time, approximately two thousand Jews had been transferred. They took Lipman to Second Corps Headquarters, where he was interrogated and scolded for having illegally taken displaced persons across the border. About ten days later, they transferred Lipman out of Czechoslovakia to the headquarters of the Fourth Armored Division in Landshut, Bavaria. Under normal circumstances, Lipman might have been court-martialed; but Neulander was a personal friend of Major General Clarence Heubner, who intervened on his behalf. Fortunately, Lipman's capture did not shut down the Prague–Pilsen–Salzburg–Italy route, which was used until 1948. Lipman continued working with Berihah, despite the risk. He also arranged for the remaining Jews in Theresienstadt (which he estimated at fifteen-to-twenty thousand) to be transported to the American zone of Germany. He then established a mail service, so that they could communicate with their relatives.[6]

The increasing number of Jews entering the American zone disturbed the army, because, it claimed, it did not have enough supplies for them and because of the constant pressure to provide Jews with the best accommodations possible. To reduce the problem, the army wanted the United States government to establish a long-range policy for dealing with these people.[7]

In an attempt to force the United States government to formulate such a policy, Berihah sent 650 Jews into Pilsen on August 21. General Patton's headquarters ordered them sent back to Poland; and when they protested, a crisis ensued. On August 23 the Jewish Telegraphic Agency published the report of Private Edward Heilbrun (a Jewish soldier from Chicago) that he was among those who loaded the Jews onto trucks bound for the train station. "My job was sickening to me," he reported. "Men threw themselves on their knees in front of me, tore open their shirts and screamed 'Kill me now!' They would say, 'You might just as well kill me now. I am dead anyway if I go back to Poland'. They kept jumping off the trucks and we had to use force." At the railroad station the troops pushed them into the train after they refused to go in by themselves. Once the train started moving, men began jumping off. The troops then fired into the air to frighten them into staying aboard.[8]

After this story appeared in the American Jewish press, letters of protest were sent to the War Department by the American Jewish Committee and other American Jewish organizations. On September 27 Arieh Tartakower, of the WJC, met with Major General Hilldring and Lieutenant Joseph Fierst of the Civil Affairs Division of the War Department in Washington to discuss the Pilsen incident. Hilldring and Fierst claimed they had not yet received a report on the incident from the army but assured Tartakower that he would be informed of the results as soon as they arrived.

When Tartakower asked what would happen if more Jews from Poland or elsewhere sought refuge in Germany, Fierst said that the army had to differentiate between individuals already repatriated and returning to Germany and those who were new arrivals. The latter group could not be admitted, he claimed, because the military had to obtain a minimum amount of food and fuel for the German population for the coming winter months. He also feared that the American zone in Germany could not absorb a large number of new people. They assured Tartakower that whatever decisions the military authorities would make, humanitarian considerations would be taken into account.[9]

General Eisenhower also responded to the criticism of the army's handling of the Pilsen incident by cabling the Orthodox Agudat Yisrael of America that compulsory repatriation of Polish Jews from Germany was not part of his instructions. He also informed them that final disposition of the Jews in Germany would be decided by authorities higher than himself.[10]

Discussions with General Hilldring continued on December 20, when Joseph Schwartz and Moses A. Leavitt of the JDC met with Hilldring to find out what was being done about infiltration of Jews into the American zone. They were informed that President Truman and Undersecretary of State Dean Acheson had taken the matter of infiltration under advisement. The State Department was apprehensive about 250,000 Jews entering the American zone (the number Judge Rifkind predicted would come); but Schwartz maintained that 50,000 was a more realistic figure. The army was willing to absorb this lesser amount, Hilldring indicated; but there was never any formal announcement to this effect. Leon Kubowitzki informed Chaplain Joseph Shubow in a letter that "We have been assured that the policy of the American Army has always been and continues to be a humanitarian one, and that the American zone has at no time been closed to our people. We are aware, however, that constant vigilance is indicated." From unofficial sources, the Jewish organizations were told that as long as the number of Jews did not exceed 5,000 per month, the army would not interfere.[11] The decision to allow 5,000 Jews a month to enter the American zone was motivated by the Harrison Report. After its publication, public opinion in the United States turned against the military's treatment of the Jews; and as a result, the military decided not to thwart Jewish survivors from entering its zone. The only effective means to stop the flow would have been to use force, and this was not a real option for moral and political reasons. It should be emphasized this action by the army was decided at the highest levels of the Truman administration.

It seems the army had agreed in principal to allow Jews to enter the American zone as early as October 1945. David Ben Gurion, then chairman of the Jewish Agency Executive in Palestine, came to Germany to meet the survivors, the representatives of the Jewish Agency and Generals Eisenhower and Bedell Smith. In October he met Eisenhower and Smith to urge that the Jews be allowed to enter the American zone of occupation and be given the status of displaced persons. Ben Gurion had hoped that the presence of a quarter of a million Jews in the American zone would force the Americans to increase pressure on the British government to allow the survivors to enter Palestine. Ben Gurion asked Eisenhower and Smith to allow the Jews to enter the American zone officially, since a large number of Polish Jews were already infiltrating anyway. Eisenhower and Smith agreed, because of the Harrison Report and their fear of additional adverse publicity.

The American military wanted the Jews in its zone to move on as rapidly as possible because their presence in Germany thwarted America's increasingly pro-German policy. The top levels of the army sanctioned this movement of Jews but did not want their troops compromised or bribed in the process. Moreover, they wanted this to be done quietly, so as not to arouse British wrath, since the British vehemently opposed the Berihah.[12]

There were occasions when the military, including Generals Eisenhower and Smith, actively assisted the Berihah. When Ben Gurion met with Eisenhower and Smith in October, he convinced Eisenhower of the need to bring additional Palestinian Jews to Germany, ostensibly to educate displaced persons. Eisenhower had no objection if these teachers happened to be Haganah immigration experts.

Most of the teachers and rabbis were killed during the war, so that instructors from Palestine were very much needed. The Jews did not wait for help from the outside, however, but established their own educational programs. The few rabbis, teachers, and others with vocational skills or the desire to teach taught classes to a wide range of groups within the community. Individual chaplains also taught classes and set up schools. Later, the JDC provided the funds, textbooks, and salaries for these schools.

Arrangements to transport Palestinian Jews to Germany were made through Eisenhower's office and then transmitted to Judge Rifkind. Before the first air force plane left for Palestine, Rifkind consulted with Ruth Kluger, who suggested that Eugene Lipman be sent as a liaison officer because he spoke Hebrew and knew the people at the Jewish Agency. Lipman was briefed by Rifkind and told by General Smith that he had one week to make the round trip. Although he succeeded in returning on time, Lipman did not bring the teachers with him. Their papers were not prepared in time by the British military, so they were not permitted to leave the country.

Although this part of his mission failed, Lipman returned with 2-1/2 tons of supplies and about $250,000 in gold sovereigns. The money, which was to be given to Ruth Kluger for the Berihah, was entrusted to him by Eliezer Kaplan, treasurer of the Jewish Agency Executive. This was not prearranged; but since Kaplan knew Lipman's uncle, a veteran Zionist from Pittsburgh, he asked him to deliver it for him. Lipman dropped the gold off at Kluger's office on his return and then reported to Rifkind. A second trip was arranged and this time he brought back thirteen teachers and more supplies. Rifkind wanted him to serve full-time on the remaining six missions but the theater chaplain refused. He claimed that the sole responsibility of the chaplains was to pray for the troops.

The Jewish Agency was so impressed by Lipman that Kluger and Rifkind attempted to enlist him as liaison between the military and the Palestinian Jews. Lipman agreed to apply for separation from the army on condition that his family be allowed to join him. Lipman was assigned to General Mickelsen's section (Civil Affairs chief for the Tenth Command). When the theater chaplain learned of this arrangement, he temporarily stopped the transfer; and Lipman wound up in Augsburg, Germany. After being discharged from the army and returning to the United States, Lipman came back to Germany in February 1947 to serve as a liaison officer between the Jewish Agency and the American military.[13]

In addition to recruiting chaplains to work in Berihah, the Palestinian Jews also asked chaplains to help supply food and other items to displaced persons, collect guns, provide radio equipment, and escort a ship of survivors to Palestine. Chaplain Herbert Eskin was one of those involved in collecting arms. He asked Jewish soldiers who came to Friday night services to bring as many weapons as they could. During July and August, large quantities of arms were stacked in the middle of the streets to be burned. These areas were off limits to army personnel; but the Jewish soldiers managed to secure large numbers of grenades, machine guns, and other weapons.

They stored everything in the basement of the Eskin house; and the next morning, the trucks of the Jewish Brigade were loaded by soldiers who had come to Saturday morning services. Eskin then led the convoy to the Italian border. He had prepared false passes and brought along Eisenhower jackets and army watches to bribe the Italian guards. This operation lasted between three and four weeks.[14]

Another chaplain recruited for collecting arms was Abraham Haselkorn. With the help of a number of Jewish soldiers stationed in Marseilles, Haselkorn amassed a large stock of guns and ammunition. Those who gathered the weapons had to be very cautions when bringing them to Haselkorn.[15] In order to avoid suspicion, one soldier used his *talit* (prayer shawl) bag whenever he smuggled guns to the synagogue.

The Palestinian Jews were also concerned about being apprehended with arms in their possession. One night they asked Haselkorn to help them avoid a potentially serious situation. They had just purchased a supply of weapons from a group of exmembers of the anti-Nazi communist underground and had no way of transporting them to their *hachshara* without being caught by French patrols. Haselkorn knew that civilians had little chance of getting through on their own, so he drove the weapons to the *hachshara* himself. Haselkorn continued work in Berihah throughout his stay in France, which ended in early 1946.[16]

On another occasion, the Palestinians approached Haselkorn to help them establish a radio link with their headquarters in Tel Aviv. With equipment secured from the army by Cy Caller, they set up an illegal radio station in Toulon, France. Messages received from Tel Aviv were brought to Haselkorn's office and transmitted by phone to the Jewish Agency office in Paris. There were few phones available, and the military system provided the best and fastest means of communication. This operation lasted six or seven weeks, until a telephone operator overheard a conversation in Hebrew and warned that only English was permitted on military phones.

At another time, the Palestinians asked Haselkorn to help them replace their malfunctioning communication equipment in Greece. Caller agreed to procure the equipment and deliver it to Greece, but he had to have a reason to travel to the Middle East. Since Caller lived in Palestine, Haselkorn arranged for him to be sent to a Tel Aviv hospital, ostensibly for rest and recuperation and to visit his family.

On his way to Palestine, Caller's military plane stopped in Italy, where he contacted the brigade. Since he wore an American Army uniform and spoke fluent Hebrew they viewed him with suspicion. Only after quizzing him about his sisters in Palestine were they convinced that he was a friend. Before leaving, they gave him messages to take to their families and friends.

From Italy, Caller flew to Palestine, with stopovers in Greece and Cairo. While in flight, he faked a toothache, so that he would be permitted to remain in Greece overnight. There he met with the brigade, gave them the radio equipment, and was given more messages. In Cairo, Caller also met with the brigade and received additional messages. After arriving in Tel Aviv, he reported to the hospital and received permission to visit his family. When his pass expired, he returned to his unit in Marseilles.[17]

When an attempt to send a shipload of about six hundred Jews to Palestine was ordered from Tel Aviv, the Palestinians contacted Haselkorn to provide enough food for six months and visas so they would be permitted to leave the country. Caller secured the food from American storehouses while Haselkorn contacted a consul from one of the Central American countries. In return for the visas, Haselkorn had the consul, who was very ill, treated by an American Army doctor.[18]

Chaplain Herbert Ribner, a twenty-eight-year-old Conservative rabbi assigned to the Twelfth Air Force stationed in Italy, reported that just before the winter of 1945/46, Palestinian Jews approached him for help to obtain warm clothing, blankets, shoes, and socks for the Jews. They were concerned about how the displaced persons would be able to survive the harsh winter ahead. Ribner immediately went to one of the largest army bases in the country, where he discussed the matter with a Jew in the Quartermaster Corps. The officer, while sympathetic, feared he would be held accountable for anything taken without permission. He suggested that Ribner seek these items at a very large base full of captured German equipment across the road.

The officer in charge of the base, a first lieutenant, was a chronic alcoholic, which Ribner used to his advantage. After receiving permission to enter the base, Ribner and his assistant filled up their jeep and trailer with blankets, sheets, sleeping bags, shoes, socks, and whatever else they could carry. They then drove to Florence, where they turned the supplies over to the Palestinians. Since the displaced persons required much more, Ribner contacted Chaplain Samuel Kaufman, a thirty-six-year-old Orthodox rabbi, to arrange for three large army trucks and trailers to be ready at the base the next day. He also obtained a special treat for the lieutenant—a bottle of scotch.

After Ribner presented the scotch to the lieutenant, the lieutenant ordered his sergeant to give Ribner whatever he required. Instead of filling out a requisition form, Ribner asked the sergeant to sign a blank form. Ribner assured him that it would be easier to fill the form in as they went along since he was not sure what he needed. The sergeant agreed, seeing only the jeep and trailer. With this signed slip, Ribner went to the gate at the other end of the sprawling base and brought in the trucks.

As the loading began with the help of German prisoners of war, Ribner told the soldier supervising the operation that the Germans should put in one hundred sheets. Since the soldier could not speak German, Ribner became the interpreter. Ribner told the soldier to write down one hundred sheets on the form, but he told the German to count out five hundred. This procedure continued with each pile they loaded. After they finished filling the trucks, Ribner left for Florence.

Ribner returned again to the base, but this time he bypassed the lieutenant and went straight to one of the soldiers. Samuel Kaufman arranged for the trucks; and Chaplain Harold Goldfarb, a forty-year-old Conservative rabbi, went along to assist. A few days later, the Americans turned the base over to the Italians.[19]

Chaplain Nathan Barack, a thirty-two-year-old Orthodox rabbi assigned to the Eighty-Eighth Division, was also approached by members of the Jewish Brigade who wanted to obtain wood for two *hachsharot* near Udine. Under normal circumstances, this would not have been difficult. However, the Eighty-Eighth Division had a strict policy of not using army supplies or vehicles for the benefit of the local civilian population. Even when the division chaplain, a lieutenant colonel in the regular army, asked for supplies for a community picnic, they denied his request. Nevertheless, Barack was determined to get them the wood. When the area commander left on an inspection tour, he requisitioned two trucks from the motor pool and had the wood delivered. It took an entire day, but the commander never found out.[20]

When the Palestinians needed someone to accompany the children from Buchenwald and Bergen-Belsen to Palestine, Ruth Kluger approached Robert Marcus. Marcus had helped many of them in Buchenwald, and they wanted him to lead their group. Marcus agreed, after obtaining permission from the army. The ship arrived in Palestine on September 8, 1945, with over a thousand survivors, thirty-five of whom were stowaways smuggled on board by Marcus, Abraham Haselkorn, Cy Caller, and several American Jewish soldiers. Marcus stayed in Palestine for ten days and then returned to Germany.[21]

Some chaplains were reluctant to discuss their involvement with Berihah even after the war. Max Braude was one of those. He worked with the brigade in Italy, where he reported securing two boats to transport Jews to Palestine. He also used his position in the constabulary to find the best border crossings and gave the brigade timetables of border patrols. When a guard became overly zealous in trying to stop the infiltration, he had the guard removed. On one or two occasions, he also directed the Palestinians to large storage depots and introduced them to the soldiers in charge.

In a letter to Philip Bernstein in early July, Braude indicated that his work was "mildly dangerous" and hoped CANRA would protect him from being court-martialed if he were caught by the army. Braude rarely wrote about his work; and when he did, as in the letter to Bernstein, he only alluded to this involvement.[22]

The Establishment of *Unzer Weg*

The chaplains also aided the survivors in establishing displaced persons newspapers in the American zone of occupation in Germany. The most widely read and influential of these newspapers was *Unzer Weg*. Within weeks and months after liberation, the survivors started publishing their own newspapers and periodicals beginning with *Techeyat Hamaytim* at Buchenwald on May 4, 1945. Because most of the Jews in Buchenwald did not remain after it became part of the Russian zone in July 1945, *Techeyat Hamaytim* was published only once. Nevertheless, it is an important document because it reveals the survivors were eager to re-establish their ties with their families and rebuild their own lives as quickly as possible.

Not long after the demise of *Techeyat Hamaytim*, newspapers in Feldafing (*Dos Fraje Wort*), Berlin (*Unzer Leben*), and Landsberg (*Landsberger Lager Cajtung*) began publication. By the end of 1945, there were eighteen local newspapers published in different cities and camps in the American zone.[23]

Unzer Weg, the Yiddish weekly newspaper sponsored by the central committee, began publication during this period. The idea of starting the paper originated with Levi Shalit, a young man who had worked as a reporter on a Yiddish newspaper in Kovno and had served as a propagandist in the Zionist movement. Some time in early July he approached Abraham Klausner with the idea, and Klausner agreed to help.

The first priority was to find Hebrew type, so Klausner arranged for Shalit to visit Frankfurt, where, in the Stempel Publishing House, Shalit found type that had been used in printing prayer books before the war. Judah Nadich obtained permission for him to take the type to Munich, Max Braude secured the authorization to have new type cast, and Klausner provided paper from the Dachau warehouse.

After returning to Munich, Shalit persuaded the owner of a German print shop to let him use two of his storehouses for the paper's editorial offices. Since there was not enough type, each page had to be set separately and then printed. They repeated this process for every page. On October 12, 1945, the first issue of *Unzer Weg* was printed; and by December 7, 1945, they were able to publish a twenty-thousand-copy edition. It was the largest Yiddish weekly in Germany and was regarded by many as their national paper. Published every Friday, the paper viewed itself as a guide through the Diaspora and exhorted the Jews to keep up their morale, encouraged them to continue fighting for their rights, and proclaimed their demands to go to Palestine.[24]

To acquaint the American military authorities with the problems of the *Shearit Hapletah*, the first edition of the paper had an English section that summarized the key articles. Some subsequent editions, too, contained English summaries of important articles.[25]

According to one JDC official,

> Within a few weeks [after publication] *Unzer Weg* found its way to editorial offices in Paris, London, New York, Tel Aviv, and Vienna. It was warmly received and letters of congratulation poured in. After the dolorous reports of the general press, this paper out of the ruins of Munich was proof of the vitality and of a faint glimmering of cultural renascence. Like a stone dropped into a pool, it engendered successive ripples of interest and enthusiasm. There was a correspondence as well as a steady stream of visitors from all corners of Europe to the tiny attic office at Alteimer Corner 19.[26]

The emergence of *Unzer Weg* and other newspapers and periodicals soon after the liberation caused one Jewish writer to wonder, "Where . . .do the . . .survivors of all these horrors find the resilience, the mental elasticity and alertness, to retain not only their sanity but their keen interest in life and their ability to read and respond so vigorously to the problems confronting them, their people, and the world?" No less impressive, the writer observed, was the presence of so many talented writers in almost every group of displaced persons.[27] *Unzer Weg*'s success continued, and the paper remained a vital link for the survivors and world Jewry. It ceased on April 1, 1949, because its purpose had ended with the departure from Germany of most of the survivors.

Vicar André and the Children of Namur

Since the problems of the survivors were ongoing, chaplains were not always able to complete the work they had initiated during their assignment in an area. One problem involved finding a way to get Jewish children out of Vicar André's supervision in Namur, Belgium. Chaplains Meyer Goldman and Harold Saperstein had learned of the orphans' being housed with the priest when they arrived in the city during the middle of 1945.

It did not become an issue until Goldman, while on a trip to Brussels, received a call from Vicar André complaining that one of his charges was about to become Bar Mitzvah. Three years before, the boy had been baptized by one of André's colleagues. The parents of the boy had taken him to Brussels, where he was being prepared for his *Bar Mitzvah*. This upset André who argued that this could not be allowed, since the boy had become Catholic. The next day, André's colleague came to Brussels to continue the debate. This priest (a Hungarian aspostate) agreed not to interfere any more when Goldman suggested that the boy would be allowed to choose which religion he wanted at age sixteen. Later, Goldman learned from the boy's teachers that the priest had told the youngster that the baptism had merely been arranged to fool the Germans.

Convinced that if these children were allowed to stay with André they would be lost to the Jewish people, Goldman and Saperstein decided to find a new home for them. After some negotiations, the children were placed in a Jewish children's home near Brussels until more permanent arrangements could be made. The vicar accepted the decision, and on October 1, the children left Namur. Both Goldman and Saperstein left Namur in late 1945, after almost half a year in the city. This concluded the work begun by Chaplain Isaac Klein.[28]

The Joint Distribution Committee and the Chaplains

Interaction between the chaplains and the JDC increased during the latter part of 1945, particularly in Germany as more representatives arrived in the country. The JDC had begun preparing their personnel to work in Europe as early as October and November 1943 when it started a course for training "selected Jewish communal workers." Approximately thirty-five individuals attended these sessions, and about eight were still working for the JDC in late 1945.[29]

The JDC recognized that many more social workers would be needed. One JDC official claimed that "time and time again" it "appealed to American Jewish social workers to come forward" and volunteer. In order not to exclude large numbers of social workers from being considered for a position, the JDC lowered some of its technical standards. Still, it complained, "for one reason or another, either [because] they were married or their communities needed them, or whatever the reason, they did not respond."[30]

The JDC had no choice but to recruit personnel from other fields and within two years it had hired 130 people. By the end of November 1945, the JDC had between fifty and sixty representatives working in the larger camps in Germany, interpreting the needs of Jewish survivors to the army and UNRRA.[31]

Given the problem of finding adequate personnel, why did the JDC not empower the chaplains to act in a semiofficial capacity until their representatives arrived or urge the chaplains to remain in Europe with the JDC after they were demobilized from the army?

This is what Chaplain Samuel Teitelbaum had suggested as early as April and May 1944.[32] The chaplains, after all, were in Europe and had proven experience and success in dealing with the survivors and the military.

To Abraham Klausner, the answer was obvious. Moses Leavitt and Joseph Schwartz, the professional leadership of the JDC, "resented the chaplains. They saw themselves as experts, and the chaplains as irritants . . . The professional staff could have, at various times, made use of the chaplains, but instead fought them again and again. . . . I remember my meeting with Leavitt, I could feel his resentment when I told him the time had come to institute a merit or compensation plan in the camps. He snapped at me, 'We're doing that!' Of course, it was never done."[33]

The chaplains had waited eagerly for the JDC because they expected it would relieve them of caring for the displaced persons. Many chaplains were disappointed, however, with the JDC workers for their lack of dedication and motivation and their low level of commitment. They claimed that a sizable portion of JDC workers lacked enthusiasm and did not have a strong Jewish identity. Without this Jewish background and commitment they could not empathize with the survivors and their suffering.[34]

Chaplain Isaac Klein found "the attitude of the [JDC] worker was that he was handling charity cases," which he deplored. Moreover, Klein noted, "the whole question of morale, of rebuilding a community, of rebuilding the morale of the people, was foreign to the mentality of many Joint Distribution Committee workers." Although Klein did not know whether he was justified in making a "sweeping statement" about Jewish social workers, he concluded that as a group they lacked warmth and did not empathize with the survivors.[35]

Robert Marcus echoed these sentiments when he declared, "We need American workers in Europe who understand the yearning of these people for a new life in lands far removed from memories of loved ones murdered and homes razed. We need workers with some understanding of Zionist aspirations who have deep earnestness and love of their people and who are tireless in their efforts to help these remnants of European Jewry." Marcus believed that by late 1945, the JDC had recognized the need to send "the right type of personnel" because he saw "more effective coordination between displaced persons and the JDC." He hoped that this trend would continue.[36]

Judah Nadich agreed with Marcus's assessment, since he, too, observed that the quality of the JDC personnel had improved considerably. Nevertheless, Nadich felt that "the Jewish social workers in this country ha[d] hardly measured up to their responsibilities";

and he challenged them to go to Europe: "If they have ideals, as I know they have, then certainly they could serve their fellow Jews in no loftier manner than by volunteering for service in Europe to take care of our people there, . . . just as our rabbis volunteered."[37]

After returning to the Untied States, Nadich spoke to Jewish social workers to find out why they and their colleagues had not gone to help the survivors. They insisted either they could not leave their positions with Jewish federation councils or Jewish social agencies because they were desperately needed or they had wives and families who needed them at home. Nadich pointed out that many chaplains had left their congregations and families behind. He believed this attitude demonstrated a "certain amount of callousness or selfishness on their part."[38]

Although many chaplains shared these criticisms of the JDC workers, there were JDC personnel for whom they had nothing but praise. Included among this list were Ann Liepah, Lavy Becker, Celia Weinberg, Abe Loskove, Joe Levine, and others who were devoted to the survivors and worked tirelessly on their behalf. These and other JDC workers bent army and JDC regulations when necessary, and the survivors regarded them as friends and were encouraged by thier concern. This was particularly important at a time when morale was low and their colleagues in the JDC did not display such sensitivity to their physical and spiritual needs.[39]

The chaplains were not alone in their criticism of the JDC representatives. Lavy Becker, a seasoned Canadian Jewish social worker whom the JDC had sent to head its United States zone operation, toured Aschau, Bamberg, Frankfurt, Deggendorf, Fürth, Heidelberg, Lampertheim, Pocking, Leipheim, Ansbach, Struth, and Stuttgart, where he found that each JDC representative had little or no prior orientation in preparing for his responsibilities and little or no supervision on the job. They were unhappy, upset, and probably not doing their very best. Becker also discovered that too many representatives were being assigned to areas that did not need them and too few were sent to places where they were in great need.[40] Other JDC representatives complained that their relief and rehabilitation programs had been too late in coming and that the experts in their organization felt too important and dignified to be "messenger boys for the displaced persons."[41]

In an attempt to raise the caliber of those working for the JDC in Germany, Edward M. M. Warburg, chairman of the JDC, asked the JWB to request the release of Abraham Klausner from the Chaplain Corps. Warburg knew of Klausner's work in Munich and realized that his experiences would be of great value to the JDC's program. Klausner agreed to join the JDC, because he never knew when the army would put an end to his activities, and he wanted to ensure his continued involvement with the displaced persons. Klausner found it significant that Warburg, rather than the JDC professionals, had asked for his transfer to the JDC; and he accepted, Klausner recalled, "only when he realized the JDC [to be] incapable of doing its work."[42]

Jacob Trobe also extended an invitation to Klausner, but only after he had asked Judge Rifkind to assess Klausner's potential as a JDC worker. Rifkind stated that Klausner was a "very dynamic young man whose energies have been directed towards helping the displaced persons with singular insight, ability, and success. He is one of those rare individuals who gets things done regardless of obstacles." Rifkind had "no doubt that he could render exceedingly useful service for the JDC and that his opportunity for service would be far greater in such a role than as a Chaplain." The army did not agree to the arrangement, because Klausner had not served with the army long enough to warrant special action by the Chief of Chaplains' Office.[43] It is not clear whether this was used as an excuse by the Chief of Chaplains' Office or whether it was routine.

It is also significant that no other chaplains were specifically requested to remain in Europe with the JDC. The JDC did inform the chaplains that it had begun recruiting additional staff for overseas work; but few, if any, of the chaplains could meet the criteria. Aside from a working knowledge of some foreign language, ideally Yiddish (which the chaplains did have), the applicant had to have been trained in Jewish communal work, with at least five years experience in either family case work, immigration service, hospital planning, loan and banking cooperatives, child care, vocational guidance, and/or organization of group and educational activities.[44]

In addition to being critical of JDC personnel and American Jewish social workers, the chaplains were disturbed that "American Jewry did not have sufficient foresight or vision in regard to this entire problem of relief to our people in Europe." "Certainly we knew from the very beginning," declared Judah Nadich,

> that someday the war would be over, that we would find a certain number of survivors and certain things would have to be done for those survivors, and I feel that not enough planning was done by the responsible American Jewish agencies in sufficient time.
>
> For example, while it is true that the army kept the [voluntary relief] agencies out until comparatively late, and while it is true also that when the army admitted the agencies, it was done on a niggardly basis, it seems to me that something might have been done in sufficient time in America, with the State Department and the War Department, so that a certain program would have been established long in advance of D-Day.

It should have been understood that on D-Day plus a certain number of other days, or upon the date of the invasion of Germany plus a certain number of other days, a certain number of Jewish relief workers would be admitted into continental Europe and that their functions would be so and so. If the Joint Distribution Committee could not have done that because it is not a political body, then the work should have been done in coordination with other American bodies that are engaged in work on the political scene, either the [American Jewish] Conference or the [World Jewish] Congress or other bodies.

Similarly I think the same lack of vision and foresight can be evidenced in the fact that there were no stock piles, or not sufficiently large stock piles, gathered together in such countries as Switzerland and Sweden where a local supply might have been purchased in advance against the day when they could have been shipped speedily into camps of Germany.[45]

Louis H. Sobel, assistant secretary of the JDC, agreed with Nadich's criticism, stating that the JDC had "failed in the face of one of the most gigantic tasks facing Jewish life in all of its history" primarily for two reasons: "because the American Jewish social workers did not respond to the JDC's call for volunteers" and for "lack of funds."[46]

Sobel pointed out:

The Joint Distribution Committee could not do a 60 million or a 75 million dollar job with the 20 million dollars made available to it in 1945, and it is beyond reasonable expectation to ask any organization to do that kind of job with the funds put at its disposal, and the responsibility for that rests squarely upon the American Jewish community. If you please, the American Jews were warned time and time again that the requirements and the needs were such that we needed untold millions of dollars more. The American Jews were told time and time again that there were many things that were not being done for lack of funds.[47]

Sobel did not mention the difficulty the JDC had in obtaining permission to enter Germany. The JDC was the first American volunteer agency to request permission to enter the country but did not receive it until the beginning of August. Even then, it was not the first volunteer agency to be allowed into the country and, like other relief agencies, it could only send its workers in when individual army commands specifically requested its help.

The constant complaints about the JDC and American Jewish organizations from "every chaplain" who returned to the United States prompted Philip Bernstein to ask whether CANRA should intervene itself. Bernstein sent the chaplains' complaints and criticisms to the JDC, the WJC and the American Jewish Conference. They received the criticism well; but still, the problem persisted.

"Do you think it would be worthwhile," Bernstein asked Chaplain David M. Eichhorn, "for someone from CANRA to come over on an official mission that would go beyond the normal military objectives and would be directed toward an overall survey of the needs and recommendations covering the total problems? The advantage of this, it seems to me, is that an official committee mission would have better contacts with the military than such non-military agencies as JDC, the [World Jewish] Congress and the [American Jewish] Conference."[48]

While nothing came of this idea, it does illustrate the concern and frustration Bernstein felt at not being in a position to do more for the survivors and the chaplains. Bernstein was especially disturbed with the JDC's handling of the situation, because he believed that "in our times the Jewish problem is not a problem of relief. It is a political problem, and relief is just one arm of the total mechanism that is required to do the job." "The Joint Distribution Committee," he argued, "fundamentally is a charity organization. You can call it fancy names, but that is what it does—it dispenses relief, it moves people from here to there as that is necessary, but the total problem of statesmanship and of planning must rest with the larger population. If the Joint Distribution Committee has a serious responsibility for failure in this area of action it is because it has seemed to preempt the job at this particular point and has seemed to discourage the other types of organizations from entering the picture." His solution was "a really effective, big, functioning American Jewish Conference of which the Joint Distribution Committee, a relief agency, will simply be an arm." Had this organization been in existence earlier, Bernstein believed, it could have "gotten a dozen Congressmen to go to work on Capitol Hill, [and] they would have moved that red tape" that could have saved Jews. Aside from relief, this organization might also have worked to resolve the larger issue of finding a permanent solution for the survivors. For this, he concluded, an effective "over-all Jewish agency" was needed "of which all other agencies" would "simply be arms."[49]

In the final analysis, as Robert Marcus pointed out, no matter what excuses or explanations were given or how many attempts were made to correct the problems, the survivors were disillusioned. "Where were their political and philanthropic representatives?" they asked:

> Where were the tons of clothes that had allegedly been gathered for them while they were still in concentration camps? Not a pair of shoes had arrived, not a package had been received, not a word of encouragement had been uttered. Did their leaders know of the thousands who had died since the liberation because of inadequate

food, care, and medical treatment, of neglect and indifference? I tried to tell them that their representatives had done their best, that they were stymied by red tape and Army regulations and indifference in high places, but this did not satisfy them. It never could satisfy people who had continued their struggle against the enemy in the streets of Warsaw, who fought on with will unbroken in the ghetto of Kovno, who carried on resistance in the shadow of the crematorium. These were people who were alive because, though enslaved by the Nazis, they had remained spiritually, innately, free.[50]

Appreciation of the Displaced Persons

That the survivors valued the assistance offered by the chaplains and the manner in which it was given can be seen in the following examples. Just before Abraham Haselkorn left France to return to the United States, Shammai Waxman presented him with a tribute that expressed the feelings of the survivors. Entitled "The Silent One," Waxman described how Haselkorn had come to them not as a rabbi or a major or even as a distant relative from America. Instead, he came as an old friend. He was "quiet and modest, serious, slightly melancholic and worried." They ate and drank together; and when they thanked him for his concern, he replied by asking questions about their welfare.

Waxman asserted:

> How different was this man and his questions from those of other visitors! How different sounded his answers! We felt that this man did not want to fill us with illusions. He does not want to fool us and gives us the truth, no matter how bad it may sound. . . . He warned against false expectations. But, he always worked with all his power and utilized all his influence to help us here on the spot, and now! He made good friends for us in the army, aroused interest in our condition among those who could help us. He brought us to those who could care for our material needs.

Now that he was returning to the United States, they were very disappointed: "Too bad, for we would like to rejoice with him a while longer, to have him with us and refresh ourselves with his warm soul, that beamed with his fire and warmed our everyday fugitive life on a strange soil in the critical period of our change from death to life".[51]

Abraham Klausner was another chaplain whom the displaced persons viewed in this way. In an article in the first edition of *Unzer Weg* entitled "One of You," Klausner summed up his feelings toward the *Shearit Hapletah* when he declared: "I have lived and grown many years during the months I have spent with the Jewish Community of Bavaria. . . . I know you well, my people. I know your thoughts and I hear your speech. I know your dreams and I behold your works and I am thankful to destiny for weaving me into the pattern of your rebirth. . . . I have during these months hoped that if not through suffering, then through my work you would accept me as one of you. And hand in hand, we would work together until we could meet on sacred soil."[52]

In the same edition of *Unzer Weg*, the editor, Levi Shalit, affirmed that Klausner had become one of them:

> To he who was the first to call for a Jewish newspaper, to he who moreover gave of himself so that the Jews of Bavaria would be infused with a new spirit, a living, growing spirit, to him we should have devoted the pages this newspaper. But, during these months in which Rabbi Klausner has been with us, he has been so woven into our life that we see him as one of us. It is he who delights in our delight and suffers from our pains. It is he who understood his duty. As father and brother he administers to us—this says more than pages of type. At present we will not thank him, we say only— "Rabbi, friend, brother, you have become one of us."[53]

Shalit compared Klausner in respect to his identification with the survivors and their response to him, to David Ben Gurion, whom Shalit had accompanied to a number of displaced persons camps in Germany. Klausner "didn't want to lead" the Jews, Shalit declared. Instead, he "worked for them and with them. . . . Whenever the leadership of the displaced persons decided something, or an individual asked him something which he might have been convinced was neither proper nor necessary, he nevertheless complied and worked for it. This was his uniqueness." That is why Klausner became the only nonsurvivor to become a member of the central committee, and on the governing board of *Unzer Weg*. "And so it came that he was called the first American member of the *Shearit Hapletah*," Shalit concluded.[54]

Other tributes to Klausner's dedication came not only from other displaced persons[55] but from his fellow chaplains. Chaplain Max Wall wrote to CANRA that Klausner "is doing one of the most important pieces of work that anyone has ever done. . . . The American community will have to decorate [him] for what he has done and continues to do, almost completely by himself."[56] Chaplain Eli Bohnen agreed with this judgment, writing to Philip Bernstein:

> The one bright gleam of hope in the whole mess is Chaplain Klausner. He has done more for the thousands of Jews in Munich and in the surrounding camps than all the agencies combined and then some. That's a mis-statement. The agencies have done practically nothing and he has, by himself, moved mountains. I cannot exaggerate the wonderful job he has done. That boy deserves the thanks of thousands upon thousands of Jews. He has literally saved hundreds of lives. How he manages to avoid a breakdown I don't know. I con-

fess I was lost in admiration for him and his achievements. If he had the resources of the JDC at his disposal he would have performed super miracles.[57]

In addition to the chaplains, a number of their assistants, including Eli Heimberg, Cy Caller, and Simon Pava also established strong relationships with the survivors. These men approached their fellow Jews as brothers, and the survivors responded by accepting them as one of them. In appreciation for his work with the Jews in Regensburg, Simon Pava was called Shimon Hazadek (Simon the Righteous).[58]

Chaplains Klein, Lipman, Bohnen, Shubow, Marcus, Ribner, Gorrelick, Saperstein, Dembowitz, Spiro, Eskin, Wall, and others also merited such recognition. There were also Jewish and non-Jewish soldiers who worked extensively with them. Much of what was accomplished by the soldiers was done quietly in order not to arouse army reaction. Klausner and Eskin, for example, were able to obtain penicillin and other badly needed drugs from soldiers; Eskin persuaded Jewish doctors and dentists to donate their off duty time to care for the survivors. CANRA was so proud of the chaplains' work with the survivors and their efforts to keep American Jewry informed of their condition that it published a special bulletin entitled "Rabbis to the Rescue" as a supplement to the *Jewish Chaplain*. In the introduction Philip Bernstein declared, "No written testimonial can possibly do justice to their devotion, their sacrifices, and their accomplishments. But this statement at least makes the basic facts known to our generation and for the future records."[59]

In France, Belgium, Italy, and Austria the chaplains were generally less involved with survivors than those in Germany. In France, Belgium and Italy, the JDC and the Palestinian Jews played a more dominant role in helping the survivors. This was particularly true in France and Belgium. In Austria, very little aside from Bohnen's activities is known. In Italy, the chaplains claimed that "they ha[d] a great deal of time on their hands and want[ed] to do some constructive refugee work." They were not aware of what the JDC was doing but wanted to coordinate activities. A special conference of chaplains was convened in Rome on November 6, 1945, to work out these arrangements.[60]

One of the ways the chaplains tried to ensure their continued involvement with the survivors was to establish good relations with the non-Jewish clergy. Unfortunately, many Christian clergy did not agree that American chaplains should be involved with European Jews. The chief of chaplains was one of the most hostile to these efforts, because he viewed this as outside the realm of military responsibilities. Although he was quite opposed to this work, Jewish chaplains managed to circumvent his directives either on their own or with the help of superior officers or Christian chaplains. Chaplains like Father Patrick Fay and others actively helped in this work and protected the chaplains from punishment.

With the creation of the position of advisor on Jewish Affairs, American Jewry felt they now had a representative in Germany who could deal directly with General Eisenhower and his successors about the plight of the survivors. To ensure that Rifkind understood what needed immediate attention, the WJC sent him a detailed memorandum before he left for Germany. The WJC continued to express its concerns and suggestions to Rifkind throughout his stay in Europe.[61] Rifkind's contribution as advisor is puzzling because of his behavior at Landsberg with Leo Srole. The army clearly tried to cover up problems at the camp, yet Rifkind sided with the military in spite of overwhelming evidence that Srole was correct.

Equally difficult to accept was Rifkind's role in trying to keep Zalman Grinberg from accepting an invitation to speak at the annual meeting of the United Jewish Appeal in Atlantic City in 1945. In December, Grinberg was invited to represent the Jews of Bavaria; but at the last moment he was informed there was no room on the plane.[62] Yossel Rosensaft, a leader from Bergen-Belsen,[63] and two representatives from France and Belgium were sent instead. Rifkind was not eager for Grinberg to go because he did not think he was objective enough or a true representative of the area. Jacob Trobe, the JDC director of Germany who succeeded Lavy Becker, attempted to cover up the incident by claiming that technical difficulties had prevented Grinberg from going.[64] The central committee was outraged at this affront and expressed its disappointment to Edward M. M. Warburg and other leaders of American Jewry. Klausner also sent letters of protest; and as a result, the WJC itself offered to bring Grinberg to America.[65]

Even after the Harrison Report and the appointment of the advisor on Jewish Affairs, the chaplains' reports were still essential to the leadership of American Jewry,[66] particularly to the WJC. Leon Kubowitzki made this point in a letter to Abraham Klausner. On December 13 Kubowitzki noted that the WJC held "an important press conference" in Washington on the problem of the Jewish displaced persons. "In presenting the case of our people in Germany," Kubowitzki declared, "we took full liberty of making full use of the information you sent us. . . . We take up daily the whole problem with the American and British authorities, as well as with UNRRA. We present all the available facts to them, offering suggestions as how to alleviate the situation and recommending drastic changes."[67]

Arieh Tartakower noted, "Day after day Jewish organizations are receiving reports from internment camps in Europe, chiefly from Jewish chaplains in the United States Army, whose admirable work incidentally deserves special mention. What they report is a continued martyrdom of the internees who, many weeks after the so-called liberation, are still suffering."[68]

Of special concern to the WJC was the problem of infiltrees, Kubowitzki observed: "We approached repeatedly the American authorities asking them to put no obstacles in the path of those, who because of the situation in various Eastern European countries, have to flee from their homelands into the American zone." Kubowitzki concluded by urging Klausner to continue keeping the WJC informed of events in Europe. He claimed that although the WJC constantly received information from a number of sources, including Judge Rifkind, many of these reports were contradictory.[69]

Until the survivors received appropriate support from American Jewry, the JDC, and the army, the chaplains would continue to be needed. They would be asked not only to provide material aid but also to listen to the problems of displaced persons, to offer them advice, to intervene with the military on their behalf, to work with the Berihah, and to continue informing American Jewry about their plight.

6

"THE JEWS ARE OUR MISFORTUNE"

Growing Tensions Between Displaced Persons, the Army, and the Germans

The chaplains had hoped that a solution to the statelessness of the survivors would be found after the cessation of hostilities or at least by the end of 1945. The Allies' failure to resolve this issue intensified existing problems and created new ones. Although the physical state of the displaced persons improved steadily, their living conditions and morale continued to deteriorate. The uncertainty of how long they would have to remain in Europe contributed to this decline, as did the growing tension between the displaced persons, the army, and the German population.[1]

Since the American military was preoccupied with enlarging the scope of German governmental authority and reviving the German and Austrian economies, the army viewed the continued presence of the Jews in Germany as a burden. One army official summed up this feeling when he remarked that Jews "have been here a long time, and we are tired of them."[2] Exasperation with the survivors led to a climate of ill feeling and conflict. Oscar A. Mintzer, the JDC legal advisor for the United States zone of Germany, conducted a study of the problem and reported that there were "frequent instances of arrests by either military or German police merely on suspicion alone, and of the conviction and imprisonment of Jews based simply on suspicion with little supporting evidence." Moreover, there were "frequent allegations of beatings, robbery, and other mistreatment of displaced persons (not only Jewish displaced persons) by arresting officers, both military and German."[3]

Mintzer also found evidence "of unjust, arbitrary and discriminatory practices by military government legal officers." Defendants were sometimes held for four to six months before they were brought to trial. Sentences were either "frivolous or out of proportion to the nature of the crime." For example, "persons were being arrested for possession of a pack of American cigarettes or a can or two of American food" and sentenced to several weeks or months in prison. Rarely were fines or bail allowed the defendants.[4]

His investigation further revealed that "certain military government laws and army directives were prejudicial and unjust as they were implemented. German police were free to enter displaced persons centers and conduct raids and searches without being required to present a supporting basis for such action." Charges of "resisting arrest and the utilization of this charge as an excuse for marks of beatings and mistreatment on the body of defendants were prevalent. Instances of entire Jewish communities feeling terrorized and fearful of both German and American alike" were also common.[5]

Under these volatile conditions it was almost inevitable that someone would be killed. On March 29, 1945, two hundred armed German police with dogs invaded the displaced persons center at Stuttgart in pursuit of alleged black-marketeers. By the time they completed their search, a thirty-five-year-old Polish Jew had been killed, and several others wounded.

On April 4 an estimated thirty-five thousand Jews in seventeen displaced persons camps throughout the American zone of Germany held a rally to protest this slaying. Judge Rifkind, who returned to the United States during the middle of March because of prior commitments, had advised the military that using Germans to police Jewish centers and camps "would lead to violence"; but his warnings went unheeded. They told him that the redeployment of American troops made it essential to use German police as a supplementary force. As a precaution, the Germans were allowed to search Jewish installations and make arrests only while under the supervision of the American military.

Rifkind countered that even with this precaution, "incidents were bound to occur." He urged the army to recruit and train Jewish displaced persons to be used as supplementary police in their own centers. This advice was also ignored; but after the Stuttgart killing, General Joseph T. McNarney, who replaced Eisenhower as commander of the United States forces in Germany after the latter left Germany in 1945, temporarily rescinded the right of German police to enter the camps. He did not, however, prohibit them from patrolling outside these centers.[6]

Jews were victimized not only by the German police but also by the German populace. During 1946, 1947, and 1948, the Germans openly expressed their anti-Semitism. Jews were blamed for food, clothing, and housing shortages and black market activities. They were abused in public, their cemeteries were desecrated, anti-Semitic songs were openly sung, and Jewish homes were stoned.[7]

According to a confidential Jewish Telegraphic Agency report prepared for the leadership of American Jewry, these anti-Semitic attitudes and behavior were thought justified by an overwhelming majority of the Germans:

> German public opinion polls have shown that today 80 per cent of the German population has pro-Nazi and anti-Semitic sentiments. In addition, Jewish displaced persons cannot expect much support from the so-called anti-Nazis. Three factors characterize the attitude of the so-called "anti-Nazis" toward the Jews: Security is the first factor. The anti-Nazis feel safe and well entrenched as they are deemed to be politically blameless and can boast of their past anti-Nazi activities. They can thus afford to act in accordance with their genuine feelings. The second factor may be called the complex of justification. As attorneys for a Germany with murder on its national conscience, they defend her, lacking other arguments of defense for the nation of murderers, by insulting the assassinated, vilifying and slandering the victims, and by attempting to persuade themselves and the occupation authorities that the Jews are criminals, dirty and unwilling to work. The third factor is the complex that: "Jews are getting extra rations; Jews are frequenting the peasant black market; Jews occupy our apartments; Jews cram the trains; *Juden sind unser Unglueck* (Jews are our misfortune)." To illustrate: in a city of the British zone a German who was formerly persecuted for political reasons, declared himself against common association with the victims of political and racial persecution by saying: "It was unjust that we were persecuted; but the persecution of the Jews was just."[8]

Matters were further complicated because of the army's negative response to the increase of Jews seeking refuge in the American zone of Germany and by the increasingly widespread fraternization between German and American military personnel.

The departure of Simon Rifkind in March 1946 left the Jews without a major spokesman. On April 16 Zalman Grinberg cabled the American Jewish Conference to send a successor. Abraham Klausner sent his own cable to the American Jewish Conference shortly thereafter. The American Jewish Conference dispatched a delegation to meet Assistant Secretary of War Howard C. Peterson, who advised them the War Department could not send an advisor without the approval of General McNarney. After consulting with McNarney, Robert P. Patterson, Secretary of War, asked Philip Bernstein to succeed Judge Rifkind.[9]

Bernstein had resigned his position at CANRA in early 1946 to return to his congregation in Rochester, New York. He had been away several years and they wanted him home. Shortly after his return, representatives of the major Jewish organizations asked Bernstein to consider Patterson's invitation. Bernstein agreed, expecting to be back in Rochester within a couple of months; in fact, he was not to return until August 1947, his successor, Judge Louis E. Leventhal, arriving from Philadelphia in July of that year. Upon Bernstein's arrival in Germany in May 1946, General Mark Clark, the commanding general of the United States forces in Austria, asked him to serve as advisor under him, as well. Clark had been sympathetic to the survivors and wanted Bernstein's guidance.[10]

Bernstein recognized that the military had little understanding of displaced persons and that they viewed them as troublemakers, irritants, and radicals. Zionism was an "anathema," and they associated it with communism. He attempted to counter their prejudices by giving a lecture on Jewish history and the plight of the displaced persons to top officers in the European command. He also initiated an orientation program for regular soldiers using the army's newspaper.

To aid him in his work, Bernstein had three assistants assigned to him. They were to act as a "buffer" between the displaced persons and the military; interpret their complaints and needs to the army; explain "the attitude, proposals and regulations of the military" to the survivors; and visit displaced persons installments in the American zones of Germany and Austria.[11]

They were to meet personnel from the army, the JDC, UNRRA, the Jewish Agency, the Organization for Rehabilitation through Training (ORT), representatives of the displaced persons, and chaplains in order to discuss the psychological state of the survivors. A full report containing recommendations for any needed changes was to be submitted at the end of each visit.[12]

His first assistant was Chaplain Emanuel Rackman, a thirty-six-year-old Orthodox rabbi. Rackman, a lawyer and political scientist, came from the United States to work on questions of reparations and restitution, an area about which Bernstein knew little. Rackman met frequently with Lieutenant General Lucius Clay, deputy military governor of the United States zone in Germany, and with Clay's legal advisor on these matters. One of several problems that were not resolved during Rackman's three-month tour of duty was what to do with the more-than-three-million books, stored in the I. G. Farben warehouse in Offenbach, that the Nazis had stolen from European Jewry.

Fearing that the army might keep the books in Germany permanently, Rackman tried to persuade General Clay's legal advisor to send the entire collection to Palestine. Before a final decision could be reached, Rackman returned to his congregation in the United States.

Rackman also played a key role in the rewriting of the central committee's constitution that lead to its formal recognition by the army as official representative of the Jewish displaced persons, in September 1946. The army had been reluctant to take this unprecendented move; but with the redeployment of its troops from a high of one million in November 1945 to less than one-third that number in April 1946, the increase of Jewish refugees from the East, the probability of the displaced persons having to remain in Europe for the foreseeable future, and the critical shortage of food and fuel for the upcoming winter months, the army feared that Jewish discontent might erupt into an embarrassing security problem. To forestall this possibility, the army wanted a representative body that would speak for the Jews. The army wanted to limit the central committee to welfare activities but the committee viewed itself as a political entity. Through Rabbi Bernstein's intervention and with Rabbi Rackman's adroit help, an agreement acceptable to both was reached.[13]

Rackman's replacement was Chaplain Herbert L. Friedman, a twenty-seven-year-old Reform rabbi who had previously been attached to Headquarters Berlin District. From July 1946 on, Friedman acted as a troubleshooter for Bernstein, visiting displaced persons installations throughout Germany and Austria and interpreting the views of the displaced persons to army officials.[14]

For his third aide, Bernstein chose Captain Abraham S. Hyman, who had been attached to the Office of the Theater Judge Advocate. On April 28, 1946, twenty Jews were arrested outside the Landsberg displaced persons camp by American military police as they were protesting the incarceration of their fellow displaced persons. They were charged with flouting the authority of the military police for shouting "Gestapo!" and "American SS!" and for entering military police headquarters to demand the release of these prisoners.

Earlier that day, a report reached the Jews at Landsberg that two guards stationed at the kibbutz at Dissen, about six miles away, had disappeared. This might not have caused alarm under normal circumstances; but in the last few weeks a fourteen-year-old Jewish boy had been murdered at Regensburg, a Jew had been killed at Stuttgart, and several boys from Landsberg were attacked and badly beaten. No report had been published or public action taken against the perpetrators, causing frustration to build among the displaced persons.

As word spread through Landsberg that the two guards were missing and presumed murdered, about 700 Jews (out of 4,200)

Remains of German bus burned in Landsberg riot. (Photo courtesy of the Mintzer Collection, Magnes Museum.)

broke out of the camp to vent their anger against the Germans in the area. About twenty Germans were attacked by approximately fifty Jews, but none of the Germans was seriously hurt. Twenty Jews were arrested by the military police.[15]

To avoid any repercussions from this mass arrest, the army assigned Herbert Friedman as an observer at the trial. Abraham Klausner also attended as official advisor to the defendants. To ensure the displaced persons received the best possible defense, Friedman asked the Office of the Theater Judge Advocate to recommend their most qualified Jewish lawyer. They suggested Hyman; and although he was scheduled to complete his tour of duty on July 31, 1946, he accepted the assignment.

Despite Hyman's efforts, nineteen of the twenty defendants were found guilty and given stiff jail sentences. Although Friedman and Klausner did not affect the outcome of the trial, Friedman did convince the army to allow the Jews to serve their time separate from American military prisoners. The displaced persons never served their complete sentences, because the sentences were either reduced or suspended. Within three months the Jews were smuggled to Palestine.[16]

At the end of the trial, Hyman agreed to become Bernstein's legal advisor. Legal problems and special cases involving displaced persons began receiving faster top-level consideration as a result.

Some of the defendants at the Landsberg trial. (Photo courtesy of the Mintzer Collection, Magnes Museum.)

Courthouse where Landsberg trial was held. (Photo courtesy of the Mintzer Collection, Magnes Museum.)

On August 31, 1946, the army officially began making a clear distinction between persecutees and displaced persons. This meant that persecutees, including all Jews, had to be brought to trial within twenty-four hours of their arrest before the nearest summary court; that a camp director could function as a summary court officer; and that sentencing had to be under military, rather than German, rule.[17]

On December 27, 1946, the army advised all military enforcement agencies to make frequent visits to displaced persons centers to establish good relations and interpret the army's policies so that the rules would be understood. The directive also stated that raids and check-and-search operations were not to be made without the direction and authority of either the commanding general of the Third Army area or the commanding general of the Office of Military Government for Germany.[18]

Immigration

Overshadowing problems between the Jewish displaced persons and the American Army was the increase of Jews entering the American zone in Germany. In June 1946, the Berihah increased the flow to pressure the Americans to allow large numbers of Jews to enter its zone without being harassed. The Anglo–American Commission on Palestine, which submitted its report on April 22, 1946, recommended that Britain immediately admit one hundred thousand immigrants into Palestine. Haim Yahil, head of the official Jewish Agency mission for Palestine in Germany, feared the Americans might make emigration to Palestine of these one hundred thousand Jews conditional on ending infiltration into the United States zone. A significant increase of infiltrating Jews, Yahil believed, might forestall the Americans from stipulating this condition.[19]

Six American and six English members on the Anglo–American Commission were asked to examine the condition of Jews in Europe and determine how many could be resettled in their former countries, in Palestine, or elsewhere. The commission began its work on January 5, 1946, with sessions in Washington and London. On February 4 they divided into four subcommittees to visit displaced persons camps in Germany. Some also visited parts of Poland, Austria, Czechoslovakia, and the Middle East.

The displaced persons camps had the most impact on them. Bartley Crum, a corporate lawyer from San Francisco and one of the American representatives, noted that as they were leaving one of the camps, a group of Jews began tipping their hats, making little speeches, and pleading for help. One man approached him with tears streaming down his face and asked: "What have I done?

Why am I here? When will you let me go? What crime have I committed?"

At another camp, a thirteen-year-old boy tugged at his coat just as they were about to leave and asked, "Mr. America, Mr. America, when are you going to let us out of here?" When Crum patted the boy on the shoulder and told him to have patience, the lad exclaimed: "Patience! How can you talk to us of patience? After six years of this war, after all our parents have been burned in the gas ovens, you talk to us about patience!"

Crum answered that he should have faith, since it was the genius of the Jewish people that they always had faith. In desperation, the young man replied: "Faith! In whom? In the British, who have been promising for 26 years that we can go home to Palestine? In the Americans, who have been following the British? We want a home!" Crum had no answer to such despair. It became clear to the delegates that the Jews overwhelmingly refused to return to their former homes and that they were anxious to emigrate to Palestine.[20] The commission submitted its final report to the British and American governments on April 22 with the recommendation that Britain admit 100,000 immigrants immediately into Palestine, so that the Jews could be removed from the displaced persons camps, and that under "suitable conditions" additional numbers of Jews ("over and above these 100,000") should be allowed to enter the country.[21]

Many Jews were eager to enter the American zone of Germany, because the commission's recommendations raised their expectations about entering Palestine. Approximately forty thousand Jews were expected to infiltrate during July, August, and September, according to Berihah estimates. Few could have anticipated that Britain would refuse to implement the unanimous recommendations of the report, which it did because it "wanted an Arab Palestine with guaranteed rights for a permanent Jewish minority under British protection."[22] Various attempts to arrive at an agreement with Britain over the commission's report were made by the United States government, but they did not succeed. By early August 1946, the report was no longer under serious consideration.[23]

The displaced persons were shattered by this turn of events. Disturbed that a committee was needed to investigate the problem, they had expected that at least some of the commission's recommendations would be accepted. Now the question of Palestine and their own future remained unresolved.

At the end of 1945 Truman tried but failed to admit some Jews into the United States. Despite the suffering endured by European Jewry, the U. S. Congress would not relax its restrictive immigration laws. Rather than initiate a protracted fight to change these statutes, Truman issued an executive order on December 22, 1945, which gave the Jews priority on existing quotas already available to displaced persons. The Polish, Austrian, and German quotas came to approximately thirty-nine thousand.

Although a large number of Jews were expected to enter the United States under this arrangement, lower-level bureaucrats in the government sabotaged this effort. Forty-five thousand displaced persons came to the United States zone between late 1945 and the Displaced Persons Act of July 1, 1948. Of these, 12,649 were Jews who arrived between May 1946 and October 1948. Nine thousand Jews left Germany legally or illegally during 1946.[24]

The major factor contributing to this influx was the Kielce pogrom. Several hundred Jews had been murdered between November 1944 and October 1945; others were attacked and wounded. Anti-Jewish riots had broken out in several cities in 1945, but in 1946 the number of riots increased dramatically. The worst of these riots took place on July 4, 1946, with the pogrom at Kielce, in which forty-two Jews were murdered for allegedly using Christian blood for ritual purposes. The Kielce pogrom had a traumatic effect on Jews in Poland because it highlighted their vulnerability and because it took place in a city of sixty thousand inhabitants, where the local bishop resided. Moreover, members of the clergy and the local militia were among the perpetrators.

Within three months, 100,000 Jews fled Poland and the surrounding countries. This movement, led by the Berihah,[25] took Jews through Czechoslovakia to Bratislava and Vienna. From Vienna they were taken to Salzburg and then either to Italy or the American zone of Germany. Another Berihah route went from Stettin (Szczecin) to Berlin and from there to the West. Berihah operations from Poland, Rumania, Hungary, Czechoslovakia, and Yugoslavia continued into 1948, transferring approximately 250,000 survivors into Austria, Germany, and Italy. It was the "largest organized illegal mass movement in the twentieth century."[26]

The prospect of continued infiltration after the summer months posed problems for the army. The displaced persons needed care and protection, but the military and UNRRA personnel were rapidly being redeployed. Furthermore, the army faced a large reduction in its budget.[27]

To make matters worse, the military suspected that this was not a spontaneous reaction to oppression but an organized mass exodus of Jews from Europe. The army's fears were confirmed by Lieutenant General Sir Frederick E. Morgan, head of UNRRA in Germany, who made this charge at a well-publicized news conference on January 2, 1946. Subsequent reports from UNRRA's research department also charged that this movement was a deliberate attempt to bring Zionism and the fate of the Jews to the forefront, adding weight to Morgan's arguments.[28] A major debate ensued on both sides of the Atlantic over Morgan's accusations, presenting Rabbi Bernstein with the challenge of persuading the military to keep open its zones in Germany and Austria.[29]

When the Berihah began increasing the number of Jews entering Germany in June 1946, Bernstein went to General McNarney to inform him that forty thousand Jews would enter the American zone during the months of June, July, and August, instead of the fifteen thousand already agreed upon. McNarney probably accepted this revised estimate in late June (shortly before the Kielce pogrom)[30] because he thought the situation temporary and still manageable.

Not long after this meeting, Bernstein informed the American Jewish Conference that this additional 40,000 Jewish infiltrees over the summer months and "the possible acceptance of a total of 100,000 to 150,000 in a year would pose no insuperable problems for the military authorities if they would receive the necessary support from Washington to carry these added responsibilities." Bernstein expected the leadership of American Jewry to ensure that these problems were fully understood in Washington.[31]

In response to this letter and two other communications that Bernstein sent to the American Jewish Conference on June 13 and 24, representatives of the American Jewish Committee, the American Jewish Conference, the JDC, the WJC, and the Jewish Agency for Palestine met in New York on July 8, 1946 to discuss his suggestions. After Meir Grossman of the American Jewish Conference reported that the War Department had notified the conference that no border closings were being contemplated, the representatives decided that there was no reason for any further discussion with the American government—at least for the time being.[32]

After the Kielce pogrom, Haim Yahil informed Bernstein that the Berihah leadership would transfer between 80,000 and 100,000 Jews from Poland. This meant that Bernstein would have to tell McNarney to revise the infiltration rate upward again. Before making specific recommendations to McNarney, Bernstein decided to see the situation for himself. With McNarney's approval, he left for Poland on July 23. Accompanying Bernstein was Chaplain Herbert Friedman. They remained in Poland until July 30th.[33]

During this visit, Bernstein met with Jewish political leaders in Warsaw, Lodz, and Lower Silesia. He reported to General McNarney that it had been impossible to obtain reliable statistics on the Jewish population in the country, since estimates, even from reliable sources,[34] ranged from 120,000 to 160,000. The higher figures were given to him by United States ambassador Arthur Bliss Lane and William Bein, director of the JDC in Poland.

Using these figures, Bernstein estimated that 100,000 Jews would leave Poland, while the balance would remain. He recommended that General McNarney be prepared to accommodate 60,000 additional Jewish displaced persons in the next three months and another 40,000 during the winter. He urged that facilities be expanded in the United States zone in Austria and the French and British zones and in France, Italy, and other countries. Moreover, he asked that the resources of the JDC and the Jewish Agency be fully utilized in this program.[35]

Apparently, McNarney had made up his mind about this influx prior to Bernstein's trip. On the day before Bernstein arrived in Poland, Undersecretary of State Dean Acheson convened a meeting in Washington of the major Jewish organizations to discuss the border situation. Among those present were Secretary of War Robert Patterson, the assistant secretary of state for occupied territories Major General John H. Hilldring, and Dean Acheson. The Jewish organizations represented included the WJC, the JDC, the American Jewish Committee, and the American Jewish Conference. The meeting had been carefully prepared. The Jewish representatives were shown elaborately detailed maps and charts of the number of Jewish displaced persons and potential displaced persons (as of July 15) in the American zone of Germany and Austria and in the British and French zones and in Poland, Czechoslovakia, Rumania, Hungary, and Italy.

A report from General McNarney was read, indicating that as of July 15, the monthly cost of food for the Jewish displaced persons in the American zone of Austria and Germany was $1,026,000. Clothing costs were $704,000. When all other expenses were taken into account, the total came to just short of $2,000,000. McNarney observed that prior to the release of the Anglo–American Commission's Report the number of Jews crossing the border had been decreasing. He predicted that by September 1, the American zone would have over 110,000 Jewish displaced persons. Not included in this figure were the 25,000 Jews living outside the camps. For McNarney this figure represented the limit the American military could accommodate for several reasons. The diversion of military personnel to the United States for separation, the lack of adequate facilities to accomodate large numbers of people, and the preferential treatment accorded Jewish displaced persons had caused considerable problems in the handling of other displaced persons and the German population. McNarney recommended that on September 1 the Americans close their border to Jews fleeing from Eastern Europe. Furthermore, he recommended the influx "of Jewish displaced persons from the French and British zones be discontinued immediately as these Jews were in no danger."[36] Acheson informed them that due to this increase, the American government had to close the border as of September 1. After a spirited discussion, he assured everyone that no action would be taken without President Truman's approval. In the meantime, the borders in the British and French zones were to be closed.[37]

The American Jewish Conference reacted by bringing their case directly to the president. John W. McCormack, majority leader of the House of Representatives, sent Truman a letter urging him to keep the borders open; a number of Senators either phoned or wrote the president expressing their concern about the border closing; Vice President Henry A. Wallace called on the president personally to discuss the problem; and Senator Robert Wagner (D–NY) asked the president to seek the advice of Judge Rifkind before making any final decision.

They approached the President "[not only on] humanitarian grounds, but also on political grounds." They pointed out that blockading the border was "no solution to the problem of military government in the American occupation zone." They viewed the situation as the seed "of a much more serious problem for the Truman administration than the mere inconvenience of feeding and housing several thousand people, in addition to those already in the zone."[38]

The intervention succeeded. A few days later, General McNarney received a cable from Secretary Patterson informing him that he could stop infiltration from the French and British zones but that under no circumstances was he to close any other borders or interfere with the large numbers of Jews fleeing from Poland.[39]

Individuals in the State Department were disturbed by this directive. In early August, General Hilldring's office began receiving cables from State Department officials in Vienna and Prague describing the dangerous increase of Jewish infiltration during the month. In this way, they had hoped to pressure the American military government to close its borders. Additional pressure came from representatives of the British military government.

General Hilldring's office responded by callling David R. Wahl, a representative of the American Jewish Conference, to help draft a cable to these diplomats. The cable informed them "in very strong terms of Secretary Patterson's cable to General McNarney that, under no circumstances, must the border be closed to persecutees." Hilldring also asked Wahl to enlist the aid of the American Jewish community, especially the JDC, to help reduce the flow of infiltrators into the American zone. Wahl told Hilldring he would do what he could but doubted "that anyone was competent to control this flow." That Hilldring and his staff believed that the American Jewish community could stem the tide of infiltration demonstrated that they did not understand the nature of this movement.[40]

While Hilldring did not succumb to pressure from the State Department and the British military government, General McNarney did. On August 6, 1946, McNarney publicly declared "all organized movement of Jewish refugees will be turned back from the American zones of Germany and Austria in the future." He maintained that the United States zone was not a "way station on the road to Palestine" and that he would "not accept movements of those who were not persecuted." Those who were persecuted would be given "temporary haven."[41] General Hilldring's office immediately informed the American Jewish Conference that these pronouncements did not signal a change in American policy. It also informed General McNarney "in no uncertain terms" that this policy was "fixed" and that "no statements should be made which would give any other impression."[42]

Though the situation in Germany was not good, the problems in Austria were much worse. On June 30 General Mark Clark reported that he did not have sufficient personnel or adequate facilities to handle any further increases of Jewish infiltrators. Moreover, he believed that serious difficulties would arise if Jews were not allowed to leave Austria and enter the American zone of Germany.[43]

During the first six days of August, about ten thousand Jews entered Austria. General Clark asked Washington to intervene diplomatically to have Poland and Czechoslavakia temporarily stop, or at least regulate, the flow. Both countries closed their borders for short periods, but only reluctantly. The Poles expressed the hope that Jews would remain in the country and wanted to appear sympathetic. The Czechs also expressed their concerns. In the end, the closings had little or no effect on infiltration.[44]

With the pressure continuing to mount, the army looked to Bernstein for relief. Bernstein tried to find an immediate solution, because he knew that even though Washington wanted to keep the borders open, the army could find excuses to have them closed. It could claim there were insufficient funds for food and housing, threats to security, or problems with the German population. These conditions, Berstein believed, constituted "an implicit danger at every stage of these crucial developments."[45]

Bernstein knew that McNarney wanted to be fair and as cooperative as possible. He had accepted Bernstein's evaluation of the problem including his estimate of the number of Jews coming into the American zone. McNarney agreed to continue offering the refugees a haven but with the understanding that American Jewry would do everything it could to divert the Jews to other areas.[46] In an attempt to find a solution, Bernstein approached the governments of Italy and Czechoslovakia to have them resettle some of these people. There were also approaches to the governments of France, Norway, Sweden, and Belgium to do the same. Nothing came of these initiatives.

Bernstein blamed the JDC for much of this failure. Had the JDC been ready to make a commitment to care for and feed the refugees from the outset, as was UNRRA and the American Army, the governments would have taken these initiatives more seriously. Without this commitment, negotiations had little chance for success. For these reasons Bernstein concluded: "It is my sober conviction that JDC is rendering minimal assistance in dealing with this current crucial situation. All parties are making definite commitments and accepting definite responsibilities; that is, all but JDC." Bernstein stressed that "the outpouring of over 100,000 Jews from Poland creates unprecedented conditions, to which the usual formulas and rationalizations for non-commitment are not applicable. Is it not infinitely wiser for the JDC to make a definite commitment to undertake a small portion of the program than for it to be compelled to assume the larger part, as it is now doing in Poland and as it would be compelled to do if the U.S. Army refused to assume any further burdens?"[47]

The failure of the JDC to adjust its policy not only thwarted a temporary solution to the problem, it also brought into question the sincerity of American Jewry's expressed intentions. Bernstein pointed out that since the attitude of the U.S. Army was "crucial to the welfare of the Jews in central Europe," it was important the JDC be viewed as competent and willing to assume its responsibility for aiding the displaced persons. On the contrary, "those officers in the USFET Headquarters who were closest to the displaced persons problem did not have a particularly high regard for the JDC."

The reason for this, Bernstein believed, was clear; and he offered his own solution to the problem:

> In this present emergency, during which we have been telling the army that the acceptance of the Polish Jewish refugees is a matter of life or death, the constant refrain is "Where is the JDC? What is the JDC doing?" In these matters JDC is Jewry and, when all that JDC offers is not commitments, but excuses and rationalizations and a sanctimonious reaffirmation of established precedents, there is the inevitable tendency for the army authorities to feel that the Jews are simply dumping the problems on the army. Although I have tried to protect the interests of the JDC in these current negotiations, the truth of its lack of active cooperation must inevitably become known and will result in a further deterioration in its position vis-à-vis the army. . . . It should be clear to New York JDC that, merely as strategy alone, it is necessary to undertake a vigorous and well-publicized program of cooperation with the army in

meeting this vast, difficult, unprecedented problem of Polish evacuation.[48]

Joseph Schwartz responded to these charges by noting that the JDC did not have the large sums of money needed for such a program and that in any event the number of Jews leaving Poland by late September was decreasing. Some Jews had even returned to Poland. Under these conditions, he believed there was no reason to pursue Bernstein's suggestions.[49]

In his attempt to improve the conditions for the Jews in transit and those who were staying in Poland, Bernstein visited Pope Pius XII on September 11 and President Truman on October 11. In his meeting with the pope, Bernstein discussed the Kielce pogrom and urged the pontiff to speak to the Polish Catholic hierarchy about preventing further violence and other acts of anti-Semitism. The Pope agreed but indicated that the Church had its own problems operating in Poland under a hostile communist regime. The pontiff also promised to speak with the Italian government about accepting ten thousand Jewish survivors into the country. Whether the pope actually intervened in Poland or Italy is not known; nothing concrete resulted in either case.[50]

Bernstein was summoned to the White House by the president, on October 11, accompanied by Secretary Patterson. During their half-hour discussion, Bernstein praised Generals McNarney and Clark for doing "a good job under difficult circumstances" and noted that they had been "thoroughly cooperative." "The top policies are good," Bernstein declared. "Such difficulties as exist develop out in the field where the human factor plays an important role."[51] Bernstein then discussed the care provided the displaced persons. Truman assured him he had instructed Secretary Patterson to "do everything possible for these unfortunate people." With regard to the morale of the displaced persons, Bernstein pointed out they had "not cracked under the strain," which was "a testimony to their character, resiliency, the care they are receiving, and the hope of resettlement in Palestine." Bernstein was concerned, however, about "what would happen if this hope were to be removed." The Jews were "becoming increasingly discouraged over the long delays in their resettlement. They see no need for all these investigations and conferences. They grow increasingly restive as they find themselves, so long after liberation, still in displaced persons centers in Europe."[52]

"Over ninety percent of these displaced Jews want to go to Palestine," Bernstein declared, because they "insist upon starting life again in their own land and on their own terms, despite hardships and dangers." Unfortunately, Bernstein found "no government in

Europe" prepared to accept them "on a permanent basis." Truman could not understand why. "The Jews," after all, "had been good citizens in the United States" and "would be assets to any country." Bernstein replied that the "world was sick" and that this attitude was "a symptom of it." Truman agreed and said he would ask Congress to liberalize United States immigration laws so that more Jews would be allowed to enter the country.[53]

Although it is difficult to determine how many Jews entered the United States zones during this exodus, one estimate placed it at 70,000 for Germany and 20,000 for Austria. An additional 4,000 Jews settled in the British zone (mostly in Germany); others settled in France and Italy. In August the United States commands in Germany and Austria decided to ease the crowding by transferring thousands of Jews from Austria to Germany. Temporary shelters were already available in Germany because in July the army had begun setting up a whole string of camps.[54]

The army decided to transport the Jews to Germany by train and assigned the Third Army Headquarters to supervise the operation. In a move probably designed to ensure cooperation of the displaced persons and forestall any criticism of the army, a Jewish chaplain accompanied each group. Assembly centers in Linz and Salzburg were the starting point. A chaplain's involvement usually began at the train station. Before departing, he explained where they were going and what to expect. The chaplain made arrangements for the care of the infants, appointed leaders in each car, selected nurses to help the sick and pregnant, and chose guards to watch out for problems. He also explained to the military personnel who these people were and why they were being taken out of Austria. The chaplains acted as troubleshooters and interpreters and tried to attend to the needs of their charges.[55]

Chaplain Yosef Miller, a twenty-six-year-old Orthodox rabbi assigned to headquarters command for the United States forces in Frankfurt, discovered on his trip from Salzburg that it was

> a very simple and natural matter for the accompanying chaplain to become a virtual train commander; and he can easily acquire the voluntary support and aid of his G.I.s by making the human element of the situation clear to them. It is almost as simple for a chaplain to become the train leader—that is of the people themselves. By conferring constantly with the inevitable leader and the heads of various groups, the chaplain can easily acquire the full cooperation of the people. In this dual capacity of military commandant and Jewish leader, the chaplain has only the emnity of the outside world to contend with—and the chances of the transport to overcome most obstacles are excellent.[56]

This did not mean that Miller was unmindful of the real problems the chaplains had to confront. They first had to obtain adequate provisions for the journey. On his trip, the army provided fifteen hundred loaves of bread and 250 cans of condensed milk as the sole ration for a thousand people for three days. At the Austrian–German border, the JDC supplied the transport with "the only real rations" they were to receive; but even these were inadequate. If it were not for the generosity of the six GIs who were on the train guard, the survivors would have arrived very hungry. The soldiers donated most of their K rations to help feed the transport.[57]

Several times, the chaplains prevented potential conflicts. When Chaplain Albert Troy, a thirty-three-year-old Reform rabbi, counted the Jews on his train, he found 372 stowaways. With the help of two JDC workers, Troy hid 325 of them so that when an official count was taken, only 47 were found. On the same trip, Troy was able to help save 52 people who were in a railroad car that caught fire. He also halted the train so that one of the women about to give birth could be taken to a hospital.

Among the complaints Troy made at the end of this journey were that the food issued at Linz was insufficient; the people needed something more substantial than the chocolate and warm beverages provided by the JDC; the trains were not equipped with water or lavatories; and the constabulary units inspecting the train at the German border were irresponsible, immature, and unsympathetic. "Under these circumstances," Troy concluded, "I am certain that without a chaplain to accompany such a large number of people, a great many of whom were undisciplined and sensitive to the least provocation, there would have been occasion for several unpleasant incidents."[58]

Once the Jews arrived at their destination, the chaplain returned to his duties or accompanied another train. There were times when the people were so disturbed by their poor accommodations that the chaplains stayed until they were settled in their new surroundings. Miller suggested to Philip Bernstein that much of the survivors' anxiety could be eliminated if they were informed about the conditions that awaited them. "The most vital problem in the minds of all the people is the kind of camp they are going to," he asserted: "If the chaplain knew the answer to this question beforehand and this answer were a satisfactory one, then all the discomforts and suffering of the trip would be bearable, there would be little complaining, and no incidents." He also maintained that it was "most important that the end of the voyage be crowned with some reward, some comfort. In several instances. . . this had not been the case."[59]

Unless adequate accommodations could be guaranteed in the future, Jews could not be persuaded to accept the intolerable conditions at these camps. At Heilbronn, where Miller's train arrived, the camp had not been prepared and probably "could not have been gotten ready for human habitation." The food situation was especially bad. People were so hungry that they were cooking potato peelings and eating green pears even after being warned by their doctor against this. A hunger strike was being organized for the following morning. By promising better conditions, which he could not be certain of, Miller succeeded in convincing the entire camp to be patient and cooperative for one week. The camp was condemned shortly thereafter.[60]

At Bad Aibling, Chaplain Eugene Cohen, an Orthodox rabbi assigned to Headquarters First Armored Division, found conditions so inadequate the Third Army agreed to stop all further shipments and promised to remove the fourteen hundred Jews already there. He remained at the camp a few days to make certain the people understood that they were to be taken to the Ludendorff Kaserne in Ulm. Bad Aibling would be used in the future, Cohen noted, but not until "several weeks engineering" made the place habitable.[61]

On September 30, a train arrived at Babenhausen, a prisoner-of-war camp near Frankfurt. When the Jews saw the substandard conditions and the barbed wire fence surrounding parts of the camp, they refused to leave the train. Army personnel, Jewish chaplains, and JDC workers rushed to the scene to convince them that they would not be harmed. That night, approximately nine hundred of the thousand Jews on the train agreed to enter the camp, but only after the army promised to remove the fence and improve the facilities. The remaining Jews were taken elsewhere.

The next day, a second train had been scheduled to arrive at Babenhausen; but it was diverted to the raiload station at Aschaffenburg, about seven miles from the camp. Trucks were sent to the station, but Chaplain Herman Dicker could only persuade 120 of them to disembark. The train then went to Babenhausen, where Chaplain Herbert Friedman met them in his capacity as assistant to Philip Bernstein.[62]

At the railroad siding near the camp, Friedman tried but failed to convince the survivors to enter the camp so they would not have to spend the night in the box cars. The next day, while he resumed negotiations, Lieutenant General Geoffrey S. Keyes, commanding general of the Third Army, appeared and persuaded most of the Jews to enter the camp. Thirty-nine refused; and the following day, they were sent back to Austria.

Friedman remained at Babenhausen until the night of October 3 to make sure that everyone received food and temporary shelter. In his report to Bernstein, Friedman praised General Keyes and the army personnel for their patience, understanding, and restraint. He was certain the whole incident could have been avoided if the

Babenhausen, October 1946. "The young pile aboard for the joy and excitement of the ride while the older people wonder, 'Where next?'" (Photo courtesy of the Mintzer Collection, Magnes Museum.)

camp had been prepared in advance and the people informed of what to expect. Succeeding groups were briefed ahead of time; and once they understood there was no alternative, they went willingly.[63]

Although the army initially expected that ten thousand Jews would arrive each month, it soon realized this was not realistic. In November the rate of Jews leaving Poland decreased to one hundred per day, while in December it dropped to fifty per day or less.[64] Philip Bernstein attributed this reduction to several factors. Most Jews who wanted to leave Poland had already left. Those who remained did so for economic or ideological reasons. Since the situation had stabilized, they were less afraid of violent anti-Semitic outbursts. Other Jews did not want a prolonged life in a displaced persons camp in Germany. Still others found it difficult to move during the winter months.[65]

Ziegenhain, September 1946. The guard tower and barbed wire serve to remind Jewish refugees that they are not home yet. (Photo courtesy of the Mintzer Collection, Magnes Museum.)

Berihah

Adding to this increase of Jews into the American zone of occupation were Chaplains Joseph Shubow, Herbert Friedman, and Mayer Abramowitz (the latter a twenty-seven-year-old Palestinian-born Conservative rabbi who worked with the Berihah in Berlin). Without their help, the operation would not have succeeded.

In 1946 the Berihah smuggled thousands of Jews into the United States sector of Berlin from Stettin (Szczecin) Poland and from there to the United States zone in Germany. Stettin was the starting point of the northern route of the Berihah in Poland. From January 1946, the American sector of Berlin became a refuge for survivors. This was not part of Haim Yahil's and the Berihah's attempt to force the Americans to keep their borders open. Nevertheless, the flow of

Jews into Berlin had this effect; for the military did not want to risk another scandal like that following the Harrison Report.

Shortly after the British closed their transfer point at Hesslingen on December 5, 1945, the Americans instructed their personnel not to allow Jews to use Berlin as a route to the United States zone in Germany.[66] Chaplain Shubow and Philip S. Skorneck, the first JDC representative in Berlin, refused to abide by this order and continued smuggling Jews into the city, causing the army to view them as the "source of much of their trouble."[67] By denying Skorneck gas allowances and mail service and subjecting him to a thorough investigation, the army tried in vain to stop him.

In January 1946 the Americans rescinded the border restrictions and set up a new displaced persons camp called Schlactensee. The military had tried to send back a group of Jewish women fleeing from the Russian zone; but when they refused, the army let them enter. This effectively broke the American resistance to Jewish infiltration into the American zone of Berlin. It did not mean, however, that Jews could enter at will. Between December 1945 and March 1946 the Palestinians smuggled eight thousand Jews into the city from Stettin.

Exit from Berlin to the United States zone of Germany also presented problems, and several different routes were established to avoid detection.

Whereas the Americans gave tacit approval to these operations the British and the Russians tried to stop them. Whenever the Russians caught a group of Jews, they were arrested and put into jail. Despite these obstacles, the Berihah succeeded in smuggling thousands of Jews into the United States sector of Berlin and from there into the United States zone in Germany. A crucial factor in their success was Chaplain Herbert Friedman, who preceeded Abramowitz in Berlin.[68] Another element was the very effective JDC team of Max Helvarg, Henry Levy, and Eli Rock.[69]

Before becoming Bernstein's assistant, Friedman had been asked by Ruth Kluger, whom he met in Paris in early January 1946, to find a way to be assigned to Berlin where he would continue the work begun by Shubow. Shubow had been the first Jewish chaplain in Berlin and had established a social and religious center which became a meeting place for Jewish soldiers, displaced persons, and Palestinians working in the city. He and his assistant, Saul Loeb, provided the Palestinians with food and lodgings and used the center as their headquarters.[70] Shubow had become so successful in helping Jews emigrate to Palestine and the United States that he became known among the displaced persons in Berlin as the "Yiddisher" general.[71]

Friedman agreed to work with the Berihah, arriving in Berlin about the first week of April. He immediately began providing the Palestinians with trucks, gasoline, cigarettes, false papers, clothing, a place to stay, and a cover for their activities. Of all these supplies, cigarettes were the most precious commodity. Since money had no value in Europe, cigarettes were used to bribe Russian soldiers smuggling Jews into Berlin. A carton of American cigarettes was valued at 1,500 marks or 150 dollars. The official rate of exchange for a dollar was ten marks; unofficially it was 300. It cost one package of cigarettes to smuggle one Jew into Berlin. Some cigarettes were given to Friedman by Jewish GIs, other Jewish chaplains, and the JDC. His greatest supplier, his father, sent five hundred cartons every couple of days.[72]

When Friedman left Berlin in July to work with Bernstein, he was replaced by Mayer Abramowitz. Abramowitz continued to help the Berihah until 1947, when the army caught him smuggling Jews from Germany. His superior officer had known about his activities; but when other Army officers learned about it, Abramowitz was exiled from Berlin and the Berihah.[73]

Eugene Cohen, Max Braude, Eugene Lipman, Samuel Burstein (a twenty-six-year-old Conservative rabbi assigned to the Wetzlar Military Post), Yosef Miller, and Abraham Klausner were some of the other chaplains who were instrumental in getting Jews out of Germany and Austria. They supplied trucks, food, gasoline, clothing, and false documents.[74]

Outside Germany and Austria, smuggling by chaplains occurred in Italy. During late September or early October 1946, Chaplain Milton Elefant, a twenty-nine-year-old Orthodox rabbi assigned to the Eighty-Eighth Infantry Division, met with Jews in Trieste who informed him of their intention to leave for Udine. From there, they would go either to Venice or Milan and then to Palestine. Since moving around without passes was illegal, Elefant had them dressed as Italian civilians. Within twenty weeks, he succeeded in smuggling forty Jews from the city. No one stopped him at the checkpoints, and the officers in his division were unaware of his activities.[75]

The army did not interfere with the chaplains involved in the Berihah unless it became an embarrassment, as with Chaplain Abramowitz. In 1947 the army knew that Eugene Cohen had been smuggling Jews on the Austrian–German border but did not stop him. Since October 1946, the Berihah without Army approval had used British uniforms in order that any investigation would have not implicated American personnel. If the Berihah had been forced to operate underground, the Army would have been deprived of its ability to "ensure some semblance of order in the camps" and on the routes bringing Jews in and out of Germany. Until 1947, the administration of the camps was in the hands of the Berihah.

Thereafter, at the request of the displaced persons, it was turned over to elected committees in each of the camps. Nevertheless, the Berihah remained the "unofficial power behind the throne."[76]

Combating Demoralization

The increase of Jews in the American zones, the hostility of the Germans, the army's lack of sympathy for the displaced persons, the absence of work, and the uncertainty of what the future would bring had a demoralizing effect on the survivors. Klausner also noticed that the spirit of the Jews had changed radically since liberation: "There is no longer an air of excitement, a darting of the eyes, a flood of questions—there is a feeling of resignation. Many leaders speak of the 'demoralization of the people'." This did not apply, however, to the children housed in centers and organized in kibbutzim. They were "fiery" and full of hope and faith.[77]

Leo Srole observed that the psychological condition of the Jews in displaced persons camps had deteriorated to the point that it compared to combat fatigue found in air force crews during the war. The Jews were jittery, excitable and anxiety-prone; suffered from pathlolgical fears; and in many instances exhibited aggressiveness to counteract these fears. "If the American Army were to withdraw today, we would all be murdered by morning"[78] remarked one survivor, illustrating the extent of this fear.

As the morale of the survivors continued to decline,[79] the chaplains struggled to combat this in a number of ways. They participated in dedicating synagogues, officiated at weddings, counseled survivors, prevented municipal authorities from taking Jewish property, reunited families through the publication of another volume of Klausner's *Shearit Hapletah,* established schools and summer camps for children, helped rebuild Jewish cemeteries, and acted as troubleshooters.

In Bremen, Jacob Kraft of the Fifteenth Air Force assisted the Jews of the community and in nearby areas by organizing a package program; aiding several Jewish orphanages, a children's camp, and the Jews at Bergen-Belsen (in the British zone); and by serving as the spiritual leader of the Bremen Jewish community.[80] In May 1946 his tour of duty ended, and he returned to the United States.

Abraham Spiro, assistant division chaplain and advisor on Jewish Affairs to the commander of the First Infantry Division, also established a package program, helped restore order in a number of displaced persons camps, convinced the army to turn over farms to the displaced persons for use as kibbutzim, and assisted in setting up a children's home. He visited these installations often and was particularly involved with the children's home, where he arranged for army doctors to check the health of the children. He continued in this position until the middle of 1948.[81]

Until the middle of March 1946, Morris Dembowitz was stationed in Heidelberg. Shortly after arriving, he learned that there were Jews in a nearby Polish displaced persons camp who wanted to be transferred but who would not acknowledge that they were Jews for fear of being harassed by Poles. Dembowitz intervened and had them removed to another installation.

On another occasion, he learned that a young girl had been trying to convert Jewish children to Catholicism at a local orphanage. The head of the orphanage promised that this would stop; but when the girl continued, Dembowitz warned her that this would not be tolerated. When she persisted, he visited the orphanage again; and this time, the girl confessed to being Jewish. Her attempts to convert the others had been a ploy to avoid detection. Dembowitz arranged for her release and had her moved to the Heidelberg Jewish community.[82]

When Chaplain Mayer Abramowitz of the Third Division Headquarters arrived at Bad Wildugen, he found an established Jewish community of approximately forty families. Like Chaplain Ernest Lorge, who had preceded him, Abramowitz provided them with army supplies. He also helped in converting a building in Marburg into a synagogue, smoothed the way for a Jewish newspaper to be published, and helped the displaced persons in trouble with the military and German police.

At least once a week, Abramowitz traveled from Kassel to Fulda visiting cities and towns in the area. During this fifteen hundred mile journey, he found many displaced persons. In Bad Hamburg, he discovered sixty to seventy young girls and gave them nylon stockings, lipstick, and cosmetics. These items, he learned, had more healing power than bread and butter. In another town, Abramowitz found a group of survivors about to be evicted from their homes. Through his intervention, they were allowed to remain. Of all the places he visited, he enjoyed Kibbutz Buchenwald the most. He officiated at their weddings; and when leaders of the kibbutz asked for fake orders authorizing them to travel to France, he readily complied. Abramowitz saw it as his responsibility to make the lives of the displaced persons better and to help them get to Palestine.

In July 1946 Abramowitz was transfered to Headquarters Berlin District. There he set up a package program, worked with the Berihah, and established an ombudsman at Schlactensee who reported all problems at the displaced persons camp to a review committee that he chaired. His cordial relationship with the provost marshal of Berlin helped the displaced persons avoid potential conflicts with the German police and the American military.

Another of the major projects he undertook was to establish one of the largest schools for children in the American zone.[83] By the end of 1946, children under the age of six accounted for 8 percent of the population. Another 12 percent were between the ages of six and seventeen. In part, this increase was a result of people arriving from Russia with their families. In addition, the survivors were eager to rebuild their lives even under these adverse conditions, and marriages proliferated. By the winter of 1946, a thousand babies were born each month.[84]

This high birthrate did not mean that they lacked information about birth control, Leo Srole observed: "Rather, it can be explained by two factors: children are needed as pillars of a normal life; and the traditional high valuation placed upon children among Jews as a foundation for group survival has been still further heightened by the slaughter of almost an entire generation of Jewish children."[85]

After finding a few teachers, he had them inform the Jews at the Schlachtensee and Tempelhof displaced persons camps and the Berlin Jewish community that a new program would be introduced to educate the Jewish children in the area. All those with educational background were asked to attend a teacher training program.

Part 1 of the weekly sessions at the chaplain's center included a lecture on pedagogical methodology. This was followed by a group discussion of the problems of living in the camps, with suggestions of how to cope with them. During the third period the trainees socialized, sang, danced, and ate. All the participants were given coffee, chocolate, cigarettes, and nylon stockings as payment for their time. In keeping with Abramowitz' philosophy of not being the visible supplier of goods, these items were distributed by the displaced persons themselves.

Within a short time, two schools were established with a joint enrollment of three thousand children. They began at the junior high level and went through high school. A number of graduates went on to the University of Berlin. Hebrew was the language of instruction so that there would be a common means of communication; for some, it would prepare them for life in Palestine. Finding textbooks became a major problem. When Abramowitz asked the JDC for help, they sent him hundreds of "old *chumashim* (bibles) and torn *siddurim* (prayer books)." Since the books could not be used, he secured thousands of reams of paper and everything else needed to reproduce these materials. He then went to a German printer and ordered him to duplicate nine different textbooks. The printer refused; but Abramowitz bribed him with coal, cigarettes, and coffee. Approximately fifteen thousand volumes were published.[86]

Abramowitz also found activities for the children during the summer. It is not known who originated the idea of setting up a summer camp, but Abramowitz played a major part in acquiring the land for the site. The Children's Summer Camp was held at Schloss Bruninglinden Kladow in the British zone and was sponsored by the British miliary government in Berlin. The JDC supported and supervised the camp together with a Jewish relief unit from England. Groups of children were rotated every few weeks so that as many as possible could attend. Abramowitz visited the camp whenever he could.[87]

Survivors who knew Abramowitz in Berlin told of the many hours he spent listening to their stories and problems, talking to them about Palestine, and teaching them Zionist songs. Some attribute their desire to emigrate to Palestine to him. His warmth and enthusiasm was contagious, and the Friday night services and the Passover Seder he conducted are still vividly remembered.[88] One Jewish offical described Abramowitz as having "actually breathed life into the displaced persons community in Berlin where he was both repected for his achievements and admired for his charming disposition. He deserves a unique place of honor in the story of the *Shearit Hapletah.*"[89]

Yosef Miller was another chaplain who worked with children in Germany on a regular basis. He, together with a group of Jewish soldiers known as the Frankfurt Jewish GI Council, spent many Sundays visiting children and adults in a number of displaced persons camps within a ninety-mile radius of Frankfurt. Among the camps visited were Zeilsheim, Bensheim, Wetzlar, Babenhausen, Lindenfels, Dieburg, Lampertheim, and Schwartzenborn. The children in these camps were taken on picnics and treated to Purim and Hanukkah parties. Books, newspapers, and other educational materials for libraries were purchased; and sports equipment was secured for the young and the adults.[90]

The chaplains attempted to raise the morale of the displaced persons also by trying to prevent incidents from arising between the survivors, the army, the Germans, and non-Jewish displaced persons. If this failed, the chaplains came to the survivors' defense. As has already been noted, the military government legal officers often treated Jews in an unjust and arbitrary manner, creating a climate in which the German population felt free to express its hostility toward the Jews, as well. In this environment, the chaplains spent much time obtaining the release of Jews from jail, having their sentences reduced, and preventing the military from launching black market raids in the displaced persons camps.

When Joseph Shubow learned that Jews were being abused by other displaced persons at the UNRRA camp in Berlin and that camp

Children's outing from Dieberg. Center, Corporal David Marcus of the Frankfurt Jewish GI Council. (Photo courtesy of the Mintzer Collection, Magnes Museum.)

officials were preventing children over the age of three from entering the facility with their families, he quickly intervened. He warned those harassing the Jews that this behavior would no longer be tolerated and he stopped UNRRA from splitting up Jewish families.

When Shubow discovered that German police and workers were insulting and mistreating Jews in a camp in the French zone of occupation, he went to the camp and demanded that the harassment end immediately. The day after Shubow returned to Berlin, Colonel Howley, head of the military government of Berlin, and General R. W. Barker, commanding general of Berlin, called him to their office to scold him for interferring in a camp outside the American sector. After Shubow explained why he went, Howley congratulated him and said, "More power to you, Chaplain, remember we are on your side. We are rooting for you."[91]

Chaplain Leo Ginsburg, a forty-six-year-old Orthodox rabbi attached to the 100th Division who replaced Herbert Eskin in Stuttgart, spent much of each day keeping Jews out of jail for dealing in the black market or for stealing German goods. He also succeeded in halting a raid the army had planned for the displaced persons living quarters in the city.[92]

Chaplain Yosef Miller adds some numbers to the door prize chart at a Purim party while his assistant David Marcus smiles. (Photo courtesy of the Mintzer Collection, Magnes Museum.)

This problem was not limited to Germany. In March 1946 Chaplain Nathan Barack became a troubleshooter when Jews in the British zone asked him to intervene with the British military. In that month he received a call from Jews in Trieste who said that several displaced persons on their way to Palestine from Yugoslavia had been caught and were imprisoned by the British. After Barack telephoned Major J. A. Kellett, the British displaced persons officer in Trieste, the Jews were released. Major Kellett arranged for them to be housed and fed and then allowed to go on their way.

Just before Passover, Barack received another phone call about the detention of Jews, but this time he went to Trieste to speak with Major Kellett personally. The Jews were released; but soon after, the British tried to put an end to Jewish infiltratrion from Yugoslavia. Early in May, Barack was informed that eighteen Jews had been imprisoned in Udine for not having passports. He was asked to intervene; but when he attempted to visit the imprisoned Jews, the request was denied. Barack turned to the JDC for help, but they could do nothing. He then spoke to the officers at the Eighty-Eighth

Division; but they felt that since it was an international matter, he should not become involved.

After waiting two months to see these incarcerated Jews, Barack went to the prison in Udine accompanied by Captain George Frederick of the 313th Medical Detachment. They found that the sanitation in the cells was primitive, that the displaced persons suffered from vitamin deficiency, that they were in a nervous state, and that they were being treated as criminals. After Barack and Frederick objected to this treatment, the British agreed to release them.[93]

Barack was one of seven chaplains in Italy at the beginning of 1946; but by August, practically all of them had returned to the United States after having finished their tours of duty. Until August, Barack remained active in the northern part of the country.

7

THE SEARCH FOR A SOLUTION

An Impasse

At times it appeared that without a resolution of their statelessness, the Jews would languish in Germany and Austria for many more years. Frustrated by this possibility, the Palestinians and President Truman continued to seek their own solutions. In 1945 and 1946 the Haganah, through the Mossad, its illegal immigration department, took control of Berihah and Haganah activities in Europe. A secret high command was established in Paris to direct the operation under Shaul Avigur, founder of the Mossad.[1]

Under extremely difficult circumstances, the Mossad purchased ships, prepared them for travel, enlisted crews composed of foreign sailors and volunteers from the Palmach, the Haganah's elite troops, and established a radio communications system. Hazardous and overcrowded conditions on small unseaworthy vessels and the danger of being caught and arrested by the British did not deter thousands of survivors of all ages from Germany, Italy, Austria, Soviet-controlled Bulgaria and Rumania, and Arab countries from risking their lives for the chance of reaching Palestine. Only a small percentage of those who wanted to make the voyage were able to do so. In 1946, 21,711 Jews arrived in Palestine aboard twenty-two ships; between August 1945 and May 1948, sixty-five ships brought 69,878 Jews. Without a large network of disguised transports and camps and the support of Yugoslavs, French, Italians, and others who opposed the British policy of preventing Jews from entering Palestine, this operation would not have been possible.[2]

In Palestine, three distinct armed Jewish groups—each with its own approach—were involved in the fight against the British. The Haganah, under the control of the Jewish Agency, was the largest, with 40,000 members in 1946. By pressuring the British, the Haganah had hoped to convince them that the Yishuv could thwart any solution it deemed anti-Zionist. The Irgun Zvai Leumi (National Military Organization—IZL), with 300 fighters and a total membership of approximately 1,500 men, had declared war against the British in 1944. Led by Menachem Begin, the IZL wanted to force the British out of Palestine and establish an independent Jewish state. The Lechi (Fighters for the Freedom of Israel)—also known as the Stern Gang, after its founder, Abraham Stern—with about 300 men, of whom 120 were fighters, was the most violent of the three. Only violence could drive the British out of Palestine, it believed.[3]

The Haganah, IZL, and Lechi joined forces during the autumn of 1945 to become the Tnuat Hameri (Jewish Resistance Movement) after concluding that the British would not allow substantial numbers of Jews to enter Palestine or permit political autonomy for the Yishuv. Military force against the British would be intensified, they decided. From autumn 1945 to July 1946 these forces sabotaged oil refineries, radar stations, railroads, bridges, airfields, and other military targets. The Haganah and IZL avoided attacking civilians and warned the British in most cases, to avoid casualties.

After the Haganah destroyed most of the bridges linking Palestine to neighboring Arab countries on the night of June 17, 1946, the British launched an intensive two-week search to apprehend the Jewish leadership. Beginning on Saturday June 29 (Black Sabbath), the British captured many Jewish Agency officials and placed them in detention. They failed, however, to find the high-ranking leadership or uncover any significant arms caches.[4]

This action, nevertheless, convinced the Jewish Agency of the futility of continuing an armed struggle against a superior military force. The Haganah decided, instead, to channel its energies into illegal immigration. Tnuat Hameri ended in July 1946, after the IZL blew up a wing of the King David Hotel in Jerusalem housing the British civil administration in Palestine. The British had been forewarned by the IZL, but the information had not been passed on to others in the building. The Haganah agreed to the operation; but when over ninety people died in the explosion, it severed its relationship with the IZL. Black Sabbath did not deter IZL and Lechi; if anything, it increased the IZL's tendency for more violence.[5]

In August the British increased its attack against the Yishuv by expelling illegal immigrants caught trying to enter the country to detention camps in Cyprus. Approximately fifty-one thousand Jews spent nearly two years in these camps, but British countermeasures seemed only to strengthen the resolve of others to reach Palestine. Moreover, the sight of the Royal British Navy scouring the seas in search of Holocaust survivors aboard decrepit ships did little to enhance its image throughout the world.[6]

By the summer of 1946, unexpected events in Europe and the Middle East forced Truman to rethink American policy toward the displaced persons. Articles in the American press about Palestine were headline news; the British government insisted that it would not implement the Anglo–American Committee's recommendations without American military and financial support and until the "illegal" Jewish and Arab armies had been stripped of their weapons and disbanded; and the number of Jewish displaced persons in Central Europe had increased significantly.[7]

Truman opposed the use of the American military in Palestine and ruled out the possibility of the United States' acting as a trustee or a cotrustee in Palestine. When British foreign secretary Ernest Bevin urged that an Anglo–American Committee of experts be appointed to reconcile the differences between the two nations, Truman agreed.[8]

The British sought American involvement in Palestine because its own general position in the Middle East was threatened. With the anticipated loss of bases in Iraq and Egypt, Britain wanted to remain in Palestine. To ensure its continued rule it needed a political solution acceptable to the Arabs that would stop Jewish resistance and curtail illegal immigration.[9]

In June 1946 Truman established the Grady Commission (a cabinet committee responsible for working with the British to implement the recommendations of the Anglo–American Committee) under the chairmanship of Henry F. Grady, an assistant secretary of state. Truman informed the commission that, if necessary, the United States could accept fifty thousand displaced persons if the British would admit a hundred thousand into Palestine. At the end of the month, Grady and his committee flew to London to meet Herbert Morrison and his group of experts for intensive discussions. During the summer, Truman also explored the possibility of having Jews admitted into Latin America and the British dominions. He met with representatives from Latin America and with members of the House and Senate immigration committees.[10]

On August 16, Truman announced his intention to ask Congress for legislation allowing an unspecified number of displaced persons into the United States. He had originally thought of suggesting three hundred thousand but decided not to indicate an exact amount. Given the American public's opposition to increased immigration, this became a wise decision. In late August, a Gallup poll revealed that 72 percent were against Truman's proposal to permit more Jews and other European refugees to enter the United States, only 16 percent approved, and 12 percent had no opinion.[11]

This proposed legislation, interpreted by many in the American Jewish community as a sign that Truman had abandoned any hope of persuading the British to allow a hundred thousand Jews to enter Palestine, caused tensions between Zionists and non-Zionists. Before Truman's proposal, the non-Zionists, who opposed the establishment of a Jewish state, supported the idea of a hundred thousand Jews going to Palestine as a humanitarian gesture. Once it appeared the Jews would not be permitted to enter Palestine, the non-Zionists launched a major initiative to bring them to the United States.[12]

With the support of many prominent non-Jews, the non-Zionists worked hard to enact the United States Displaced Persons Acts of 1948 and 1950, which brought more than four hundred thousand displaced persons to the United States by the end of 1952;[13] approximately sixty-eight thousand of whom were Jews. Between this legislation and the Truman directive, less than a hundred thousand Jews came to the United States.[14] Had it not been for Patrick McCarran (D), senior Senator from Nevada, more would have reached America. As chairman of the Senate Judiciary Committee, McCarran effectively delayed displaced persons legislation so that by the time it passed, most Jews had immigrated to Israel and other countries. McCarran, an isolationist who viewed himself as guardian of the national interest, did not like Jews and had an ongoing dislike for the president since the 1930s.[15]

On July 31, 1946, the Morrison–Grady Committee submitted its report to the British Parliament. It proposed that Palestine be divided into separate Arab and Jewish provinces with each community maintaining self-rule in domestic affairs and with the British in control of foreign relations, defense, the courts, police, customs, and communications. A hundred thousand Jews would be admitted to Palestine during the first year the plan was implemented, but any future immigration would be determined by the British.[16]

Fearing that the adoption of the plan would prevent the establishment of a sovereign Jewish state, the Jewish Agency executive called a meeting in Paris on August 2, 1946, to formulate a Zionist response. Given the increasing number of Jews fleeing into the American zone, the growing demoralization in the displaced persons camps, and the fear the Americans might stop trying to influence the British, the Zionist executive agreed that a viable partition plan was their best alternative proposal. Their other options were binationalism, trusteeship, and partition.[17] Nahum Goldmann, chairman of the Jewish Agency's American section, argued in favor of partition and against the other alternatives. Binationalism would be impractical, since the Arabs would not agree to parity; and even if they did, there would be no unanimity on political issues. Trusteeship would require a British presence, and the British were anti-Zionist. Partition was the only solution because it would separate Jews and Arabs, thus reducing potential conflict and simultaneously promoting economic competition.[18]

Goldmann brought the partition proposal to the American government and convinced key members of the Truman administration and the American Jewish Committee of its wisdom. Truman informed the British on August 12 that he rejected the Morrison–Grady Plan because "the opposition in this country to this plan has become so intense that it is now clear it would be impossible to rally in favor of it sufficient public opinion to enable this government to give effective support." Truman assured them that he would continue to seek a solution and indicated the American Embassy's willingness to discuss the partition plan that Nahum Goldmann had advanced.[19]

On August 30, 1946, Goldmann asked either Truman or Dean Acheson, acting secretary of state, for a statement endorsing partition. The State Department and the joint chiefs of staff approved the suggestion out of fear of antagonizing the British and alienating the Arabs. Truman's response came on October 4, the eve of Yom Kippur, in his annual greetings to American Jewry. He endorsed the idea of partition and called for a "substantial" increase in immigration to Palestine to begin immediately.[20]

Realizing they could not reach a joint solution with the Americans, the British turned to the Jews and Arabs for a last attempt at imposing a new British plan. Each group rejected the proposal—the Jews because it offered "neither an independent state nor an autonomous province," the Arabs because it allowed for more Jewish immigration.[21] Britain was clearly at an impasse. It could neither sanction the creation of a Jewish state without fear of losing its influence nor establish an independent Arab state in Palestine, thus shutting the door to hundreds of thousands of Jewish displaced persons. Without a policy acceptable to both, the British "drifted along aimlessly," satisfying neither party "yet arousing the ire of each."[22]

Tension Between Chaplains and the Army

The military often overlooked much of what the chaplains did for displaced persons if they remained discreet, did not cause them embarrassment, and were not neglecting their military duties. When supplies from the package program began appearing on the black market, the army began an investigation. Throughout the postwar period the black market had been a problem for the army because so many of its own personnel were involved.

In one month alone, the GIs in Berlin sent to the United States "84,000,000 more dollars than they earned." The biggest operators were generally the officers. It was not uncommon for them to leave "the work on their desks to make deals in the street." The army was slow to react to this problem because "the practice was so prevalent and involved so many high ranking officers," that it became difficult "to know where and how to start a stiff program of correction." The army could not ignore it completely, since it was part of an overall breakdown in discipline among the American military in Germany.[23]

Even before General McNarney started a crackdown on discipline in the army in April 1946, investigations into the package programs had begun. The military had assumed that since the packages were addressed to chaplains, they were responsible for what was happening. Most chaplains had very little to do with the packages once they arrived. Chaplain Max Wall, for example, received several tons of material each day that he immediately turned over to a special group of displaced persons responsible for distributing them.

Although the chaplains knew the packages ended up in the black market, they understood that the displaced persons had no other means to obtain the items they needed. Many agreed with Leo Srole that this phenomenon had to be viewed in its proper perspective: "In the first place no controlled, rational economy operating under acute shortages of necessities had ever been free of clandestine trade. Nor are any elements now in occupied Germany immune to the temptations it offers. However, . . . among all elements so engaged, the displaced Jews, being legally destitute, have least to contribute to the commodities that are the traffic of the market. If all the displaced persons in Germany were resettled tomorrow, the traffic would be diminished in no important way."[24]

In early 1946, Max Wall came under investigation because packages addressed to him were being used in black market transactions. Fortunately for Wall, one of those involved in the inquiry was the former inspector general of the Ninth Infantry. He knew Wall and convinced his colleagues that there had been no criminal intent. All charges were dropped and Wall left Germany on April 16, 1946. Before departing, Wall signed a statement absolving the postal system from any further responsibility for the packages. Had he been convicted, Wall could theoretically have been sent to prison.[25]

To ensure that the mails would not be misused again, Chaplain Paul Gorin instructed Jewish chaplains in the Third Army to turn over all unauthorized packages to the JDC and inform the senders not to post any more packages. Although other chaplains were investigated for alleged misuse of the mails, none received more than a formal reprimand.[26]

Many chaplains informed their sources to cease sending packages, but others continued to receive and distribute them. The GI Council, for example, initiated a package program in July or August that continued for about a year. The council had been established in June 1946 by David Bar-El (Schachter) and Eliezer Dembitz with the aid of Chaplain Yosef Miller. Both Bar-El and Dembitz were American-born Jews who lived with their parents in Palestine. As United States citizens they were drafted into the American military and arrived in Germany in April 1946.

The council, which began with twenty-five GIs, was dedicated to helping all Jewish displaced persons within a "reasonable radius" of Frankfurt. During the first year they emphasized direct relief. The needs of the Jews in the displaced persons camps were determined, and supplies were secured. At first, most of the provisions were obtained from packages sent to GIs by parents and relatives; from the local army supply depot, which unofficially provided blankets, sheets, and underwear; from the PX, which often gave Chaplain Miller toys, candy, and toothpaste; and from GIs, who bought supplies from the PX with monies accumulated from bingo games and a nylon stocking raffle.[27] But much more was needed. In his Friday evening sermons Chaplain Miller described the terrible conditions in the displaced persons camps and asked for help. In requesting assistance, the council stated that it was not its "aim to try and outdo the many excellent organizations already working to solve the many problems of supply." It merely wanted to supplement these efforts.[28]

After one service, Johnny Low (Yehuda Lev), a Jewish GI, told Miller that he could obtain much of what they needed from the Forest Hills Jewish Community Center in New York, where his parents were members. Ben Zion Bokser, rabbi of the center, urged his congregation to help and also enlisted the support of the local churches. Initially, hundreds of twenty-two-pound packages were sent each week. Within a short time a more efficient means of transportation had to be found. Mrs. Rosamund Low, who had maintained a collection point for supplies in her home, approached the JDC, which agreed to provide the shipping. Almost twenty-three tons were sent via the JDC.[29] On Sundays, the packages were distributed by Miller and the soldiers to the survivors at nearby displaced persons camps. Along with providing relief, the council wanted "to instill some hope for the future into persons deadened by the past"[30] and to demonstrate that American Jews cared for

Basement of Mr. and Mrs. Sol Low in Forest Hills, New York. There, they and their friends packed hundreds of packages for the Frankfurt Jewish GI Council. (Photo courtesy of the Mintzer Collection, Magnes Museum.)

them. The soldiers engaged the survivors in recreational activities, visited the sick, and listened to their stories.

The overwhelming response to the council's request for packages became a source of embarrassment to the JDC despite its own involvement in shipping them. In April 1947, the JDC admonished the council and Miller for soliciting packages, since many American Jews questioned the need for this project in the light of the JDC's own activities in Germany. The council terminated the program sometime in late February or early March 1947, when David Marcus (Rabbi Miller's assistant) received a reprimand from the United States government for illegally using the mails.

With the end of the package program, the council shifted its emphasis to rehabilitation, following the pattern of the major relief organizations. The council continued until the early 1950s, when most of the displaced persons and army personnel left. Although Miller remained in Frankfurt only until early 1947, David Marcus and other GIs carried on in the direction that he had set.[31]

Chaplains Abraham Klausner, Herbert Friedman, and Meyer Goldman also came under investigation by the military, but for different reasons. Klausner had tried unsuccessfully to send Zalman

Grinberg to the United States in late 1945 to speak to the leadership of American Jewry about the survivors. Although Klausner's initial attempt had been thwarted by Jacob Trobe of the JDC and Judge Rifkind, Klausner managed to have Grinberg invited to the United States in early 1946 by the American Jewish Conference. Since Grinberg had no means of traveling to America, Klausner prepared an identity card and travel documents authorizing him to proceed by "first available air transportation"[32] to New York via Paris. In Paris, Grinberg was stopped because displaced persons were not allowed to fly on military planes. Inquiries were made to Munich; and as a result of a change in travel procedures and the help of an American officer, Grinberg managed to elude further detection.

When he arrived in the United States the Federal Bureau of Investigation detained Grinberg after it discovered that his travel documents were forgeries. Only after the American Jewish Conference intervened did they allow him to remain in the country.[33] During his twenty-three-day stay, Grinberg spoke at the third session of the American Jewish Conference and addressed the biennial council of the Union of American Hebrew Congregations in Cincinnati. He also delivered a major speech at a mass meeting held by the American Jewish Conference in New York and met with representatives of the JDC, the WJC, Hadassah, the Federation of Temple Sisterhoods, the (Reform) Jewish Institute of Religion (the oldest rabbinical seminary in the United States) and the press.

In Washington, Grinberg met with Major General John S. Hilldring; Herbert H. Lehman, director general of UNRRA; George L. Warren, assistant to the secretary of state and advisor on refugees and displaced persons; and Jewish members of Congress. His views on the conditions in the camps were incorporated into an American Jewish Conference memorandum submitted to a congressional subcommittee studying the problem of the displaced persons.

I. L. Kenen, executive secretary of the American Jewish Conference, hailed Grinberg's visit as a success: "He made a profound impression, not only on Government officials, but on the American Jewish Conference and every other audience he addressed." One of Grinberg's most significant achievements, Kenen believed, was that "he did a great deal to neutralize many who have hitherto been antagonistic to our viewpoint" concerning Palestine.[34]

In his speeches, Grinberg asserted that the majority of the survivors wanted to emigrate to Palestine. He delivered his most persuasive speech at the convention of the Union of American Hebrew Congregations. Graphically describing conditions in the camps, he told of the despair and disillusionment among the survivors: "Liberation was the greatest disillusionment of all. It is better today in Germany to be a conquered German than a liberated Jew. There is no ground under our feet, no permanent roof over our heads. . . . We can not think of tomorrow. We think only of yesterday. We live still with the dead."

The solution to the problem, Grinberg believed, was Palestine: "We wish to go to Palestine. We want to leave the soil of Europe forever. Every day spent on the soil of Europe is a day spent with our past. . . . We believe we have learned what is best for us." All he wanted was that they "should do nothing to make our task more difficult." He knew there were non-Zionists and anti-Zionists in the audience but asked that they not place any obstacles in their way.

This plea moved Alfred Segal, a writer for the Anglo–Jewish press. In "The Man from Dachau," an article reviewing Grinberg's speech at the Union of American Hebrew Congregations, Segal described his personal reactions. Although he opposed the idea of a Jewish state in Palestine, he decided, "I don't have to make a fight about it, to stand in the way of those homeless people striving toward a safe place. The little man from Dachau certainly had a right to command me to get out of the way and keep still."[35]

Grinberg was moved by the warm reception he received in the United States but disturbed that the American Jewish community did not understand the problems facing the survivors. The Jews of America "are a good people and want to do what they can to assist us," declared Grinberg upon his return to Germany. "Unfortunately, not many of them understand us nor begin to conceive of the tragedy we experienced. Let us do what we can to awaken them in our cause."[36] Grinberg's observations convinced Klausner even more that American Jewry had to be constantly informed about the problems of the displaced persons.

When the American military learned how Grinberg reached the United States, Klausner came under investigation because he had demonstrated that security was lax. The army was particularly embarrassed by its inability to prove that Grinberg had returned to Germany. They assigned an officer to the case; and after investigating Klausner, he found that nothing sinister had been intended.[37]

Another episode involving Klausner that came to the attention of the army was the establishment of a Jewish hospital in Munich. Dr. Pesachowitz, chairman of the Health Committee of the central committee, had urged Klausner to establish a hospital because of the survivors' psychological fear of being treated by German physicians. During early 1946, when Klausner was officially assigned to the Ninety-Eighth General Hospital, he approached his superiors with the idea. After they rejected the project, he learned about the Bogenhausen Hospital run by a Catholic religious order. Since the hospital had been established during the war, he felt that the Jews had certain claims to it as well.

On his own, Klausner began moving Jewish patients and doctors into the hospital. When Dr. Pesachowitz asked to be placed in charge of the institution, Klausner approached Major Marvin Linick, an American Jewish GI, who controlled the hospital.[38] Linick rejected the proposal because he did not want to single Jews out for special treatment. The Nazis had made everything a Jewish issue; he did not want to do the same. Furthermore, he felt that since there were non-Jews who fought against Hitler, it would be wrong to deny them access to the hospital.[39]

Klausner was determined to secure the hospital and enlisted the help of Ann Liepah,[40] who had assisted him on previous occasions. Liepah went to see Linick and persuaded him to turn the hospital over to them. His only stipulation was that it not become a Jewish hospital. They formally took charge during the week of April 25, 1946. Within a short time thereafter, Klausner turned the hospital into a Jewish facility.[41]

When Jack Whiting, zone director of UNRRA, heard of Ann Liepah's role in obtaining the hospital, he complained to Leo Schwarz, his counterpart in the JDC. Schwarz investigated and found that Liepah had been "the source of considerable criticism on the part of UNRRA and Army officials in the Third District" because of her "buccaneer behavior" and inability to work within the military system. To avoid further problems, he ordered her demobilized. Klausner and Liepah reacted to Schwarz's order by threatening to have the central committee organize protests against him. Moreover, they and the committee made representations to UNRRA.[42] Although the central committee sided with Klausner and Liepah, it did not really matter, since both would soon be transferred out of the area.

The army and UNRRA had enough of Klausner and his unorthodox approach to helping the displaced persons. When Klausner requested an extension of his military tour of duty (which he completed in the latter half of 1946), he was turned down. To keep Klausner in Europe, Haim Yahil agreed to assign him to the Jewish Agency; but after Jack Whiting raised objections, Yahil withdrew the offer. Klausner had no alternative but to leave.[43] From the United States, he would plan his return to Germany.

The central committee was so distressed by Klausner's departure that it appealed to its friends in the United States to send him back, declaring:

From the moment of our long awaited liberation to this day, our Chaplain Klausner, responsibly and energetically has waged an incomparable battle in our behalf. His sacrifice has been without parallel in this recent page of Jewish history. Chaplain Klausner has worked with us and for us and through his work has become a friend of the suffering, daily carrying their burdens and alleviating their pains. In addition, the Chaplain has been the life giving spirit of the organized Jewish existence. His unexpected departure leaves a vacancy that can not be filled. We express our sincerest hope, a wish and a prayer and trust that on their wings, Chaplain Klausner will be brought back to us. During his absence we will constantly think of him as one of us. We know that wherever he will go, he will labour proudly on behalf of the many problems that face his *Shearit Hapletah*.[44]

By the time Klausner was released from the army on October 24, 1946,[45] a number of projects he initiated were either being completed or were already finished. A building at 11 Neuberghauser Strasse was requisitioned and plans called for it to house a school, a kitchen, a theater, a synagogue, a *mikveh* (ritual bath) and a yeshiva; sixty *sifrei Torah* were delivered to the JDC religious director of Germany; a number of businesses and factories run by displaced persons were in operation; and a press for *Unzer Weg* was to be transferred to the central committee. In addition, Klausner had encouraged and supported the Munich Writers' Union and was involved with the central committee's Historical Commission.[46]

In August 1946 the commission began publishing *Fun Letzten Churben* (Of the Recent Destruction) under the editorship of Israel Kaplan, a Lithuanian Jew. This was the first time the survivors dealt with the destruction of European Jewry in a systematic manner. Articles in the first issue discussed Jewish folklore during the Nazi regime, ghetto songs, and the first concert in the Vilna ghetto. It also presented eyewitness accounts of what happened in Radom, Poland; a list of articles about Jewish life under the Nazis that appeared in the *Shearit Hapletah* press; Nazi documents; and pictures of Jews during the Holocaust.[47] Another project undertaken by the commission was to record ghetto and concentration camp songs.[48]

Throughout his stay in the United States, Klausner received detailed accounts about the displaced persons and requests for aid from JDC personnel, who were eager for him to return. The letters were full of requests for aid from displaced persons urging his immediate return. With help from Chaplain Morris Dembowitz, he arranged to send a million units of penicillin each week.[49]

Herbert Friedman also came under the intense scrutiny of the military and almost faced court-martial for violating army regulations. At the end of the war, the American Army found hundreds of thousands of Jewish books and ritual objects in Germany and brought them to the I. G. Farben warehouse in Offenbach. After months of negotiation with Chaplain Emanuel Rackman, the army eventually decided that whenever possible, identifiable items would be returned to their former owners. Books and objects that remained were given to the Cultural Reconstruction Corporation, which was assigned to distribute them according to criteria that had not yet been established.

Thousands of books were loaned to displaced persons camps under a program administered by Koppel S. Pinson of the JDC. Although only Pinson was authorized to sign for these books, there was concern about how the Germans working in the warehouse were handling them. During the latter part of 1946, Gershon Scholem, world-renowned scholar and professor of Jewish mysticism and Kabbalah at the Hebrew University in Palestine, arrived to sort out the most valuable of these items. Eleven hundred were selected and put into five crates.

Herbert Friedman was so concerned about the welfare of this valued treasure that he decided to do something about it on his own. On December 30, 1946, he went to the Offenbach warehouse with an ambulance borrowed from the JDC and with the help of Captain Isaac Bencowitz, the director of the depot, loaded the crates on to the vehicle. He then took the books by train to the Jewish Agency office in Paris, where they were sent to Scholem in Jerusalem.

The army discovered that the books were stolen; and an investigation linked the theft to Friedman. Before acknowledging his guilt to army investigators, he informed Philip Bernstein; and together they went to see General Clay. After this meeting, court-martial proceedings against Friedman were dropped, and no disciplinary action was taken against him. He did, however, receive an administrative admonition stating that his usefulness to the army had come to an end. At Friedman's suggestion, the books were turned over to the U. S. Consulate in Jerusalem, where they remained until a final decision about their disposition could be reached.

Friedman left Germany in May 1947 and was supposed to report to Camp Kilmer in New Jersey for discharge. When he arrived in the United States, Henry Morgenthau, Jr., former secretary of the treasury, asked him to speak at an emergency United Jewish Appeal (UJA) conference in Pennsylvania. He had arranged with the secretary of war for him to take this assignment. Friedman's talk was so successful that Morgenthau, who was then national chairman for the UJA, decided to have him speak around the country for the next month. At the end of the month, Friedman reported to Camp Kilmer where he was immediately arrested for being absent without leave. For four days, he sat in the post jail until a cable arrived from the secretary of war explaining that he had been authorized to speak for the UJA. On July 18, 1947, Friedman was officially discharged from the army and became executive director of the UJA.[50]

The Stars and Stripes article describing Chaplain Friedman's removal of rare Jewish books from Offenbach storehouse. (Photo courtesy of the Mintzer Collection, Magnes Museum.)

While most chaplains avoided bringing attention to their work with the survivors, Meyer Goldman chose to make an issue of his not being allowed to visit displaced persons installations. For some time, Goldman had been the only Jewish chaplain serving with the American Air Force in the entire European theater. During this period he asked permission to visit several displaced persons camps in his area. The acting staff chaplain denied his request, claiming that Goldman had enough work with the Jewish personnel in the military to keep him occupied.

Goldman complained; and when the acting staff chaplain brought the problem before the chief of staff, Goldman "was directed by the Chief of Staff to focus his attention on the military." The air force was annoyed with Goldman but wanted to avoid any misunderstandings about the incident with CANRA. Therefore, Charles I. Carpenter, a high-ranking chaplain at Air Force headquarters in Washington, sent a letter to Philip Bernstein—at that point still CANRA's executive director—explaining what had transpired.[51] Bernstein responded that "no Jewish chaplain would be worthy of the name and office, who did not do whatever he could to help these people in distress." Furthermore, it was Bernstein's understanding "that on the whole, the military authorities in Europe are sympathetic and cooperative in such matters." Bernstein reiterated his belief that "the Jewish Chaplain must not neglect his military responsibilities. It resolves itself, therefore, into a matter of judgement, tact, experience, etc., as to where the line is to be drawn."[52]

Bernstein promised Carpenter that CANRA would continue to be understanding and helpful in such matters. As a result of this correspondence, Carpenter sent a letter to the air force staff chaplain explaining Bernstein's views and suggested that the staff chaplain adopt a policy allowing the chaplains to care for the displaced persons within the areas to which they were assigned. "This approach," Carpenter assured Bernstein, "should handle the situation and accomplish what your organization feels should be accomplished and still meet the needs of the military personnel."[53]

DP Chaplains

The incident with Chaplain Goldman convinced Bernstein that problems with the military would continually occur unless the army officially sanctioned chaplains' working exclusively with the survivors. Such an arrangement was needed immediately because of the deteriorating condition of European Jews. At a meeting with Jewish chaplains in Frankfurt in August 1946 Bernstein underlined this concern when he warned: "This promises to be a grim, bitter winter for those people. Although the basic necessities of life are being provided by the army, with supplementary assistance of UN-

RRA and the JDC, the people are essentially miserable. Life in DP centers tends to be barren and drab. The normal necessities of life are absent. The prolonged delay of resettlement have [sic] robbed the people of hope."[54]

The chaplains responded to Bernstein's call by asking General McNarney to "issue a directive giving official approval to unit commanders to utilize Jewish chaplains for DP work, as necessary" and by asking the general to "request ten additional Jewish chaplains exclusively for DP work."[55] This increase was imperative, the chaplains asserted, particularly during the critical winter months of 1946/47.

After some negotiation, McNarney agreed to the request for ten additional chaplains. Bernstein observed in a letter to the chief of chaplains that McNarney understood that displaced persons work required "a tremendous amount of attention and careful handling from the military and, also, that the Jewish chaplain, combining within himself the office of rabbi and the role of American military officer, is the most effective person to handle delicate, difficult, tense situations."[56]

In early October, Luther D. Miller, chief of chaplains, informed the JWB that the army did not have the men on duty that McNarney wanted and asked that they provide them.[57] According to the agreement, the DP chaplains were to be in Europe during the winter. At the end of six months, their service could be extended if General McNarney and the chaplains requested it. A call went out to the American rabbinate; and although a number of former chaplains expressed interest in this assignment, only three actually came forward. An additional three were recruited from those already in Europe, whose military service had ended. A special agreement was reached whereby they were permitted to remain.[58]

While Bernstein saw this tour of duty as a "rare opportunity for direct service to the group of Jews most in need of such help,"[59] he was not overly concerned by this poor response. He had requested ten rabbis; although only six volunteered, the Jews did not suffer. The army made sure that no Jew died of cold or hunger in the American zones of Germany and Austria during the winter months. Furthermore, Bernstein realized that there were problems in getting chaplains on such short notice.

Only a limited number of chaplains could be approached. Older rabbis could not be considered because the military rarely commissioned chaplains in their late thirties or early forties even during war time. Until November 1946, the army refused to take recent seminary graduates directly from civilian life. Since several months were needed to train these men, it served no purpose to bring them over at that time.[60] This meant that only those chaplains who had recently served in Europe could be asked.

Many of these men had left their families for two, three, and four years or had recently married and were under family pressure to remain at home. Some chaplains inquired about taking their families with them; and had this been a possibility, more would have volunteered to return.

Since many chaplains had embarked on new careers, anyone who chose to return to Europe would lose his position. The congregations could have encouraged their rabbis to assume this responsibility without losing their pulpits—but failed to do so. Interestingly, the leadership of American Jewry did not ask the congregations to make this sacrifice. The failure of the congregations to encourage their rabbis to go to Europe and their unwillingness to hold positions open for them (except for rabbis like Philip Bernstein, who had been with his congregation for many years) shows an insensitivity to the needs of the survivors. Without this backing, the chaplains had to decide whether it was worth uprooting themselves and their families.

Some rabbis decided that it was not worth losing their position or causing friction with their families. Others felt that with the army, the JDC, and other relief organizations in place, they could be of little service. There were those who had no interest in returning because they had done little while in Europe even when they had the opportunity to do so. Still others may have wanted to return but were unsure about their own role, since they may not have been especially effective in working with the displaced persons.[61]

If it were not possible to enlist more chaplains, Bernstein's second choice was Jewish social workers: "The best qualified American Jewish professional personnel should be working in Germany. It is shocking to find [that] our most experienced and ablest Jewish social workers remain at home." He suggested that Jewish organizations make the same "arrangements for temporary, emergency services as congregations made for Jewish chaplains during the war."[62]

Disillusionment with Displaced Person Work

Some chaplains who did return to Europe felt that it had not been worth their time. One of the most disillusioned and embittered was Abraham Klausner. Klausner returned to Germany in February 1947 through the efforts of Senator Robert A. Taft (R–Ohio). A friend had suggested that he write to the senator; and as a result Klausner received orders on January 21, 1947 recalling him to duty.[63]

Although Klausner had preferred to be stationed in Munich because it was the "nerve center" of Jewish relief activity, the military viewed him as persona non grata.[64] They assigned him to Kassel, where he served as the post chaplain. He had a good working relationship with the commanding officer, the JDC field representatives, UNRRA, and other relief agency personnel. He organized schools, had textbooks published for the children, and had time to spend individually with the displaced persons. While in Munich, Klausner did not have time for much personal contact, since he had been too busy dealing with displaced persons as a group.[65]

Klausner was appalled by the condition of the Jewish displaced persons, which had rapidly deteriorated during his six months in the United States. In a report to the executive committee of the American Jewish Conference, Klausner charged: "The rehabilitation of the people, as anticipated, had not materialized. The demoralization of the people increased rapidly. There is hardly a moral standard to which people adhere. Nothing seems to be wrong and everything can be excused, no matter how serious with a shrug of the shoulder or the oft heard comment, 'he is still a Jew'."[66]

"Step by step," he wrote, "our people are marching out of the living world, taking their places on the beggar's line with all the rights and prerogatives becoming a professional beggar. Unknowingly, all of us, the sane and the insane, the wise and the ignorant, Committee leaders and remote control executives, social workers and politicians of all shades and stripes, persist in whipping the mass towards the beggar's line." He was particularly distraught that "one third of each camp population now consists of youngsters slowly being yoked to ignominy which will strangle growth and hump each character to unfit him for participation in cooperative living. . . . The cost will be recorded in the days to come. It will be noted as a material cost and a spiritual cost."[67]

Of the approximately one hundred thousand Jewish displaced persons in the American zone, more than 80 percent were Polish Jews who had fled from Poland with the Russian Army before the Nazi invasion. After the war, they returned to Poland but in the wake of the upsurge in anti-Semitism in that country fled to Germany. A great majority of these people were idle. The Organization for Rehabilitation through Training (ORT) established rehabilitation programs in the camps but while vocational training was available, there was little opportunity for putting any skills to use.[68] "Time is healing many wounds," Klausner observed: "Slowly the Jew forgets his past sufferings and slowly he binds himself to a system that will again strangle him. He rationalizes, 'It is only for the moment'; he disbelieves his own rationalizations."[69] Some Jews found their way into "every sordid aspect of German society," including prostitution and large-scale black market transactions. Government representatives and police officials in several German communities were also involved in these illegal operations.[70]

Although not a Zionist himself, Klausner believed that the only viable solution was to send the Jews to Palestine: "There is no social force in the world today [that is] as capable as that of Palestine to mold [these people] into positive members of a Jewish society." It was difficult to convince them to emigrate, however, because as a group they were not eager to go. Judging from recent experiences of the Palestinians to recruit displaced persons for the Haganah and register them for immigration to Palestine, Klausner concluded that perhaps only 30 percent would emigrate there. Of these, many had begun to believe it unwise to leave without funds; "and since Germany is a source of 'easy money', it would be better to remain in Germany for a year or two in order to earn sufficient funds to facilitate their establishment in Palestine."[71]

To counter this attitude, Klausner urged world Jewry to insist that the displaced persons go to Palestine when given the opportunity. If they refused, they should be told they "are no longer to be wards of the Jewish community to be maintained in camps and fed and clothed without their having to make any contribution to their own subsistence." If this were not enough, Klausner advised that the Haganah should harass them and that the DP chaplains, the advisor on Jewish Affairs, and Jewish Agency personnel should be withdrawn from Europe. Jews with visas to the United States would be allowed to emigrate there.[72]

Klausner urged the American Jewish community to purchase and equip forty ships to take the displaced persons to Palestine immediately. The possibility that the English would stop the ships and imprison the Jews on Cyprus did not bother him, since there was inadequate space for everyone on the island. Even if the British found another area to imprison the survivors, it was questionable how long they would be able to be kept there. "Once out of Germany," Klausner believed, "there is no question but that the people will soon be settled in Palestine."[73]

Klausner hoped this solution would be acceptable to the American Jewish community: "He who is concerned with the huge sums of money directed towards European relief can be sold on the cheapness of the plan—fifteen million today, nothing tomorrow. He who is concerned with anti-Semitism will be relieved to know that the Jews will no longer be blamed for black marketing and the failure of the German economy. And he who is anxious to invest in the German economy could precede without qualms of conscience."[74]

"It must be borne in mind," Klausner concluded, "that we are dealing with a sick people. They are not to be asked, but to be told what to do. They will be thankful in years to come. Too many times have I been cursed in the evening, while moving masses of people, only to be thanked the following morning for having transferred them from an abominable site to a more comfortable location."[75]

Klausner did not blame the survivors alone for their present status. UNRRA and the JDC were also responsible for having failed to respond adequately to the needs of the survivors. Shortly before UNRRA turned over its responsibilities to the International Refugee Organization (IRO) on July 1, 1947, Klausner remarked: "It is too late to play with the 'If' of UNRRA history. Nevertheless, be it noted that had the people and the attitude now with the UNRRA been with the displaced peoples during the trying months following the liberation, many of the sufferings and hardships would not have come to pass."[76]

While UNRRA was past history, the problems of the JDC still remained. Klausner complained that the JDC continued "in its disorganization and consequently its limited effectiveness." Leo Schwarz had just returned to the United States after nine months "of intensive effort" to make the JDC run effectively. His departure meant that within the span of twenty months there were four directors, including his successor.[77] "Problem number one," Klausner believed, was that "of adequate personnel. A study of the turnover of employees reveals the comparatively short periods of time individuals have remained with the program, and the much shorter period of time individuals have remained with one assignment. Case after case of dissatisfaction and bickering and reassignment could be noted. Suffice it to say that with few exceptions the staff of the A[merican] JDC has not been radically improved."[78]

Leo Schwarz had made some of these same points earlier in a letter to Joseph Schwartz. Leo Schwarz had been reluctant to express his "dissatisfaction with the situation in the United States Zone," he said, because he "did not want to join the chorus of complainers and add to the complications" of "your onerous tasks." Nevertheless, he felt compelled to speak out at this point "not only for personal reasons but above all, for the best of the program."[79]

Leo Schwarz asserted:

> If I have managed to build any sort of organization in the United States Zone the results have been achieved at a huge personal cost. From the very beginning I found no policy, no guidance, no decisions and no organization. I accepted this challenge, . . . but the unwillingness of responsible personnel in all echelons of the organization to face realities in terms of handling unsuitable personnel and establishing administrative practices, complicated and almost nullified my efforts. . . . If my major energies had not perforce been diverted in trying to convert an unoriented, undisciplined staff into the semblance of a professional organization, and in trying to clear the administrative lines [with Paris], this objective might have

been achieved in four rather than in eight months; and as a consequence, we would have been in an even stronger position to cope with the increasingly complex problems of this operation.

For these reasons Leo Schwarz felt the need to explain why he "could no longer continue to carry on under the present conditions."[80]

Klausner also found fault with the JDC with regard to supply. "This problem actually is twofold," he maintained, "namely arrival and distribution of supplies." The quality of supplies remained inadequate:

> Although Joint officials are always in agreement with the contention that more is needed, I maintain that the allocations made by the Joint are sufficient if they are adequately translated into supplies. According to the 1947 allocation of 17,500,000 dollars, there should be a sufficiency in Germany in all matter of supplies. Yet, the first three months of 1947, entitled to a minimum of 3,000,000 dollars worth of supplies, had hardly received a fraction of that figure.[81]

To further "indicate the degree to which the Joint failed in its job of supply," members of the central committee brought the following examples to the attention of the leadership of American Jewry:

> The Joint was made aware of the anticipated needs created by the sudden flood of newly born children, the supplies for these children did not and have not yet arrived in any measurable quantity. The story of layettes has been told and retold, but the fact remains that even Dr. Joseph Schwartz had to report at a conference in Atlantic City that children were being wrapped in newspapers upon birth. There is no excuse for this and not even the shipping strike can justify the failure of the Joint on this particular item. Children's shoes have been needed and have not been supplied. It has been pointed out again and again that many of the children arriving from Poland had to be kept indoors because of the lack of shoes. This need is still great and is still not being met by the American JDC. Likewise, typewriters and type, often requested have still not been supplied and the matter of penicillin caused some great difficulties before that supply was made sufficient for the hospitals in Germany. Educational materials are still inadequate and since no planned program exists, such supplies are not received in sufficient quantities or according to the items of greatest need.[82]

> The quality of the clothes received was generally poor. It was impossible and it continued to be impossible for the Central Committee to contribute such garments which definitely lack dignity for the use of an individual. Consequently, in many cases, when items are distributed, the individual instead of using the particular item, manages to exchange it on the black market in addition to some other items for other articles which he will wear which will give him

the feeling of dignity in the community. It is safe to say that every decent suit being worn by the displaced Jews in Germany was either manufactured or purchased by the Central Committee, or received by the individual through an exchange on the black market.[83]

Klausner concluded:

> Any discussion of the AJDC in Germany must recognize the importance of the AJDC program especially at this time when it is anticipated that the UNRRA program will come to an end. It must also be noted that there are a number of individuals on the Joint staff doing an excellent job and rendering invaluable services to the people they serve. Nevertheless, it must likewise be emphasized that the confidence placed in the Joint, and the contributions made to the Joint, are not justified by the present program of the Joint in Germany.[84]

Since his inability to change these conditions became too frustrating for Klausner, in late 1947 he left Germany and the military. He explained his reasons in a letter to Philip Bernstein on October 10, 1947: "I must leave Germany! I do not want to, but the heartache which of late has become my companion, has the same driving force which brought me back to Germany. A hundred times a day I swear—no more! And each day as many questions appear to challenge my oaths. . . . The Jew has become his deadliest enemy here in Germany [and] I cannot battle the Jew for the sake of the Jews."[85] In another letter to Bernstein he claimed he would love to stay and work if he could "feel that we are on our way out, our way up—but this is not so, we are on our way down—we are lost and being led in that direction. . . . I can go no further for I no longer know the way."[86]

Although Klausner left disillusioned with the displaced persons, he did not abandon their cause. To ensure that his views received a hearing in the American Jewish community, Klausner met with Judges Rifkind and Levinthal and sent reports of his observations and recommendations to the American Jewish Conference. This disturbed William Haber, professor of economics at the University of Michigan, then the advisor on Jewish Affairs. Bernstein had left Germany in August 1947 to return to his pulpit in Rochester and was succeeded in July by Judge Louis Levinthal from Philadelphia. Haber succeeded Levinthal in 1948. In letters to American Jewish leaders Haber charged that while Klausner had the "zeal of a prophet," he had exaggerated the shortcomings of the displaced persons, had ascribed the moral aberrations of a few to all, and had failed to mention "the positive and constructive aspects" of Jewish life in the camps. Moreover, Klausner's solution was "unquestionably premature."[87]

In spite of Haber's denunciations, a special meeting was held in New York on May 4, 1948, at which Klausner's report was discussed and debated by representatives of the American Jewish Committee, the American Jewish Conference, the Jewish Agency for Palestine, the WJC and the JDC. Rabbis Bernstein and Klausner and Judge Levinthal were also present. While most participants felt that Klausner's proposals were unrealistic, Simon Segal of the American Jewish Committee and Philip Bernstein believed that the report had raised some very serious problems requiring immediate attention. Since no final decisions were made at the meeting, they decided to meet again.[88]

In a letter to Klausner on May 9, Samuel Steinberg, the ORT director for the United States zone in Germany from 1947 to 1948 expressed his wholehearted agreement with Klausner's main conclusions and recommendations. Steinberg believed that the vocational training program run by ORT was "overrated both qualitatively and quantitatively" because of the "lack of competent teachers, and the diffusion of effort and materials by unscrupulous leaders whose sole interest has been a paper record account for this fact." The young suffered the most because they did not receive "positive" training. For this reason, Steinberg wanted to "curtail and consolidate" the vocational training program. Fifty per cent of the funds being spent were "not only a tragic waste" but harmful to the displaced persons. The rehabilitation program had also failed, because work incentives were not strong enough, the German economy had been slow to recover, and the displaced persons found that the "attractions of the black market more compelling than the rewards of work."

Steinberg also agreed that the Jews were involved in all sorts of illegal activity, particularly in Munich, Berlin, and Frankfurt; but he did not believe they were sick. They were perplexed, bewildered, and badly frightened. Instead of harassing them into emigrating to Palestine, Steinberg suggested, "all that is needed under the circumstances is a bit of *salutary neglect.*"[89]

Steinberg also urged that "if a commission is to be appointed to go over to make a rapid, thorough, and honest survey, let men and women be chosen who are not agency career persons, who are not sentimental do-gooders, but trained individuals, qualified scientifically and Jewishly, who will be able to 'see' and 'understand' what they see and interpret their findings for the American Jewish community."[90]

Abraham Hyman, too, took issue with Klausner's solutions but shared his conviction that Jews were "rotting in the camps." As assistant to Bernstein, Levinthal, and Haber and as the last advisor on Jewish Affairs, Hyman respected Klausner as a friend and colleague.[91] Hyman agreed that the environment in Germany was debilitating and that everything should be done "to liquidate camp life the first moment that liquidation is possible." He disagreed on the timing. "In the first place," he asked Klausner, "why do you assume that our people in the camps want to continue their listless existence? When did these people have a genuine opportunity to quit the camps and when did they turn down that opportunity? Can you really blame them for not taking the illegal route when they know that some of their kin were returned to Germany, and those who were not are still living behind barbed wire in Cyprus."[92]

This discussion became a secondary issue with the establishment of the State of Israel on May 14, 1948. In February 1947 the English had asked the United Nations to help resolve the question of Palestine, expecting it to adopt Britain's solution. It foresaw no opposition from Western Europe, the Soviet Union, or Latin America. As anti-Zionists, the Russians would oppose a Jewish state, while the countries of Latin America would follow the Vatican lead in not wanting Jewish sovereignty in Palestine.

The British were mistaken. The struggle of the survivors to reach their ancient homeland had gained public sympathy in Western Europe. The Russians were prepared to support the creation of other independent states in the region if this meant the end of British rule in Palestine. The Vatican was open to compromise so long as the holy places remained accessible and internationalized, thus leaving the Latin American countries free to decide for themselves.[93]

During the summer of 1947, the United Nations established the United Nations Special Committee on Palestine (UNSCOP), an eleven-nation investigative board, to recommend a solution to the problem of Palestine. While deliberating the future of the country, a dramatic confrontation between the survivors and the British highlighted the urgency of UNSCOP's mandate.

In July 1947 the Berihah arranged a transport of forty-two hundred Jewish survivors to leave for Palestine from France on board the *President Warfield,* an American ferry renamed *Exodus, 1947.* Seventeen hundred of the Jews had French visas and arrived from Germany by train; the rest were illegally transported in motorcades.

A British escort shadowed the *Exodus* until it reached Palestine territorial waters. The British then boarded the ship and, using machine guns and gas bombs, quelled those who resisted, leaving 3 Jews dead. Another 146 were injured, 28 of whom had to be hospitalized. After the British rammed the ship, the crew of the *Exodus* surrendered, fearing it would sink if the ramming continued. The Jews were taken to the port of Haifa where they were forcibly removed and put on three British caged prison ships. Members of

UNSCOP, who were in Palestine at the time, watched this spectacle; but neither they nor the foreign press were permitted to speak with the passengers.

The Jews were sent back to France on the British prison transports arriving on August 2. They refused to disembark and the French would not force them to leave the ships. During an impasse lasting several weeks, the Jews remained on board the vessels anchored off the shores of Port-de-Bouc during the heat of the summer. The fear of an epidemic eventually prompted the French to order the ships to leave the country. The British decided to return them to Germany.

While the drama of the *Exodus* captured headlines throughout the world, UNSCOP continued its deliberations in Europe. On August 8 a subcommittee of UNSCOP arrived in Munich to investigate the situation of the displaced persons in Germany. On August 31, UNSCOP completed its report, which called for the partition of Palestine.

On September 7 the Jews from the *Exodus* arrived in Hamburg, where British troops, using hoses and clubs, carried off those who had refused to disembark. They were taken to the Poppendorf and Am Stau internment camps in the British zone, where they were once again surrounded by familiar sights and sounds: double barbed wire fences and armed guards.[94]

The Nuremburg correspondent of *Unzer Weg* arrived at Poppendorf (a former prisoner-of-war camp and the worst of the two) on the eve of Yom Kippur. He found Jews living in "broken down barracks and in . . . tents that seemed ready to topple in the first breeze." Hundreds of people were living in one barrack. Many beds had no legs, so people had to sleep on the floor. Food and water were in short supply. One young girl observed that "the boys are all hungry. The bread is terrible and unfit to eat. Many suffer from stomach trouble."[95]

Rabbi Abraham Klausner also arrived at Poppendorf on Yom Kippur eve. Shortly before the High Holidays one of the Palestinians had asked him to visit the camps to discuss plans to smuggle Jews to the American zone and from there to Palestine. Because these camps were in the British zone, Klausner needed a valid reason for the trip, especially since he was expected to conduct services for the American Jewish personnel stationed in the Kassel area.

For some inexplicable reason, the chaplain's office in Frankfurt agreed to his request to be transferred to Bremen, an American enclave in the British zone, ostensibly to conduct High Holiday services in the city. The army even assigned him a special vehicle for transportation. In Bremen, Klausner arranged a visit to Poppendorf, claiming he needed to bring the Jews at the camp a supply of prayer books.

At Poppendorf, the commanding officer refused him entry to the camp. When the officer assured him that the prayer books would be distributed, Klausner protested that they needed his guidance to use them. The officer then sent for the religious leaders of the group. One of the two men, a rabbi from Munich, knew Klausner.

After being admitted to Poppendorf, Klausner met with the leadership of the camp. Together, they discussed a plan to transport the people to Munich, once they had managed to reach Kassel, the first city in the American zone where they could be housed in groups. From Munich, the Berihah would attempt to take them to Palestine.

On November 7 the British moved the Jews to two camps allegedly more suitable for the winter months. When the British relaxed their guard at these camps, the Jews were smuggled to Kassel, where Klausner illegally provided them with housing for a night or two, food, and clothing, including blankets from the JDC. When the JDC realized that the blankets would not be returned because the Jews either took the blankets with them or cut them up for garments, it refused to deliver any more. To convince the JDC to cooperate, Klausner had a six-by-six army truck positioned outside the JDC's warehouse, preventing the use of the building. From then on, Klausner reported, "we had no problem with blankets."

From Kassel, Klausner arranged for the people to be transported to Munich by train. The army transportation officer was so eager to get rid of the displaced persons that he willingly attached extra cars to the train to accommodate them. Klausner also provided travel papers for each displaced person. By May 1948, more than half of them had reached Cyprus or Palestine.[96]

For the Berihah, the movement of the Jews of the *Exodus* was its last major undertaking. UNSCOP had called for the partition of Palestine into Jewish and Arab states in late August; and on November 29, 1947, the General Assembly of the United Nations voted by a two-thirds majority to approve the partition. The Arabs opposed the decision, and the Israeli War of Independence began.[97]

Once the Israelis took the initiative against the Arabs, William Haber found that the survivors "began to flock to the Jewish Agency offices for the early opportunity to migrate to Israel. They dropped their complaints that they were 'trapped' and 'imprisoned' in Germany and Austria and went about their business of preparing themselves for migration to that country."[98] Many survivors decided to go to Israel because they were "convinced that their hope to migrate to the States was illusionary" since the Congress had failed to enact legislation to allow significant numbers of them to enter the country. In other words, this decision by the Congress "helped to crystallize the thinking of these people as to where they *had* to go."[99]

Haber also observed: "at the same time that the prevailing mood of the DP changed, the attitude of the military authorities softened. The constant criticism of the DP that one heard on the highest levels yielded to an intense interest in helping the migration out of Germany."[100]

Since not all the survivors were able or willing to leave Germany, the need for DP chaplains remained. The army, however, had some reservations about the program. In 1948 Chaplain Samuel Burstein complained of having his movements restricted by the military. Chaplain Leon Adler, a twenty-seven-year-old Reform rabbi who had arrived in Germany in late 1947, claimed that the army did not understand the role of displaced persons chaplains. Adler called for a directive defining their duties and urged the formation of a coordinating council to determine how displaced persons problems should be handled.[101]

Nothing came of Adler's suggestion because the army began its own reassessment of the program. At its height, there were nine DP chaplains. By June 1948 there were six. Four of the remaining chaplains were to be redeployed or transferred. The other two were to stay in the area. One of those asked by Haber to remain was Chaplain Louis Barish, a thirty-six-year-old Reform rabbi assigned to work in his office.[102] Barish had previously been in the Stuttgart area and had impressed Haber with the "quality" of his work. Arrangements were also made to have Chaplain Burstein and Chaplain Hersh Livazer stay until their tours of duty had expired. This meant that three chaplains would be involved with the displaced persons.

The army had been reluctant to continue the program for several reasons. The commands to which the chaplains were assigned complained that their presence reduced the number of officers available to them for general duty. Moreover, since there had been a reduction of approximately 50 percent in the number of Christian chaplains in the European theater, the army expected that there should be a proportional reduction of Jewish chaplains, as well. Finally, the army argued that the displaced persons situation had stabilized and that chaplains were not needed to work exclusively in this area.[103]

Haber could have refuted these arguments by pointing out that the problems within the displaced persons camps were "likely to increase as the leadership migrates and men of lesser stature are left behind in charge of committees and other administrative duties." Although Haber wanted "a half dozen high-grade chaplains who could be of assistance in such situations," he chose not to press the army for several reasons.[104] Haber was not sure he could succeed even if he took a strong stand. Furthermore, he could not, in good conscience, endorse the retention of all those who asked to remain as DP chaplains. Some of these chaplains were "not men from whom any significant contribution" could be expected. They either lacked "vigor and resourcefulness" or developed other interests that had a priority on their time.[105]

While Haber decided not to ask the army to retain the DP chaplains, he did leave the matter open so that he could recommend an increase provided the candidates were "of such caliber that they can be of real service to the DP."[106] Fortunately, the situation never became serious enough for Haber or his successors to call the chaplains back for special service. In early 1949, the war in the Middle East ended with an armistice. By that time, sixty-five hundred Palestinian Jews (about 1 percent of the Jews in the country) had died. By 1950–51, two-thirds of the survivors came to Israel; the rest went to other countries.[107]

While there were several factors that contributed to bringing the issue of Palestine to the United Nations, it was the presence of Jewish survivors in Germany and Austria that became "a mighty force in pressing for the opening of Palestine to immigration. Residence in camps had ceased to be a temporary phenomenon";[108] and American Jewry maintained its pressure upon "a receptive American public" and the American government. The pressure on the government succeeded; and it, in turn, "prevented Britain from implementing her anti-Zionist policy." Furthermore, the American government pressured the British to resolve the issue of Palestine in the United Nations. The establishment of the State of Israel was "to a large degree" made possible by Jews in the Diaspora, the survivors who organized groups such as the Berihah, and American Jewry.[109]

There is no doubt that the chaplains played a significant part in helping American Jewry shape its response to the *Shearit Hapletah.* According to Edward M. M. Warburg, chairman of the JDC, the information they provided "sharpened the awareness of the American Jewish communities to their responsibility for their brethren in the camps."[110] While the chaplains worked on temporary solutions in Europe, they pressed American Jewry to find a permanent solution. Even when the chaplains became disillusioned with their work, they never lost sight of their ultimate objective. For many survivors, the chaplains were seen as "an oasis in an alien, parched land—a beacon in a darkened world—a friend in a hostile territory—a voice of authority for a frightened people—an undaunted champion for an unwanted folk—our friend."[111]

CONCLUSION

I HAVE ATTEMPTED to analyze the impact the European Jewish survivors had on the American Jewish chaplains and, through them, on American Jewry. The chaplains were among the first Jews in Europe to meet the survivors; and although they had not been expected by either the American Army or the American Jewish community to assist the displaced persons, many chose to do so. Since the chaplains were not acting as official representatives of the American rabbinate or any organization while engaged in this activity, each chaplain had to decide the extent of his own involvement.

My concern has been the general issue of the American Jewish community's response to the survivors and their plight in areas under American military control during the period of liberation from 1944 through 1948. The work has focused on the interaction of the chaplains and survivors in efforts to keep American Jews informed about conditions in Europe and the response of the American Jewish community; attempts to persuade the American Army to recognize Jews as a separate entity requiring special treatment; contributions to the organization of the displaced persons as a political force; and influence by involving Jewish soldiers in displaced persons work. In addition, I have examined the chaplains' role in the crystallization of displaced persons society, in the displaced persons' struggle to emigrate, and in their attempt to "reclaim their full rights as free men."

Conclusion

The displaced persons period was a decisive era in contemporary Jewish history. During this time the fate of the survivors and the future of Palestine was determined. The struggle of the survivors to regain their freedom and the quest to establish a Jewish state involved not only world Jewry but much of the non-Jewish world as well. By examining the American Jewish chaplains' involvement with the remnants of European Jewry, a new perspective has been gained about the response of the American Jewish community to the Holocaust and to the period of liberation. Much has also been learned about the attitude of the American government and military toward the displaced persons.

It is clear the leadership of American Jewry understood that at the end of the war the American Jewish community would have to aid European Jews and began preparations even without knowing the full extent of the catastrophe or the severity of the problems. In 1943 the JDC started recruiting and training personnel for duty in Europe. At the same time, leaders of American Jewry began publicly discussing the enormous financial burden the community would have to bear.

This awareness did not adequately translate into deeds. The JDC's attempts were thwarted not only by the American military but by the failure of American Jewry to provide qualified personnel and sufficient funds. Lacking competent social workers and adequate funding, the JDC's operation floundered for some time.

It is important to note that American Jewry could have provided the qualified social workers and the funding the JDC required. The failure of Jewish social workers to respond to calls for assistance cannot be explained by their inability to assimilate the magnitude of the horror. Perhaps Judah Nadich was correct in saying that Jewish social workers were unwilling to take temporary leaves of absence from Jewish federations and other Jewish social agencies because they were "callous" and "selfish." Perhaps this can also be said about much of American Jewry, who refused to react adequately to pleas for financial aid. To their credit, there were Jewish social workers who enlisted in the JDC and did yeoman work on behalf of the survivors. They also worked in concert with the chaplains and were willing to bend the rules when necessary.

While individual JDC personnel worked with chaplains, the JDC did not utilize them in an effective manner. After the chaplains began sending information about the conditions in Europe, it became clear they could play a constructive role in displaced persons work. The JDC acknowledged the importance of their help but rarely shared information with the chaplains or kept them abreast of its activities. More importantly, the JDC neither empowered the chaplains to work on its behalf before it was allowed to enter Europe nor actively encouraged them to enlist in the JDC at the end of their tours of duty.

Chaplains were not only not encouraged to join the JDC, they were informed as early as May and June 1944 that even if they had background in community organization, psychiatric social work, or some similar field (which the JDC considered essential for this type of work), they could not be guaranteed a position in the JDC after being demobilized. In view of the acute shortage of trained personnel, this policy seems incomprehensible.

If the JDC had asked individual chaplains to remain in Europe, it is likely that some would have agreed to do so. A number had been searching for ways to stay and continue their work. The failure actively to recruit these chaplains deprived the JDC of dedicated, competent, and Jewishly committed individuals who already had firsthand experience with the survivors and knew how to function within the military.

Although the JDC had been reluctant to use chaplains in displaced persons work, CANRA encouraged them and publicly praised their efforts. To its credit, CANRA also kept constant pressure on the JDC to bring relief to European Jewry. CANRA had to be cautious in these discussions because of the JDC's sensitivity to other Jewish organizations becoming involved in relief work. Had the JDC been less concerned about organizational jurisdiction, it might have increased the effectiveness of its operation and avoided embarrassment when the chaplains' activities raised questions about the efficacy of JDC programs.

In view of the JDC's attitude toward the chaplains, it is not surprising that prior to going to Europe, the chaplains had not been asked by the JDC to send back information about the condition of European Jewry. It is also significant that the chaplains themselves had not anticipated the possibility of meeting survivors. It vividly illustrates the extent to which the impact of the Holocaust was not understood.

What impact did the chaplains have on the survivors in shaping American Jewry's response to the survivors, influencing American policy toward the displaced persons, and mobilizing Jewish soldiers to work with them? The chaplains had a direct and indirect impact on the survivors. They touched the lives of many survivors on an individual basis or in groups by assisting with personal problems, particularly with the army. They also provided food and material goods; helped locate families; established communication links with relatives abroad; returned children hidden by the church; served as escorts aboard trains that took children out of Buchenwald and aboard trains that transferred Jews from Eastern Europe to the American zone of occupation and aboard ships that took Jewish children to Palestine; intervened with the military to have displaced persons released from jail; had their sentences reduced and prevented the army from launching black market raids in displaced persons camps; conducted services, performed weddings, and at times served as rabbis of communities; and helped establish schools and summer camps.

Since there were so few chaplains and so many survivors, thousands of displaced persons had little or no personal contact with them at all. Yet a number of chaplains played an indirect role in many of their lives. Through the Berihah chaplains actively assisted thousands of Jews to leave Europe for Palestine. Abraham Klausner played a key role in the creation of the Central Committee of Liberated Jews in Germany, which represented the Jews in dealing with the American military. Klausner had also been instrumental in establishing separate Jewish camps and hospitals, the publications *Unzer Weg* and *Fun Letzten Churben,* a library, and many other cultural and business enterprises. These gave the survivors a sense of self-worth, enabled them to become a political force, and provided them with vehicles to express their creative energies.

In the end, however, the displaced persons themselves were responsible for developing communities in the camps, struggling to rebuild their lives, gaining recognition for themselves, and emigrating to Palestine. The chaplains, the JDC, and the Palestinians each in their own way contributed to this effort; but it was the survivors' will to live and reconstruct their lives that provided the major impetus to their success.

By keeping the American Jewish community informed of events in Europe and of the attitude of the American Army toward the displaced persons, the chaplains influenced the response of American Jewry to plight of the displaced persons. Through the Harrison Report, Abraham Klausner brought the problems facing the survivors to the attention not only of American Jews but also the American government and public.

Harrison's findings persuaded President Truman to demand changes in the army's treatment of the Jews and created much discussion in the United States about their plight. Until then, the American government had not understood the nature of the problem. As a result of the report, the United States recognized the unique position of the Jews, while the military became more cautious of its treatment of them in part to avoid adverse publicity. While the chaplains helped alert the leadership of American Jewry to problems encountered by displaced persons, none of the chaplains' pleas for help raised large sums of money or convinced the Jewish social workers to come to Europe.

The chaplains' influence had limitations in Europe, too. They generally could not change army policy. The chaplains did succeed in individual cases where they directly intervened in requesting that an exception be made. Abraham Klausner succeeded in forcing the military to change its policy when it agreed to establish all-Jewish displaced persons camps. The problem the chaplains faced with the military was that it had not formulated a long-range policy to deal with the displaced persons. Without such guidelines, the army was unsure of what to do, causing itself embarrassment and unnecessary hardships and problems for the survivors.

Although much can be said against the American Army's treatment of the Jews, it must also be acknowledged that Jews fled to the American zones of Germany and Austria because they were treated better there than in the French, British, or Russian zones. In spite of the army's attempt to stop individual chaplains from working with survivors, there were army officers who looked the other way or openly cooperated. In the final analysis, no other army permitted chaplains to operate in this manner; and although the American military may not have been aware of the full extent of these activities, it knew enough to curtail them if it had chosen to do so. In general, the army grudgingly yielded to—and at times even cooperated in—these efforts.

Of all the groups the chaplains dealt with in displaced persons work, they had the least impact on the Jewish soldiers. This is paradoxical, since it was this group with whom they were officially charged to work. It was rare for the chaplains actively to recruit GIs except for special projects and then generally from those who attended synagogue services. The chaplains simply did not have the time or inclination to recruit people they did not know for work considered illegal by the military. Under these circumstances, they preferred to do it themselves.

It is difficult to assess the role of the Jewish soldiers because the chaplains disagree about the level of commitment these men had toward the survivors. Some chaplains praised their dedication; others complained that they could rarely rely on them to offer more than minimal assistance. While many soldiers were involved in their own efforts to assist the displaced persons, it appears that a large number were not interested enough to help in any way.

In assessing the chaplains' accomplishments, it is essential to remember that each chaplain worked on his own or (at times) with other chaplains, not as part of an organized effort. CANRA encouraged the chaplains but did not coordinate their activities. While not official representatives of American Jewry, chaplains reluctantly assumed this position in the absence of the JDC and other Jewish relief agencies to better represent the needs of the survivors to the army.

This was a unique position for the chaplains and unprecedented in American Jewish history. For the first time, chaplains were representing the American Jewish community outside the military while still serving in the army. In doing so, the chaplains acted openly on behalf of American and European Jewry.

Nothing in the religious training of these men provided any clue as to how they would respond to the survivors. No sect was more responsive to their needs than another: there were no differences in the level of commitment and dedication between the Reform, Conservative, and Orthodox chaplains.

What emerges from this study, despite all the qualifications, is that when the *Shearit Hapletah* desperately needed help, it received it from an unexpected source—American Jewish chaplains. Through their devotion and dedication to the survivors, they tried to show that American Jewry cared and that they were no longer alone. This experience had a lasting impact on the chaplains and strengthened their commitment to the Jewish people. In some cases it even persuaded them to Zionism.

The presence of the survivors in Europe so long after the end of the war convinced them that although they had reservations about the need for a Jewish state, it was the only solution for these Jews. Interestingly, aside from discussing their activities with congregants and friends after returning from Europe, most chaplains no longer spoke about these experiences. Their reluctance to speak deprived the American Jewish community of a perspective that sheds additional light on the remnants of European Jewry and on the response of American Jewry to a major tragedy and crisis. The accomplishments of the chaplains in themselves deserve much praise; in view of the magnitude of the obstacles they surmounted, theirs was a successful effort.

Biographical Notes

The following are biographical notes on the army (with one exception) chaplains who appear or have been interviewed for this book. The information is taken from the *American Jewish Yearbook* 47 (1945–1946): 179–200. Ind. = "inducted"; M.H.L. = Master of Hebrew Literature; for other acronyms and abbreviations, see pages xi and xii.

Abramowitz, Mayer; b. Palestine, Dec. 13, 1919; in U.S. since 1928; single; A.B. Yeshiva College '40; rabbi, JTS '44; mem. RAA; ind. July 1945.

Adler, Leon; b. U.S., Aug. 12, 1921; single; B.S.S. CCNY '41; rabbi, JIR '45; mem. CCAR; ind. Sept. 1945.

Barack, Nathan A.; b. Russia, July 2, 1913; in U.S. since 1923; married, 1 child; B.S. Lewis Institute '34, rabbi, HTC '36; mem. RCA; ind. June 1944.

Barish, Louis.; b. U.S., Dec. 22, 1912; married, 1 child; B.A. CCNY '33; M.A. Columbia '42; rabbi, JTS '42; mem. RAA; ind. Mar. 1944.

Bohnen, Eli Aaron; b. Canada, Sept. 16, 1909; in U.S. since 1931; married, 2 children; B.A. U. of Toronto '31; rabbi, JTS '35; mem. RAA; ind. Oct. 16, 1943.

Braude, Max A.; b. U.S., Sept. 26, 1913; married; B.A. U. of Pittsburgh '33; rabbi, HTC '36; mem. RCA; ind. May 1941.

Breslau, Isadore; b. Russia, Jan. 20, 1897; in U.S. since 1906; married, 2 children; B.A. NY State Teachers' College '22; rabbi and M.H.L., JIR '28; mem. CCAR; ind. Mar. 12, 1943.

Brodey, Arthur; b. Canada, Oct. 28, 1900; in U.S. since 1930; married; B.A. U of Toronto '23; LL.B. Osgood Law School '26; rabbi and M.H.L., JIR '34; mem. CCAR; ind. Jan. 22, 1943.

Cohen, Eugene J.; b. U.S., Aug. 22, 1918; single; rabbi, ETS '42; mem. RCA; ind. July 1945.

Biographical Notes 199

Decter, Aaron; b. Russia, July 26, 1912; in U.S since 1919; married, 1 child; B.A. U. of Pittsburgh '33; rabbi, JTS '37; mem. RAA; ind. Aug. 14, 1943.

Dembowitz, Morris V.; b. U.S., May 15, 1915; married; B.A. Yeshiva College '39; rabbi, JTS, 41; mem. RAA; ind. Feb. 1944.

Dicker, Herman; b. Czechoslovakia, Jan. 30, 1914; in U.S. since 1938; married; Ph.D. U. Berlin and Zurich '37; rabbi, Hildesheimer Sememinary (Berlin) '36; mem. RCA; ind. June 2, 1943.

Eichhorn, David M.; b. U.S., Jan. 6, 1906; married, 4 children; B.A. U. of Cincinnati '28; rabbi, HUC '31; D.D. HUC '38; mem. CCAR; ind. July 3, 1942.

Elefant, Milton H.; b. U.S., Aug. 21, 1917; single; B.A. Yeshiva College '39; rabbi, ETS '42; mem. RCA; ind. May 1945.

Ellenbogen, Edward; b. U.S., Jan. 13, 1912; married, 1 child; Ph.D. U. of Chicago '31; rabbi, HUC '37; mem. CCAR; ind. Dec. 1940.

Eskin, Hebert S.; b. Russia; in U.S. since 1923; single; A.B. Detroit Inst. Tech. '32; rabbi by private ordination; mem. RCA; ind. May 19, 1943.

Essrig, Harry; b. Palestine, Aug. 16, 1912; in U.S. since 1920; single; B.S. Columbia '34; rabbi and M.H.L., HUC '40; mem. CCAR; ind. Oct. 3, 1942.

Fine, Alvin I.; b. U.S., Oct. 25, 1916; single; B.A. Reed '37; rabbi and M.H.L., HUC '43; mem. CCAR; ind. May 18, 1943.

Friedman, Hebert A.,; b. U.S., Sept. 25, 1918; married; B.A. Yale '38; rabbi, JIR '38; mem. CCAR; ind. May 1945.

Ginsburg, Leo; b. U.S., Mar. 2, 1899; married; B.Litt. U. of Oxford '36; rabbi by private ordination '34; m. RCA; ind. Sept. 1943.

Goldfarb, Harold; b. U.S., Oct. 17, 1905; single; A.B. Columbia '26; rabbi, JTS '33; m. RAA; ind. Jan. 1943.

Goldman, Meyer J.; b. U.S., July 18, 1901; married, 1 child; M.S. CCNY '35; rabbi, ETS '29; mem. RCA; ind. Oct. 1942.

Gorin, Paul; b. U.S., Mr. 25, 1911; single; B.A. U. of Chicago '35; rabbi and M.H.L., HUC '39; mem. CCAR; ind. Sept. 17, 1943.

Gorrelick, Benjamin H.; b. Poland, June 4, 1906; in U.S. since 1921; married, 1 child; B.A. CCNY '30; rabbi, JTS '33; mem. RAA; ind. Mar. 1944.

Haselkorn, Abraham; b. U.S., Oct. 17, 1905; married; B.S. NYU '26; rabbi and M.H.L., JIR '32; mem. CCAR; ind. Nov. 1941.

Hyman, Irwin I.; b. Latvia, Feb. 16, 1909; in U.S. since 1921; married, 1 child; M.A. Columbia '33; rabbi, JTS '35; mem. RAA; ind. Feb. 1943.

Kaufman, Samuel; b. U.S., Nov. 14, 1909; single; B.A. CCNY '32; rabbi, ETS '41; mem. RCA; ind. Sept. 1942.

Kertzer, Morris N.; b. Canada, Oct. 18, 1910; in U.S since 1930; married, 1 child; B.A. (honorary) U. of Toronto '30; M.A. U. of Illinois '39; rabbi, JTS '34; mem. RAA; ind. Mar. 1943.

Klausner, Abraham J.; b. U.S., Apr. 22, 1915; single; M.A. U. of Denver '38; rabbi and M.H.L., HUC '43; mem. CCAR; ind. June 1944.

Klein, Bert A.; b. Hungary, May 30, 1902; in U.S. since 1924; single; Matura Degree, Collegium Zillan, Hungary '22; rabbi by private ordination.

Klein, Isaac; b. Hungary, Sept. 5, 1905; in U.S. since 1921; married, 3 children; B.A. CCNY '31; M.S. Mass. State '37; rabbi, JTS '34; mem. RAA; ind. July 1942.

Kraft, Jacob; b. Poland, Feb. 12, 1904; in U.S since 1908; married, 1 child; A.B. Harvard '25; rabbi, JTS '30; mem. RAA; ind. Oct. 1943.

Lefkowitz, David, Jr.; b. U.S., Aug. 8, 1911; married, 2 children; A.B. U. of Cincinnati '32; rabbi, HUC '37; mem. CCAR; ind. Mar. 30, 1943.

Lefkowitz, Sidney M.; b. U.S., Sept. 11, 1908; married; B.A. U. of Cincinnati '30; rabbi, HUC '33; mem. CCAR; ind. May 8, 1942.

Lev, Aryeh; b. Palestine, June 6, 1912; in U.S since 1918; married, 2 children; B.S. Columbia '34; rabbi and M.H.L., JIR '37; mem. CCAR; ind. Nov. 1940; office chief of chaplains, Washington.

Lifschutz, Oscar Michael; b. U.S., Apr. 10, 1916; single; M.A. Northwestern U. '42; rabbi, HTC '45; mem. RCA; ind. July 1945.

Lipman, Eugene Jay; b. U.S., Oct 13, 1919; married; A.B. U. of Cincinnati '41; rabbi and M.H.L., HUC '43; m. CCAR; ind. Aug. 1944.

Livazer, Hersch; b. Poland, Dec. 15, 1904; in U.S. since 1930; married; rabbi, Yeshiva of Lomza '27; mem. RCA; ind. Aug. 1943.

Lorge, Ernst Mordecai; b. Germany, May 26, 1916; in U.S. since 1936; married, 1 child; B.A. U. of Cincinnati '38; rabbi and M.H.L., HUC '42; mem. CCAR; ind. Mar. 1944.

Marcus, Robert S., Army: b. U.S., Dec. 26, 1909; married, 2 children; J.D. NYU '35; B.S.S. CCNY '31; rabbi, ETS '31; mem. RCA; ind. Sept. 1942.

Messing, Joseph B.; b. U.S., Jan. 24, 1920; married; A.B. Brooklyn College '41; rabbi, JIR '45; mem. CCAR; ind. July 1945.

Milgrom, Louis; b. Poland, Dec. 11, 1909; in U.S. since 1921; married; B.S. Lewis Institute '30; rabbi, HTC '34; mem. RCA; ind. Mar. 1943.

Miller, Carl Isaac; b. U.S., June 10, 1906; married, 2 children; A.B. U. of Cincinnati '29; rabbi, HUC '31; mem. CCAR; ind. May 1944.

Miller, Joseph; b. Poland, Apr. 5, 1920; in U.S. since 1928; married; LL.B. De Paul U. '43; rabbi by private ordination '43; mem. RCA; ind. June 1945.

Miller, Meyer; b. U.S., July 4, 1904; married, 2 children; B.S. NYU '30; rabbi and M.H.L., JIR '36; mem. CCAR; ind. May 1942.

Nadich, Judah; b. U.S., May 13, 1912; single; A.B. CCNY '32; M.A. Columbia '36; rabbi, JTS '36; mem. RAA; ind. Apr. 1942; in Aug. 1945 named advisor on Jewish Affairs to Gen. Eisenhower.

Paperman, Aaron; b. U.S., Jan. 17, 1914; married, 1 child; rabbi, Rabbinical Seminary of Telshe, Lithuania '37; mem. RCA; ind. Sept. 1942.

Plaut, W. Gunther; b. Germany, Nov. 1, 1912; in U.S. since 1935; married, 1 child; J.D. U. of Berlin '34; rabbi and M.H.L., HUC '39; mem. CCAR; ind. July 5, 1943.

Poliakoff, Manuel M.; b. U.S., Mar. 18, 1914; single, B.A. Johns Hopkins U. '44; rabbi, Rabbinical Seminary of Telshe, Lithuania '39; mem. RCA; ind. May 17, 1943.

Rackman, Emanuel; b. U.S., June 24, 1910; married, 2 children; LL.B. Columbia '33; rabbi, ETS '34; mem. RCA; ind. May 1943.

Rackovsky, Isaiah; b. Palestine, Sept. 14, 1906; in U.S. since 1917; married; rabbi, ETS '29; mem. RCA; ind. May 14, 1943.

Reznikoff, Marvin Meir; b. U.S., Dec. 9, 1910; married, 1 child; A.B. Wesleyan '34; rabbi and M.H.L., JIR '38; mem. CCAR; ind. Apr. 27, 1943.

Ribner, Hebert; b. U.S., Nov. 8, 1917; married; M.A. Columbia '39; rabbi, JTS '42; mem. RAA; ind. Aug. 27, 1943.

Biographical Notes 201

Rosen, Samuel; b. Poland, Feb. 12, 1907; in U.S. since 1920; married, 1 child; B.S. CCNY '33; rabbi, ETS '29; mem. RCA; ind. Jan. 1942.

Rubin, David; b. U.S., July 6, 1910; single; B.A. CCNY '31; M.A. Columbia '33; rabbi, ETS '31; mem. RCA; ind. Apr. 1942.

Ruslander, Selwyn D., Navy; b. U.S., Jan. 7, 1911; married, 1 child; A.B. U. of Cincinnati '32; rabbi, HUC '35; mem. CCAR; ind. July 1942.

Sandhaus, Morris; b. Poland, Feb. 25, 1912; married, 1 child; B.S. CCNY and Columbia '42; rabbi, Mesifta Talmudic Academy '35; mem. RCA; ind. June 1942.

Sandrow, Edward T.; b. U.S., Dec. 23, 1905; married, 1 child; B.A. U. of Pennsylvania '29; M.A. Columbia '40; rabbi, JTS '33; mem. RAA; ind. July 18, 1942.

Saperstein, Harold I.; b. U.S., Dec. 9, 1910; married; B.A. Cornell '31; rabbi and M.H.L., JIR '35; mem. CCAR; ind. May 29, 1943.

Schacter, Herschel; b. U.S., Oct. 10, 1917; single; B.A. Yeshiva College '38; rabbi, ETS '41; mem. RCA; ind. Nov. 9, 1942.

Schenk, Emanuel; b. U.S., Mar. 22, 1908; married, 2 children; A.B. NYU '35; rabbi and M.H.L., JIR '39; mem. CCAR; ind. Apr. 24, 1941.

Segal, Jacob Elchanan; b. Palestine, Sept. 1, 1913; in U.S since 1920; married, 1 child; B.A. CCNY '35; M.A. Columbia '39; rabbi, JTS '39; mem. RAA; ind. Mar. 9, 1943.

Shubow, Joseph Shalom; b. Lithuania, Sept. 26, 1899; in U.S. since 1907; married, 2 children; M.A. Harvard '21; rabbi and M.H.L., JIR '33; mem. CCAR; ind. Oct. 20, 1943.

Spiro, Abraham; b. Poland, May 28, 1912; in U.S. since 1937; single; B.A. Hebrew U. (Jerusalem); rabbi, Yeshiva of Mir '31; mem. RAA; ind. June 1944.

Stone, Earl E.; b. U.S., July 2, 1914; married; B.A. Syracuse U. '35; rabbi and M.H.L., JIR '39; mem. CCAR; ind. Aug. 1941.

Teitelbaum, Samuel; b. Galicia, Austria, Apr. 28, 1901; in U.S. since 1908; married; B.A. Harvard '22; rabbi and M.H.L., JIR '27; mem. CCAR; ind. Apr. 16, 1942.

Tofield, Aaron Judah; b. Poland, Oct. 8. 1912; in U.S. since 1923; married, 1 child; B.S. Tulsa '34; M.A. Columbia '37; rabbi, JTS '39; mem. RAA; ind. Oct. 8, 1943.

Troy, Albert Nathaniel; b. U.S., May 23, 1913; single; B.A. Yeshiva College '34; rabbi, JIR '43; mem. CCAR; ind. Nov. 4, 1944.

Vida, George; b. Hungary, July 31, 1906; in U.S. since 1939; married, 2 children; Ph.D. U. of Breslau '29; rabbi, JTS (Breslau) '32; mem. RAA; ind. Dec. 17, 1943.

Wall, Max B.; b. Poland, July 23, 1915; in U.S. since 1921; married, 1 child; B.A. Yeshiva College '38; rabbi, JTS '42; mem. RAA; ind. Nov. 3, 1943.

Ziskind, Bernard Hyman; b. Lithuania, Oct. 27, 1900; in U.S. since 1910; married, 2 children; B.A. Ohio State '23; rabbi, JTS '27; mem. RAA; ind. Oct. 23, 1943.

Interviews

I interviewed the following individuals. The organizational affiliation is listed after each name. C designates chaplains, GI indicates American Jewish soldier, S stands for Holocaust survivor, and British Army represents chaplains serving with the British military forces. For other acronymns, see pages xi and xii. Others interviewed include prominent American Jewish leaders, chaplains' assistants, workers for the Jewish Agency for Palestine, and relatives of chaplains and GIs. The organizational affiliation of each chaplain is also included.

Mayer Abramowitz, C, Conservative
Leon Adler, C Reform
Shmuel Atzmon, S
Nathan A. Barack, C, Orthodox
David Bar-El, GI
Louis Barish, C, Conservative
Gary Bernstein, GI
Philip S. Bernstein, C, Reform (advisor on Jewish Affairs)
Zeev Birger, Palestinian Jew
Solomon H. Blondheim, GI
Eli A. Bohnen, C, Conservative
Ann Borden (Liepah), JDC
Max A. Braude, C, Orthodox
Isadore Breslau, C, Reform
William W. Brickman, GI
Arthur Brodey, C, Reform
Israel Brodie, C, British Army
Sidney Burke (Berkowitz), (GI)
Samuel Burstein, C, Conservative
Simon Caller, GI
Eugene J. Cohen, C, Reform

Sydney Davidson, GI
Eliezer Dembitz, GI
Morris V. Dembowitz, C, Conservative
Herman Dicker, C, Orthodox
Milton H. Elefant, C, Orthodox
Benjamin J. Elsant, C, Conservative
Herbert S. Eskin, C, Orthodox
Harry Essrig, C, Reform
Stanley Evans, GI
Patrick B. Fay, C, Catholic
Joseph Fink, JDC
Paulette Fink, JDC
Harold Fishbein, UNRRA
Leon D. Fisher, JDC
Chava Frank (Eva Kuntsman), S
Bernard Freilich, S
Herbert A. Friedman, C, Reform
Leo Ginsburg, C, Orthodox
Joseph Glatzer, S
Harold Goldfarb, C, Conservative
Ralph Goldman, JDC

Interviews

Israel Goldstein, prominent American Zionist and Jewish leader
Louis Goldstein, S
Paul Gorin, C, Reform
Benjamin H, Gorrelick, C, Conservative
Mrs. Benjamin Gorrelick, wife of chaplain
Aaron Goryn, S
Adele Goryn, S
Melvin Greenbaum, GI
Zalman Grinberg, S
Samuel Haber, JDC
William Haber, advisor on Jewish Affairs
Robert Handwerger, chaplain's assistant
H. L. Hardman, C, British Army
Abraham Haselkorn, C, Reform
Mrs. Abraham Haselkorn, wife of chaplain
Dixie Heim, Jewish Relief Unit worker
Eli Heimberg, GI
Max Helvarg, JDC
Haskell Hollander, GI
Albert Hutler, GI
Abraham S. Hyman, asst. to the advisor on Jewish Affairs, then advisor on Jewish Affairs
Irwin Hyman, C, Conservative
M. Jacob Joslow, JDC
Ben Kaplan, JDC
Robert L. Katz, C, Reform
Samuel Kaufman, C, Orthodox
Morris N. Kertzer, C, Conservative
Abraham J. Klausner, C, Reform
Bert A. Klein, C, Reform
Isaac Klein, C, Conservative
Ruth Kluger (Aliav), Jewish Agency for Palestine
Jacob Kraft, C, Conservative
Lola Kublanoff, Palestinian Jew
Sidney M. Lefkowitz, C, Reform
Baruch Leizerowski, S
Aryeh Lev, C, Reform
Yehuda Lev, GI
Jack Levin, S
Bertram Levine, JWB worker
Joseph Levine, JDC
Avram Levinson, GI
Louis Levinthal, advisor on Jewish Affairs
Gershon Levy, C, British Army
Henry Levy, JDC
Isaac Levy, C, British Army
Oscar M. Lifshutz, C, Orthodox
Marvin Linick, GI
Eugene J. Lipman, C, Reform
David Lippert, GI
Saul Loeb, GI
Ernst M. Lorge, C, Reform
Abe Loskove, JDC
Rosamund T. Low, mother of GI
David Marcus, GI
Milton Marcus, GI
Laura Margolis, JDC
Max Meletzer, S
Joseph B. Messing, C, Reform
Gunther Meyer, S
Ernest Michel, S
Louis Milgrom, C, Orthodox
Carl I. Miller, C, Reform
Joseph Miller, C, Orthodox
Kay Miller, wife of chaplain
Meyer Miller, C, Reform
Paul Montag, GI
Judah Nadich, C, Conservative, first advisor on Jewish Affairs
Aryeh Nesher, S
Aaron Paperman, C, Orthodox
Simon Pava, chaplain's assistant
Joel Philips, chaplain's assistant
Manuel M. Poliakoff, C, Orthodox
Efraim Poremba, S
L. I. Rabinowitz, C, British Army
Emanuel Rackman, C, Orthodox, asst. to the advisor on Jewish Affairs
Isaiah Rackovsky, C, Orthodox
Marvin M. Reznikoff, C, Reform
Herbert Ribner, C, Conservative
James P. Rice, JDC
Eli Rock, JDC
Harold Saperstein, C, Reform
Herschel Schacter, C, Orthodox
Emanuel Schenk, C, Reform
Morton Shanok, chaplain's assistant
David D. Shor, C, Reform
Leo Srole, UNRRA
Seymour S. Stern, C, Reform

Earl Stone, C, Reform
Bruce Teicholz, S
Samuel Teitelbaum, C, Reform
Aaron J. Tofield, C, Conservative
Harold Trobe, JDC
Jacob Trobe, JDC

George Vida, C, Conservative
Max B. Wall, C, Conservative
Rosalie Westreich, JDC
Isaac Zaelon, chaplain's assistant
William Zimmerspitz, S

Notes

Introduction

1. U. S. President's Committee on Religion and Welfare in the Armed Forces, *The Military Chaplaincy*. (Washington: GPO, 1950), p. 18.

2. Louis Barish, *Rabbis in Uniform* (New York: Jonathan David, 1962), pp. 1–52; Philip S. Bernstein, *Rabbis at War* (Waltham: American Jewish Historical Society, 1971), pp. 1–10.

3. Barish, *Rabbis in Uniform*, pp. 21–22, 49–103; interviews with Samuel Teitelbaum and Earl Stone, OH.

4. Samuel Burstein, *Rabbis with Wings: A Story of a Pilot* (New York: Herzl, 1965); Morris Kertzer, *With an H on My Dog Tag* (New York: Behrman House, 1947); Isaac Klein, *The Anguish and the Ecstasy of a Jewish Chaplain* (New York: Vantage, 1974); Hersh Livazer, *Berchato Shel Harabi* (Jerusalem: Boys Town, 1977); Judah Nadich, *Eisenhower and the Jews* (New York: Twayne, 1953); George Vida, *From Doom to Dawn* (New York: Jonathan David, 1967).

5. Yehuda Bauer, *Flight and Rescue: Brichah* (New York: Random House, 1970); idem, "The Initial Organization of Holocaust Survivors in Bavaria," *Yad Vashem Studies* 8(1970): 127–57; Meyer Levin, *In Search* (New York: Horizon, 1950); Leo Schwarz, *The Redeemers* (New York: Farrar, Straus and Young, 1953); Barish, *Rabbis in Uniform;* Lee Levinger, "Rabbis to the Rescue," 1946; idem, "The Jewish Chaplains and CANRA," 1946, JWB; Bernstein, *Rabbis at War*.

6. Yehuda Bauer, "The Holocaust and the Struggle of the Yishuv as Factors in the Establishment of the State of Israel," in *The Catastrophe of European Jewry*, ed. Yisrael Gutman and Livia Rothkirchen (Jerusalem: Yad Vashem, 1976), pp. 630–32.

7. Yehuda Bauer, *My Brother's Keeper: A History of the American Jewish Joint Distribution Committee 1929–1939* (Philadelphia: Jewish Publication Society of America, 1974), p. 248; Naomi Cohen, *Not Free To Desist* (Philadelphia: Jewish Publication Society, 1972) pp. 219, 221–22.

8. Oscar I. Janowsky, *The JWB Survey* (New York: Dial, 1948), pp. 1–2, 51; Bernstein, *Rabbis at War*, pp. 1–2; Barish, *Rabbis in Uniform*, p. 80.

9. Levinger, "Jewish Chaplains," p. 50.

10. State and War Department files were not consulted for this study. The chaplains were not directly involved with either of these institutions, and the correspondence with American Jewish organizations relating to the displaced persons from these departments was found in the archives of the WJC, YIVO, and the JDC. Army directives concerning the displaced persons were also found in a number of these archives, as well as in AH.

Chapter 1

1. Bernstein, *Rabbis at War*, pp. 1–10; CANRA Section of JWB Annual Report, CJC Minutes 1946, pp. 1–5; idem, "Jewish Chaplains in World War II," *JE*, Feb. 1, 1946, p. 5; idem, "American Jewish Chaplains in World War II," *AJYB* 47(1945/46): 173–200; Executive Directors Report, CJC Minutes, Aug. 1945, pp. 2–5; ibid., Aug. 27, 1945, pp. 1–2; ibid, Aug. 28, 1945, pp. 1–52; Barish, *Rabbis in Uniform*, pp. 1–52.

2. Barish, *Rabbis in Uniform*, p. 8; Bernstein, *Rabbis at War*, pp. 1–2; Janowsky, *JWB Survey*, pp. 45–156.

3. Janowsky, *JWB Survey*, pp. 60, 114–15; Bernstein, *Rabbis at War*, intro.

4. Janowsky, *JWB Survey*, p. 115.

5. Ibid.

6. Ibid. pp. 115–116.

7. Ibid. pp. 116–117.

8. Ibid. p. 117.

9. Bernstein, *Rabbis at War*, p. 8.

10. Ibid.

11. Bernstein, *Rabbis at War*, pp. 7–10; Bernstein, CANRA Section of JWB Annual Report, p. 1.

12. Bernstein, *Rabbis at War*, pp. 7–8.

13. Roy J. Honeywell, *Chaplains of the United States Army* (Washington: Office of the Chief of Chaplains, 1958), p. 2.

14. Bernstein, *Rabbis at War*, p. 8; Janowsky, *JWB Survey*, p. 124.

15. *AJYB* 47(1945/46): pp. 179–200. See Biographical Notes.

16. Janowsky, *JWB Survey*, pp. 122–24.

17. U.S. War Department, *Military Education: The Chaplains' School* (Washington: War Department, 1926), p. 2.

18. Bernstein, *Rabbis at War*, p. 11; Janowsky, *JWB Survey*, p. 24.

19. Interview with Aryeh Lev, OH.

20. Bernstein to author, Oct. 25, 1976, PM.

21. Interview with Herschel Schacter, OH.

22. Judith Elizur's interview with Eugene Lipman, OH.

23. Yehuda Bauer, *American Jewry and the Holocaust* (Detroit: Wayne State University Press, 1981), pp. 294–96.

24. Barish, *Rabbis in Uniform*, pp. 21–22, 37–38.

25. Interviews with Samuel Teitelbaum and Earl Stone, OH; Barish, *Rabbis in Uniform*, pp. 99–102.

26. Earl Stone to Philip Bernstein, Oct. 5, 1943, CJC, box 3, file A.

27. Philip Bernstein to Earl Stone, Nov. 30, 1943. CJC, box 3, file A; Philip Bernstein to Camillus Angel, Aug. 31, 1944, CJC, box 3, file A; Nathan Witkin to Joseph Hyman, May 5, 1944, CJC, box 3, file A; Janowsky, *JWB Survey*, p. 129.

28. Philip Bernstein to Louis Kraft, Nov. 30, 1943, CJC, box 3, file A.

Notes to Chapter 1

29. Ben Rabinowitz to Louis Kraft, Nov. 22, 1944, CJC, box 3, file A.
30. Janowsky, *JWB Survey*, pp. 51–57, 106–14.
31. Interviews with Herbert Ribner, Abraham Klausner, and Eugene Lipman, OH.
32. Alex Grobman, "What Did They Know? The American Jewish Press and the Holocaust, September 1, 1939–December 17, 1942," *American Jewish History*, Mar. 1979, pp. 327–52; Haskel Lookstein, *Were We Our Brothers' Keepers? The Public Response of American Jews to the Holocaust, 1938–1944* (New York: Hartmore House, 1985).
33. Deborah E. Lipstadt, *Beyond Belief* (New York: Free Press, 1986); Robert W. Ross, *So It Was True: The American Protestant Press and the Nazi Persecution of Jews* (Minneapolis: University of Minnesota Press, 1980).
34. Yehuda Bauer, "When Did They Know?," *Midstream*, 14, no. 4 (Apr., 1968): 51–58. See also Walter Laqueur, *The Terrible Secret* (Boston: Little, Brown, 1980); Marie Syrkin, "Reaction to News of the Holocaust," *Midstream*, May 1968, pp. 62–64; idem "What American Jews Did During the Holocaust," *Midstream*, Oct. 1982, pp. 6–10. David Kranzler, *Thy Brother's Blood: The Orthodox Jewish Response During the Holocaust* (Brooklyn, N.Y.: Mesorah, 1987), pp. 90–94.
35. Grobman, "What Did They Know?," pp. 346–52; David Wyman, *The Abandonment of the Jews* (New York: Pantheon, 1985); Monty Penkower, *The Jews Were Expendable* (Urbana–Champaign: University of Illinois Press, 1983); Martin Gilbert, *Auschwitz and the Allies* (New York: Holt,, Rinehart, and Winston, 1981).
36. Yehuda Bauer, *The Holocaust in Historical Perspective* (Seattle: University of Washington Press, 1978), pp. 19, 28; Walter Laqueur, "Jewish Denial and the Holocaust," *Commentary*, Dec. 1979, pp. 44–55.
37. Interview with Abraham Klausner, OH.
38. Vida, *Doom to Dawn*, pp. 5–6, 10.
39. Jan Karski, *Story of a Secret State* (Boston: Houghton Mifflin, 1944).
40. Ken Adelman, "Seeing Too Much," *Washingtonian*, July 1988, p. 66.
41. Syrkin, "What American Jews Did," pp. 6–7.
42. Lucy S. Dawidowics, *The War Against the Jews* (Philadelphia: Jewish Publication Society of America, 1975), pp. 369–371; Nicholas A Stigliani and Antoinette Marzotto, "Fascist Anti-Semitism and the Italian Jews," *Wiener Library Bulletin*, 28(1975): 41–49; *JTA* Dec. 14, 1944, pp. 3–4; Moses A. Leavitt, "Report of the Secretary," prob. late 1944, CJC, box 3, file A, p. 12.
43. Kertzer, *With An "H"*, pp. 53–58; *JTA* June, 16, 1944; Harold Goldfarb to CANRA, June 7, 9–11, 1944, JWB, box 205; interview with Harold Saperstein, OH; "The Symbol of Liberation," *Jewish Chaplain* supp., Dec. 1944, p. 1; interview with Aaron Paperman, OH.
44. Interview with Morris Kertzer, OH.
45. Michael J. Cohen, *Palestine: Retreat from the Mandate* (New York: Holmes and Meier, 1978), pp. 98–124.
46. Louis Sobel to Marvin Reznikoff, Nov. 20, 1945, CJC, box 3, file A, p. 2; Marvin Reznikoff, "JDC Report re: Italy," prob. late 1945/early 1946, CJC, box 3, file D, p. 102; S. D. Wolkowicz, "Report on the Situation of the Refugees in Southern Italy," June 14, 1944, WJC–NY, file 40, drawer 274, pp. 1–10; *JTA* June 30, 1944, p. 2. One training farm was obtained by bartering a case of liquor (Marvin Reznikoff to author, Dec. 9, 1974, PM).
47. Ephraim Dekel, *B'riha: Flight to the Homeland* (New York: Herzl, n.d.), pp. 10, 340; Martin Gilbert, *Exile and Return: The Struggle for a Jewish Homeland* (New York: Lippincott, 1978), p. 268.

48. Reznikoff, "JDC Report," pp. 1–3; Louis Sobel to Marvin Reznikoff, Nov. 20, 1945, CJC, box 3, file A, p. 3; *JTA* June 29, 1944, p. 2; ibid., July 2, 1944, p. 4; ibid., July 25, 1944, p. 3; Malcolm J. Proudfoot, *European Refugees* (London: Faber and Faber, 1957), pp. 65, 140–41. In the summer of 1944 UNRRA contributed $30,000 to the JDC for this work.

49. The Intergovernmental Committee on Refugees was established after the Evian Conference in July 1938 to help refugees from Nazism.

50. S. D. Ruslander to Philip Bernstein, Sept. 11, 1945, CJC, box 3, file D; Telephone interview with Dr. Paul Montag, a senior medical officer at the naval base at Salerno. Ruslander had worked with some of these Palestinians earlier in southern Italy, and they therefore called upon him in this situation.

51. Interviews with Herbert Ribner, Morris Kertzer, and Samuel Teitelbaum, OH.

52. Samuel Teitelbaum to Philip Bernstein, Feb. 16, 1944, CJC, box 3, file A; Samuel Teitelbaum, monthly chaplain's report, Feb. 1944, NA-SW.

53. Samuel Teitelbaum to Philip Bernstein, Feb. 16, 1944, CJC, box 3, file A.

54. Philip Bernstein to Samuel Teitelbaum, Mar. 16, 1944, CJC, box 3, file A.

55. Leon Kubowitzki to Samuel Teitelbaum, Feb. 4, 1944, Apr. 6, 1944, June 9, 1944, WJC–NY, file 12, drawer 272; Samuel Teitelbaum to Leon Kubowitzki, Apr. 23, 1944, May 3, 1944, WJC–NY, file 12, drawer 272.

56. See WJC–NY files 12, 67, 76, drawer 272.

57. Samuel Teitelbaum to Leon Kubowitzki, Apr. 23, 1944, May 3, 1944, WJC–NY, file 12, drawer 272.

58. Edward N. Peterson, *The American Occupation of Germany: Retreat to Victory* (Detroit: Wayne State University Press, 1977), p. 32.

59. Robert H. Dunlop to Leon Kubowitzki, May 23, 1944, WJC–NY, file 12, drawer 272.

60. Leon Kubowitzki to Samuel Teitelbaum, June 9, 1944, WJC–NY, file 12, drawer 272.

61. John Sills to Louis Kraft, May. 26, 1944; Louis Kraft to John Sills, June. 8, 1944; Louis Kraft to Joseph Hyman, May 31, 1944, July 10, 1944, CJC, box 3, file A. This whole episode was the result of a cable inquiry from John Sills (a JWB representative) about whether the JDC was willing to give chaplains money to help Jewish refugees.

62. Arieh Tartakower to John Hilldring, Nov. 13, 1944, WJC–NY, file 43, drawer 274.

63. Peterson, *American Occupation*, pp. 31–34.

64. Harry D. Biele to Philip Bernstein, Nov. 2, 1944, CJC, box 3, file A.

65. Northeastern Regional Chaplain's Conference proceedings, Feb. 4–6, 1946, CJC, box 20.

66. Henri Michel, *The Second World War* (New York: Praeger, 1975), vol. 2, pp. 630–81.

67. J. C. Hyman to Louis Kraft, Sept. 25 and Sept. 29, 1944, CJC, box 3, file A.

68. J. C. Hyman to Louis Kraft, Sept. 29, 1944, CJC, box 3, file A.

69. Philip Bernstein to the chaplains, Nov. 2, 1944, CJC, box 3, file A.

70. Philip Bernstein to Frank Weil, Nov. 14, 1944; Ben Rabinowitz to Louis Kraft, Nov. 22, 1944, CJC, box 3, file A.

71. Philip Bernstein to the chaplains, June 2, 1944, CJC, box 3, file A.

Notes to Chapter 1   209

72. Philip Bernstein to Frank Weil and Walter Rothschild, Nov. 14, 1944, CJC, box 3, file A.

73. Ben Rabinowitz to Louis Kraft, Nov. 22, 1944, CJC, box 3, file A.

74. David M. Eichhorn, "Autobiography," AJA, p. 31.

75. Nili Keren, "Hazalat Yeladin Betsarfat Bitkufat Hakibush Hagermani 1940–1944 Al-Yedeh Eargunim Yehudim," master's thesis, Institute of Contemporary Jewry, Hebrew University, Jerusalem, 1975.

76. Interviews with Abraham Haselkorn and Morton Shanok, OH; *JA*, Nov. 16, 1944, 2d ed., p. 1; Abraham Haselkorn to Philip Bernstein Sept. 22, 1944, CJC, box 3, file A; Morton Shanok to Louis Shanok, Nov. 22, 1944, PM; *The Bulletin* (pub. Jewish Community of Staten Island), May. 24, 1946, PM, p. 2.

77. Before going to Europe, Haselkorn received several hundred dollars from Sigmund Thau, a European Jew who asked that it be used to help Jewish survivors. (interview with Abraham Haselkorn, OH; memorandum of his activities in Europe, n.d. PM.

78. Levin, *In Search*, pp. 182–89; Abraham Haselkorn to Philip Bernstein, Oct. 15, 1944, CJC, box 3, file A.

79. Excerpts from Judah Nadich's diary, CAH.

80. *JA*, Nov. 16, 1944, p. 1.

81. Abraham Haselkorn to Philip Bernstein, Sept. 22, 1944.

82. Philip Bernstein to Abraham Haselkorn, Nov. 2, 1944, CJC, box 3, file A.

83. Interviews with Abraham Haselkorn and Morton Shanok; *JA*, Nov. 16, 1944, p. 1.

84. *JA*, Nov. 16, 1944, p. 9.

85. *Der Tog*, Nov. 2, 1944, See also *Forward*, Sept. 6, 1944, p. 4.

86. Office of the Chief of Chaplains circular letter no. 292, Jan. 1, 1945, JWB, pp. 1–2.

87. Interviews with Chaplains Abraham Haselkorn, Herman Dicker, Morris Kertzer, Morris Dembowitz, Judah Nadich, Isadore Breslau, and Herbert Eskin, OH.

88. Klein, *Anguish and Ecstasy*, pp. 104–11, 114–32; Isaac Klein to Philip Bernstein, Oct. 19, 1944, CJC, box 3, file A; Yehuda Bauer's interview with Isaac Klein, OH.

89. Interview with Morris Dembowitz, OH.

90. David M. Eichhorn, monthly report, Dec. 1944, JWB, box 199; *JTA*, Dec. 15, 1944, p. 2; Judah Nadich to Philip Bernstein, Oct. 2, 1944, JWB, box 221; Herbert Eskin, monthly reports, Oct.–Dec. 1944, and Feb. 1945, JWB, box 201; interview with Herbert Eskin and Aaron Tofield, OH.

91. Levinger, "Jewish Chaplains and CANRA," p. 97; Aaron Decter, "Report on Activities While on TD, October 1944," JWB, box 199.

92. David M. Eichhorn, monthly report to CANRA, Oct. 1944, JWB, box 199; Jacob Ott to Philip Bernstein, Sept. 13, 1944, CJC, box 3, file A; Morris Sandhaus to Philip Bernstein, Oct. 12, 1944, CJC, box 3, file A; Herman Dicker, monthly report, Aug. 1944, JWB, box 199; interview with Judah Nadich, OH; excerpts from the diaries of Judah Nadich, OH; Leon Kubowitzki to Robert Marcus, Sept. 21, 1944; Judah Nadich to Philip Bernstein, Oct. 2, 1944, JWB, box 221.

93. *JA*, Mar. 29, 1945, p. 14; Robert Marcus to Maurice Brenner, Nov. 6, 1944, CJC, box 3, file A; Meyer Goldman, memorandum, n.d., CHS.

94. Leo Friedman to Leon Kubowitzki, Nov. 24, 1944, WJC–NY, file 53, drawer 272.

95. Leon Kubowitzki to Robert Marcus, Oct. 16, 1944, WJC–NY, file 67, drawer 272.
96. Robert Marcus to Jewish Publication Society, Oct. 18, 1944, CAH; Louis Kraft to Maurice Jacobs, Dec, 26, 1944, JWB, box 219.
97. Interview with Manuel Poliakoff, OH.
98. *Congress Weekly*, Apr. 20, 1945, pp. 8–10.
99. Interview with Max Wall, OH.
100. Ibid.

Chapter 2

1. Peterson, *American Occupation*, pp. 54–55.
2. William Hardy McNeill, *Survey of International Affairs 1939–1946* (London: Oxford University Press, 1953), p. 582.
3. Peterson, *American Occupation*, p. 55.
4. John Gimbel, *The American Occupation of Germany: Politics and the Military 1945–1949* (Stanford: Stanford University Press, 1968), p. xiii.
5. Peterson, *American Occupation*, p. 114.
6. Proudfoot, *European Refugees*, pp. 98–110.
7. *NYT*, Apr. 22, 1945, sec. 4, p. 5; ibid., Apr. 25, 1945, p. 1; Ibid., May 29, 1945, p. 6; Bauer, *Flight and Rescue*, pp. 47, 50–51.
8. Proudfoot, *European Refugees*, p. 324.
9. *Jewish Spectator*, Nov. 1945, p. 22; *Indiana Jewish Chronicle*, Feb. 1, 1946, p. 2; *NYT*, Apr. 17, 1945, p. 4; June 27, 1945, p. 6; *Time*, Apr. 30, 1945, p. 43.
10. Max Braude to Judah Nadich, May 11, 1945, WJC–NY, drawer 272, file 64; Eichhorn, "Autobiography," p. 45.
11. Interviews with Eli Bohnen and Eli Heimberg, OH; "Letter from Eli Bohen," CJC, box 3, file D; Marcus J. Smith, *The Harrowing of Hell* (Albuquerque: University of New Mexico Press, 1972), p. 98; Eli Heimberg to wife, May 12, 1945, OH; Barish, *Rabbis in Uniform*, pp. 82–86.
12. From my notes of interview with Max Braude.
13. Louis Barish, *Rabbis in Uniform*, pp. 63–70; Chester Kaplan to CANRA, June 21, 1945, CJC, box 2, file B.
14. Interview with Max Braude, OH; Max Braude to Judah Nadich, May 11, 1945, WJC–NY, file 64, drawer 272.
15. Max Braude to Eunice Braude, May 6, 14, 15, 28, and June 7, 1945, CJC, box 3, file D.
16. Yehuda Bauer's interview with Abraham Klausner, OH.
17. Interview with Emanuel Schenk, OH.
18. Interviews with Herschel Schacter and Benjamin Elsant, OH.
19. Interview with Herschel Schacter, OH.
20. Chaim Finkelstein to office committee, July 5, 1945, WJC–NY, file 67, drawer 272; *Jewish Spectator*, Nov. 1945, pp. 21–23. This differs from both the data that Yehuda Bauer found (see *Flight and Rescue*, p. 54) and an observation by Kieve Skidell, a former member of Habonim (American Pole Zion youth organization) who was serving in the U. S. Army in Germany. Skidell remarked that the Jews in Poland had not lost hope that their families were alive (*Yiddisher Kempfer*, July 16, 1945). Yet judging from articles in *T'khias Hamesim* (a newspaper published by the Jews in Buchenwald) May 4, 1945, WJC–NY, drawer 27, a number of people talked about being the sole surviving members of their families.

21. Chaim Finkelstein to office committee, July 5, 1945, WJC–NY, file 67, drawer 272.

22. *World Telegram*, Feb. 1–2, 1946; *Morgen Journal*, May 15, 1945; *Congress Weekly*, Apr. 20, 1945, pp. 8–10; ibid., May 11, 1945, pp. 11, 16; ibid., June 15, 1945, pp. 5–6; ibid., June 29, 1945, pp. 13, 16; ibid., Aug. 17, 1945, pp. 6–8; ibid., Oct. 6, 1945, pp. 5–6.

23. *JTA*, Apr. 22, 1945, p. 1; ibid., June 29, 1945, p. 2.

24. Yehuda Bauer, *A History of the Holocaust* (New York: Franklin Watts, 1982), pp. 337–38.

25. Leo Schwarz, *The Root and the Bough* (New York: Rinehart, 1949), p. 310; *Yiddisher Kempfer*, June 16, 1945; *Forward*, June 15, 1945; *T'khias Hamesim*, May 4, 1945.

26. Dorothy Rabinowitz, *New Lives* (New York: Alfred A. Knopf, 1976), p. 61; *Atlantic Monthly*, July 1945, pp. 87–90; *JTA* June 10, 1945, p. 4; ibid., June 22, 1945, p. 4; Bauer, *Flight and Rescue*, p. 50; Joseph S. Shubow to Stephen S. Wise, May 23, 1945, WJC–NY, file 56, drawer 272.

27. *Congress Weekly*, Nov. 30, 1945, pp. 7–8.

28. Leonard Dinnerstein, *America and the Survivors of the Holocaust* (New York: Columbia University Press, 1982), p. 11.

29. Schwarz, *Root and the Bough*, p. 311.

30. Dinnerstein, *America and the Survivors*, p. 28.

31. Dinnerstein, *America and the Survivors*, p. 13.

32. Interviews with Abraham J. Klausner, Ann Borden (Liepah), and Marvin Linick, OH.

33. Revised administrative memorandum no. 39, Apr. 16, 1945, AH.

34. Abraham Klausner, "A Detailed Report on the Liberated Jew as He Now Suffers His Period of Liberation Under the Discipline of the Armed Forces of the United States," June 24, 1945, CAH.

35. Peterson, *American Occupation*, p. 87; interviews with Sylvia Neulander, Herschel Schacter, and Eli Bohnen, OH.

36. Peterson, *American Occupation*, pp. 86, 90.

37. Ibid.

38. Dinnerstein, *America and the Survivors*, p. 12.

39. Earl Stone to Philip Bernstein, Oct. 5, 1943, CJC, box 3, file A.

40. U. S. Department of the Army, *Fraternization with the Germans in World War II* (Frankfurt am Main: Department of the Army, 1947), pp. 1–18, 194–95.

41. Harold Zink, *American Military Government in Germany* (New York: Macmillan, 1948), pp. 237–43.

42. "L.F.," [pseud.], "There Is Still Something Wrong," Aug. 2, 1945, WJC–NY, file 35, drawer 274.

43. Interview with Chaplain Irwin Hyman, OH; Aryeh Lev's trip folder for 1943–45, June 4, 1945, CJC, Aryeh Lev's personal file.

44. Shearit Hapletah–Germany, YIVO, file 66; *Indiana Jewish Chronicle*, June 15, 1945, p. 4; Robert J. Northshield to WJC, June 8, 1945, WJC–NY, file 272, drawer 272; Sheldon Lutz to CANRA, Box 33, file 3.

45. Smith, *Harrowing of Hell*, pp. 98, 128.

46. Interviews with Abraham Haskelkorn, Albert A. Hutler, and Ernest Michel (one of the survivors whom Haselkorn helped), OH; Albert Hutler file, CAH; Albert Hutler to author Nov. 8, 1975, PM. To show their appreciation for this aid, the Jews from Vaihingen concentration camp wrote Abraham Haselkorn a poem with the inscription, "To Mr. Chaplain Abraham Haselkorn as a sign of profound

gratitude for the great help and everything what [sic] he made in the interest of the political ex-prisoners from the concentration camp in Vaihingen," PM.

47. Interview with Herschel Schacter, OH.

48. Schwarz, *Root and the Bough*, p. 319.

49. Robert Marcus to Stephen S. Wise, July 5, 1945, WJC–NY, file 92, drawer 272; Robert Marcus to Stephen S. Wise, July 3, 1945, WJC–NY, file 55, drawer 272; Schwarz, *Root and the Bough*, pp. 314, 317, 319; interview with Herschel Schacter, OH.

50. Interviews with Ernst Lorge and Isaac Zaleon (Lorge's assistant), OH; Ernst Lorge to Judah Nadich, May 1, 1945, WJC–NY, file 64, drawer 272.

51. Interview with Herbert Eskin, OH; Herbert Eskin to CANRA, July 1945, JWB, box 201; *Corps News*, n.d., JWB, box 201.

52. Eugene J. Lipman, "Summary of War Experiences," n.d., AJA; Eugene Lipman to Philip Bernstein, June 5, 1945, JWB, box 218.

53. Charles I. Schottland, "Memorandum on Stateless and Non-Repatriables," Aug. 5, 1945, AH.

54. Interview with Sylvia Neulander, OH; *Congress Weekly*, June 22, 1945, p. 4; ibid., June 9, 1945, pp. 13–14; *JTA*, May 7, 1945, p. 4; ibid., May 27, 1945, p. 4; *NYT*, June 9, 1945, p. 4.

55. *Congress Weekly*, June 9, 1945., pp. 13–14.

56. *JTA*, May 27, 1945, p. 4; ibid., June 11, 1945, p. 2; Robert Marcus to Stephen S. Wise, July 3, 1945, WJC–NY, file 55, drawer 272.

57. *New York Herald Tribune*, June 9, 1945, pp. 1–2 (also in *Jewish Exponent*, June 15, 1945, p. 1 and *Jewish Advocate*, June 14, 1945); interview with Sylvia Neulander, OH; Joel S. Fishman, "Jewish War Orphans in the Netherlands: The Guardianship Issue, 1945–1950," *Wiener Library Bulletin* 26 (1973–74): 31–36; idem, "The Annelce Beekman Affair and the Dutch News Media," *Jewish Social Studies*, 40(Winter 1978): pp. 3–24.

58. *Congress Weekly*, June 22, 1945.

59. *JTA*, June 15, 1945, p. 4; report of the first JDC team in Germany; Arthur Greenleigh to JDC, New York office, June 16, 1945, JDC, Germany Displaced Persons File; Ernst Lorge to CANRA, July 4, 1945, CJC, box 3, file D; interview with Herschel Schacter, OH; *NYT*, June 26, 1945, p. 4; WINS (New York), radio program transcript, Nov. 14, 1945, PM; *JTA*, Jan. 29, 1945, p. 2.

60. Gerhart M. Riegner to Chaplain Schacter, June 27, 1945, PM; minutes of meeting, June 27, 1945, PM; Gerhart Riegner to Leon Kubowitzki, June 29, 1945, WJC-GA; Gerhart Riegner to Leon Kubowitzki, July 10, 1945, WJC-GA.

61. Harold Saperstein to Stephen S. Wise, June 22, 1945, WJC–NY, file 53, drawer 52; interview with Harold Saperstein, OH.

62. Arieh Tartakower to Judah Nadich, Robert Marcus, and Joseph S. Shubow, June 25, 1945, WJC–NY, file 64, drawer 272.

63. Levinger, "Rabbis to the Rescue," p. 3.

64. Abraham Klausner to Philip Bernstein, June 11, 1945, CAH.

65. Interview with Herschel Schacter, OH.

66. *NYT*, Apr. 13, 1970; *New York Daily News*, Apr. 13, 1970.

67. Interview with Abraham Klausner, OH. For a description of the work done by the army see Smith, *Harrowing of Hell*.

68. Klausner file, CAH.

69. *Shearit Hapletah*, vol. 1, PM; Abraham Klausner to Philip Bernstein, prob. late June 1945, CJC, box 3, file D; Abraham Klausner to Philip Bernstein, June 11, 1945, CJC, box 3, file D.

Notes to Chapter 3   213

70. Proudfoot, *European Refugees,* p. 97.
71. Interview with Abraham Klausner, OH.
72. Zalman Grinberg, *Schuchranu MeDachau* (Herziliya: Massada, 1948), pp. 44–46; Leo W. Schwarz, *The Redeemers* (New York: Farrar, Strauss, and Young, 1953), pp. 3–6; *Congress Weekly,* Feb. 15, 1946, pp. 6–8; interview with Abraham Klausner, OH.
73. *New Palestine,* Oct. 12, 1945, p. 8; *Indiana Jewish Chronicle,* June 22, 1945, p. 2; ibid., Oct. 26, 1945, p. 1; Max Braude to Eunice Braude, May 6, 1945, CJC, box 3, file D; The Jewish Community of Bavaria, Shearit Hapletah–Germany, YIVO, file 209; G. R. More to Arieh Tartakower, May 2, 1945, WJC–NY, file 91, drawer 272; Abraham Klausner to Philip Bernstein, June 11, 1945, CJC, box 3, file D; *Center Courier,* March 1946, PM, p. 3.
74. Interviews with Abraham Klausner and Sidney Burke, OH.
75. Interviews with Benjamin Elsant, Benjamin Gorrelick, Emanuel Schenk, and Isadore Breslau, OH; *Congress Weekly,* May 11, 1945, pp. 11, 16; June 15, 1945, pp. 5–6; *JTA,* June 10, 1945, p. 3; Max Braude, JWB, box 196; Joseph Shubow, May 8, 1945, WJC–NY, file 56, drawer 272; Herman Brotman to WJC–NY, Apr. 27, 1945, file 43, drawer 272; "The Jewish Community of Frankfurt," June 10, 1945, WJC–NY, file 43, drawer 274.
76. Klein, *Anguish and Ecstasy,* pp. 170–95, 198–213.
77. Interview with L. H. Hardman, OH; Aryeh Lev's trip folder for 1943–45, June 4 1945, CJC, Aryeh Lev's personal file.
78. Robert Marcus to Stephen S. Wise, May 12, 1945, WJC, file 67, drawer 272, p. 16.
79. Interview with L. H. Hardman, OH; Aryeh Lev's trip folder for 1943–45, June 4, 1945, CJC, Aryeh Lev's personal file.
80. Shearit Hapletah–Germany, YIVO, file 66; "Germany DPs General 1945," 1945 JDC.
81. Aryeh Lev's trip folder for 1943–45, June 4, 1945, CJC, Aryeh Lev's personal file.
82. Interview with Herschel Schacter, OH.

Chapter 3

1. Abraham Klausner to Philip Bernstein, mid-June 1945, CAH.
2. Klauser, "Detailed Report." June 24, 1945, CAH.
3. Stephen S. Wise to Abraham Klausner, July 16, 1945, CAH.
4. Stephen S. Wise to Abraham Klausner, July 25, 1945, CAH.
5. Robert Marcus to WJC, May 12, 1945, WJC–NY, drawer 272.
6. Joseph S. Shubow to Stephen S. Wise, May 23, 1945, WJC–NY, file 43, drawer 272.
7. "The Challenge of Suffering European Jewry," *Jewish Spectator,* July 1945.
8. Philip Bernstein to Abraham Klausner, Aug. 27, 1945. The long delay between Klausner's letter and Bernstein's reply was due to the death of Bernstein's father.
9. Max Braude to Philip Bernstein, June 29, 1945, JWB, box 211, Klausner file.
10. Aryeh Lev's trip folder for 1943–44, June 4, 1945, CJC, Aryeh Lev's personal file.
11. Arieh Tartakower to Judah Nadich et al., June 25, 1945.
12. The American Jewish Conference was convened in September 1943 by major Jewish organizations to prepare postwar Jewish demands.

13. Emanuel Celler et al. to Dwight D. Eisenhower, May 10, 1945, CAH; *American Jewish Conference Bulletin*, Oct. 2, 1945, pp. 1–2.

14. J. A. Ulio to Emanuel Celler, May 29, 1945, CAH.

15. *American Jewish Conference Bulletin* July 13, 1945, p. 2.

16. Interviews with Judah Nadich and Irwin Hyman, OH; excerpts from the diaries of Judah Nadich. The Truman Library in Independence, Missouri does not have the memorandum or any related information. Neither Nadich nor Hyman had a copy or could remember anything more about this mission or its repercussions. Nor did Mrs. Rosenberg remember anything about this episode.

17. Leonard Dinnerstein, "The United States Army and the Jews: Policies Toward the Displaced Persons After World War II," *American Jewish History*, March 1979, p. 356; Harry S. Truman, *Memoirs: Years of Decision* (New York: Doubleday, 1955), p. 311; M. Madeline, "America's Response to Europe's Displaced Persons, 1945–1952: A Preliminary Report," Ph.D. diss., St. Louis University, 1964, p. 56; Dinnerstein, *America and the Survivors*, pp. 34–36.

18. Gemma Newman, "Earl G. Harrison and the Displaced Persons Controversy: A Case Study in Social Action," Ph.D. diss., Temple University, 1973, p. 160.

19. *NYT*, Sept. 29, 1945, p. 38.

20. Interview with Abraham Klausner, OH.

21. Newman, "Earl G. Harrison," pp. 160–61; interview with Abraham Klausner, OH.

22. *NYT*, Sept. 29, 1945, p. 38.

23. Klausner, "A Detailed Report," p. 3.

24. *NYT*, Sept. 29, 1945, p. 38.

25. Klausner, "Detailed Report," p. 4.

26. *NYT*, Sept. 29, 1945, p. 38.

27. Klausner, "Detailed Report," p. 4.

28. *NYT*, Sept. 29, 1945, p. 38.

29. *NYT*, Sept. 29, 1945, p. 38.

30. Klausner, "Detailed Report," p. 4.

31. *NYT*, Sept. 29, 1945, p. 8.

32. Ibid.

33. Ibid.

34. Ibid.

35. Ibid., p. 38.

36. Ibid.

37. Ibid.

38. Ibid.

39. Nadich, *Eisenhower and the Jews*, pp. 33–36; *JTA*, Aug. 26, 1945, p. 2.

40. Leon Kubowitzki to Stephen S. Wise and Nahum Goldmann, Aug. 3, 1944, WJC–IJA; Stephen S. Wise to Dwight D. Eisenhower, Aug. 3, 1945, WJC–NY, file 102, drawer 271.

41. Dwight D. Eisenhower to Stephen S. Wise, Aug. 10, 1945, WJC–NY, file 102, drawer 271; file 47, drawer 273.

42. Judah Nadich asserted that Eisenhower did not like the term *liaison officer* in this context, because a liaison officer "was a military officer of a foreign army, appointed by his own national government to represent the interests of citizens of that foreign government within the orbit of General Eisenhower's command"; the Jewish displaced persons "as a group, therefore, could not be

represented by a 'liaison officer', for they come from various countries; they had no government of their own to represent them, no army of their own from which a liaison officer could be selected" (*Eisenhower and the Jews*, pp. 32, 38).

43. Interview with Jacob Trobe, OH.
44. Robert Marcus to Stephen S. Wise, July 5, 9, and 16, 1945, WJC–NY, file 92, drawer 272; Robert Marcus to Arieh Tartakower, July 29, 1945, WJC–NY, file 67, drawer 272; Robert Marcus to Colonel Schottland, July 11, 1945, WJC–NY, file 67, drawer 272; "Report of the First JDC Team in Germany."
45. Interview with Jacob Trobe, OH.
46. *Jewish Post*, Sept. 21, 1945.
47. Nadich, *Eisenhower and the Jews*, pp. 48–127.
48. Twenty-Third Army Corp, record group no. 338, NA–SM, box 8017.
49. Nadich, *Eisenhower and the Jews*, pp. 129–30; Schwarz, *Redeemers*, pp. 38–39.
50. Peterson, *American Occupation*, p. 55.
51. Zink, *American Military Government*, p. 25.
52. *JTA*, Sept. 23, 1945, p. 2; *JA*, Sept. 27, 1945, p. 8.
53. Nadich, *Eisenhower and the Jews*, pp. 129–30.
54. Eisenhower to all subordinate commanders, Sept. 20, 1945, WJC–NY, file 102, drawer 271.
55. Nadich, *Eisenhower and the Jews*, p. 133.
56. Ibid., Oct. 2, 1945, pp. 1, 18.
57. Ibid., Oct. 1, 1945, p. 2.
58. Ibid., Sept. 23, 1945, p. 1.
59. Martin Blumenson, ed., *The Patton Papers 1940–1945* (Boston: Houghton Mifflin, 1974), pp. 744, 751, 755. Ironically, the *New York Post* reported on October 20, 1945 that Patton denied that he "ever made any statement contrary to the Jewish or any other religious faith," p. 36.
60. *NYT*, Oct. 17, 1945, p. 8; *JE*, Oct. 19, 1945, pp. 1, 8.
61. *NYT*, Oct. 2, 1945, pp. 1, 8.
62. *The Record*, October 1945, p. 13.
63. *NYT*, Oct. 18, 1945, p. 13; *JTA*, Oct. 18, 1945, p. 4.
64. *NYT*, Oct. 28, 1945, p. 3.
65. *NYT*, Oct. 16, 1945, p. 7; ibid., Oct. 20, 1945, p. 5; ibid., Oct. 26, 1945, p. 6.
66. *JTA*, Nov. 29, 1945, p. 6.
67. *NYT*, Nov. 20, 1945, p. 20; ibid., Nov. 21, 1945, p. 20; ibid., Nov. 22, 1945, p. 21; *JA*, Dec. 6, 1945, p. 8; Sadie Sender to JDC, Feb. 20, 1946, Shearit Hapletah–Germany, YIVO, file 210; Abraham Klausner to Leon Kubowitzki, Nov. 16, 1945, WJC–NY, file 74, drawer 272; YIVO, Shearit Hapletah-Germany, File 66; "Plight of the Jews in the Nazi Camps Under Americans Called Terrible," WJC–NY, file 43, drawer 274; Eric Maier to Leon Kubowitzki, Oct. 22, 1945, WJC–NY, file 59, drawer 272; Eric Maier to WJC, Dec. 2, 1945, WJC–NY, file 59, drawer 272; Jean Gafan to JDC, prob. late 1945, Shearit Hapletah–Germany, YIVO, file 71; Abraham Klausner, Nov. 16, 1945, CAH; WJC to Simon Rifkind Jan. 12, 1945, WJC–NY, file 59, drawer 272; *Congress Weekly*, Oct. 19, 1945, pp. 4–5; ibid., Nov. 30, 1945, pp. 4–5; *New Palestine*, Oct. 12, 1945.
68. *JTA*, Nov. 23, 1945, p. 5; *NYT*, Nov. 22, 1945, p. 21; *Nassau Review Star*, Nov. 24, 1945. The news conference also received wide coverage in the

Jewish press for Nov. 30, 1945 throughout the United States, including *Jewish News, Jewish Review and Observer, Jewish Criterion, Jewish Record, Jewish Independent, Jewish Standard, Jewish Post.*

69. *Congress Weekly,* Feb. 15, Mar. 18, 22, and 29, Apr. 3, and 10, and Nov. 1, 1946 and Mar. 26, 1948.

70. Abraham Klausner to Leon Kubowitzki, Nov. 16, 1945.

71. Zalman Grinberg to WJC, Sept. 26, 1945, WJC–NY, file 43, drawer 274; *Congress Weekly,* Nov. 2, 1945. See also Herman Dicker to friends, Sept. 14, 1945, CJC, box 3, file C.

72. Zalman Grinberg to WJC, Sept. 26, 1945, WJC, file 43, drawer 274.

73. Sadie Sender to JDC; Yehuda Bauer's interview with Eli Bohnen, OH.

74. *JA,* Oct. 11, 1945, pp. 6, 10; Eric Maier to Leon Kubowitzki, Jan. 22, 1945, WJC–NY, file 71, drawer 272; Abraham Klausner to Oscar Karbach, Mar. 11, 1946, WJC–NY, file 74, drawer 272.

75. *American Jewish Conference Bulletin,* Oct. 19, 1945, p. 3.

76. *Indiana Jewish Chronicle,* Oct. 12, 1945, p. 4.

77. *JE,* Nov. 5, 1945, p. 1.

78. Ibid.

79. *JTA,* Oct. 18, 1945, p. 5; see also *Congress Weekly,* Oct. 26, 1945, p. 4.

80. *NYT,* Oct. 3, 1945, p. 18.

81. "Northeastern Regional Chaplains' Conference," CJC, box 20.

82. Minutes of CANRA Executive Committee, Dec. 21, 1945, AJA.

83. Nadich, *Eisenhower and the Jews,* p. 236.

84. *The Record,* October 1945, p. 14; *Bulletin of Activities and Digest of the Press* (American Jewish Conference), Oct. 2, 1945, pp. 1–2; American Jewish Conference representatives in American zone of Germany, interim report, Dec. 13, 1945, Harry S. Truman Library and AJA; Samuel L. Sar, "Supplementary Report to the American Jewish Conference," Feb. 4, 1946, PM; Alfred Fleishman and Samuel Sar, report, Nov. 10, 1945, PM; supplement to bulletin no. 77, Nov. 30, 1945, WJC–NY, file 43, drawer 274.

85. Francis Williams, ed., *Twilight of Empire: Memoirs of Prime Minister Clement Attlee* (New York: Barnes, 1962), p. 188.

Chapter 4

1. *The Record,* March 1946, p. 14.

2. *Unzer Weg,* suppl. no. 1, Oct. 12, 1945, p. 1.

3. *JE,* June 28, 1946.

4. Newman, "Earl G. Harrison," p. 179.

5. Peterson, *Occupation of Germany,* p. 114.

6. Abraham Spiro to Philip Bernstein, JWB, box 272; William Jordy, "Refuge," *Stars and Stripes,* gen. ed., Nov. 14, 1945; Joseph Levine to Leo Schwarz, Aug. 19, 1946, Shearit Hapletah–Germany, YIVO, file 25. One of Liepah's most successful exploits was to convince the army to turn over the farm belonging to Julius Streicher, editor of the infamous Nazi anti-Semitic newspaper *Der Stuermer,* for use as a training farm to prepare the survivors for life in Palestine (interview with Ann Liepah, OH).

7. Interview with Herbert Eskin, OH; Herbert Eskin to CANRA, Sept. 1, 1945, JWB, box 201.

8. Interview with Morris Dembowitz, OH; Saul Elgart, "Report of JDC Activities, Western Military District," 1945, Shearit Hapletah–Germany, YIVO, file 11, pp. 10–11.

9. Interview with Chaplain Manuel Poliakoff, OH.
10. Lipman, "Summary of War Experiences," pp. 5–7.
11. Interviews with Isadore Breslau, David Lefkowitz, Jr., and Ernst Lorge, OH; George Vida, *From Doom to Dawn;* Bert Klein to author, Dec. 30, 1974, PM; Saul Elgart, "Report of JDC Activities, Western Military District," Shearit Hapletah–Germany, YIVO, pp. 10–11; Irving Ganz to parents, Jan. 19, 1945, PM.
12. Herman Dicker to friends, Sept. 14, 1945, CJC, box 3, file C; Meyer Goldman, "Memorandum," n.d., Center for Holocaust Studies, New York, p. 24.
13. Interview with Chaplain Abraham Klausner, OH.
14. Jean Gafan to JDC, prob. late Dec. 1945 or early 1946, PM.
15. Interviews with Abraham Klausner and Leo Srole, OH; report from Camp Fahrenwald, Sept. 20, 1945; Oct. 20, 1945, Shearit Hapletah–Germany, YIVO, file 11.
16. *NYT*, Dec. 6, 1945, p. 7; *JTA*, Dec. 6, 1945, p. 3. For Heymont's view of what transpired, see Jacob Rader Marcus and Abraham J. Peck, eds., *Among the Survivors of the Holocaust—1945: The Landsberg DP Camp Letters of Major Irving Heymont, United States Army* (Cincinnati: American Jewish Archives, 1982), pp. 103–7.
17. *NYT*, Dec. 7, 1945, p. 5; "Digest of the Jewish DP Camp Newspapers," Jan. 16, 1945, WJC–NY, file 92, drawer 272; *Chronicles* (American Jewish Committee), Feb. 1946, pp. 11–12; *Jewish Frontier*, Jan. 1946, p. 24.
18. *NYT*, Dec. 8, 1945, p. 8.
19. Interview with Leo Srole, OH.
20. Simon Rifkind to Stephen S. Wise, Jan. 2, 1945 (error for 1946), WJC–NY, file 59, drawer 272.
21. In particular, Rifkind was upset with a number of reports in the Yiddish press allegedly made by Robert Marcus about the Allied military government. According to these reports, Marcus charged that "between twenty-five to thirty thousand displaced persons in Europe died since VE Day largely because members of the Allied Military Government are incompetent and disinterested." Ruth Kluger of the Jewish Agency also reacted negatively to this charge and cabled Stephen S. Wise to have it withdrawn: "otherwise important plans will fall through." It is not clear what plans in particular she was referring to: but since the Jewish Agency counted on the good will of the American Army to carry on activities on behalf of the survivors, this created a bad climate in which to work. In a letter to Rifkind on March 1, 1946, Marcus assured him that he had been misquoted. The conditions referred to the British zone and the Bergen Belsen camp in particular. See Ruth Kluger to James Heller, WJC–NY, file 59, drawer 272; Leon Kubowitzki to Abraham Klausner, Dec. 19, 1945, WJC–NY, file 74, drawer 272; Leon Kubowitzki to Simon Rifkind, Nov. 28, 1945, WJC–NY, file 59, drawer 272; Simon Rifkind to Leon Kubowitzki, Dec. 7, 1945, WJC–NY, file 59, drawer 272; Robert Marcus to Simon Rifkind, Mar. 1, 1946, WJC–NY, file 68, drawer 272; Robert Marcus to Simon Rifkind, Mar. 1, 1946, WJC–NY, file 74, drawer 272; Erich Maier to Leon Kubowitzki, Nov. 9, 1945, WJC–NY, file 74, drawer 272; *JTA*, Nov. 23, 1945, p. 5; *Congress Weekly*, May 3, 1946, p. 3; *Jewish Post*, Nov. 30, 1945; *JTA*, Dec. 9, 1945, p. 3; ibid., Dec. 13, 1945, p. 4; Sadie Sender, "Report on Zeilsheim," Oct. 27, 1945, Shearit Hapletah–Germany, YIVO, file 209; Rabbi Alexander Rosenberg to J. L. Trobe, Dec. 4, 1945, Shearit Hapletah–Germany, YIVO, file 209.
22. Simon Rifkind to James Heller, Dec. 17, 1945, WJC–NY, file 59, drawer 272; Simon Rifkind to E. M. M. Warburg, Dec. 17, 1945, Shearit Hapletah–

Germany, YIVO, file 65; Simon Rifkind to Nahum Goldmann and Stephen S. Wise, Dec. 17, 1945, WJC–NY, file 54, drawer 272.

23. Simon Rifkind to Stephen S. Wise, Jan. 2, 1946, WJC–NY, file 59, drawer 272.

24. "Interim Report of American Jewish Congress Representatives in American Zone of Germany," Dec. 13, 1945, Harry S. Truman Library and AJA; Samuel L. Sar, "Supplementary Report to the American Jewish Conference," Feb. 4, 1945, PM; Alfred Fleishman and Samuel Sar, report, Nov. 10, 1945, PM; Bulletin no. 77, suppl. Nov. 30, 1945, WJC–NY, file 43, drawer 274.

25. Leon Kubowitzki to Robert Marcus, Dec. 19, 1945, WJC–NY, files 59 and 67, drawer 272.

26. Interview with Leo Srole, OH. Although Smith's mother was Jewish, he was raised as a Catholic.

27. Lavy Becker to Jacob Trobe, Dec. 16 and 17, 1945, PM; Blanche Bernstein to Joseph Schwartz, Feb. 19, 1946, PM; Jean Gafan, report, *JA*, Dec. 20, 1945, pp. 1, 15; *NYT*, Dec. 7, 1945, p. 5.

28. *JTA*, Dec. 11, 1945, p. 2.

29. Interviews with Eli Bohnen and Eli Heimberg, OH; Yehuda Bauer's interview with Eli Bohnen, OH.

30. Mark W. Clark, *Calculated Risk* (New York: Harper and Brothers, 1950), p. 454.

31. Interviews with Eli Bohnen and Eli Heimberg, OH; Yehuda Bauer's interview with Eli Bohnen, OH.

32. Eli Bohnen to Philip Bernstein, Aug. 15, 1945, CJC, box 3, file D.

33. Bauer, *Flight and Rescue*, pp. 82–86.

34. Interviews with Eli Heimberg and Eli Bohnen, OH; Eli Heimberg, *Englisch für Jedermann*, PM; Harry J. Collins to Eli Heimberg, Nov. 8, 1945, PM.

35. Eli Bohnen to Philip Bernstein, Nov. 12, 1945; Dec. 3, 1945, CJC, box 3, file C.

36. Northeastern Regional Chaplains Conference, proceedings, Feb. 4–6, 1946, CJC, box 20.

37. Lipman, "Summary of War Experiences."

38. *JA*, Oct. 4, 1945, p. 4; *New York Post*, Oct. 9, 1945; ibid., Jan. 17, 1946, p. 13.

39. Erich Maier to WJC, Sept. 18, 1945, WJC–NY, file 71, drawer 272.

40. Interview with Abraham Klausner, OH; Abraham Klausner to Euton Place Temple, Mar. 6, 1946, CAH, Klausner file; Abraham Klausner to Kurt Grossman, Nov. 16, 1945, WJC–NY, file 92, drawer 272; Abraham Klausner to chaplains Decter and Segal, Jan. 8, 1946, CAH; Sol (no last name) to Morris Gershbaum, Dec. 27, 1945, PM; inventory and financial statement, May 10, 1946, CAH; Abraham Klausner to Rabbinical College of Celse, Nov. 6, 1945, CAH.

41. Abraham Klausner to American Federation of Lithuanian Jews, Jan. 8, 1946, CAH.

42. Lipman, "Summary of War Experiences," pp. 5–6.

43. Interview with Louis Milgrom, OH.

44. Paul Gorin file, PM; Vida, *Doom to Dawn*, p. 46.

45. Harry Segal to his family, Sept. 9, 1945, CJC, box 3, file D; *Community Council Commentator* (Jacksonville, Flor.), Sept. 27, 1945; interviews with Eli Bohnen and Eli Heimberg, OH.

46. Interview with Benjamin Gorrelick, OH; Benjamin Gorrelick to his wife, PM.

47. Interviews with Abraham Haselkorn and Mrs. Haselkorn, OH; "Restrictions on Overseas Shipments to Army Personnel Order No. 19687," CJC, box 3, file C.
48. Interview with Robert Handwerger, OH.
49. Herman Dicker monthly report, Nov. 1945, JWB, box 199; Herman Dicker to Aryeh Lev, Feb. 19, 1946, CJC, box 33, folder 3.
50. Louis Kraft to Philip Bernstein, Oct. 9, 1945, CJC, box 3, file C.
51. Aryeh Lev to Louis Kraft, Oct. 9, 15, and 18, 1945, CJC, box 3, file C.
52. Rita Sadev to Philip Bernstein, Oct. 31, 1945, CJC, box 3, file C; Joseph Hyman to Philip Bernstein, Oct. 30, 1945, CJC, box 3, file C.
53. Interviews with Benjamin Gorrelick and Haskell Hollander, OH.
54. Lipman, "Summary of War Experiences," pp. 6–7.
55. Interviews with Abraham Haselkorn and Cy Caller, OH.
56. Interview with Jacob Kraft, OH; Jacob Kraft file, DJHS; Jacob Kraft and Bernard Ziskind to Kalman Stein, Nov. 4, 1945, WJC–NY, file 12, drawer 272; Kalman Stein to Jacob Kraft, Dec. 16, 1945, WJC–NY, file 12, drawer 272.
57. Schwarz, *Redeemers*, pp. 17–23; interview with Abraham Klausner, OH; Bauer, *Yad Vashem Studies*, vol. 8, pp. 148–51.
58. Conference of Liberated Jews in Germany, "Minutes of the Business Section," July 25, 1945, WJC–NY, file 43, drawer 274; Schwarz, *Redeemers*, p. 31.
59. Bauer, *Yad Vashem Studies*, vol. 8, p. 155.
60. Conference of Liberated Jews in Germany, "Minutes of the Business Section," July 25, 1945, WJC–NY, file 43, drawer 294; Bauer, *Yad Vashem Studies*, vol. 8, p. 54.

Chapter 5

1. Bauer, *Flight and Rescue*, pp. 3–42; Yehuda Bauer, *The Emergence from Powerlessness*. (Toronto: University of Toronto Press, 1974), pp. 62–63; Michael Bar-Zohar, *The Avengers* (London: Arthur Barker, 1968).
2. Bauer, *Flight and Rescue*, pp. 3–42; idem, *Jewish Emergence*, pp. 62–63.
3. Dekel, *B'riha*; *Encyclopedia Judaica*, vol. 4, pp. 622–630.
4. Schwartz, *Redeemers*, p. 15.
5. Bauer, *Flight and Rescue*, pp. 96–99.
6. Lipman, "Summary of War Experiences"; interview with Sylvia Neulander, OH.
7. *NYT*, Dec. 7, 1945, p. 8.
8. *JTA*, Sept. 20, 1945, p. 2; ibid., Oct. 3, 1945, pp. 1–2; ibid., Oct. 3, 1945, p. 5.
9. Arieh Tartakower to WJC Office Committee, Sept. 28, 1945, WJC–NY, file 91, drawer 272.
10. Louis Lipsky to John J. McCloy, Sept. 24, 1945, PM.
11. Bauer, *Flight and Rescue*, p. 84. Office of the Military Government DP Division to Joint Anglo–American Committee of Inquiry, prob. early 1946; Nahum Goldmann to Stephen Wise, Jan. 8, 1946; Gruenbaum to Stephen Wise, Jan. 8, 1946, WJC–NY, file 59, drawer 272; Leon Kubowitzki to Joseph Shubow, Jan. 24, 1946—all of which are in WJC–NY, file 56, drawer 272.
12. Bauer, *Jewish Emergence*, pp. 66–69.
13. Lipman, "Summary of War Experiences."
14. Interview with Herbert Eskin, OH.

15. Interview with Cy Caller and Abraham Haselkorn, OH; Haselkorn, memorandum, CAH.
16. Interview with Hillel Blondheim and Abraham Haselkorn, OH.
17. Interview with Cy Caller, OH.
18. Interviews with Abraham Haselkorn and Cy Caller, OH; *JA*, Sept. 11, 1947, pp. 8B, 11B.
19. Interview with Herbert Ribner, OH.
20. Nathan Barack to author, n.d., PM.
21. Interview with Abraham Haselkorn and Cy Caller, OH; *World Telegram*, Feb. 1, 1946, p. 1; *Congress Weekly*, Oct. 6, 1945, pp. 5–6; Schwarz, *Root and the Bough*, pp. 329–32; *JTA*, Aug. 24, 1945, p. 3.
22. Interview with Max Braude, OH; Max Braude to Philip Bernstein, July 4, 1945, CJC, box 3, file D.
23. Tsemah Tsamriyon, *Haetoenoot Shel Shearit Hapletah BeGermania Kebetooyeh LeBayoteha*, (Organization of Holocaust Survivors from the British Zone, 1970), pp. 64–68.
24. Interview with Abraham Klausner, OH; Levi Shalit to author, Feb. 26, 1976, PM; Schwarz, *Redeemers*, pp. 10–11; *Jewish Spectator*, Sept. 1947, pp. 9, 16.
25. Tsamriyon, *Haetoenoot Shel Shearit Hapletah*, p. 87.
26. Schwarz, *Redeemers*, p. 61.
27. *Congress Weekly*, Feb. 8, 1946, p. 7.
28. Harold Saperstein to Philip Bernstein, Oct. 18, 1945, CJC, box 3, file C; Harold Saperstein to author, May 5, 1975, PM; Meyer Goldman to CANRA, Aug. 3, 1945; Sept. 5, 1945, CJC, box 3, file D; Arthur Burak to JWB, Feb. 12, 1946, CJC, box 33, file 3; Sophie Pearlman to Leon Kubowitzki, July 6, 1945, WJC–NY, file 43, drawer 274.
29. Northeastern Regional Chaplains Conference proceedings, Feb. 4–6, 1946, CJC, box 20.
30. Ibid.
31. Ibid.
32. Samuel Teitelbaum to Leon Kubowitzki, Apr. 23 and May 3, 1944, WJC–NY, file 12, drawer 272; John Sills to Louis Kraft, May 26, 1944; Louis Kraft to John Sills, June 8, 1944; Louis Kraft to Joseph Hyman, May 31 and July 10, 1944, CJC, box 3, file A.
33. Abraham Klausner to author, Nov. 24, 1989, PM.
34. Northeastern Regional Chaplains Conference, proceedings, Feb. 4–6, 1946, CJC, box 20.
35. Ibid.
36. Ibid.
37. Ibid.
38. Ibid.
39. Ibid. See also Robert Marcus to Arthur Greenleigh, July 16, 1945, WJC–NY, file 92, drawer 272; Robert Marcus to Arthur Greenleigh, Aug. 8, 1945, WJC–NY, file 67, drawer 272. Abraham Spiro remarked that he "looked for JDC representatives but never could find them, they were *elusive* obstacles, they existed on paper, they were available, maybe, where there was glamor" (Abraham Spiro to Philip Bernstein, CAH).
40. Lavy Becker, summary report, Shearit Hapletah–Germany, YIVO, file 211; Lavy Becker to Jacob Trobe, Dec. 16, 1945, YIVO, file 211; Irving Sherman to Paul Baerwald, July 25, 1945, JDC-DP General; Lavy Becker to Joseph J. Schwartz, Feb. 9, 1946, PM.

41. Sadie Sender and Irving Krasnik, Dec. 25, 1945, Shearit Hapletah–Germany, YIVO, file 209. See also *Indiana Jewish Chronicle*, Sept. 21, 1945, p. 2; Joseph Levine to Leo Schwarz, Aug. 19, 1946, Shearit Hapletah–Germany, YIVO, file 25.

42. Abraham Klausner to author, Nov. 24, 1989, PM.

43. Edward M. M. Warburg to JDC, Nov. 2, 1945, CAH; Philip Bernstein, memorandum, Nov. 7, 1945, CAH; Philip Bernstein to Abraham Klausner, Nov. 7, 1945, CAH; Simon Rifkind to Jacob Trobe, Nov. 26, 1945, CAH; Jacob Trobe to Abraham Klausner, Nov. 5, 1945, CAH.

44. "Schmooze Sheet for Chaplains," Jan. 11, 1946, PM, p. 5.

45. Northeastern Regional Chaplains Conference, proceedings, Feb. 4–6, 1946, CJC, box 20.

46. Ibid.

47. Ibid; Bauer, *American Jewry*, p. 458.

48. Bernstein to Eichhorn, Aug. 17, 1945, JWB, box 199.

49. Northeastern Regional Chaplains Conference, proceedings, Feb. 4–6, 1946, CJC, box 20.

50. Ibid.

51. *Jewish Centergram*, March 1950, pp. 5, 14.

52. *Unzer Weg*, Suppl. no. 1, Oct. 12, 1945, p. 1.

53. Ibid.

54. Levi Shalit to author, PM.

55. B. Konichsky, an engineer who worked at the central committee, remarked that "towards the end of July . . . I was at a meeting in St. Ottilien. . . . There I saw you for the first time. At the same meeting there appeared a guest from Palestine. Although he found warm words, . . . I felt the existence of a wall between us, . . . an abyss to be bridged. I heard your words. . . . You were one of us, as you entitled your article in *Unzer Weg* later on" (B. Konichsky to Abraham Klausner, Dec. 18, 1945, PM); interview with Jack Levin, OH.

56. Max Wall to CANRA, Aug. 1, 1945, JWB, box 236.

57. Eli Bohnen to Philip Bernstein, Aug. 15, 1945; Philip Bernstein to Abraham Klausner, Sept. 9, 1945, CAH.

58. Interviews with Simon Pava, Eugene Lipman, Eli Heimberg, Eli Bohnen, and Abraham Haselkorn, OH.

59. Levinger, "Rabbis to the Rescue." (Philip Bernstein reiterated this expression of pride when he wrote to David M. Eichhorn: "I cannot begin to tell you what a sense of satisfaction we have derived from the knowledge that our Jewish chaplains were on the spot. They have certainly earned for themselves an honored place in Jewish history," Aug. 17, 1945, JWB, box 199.)

60. Benjamin Brook to Reuben Resnick, Oct. 24, 1945, CJC, box 3, file C.

61. Memorandum to Simon H. Rifkind, Jan. 12, 1945, WJC–NY, file 59, drawer 272; Leon Kubowitzki to Simon Rifkind, Nov. 1, 1945, WJC–NY, file 59, drawer 272.

62. Abraham Klausner to James Heller and Jonah B. Wise, Dec. 3, 1945, CAH; Abraham Klausner to Leon Kubowitzki, Dec. 20, 1945, Shearit Hapletah–Germany, YIVO, file 670.

63. Jacob Trobe considered him the Abraham Lincoln of Jewry and arranged to smuggle him out of the British zone in Germany. The British were very disturbed because they saw it as a hostile propaganda move designed to complicate their problems with the Mandate. Interview with Jacob Trobe, OH;

for a review of the proceedings of the conference, see *JTA*, Dec. 17, 1945, pp. 1–4; *JE*, Dec. 28, 1945, p. 7.

64. Herbert Katzki to JDC, Paris, Jan. 14, 1946, Shearit Hapletah–Germany, YIVO, file 159.

65. Central Committee of Liberated Jews in Bavaria to Lavy Becker, Dec. 28, 1945, Shearit Hapletah–Germany, YIVO, file 209; Abraham Klausner to Leo Jung, Jan. 6, 1946, Shearit Hapletah–Germany, YIVO, file 209; see Klausner file, CAH; Kalman Stein to Leon Kubowitzki, Jan. 11, 1946, WJC–NY, file 75, drawer 272; Leon Kubowitzki to Abraham Klausner, Jan. 24, 1946, WJC–NY, file 74, drawer 272.

66. See also reports in the American Jewish press about them or their activities: *Jewish Frontier*, Aug. 1945, pp. 7–14, and the series of articles by Herbert Friedman in *Intermountain Jewish News*, fall 1945.

67. Leon Kubowitzki to Abraham Klausner, Dec. 19, 1945, WJC–NY, file 74, drawer 272.

68. *Jewish Frontier*, July 1945, p. 13.

69. Leon Kubowitzki to Abraham Klausner, Dec. 19, 1945, WJC–NY, file 74, drawer 272.

Chapter 6

1. *JE*, June 28, 1945, p. 4; Philip Bernstein to WJC, AJC, JDC, American Jewish Conference, and Jewish Agency for Palestine, prob. after May 1947, AH.

2. William Haber to WJC, AJC, JDC, American Jewish Conference, and Jewish Agency for Palestine, Apr. 1, 1948, Shearit Hapletah–Germany, YIVO, file 120; Clifford Townshend to commanding generals, July 7, 1947, AH.

3. Oscar Mintzer, "The Legal Situation of Jewish DPs in the American Zone, Germany," Sept. 23, 1946, Shearit Hapletah–Germany, YIVO, file 170. For more details, see Irving Krasnik, "Report on Lampertheim," Feb. 20, 1946, Shearit Hapletah–Germany, YIVO, file 210; Henry Cohen to WJC, Nov. 9, 1946, Shearit Hapletah–Germany, YIVO, file 65; Oscar Mintzer to Leo W. Schwarz, Apr. 20, 1946 and June 20, 1946, Shearit Hapletah–Germany, YIVO, file 171; "Survey of Anti-Jewish Acts and Excesses in the American Occupied Zone in Germany," CAH; *JE*, June 28, 1946, p. 29; ibid., Sept. 27, 1946, p. 15; ibid., Dec. 13, 1946, p. 6; *JTA*, Mar. 27, 1946, p. 2; ibid., May 9, 1946, p. 1; ibid., June 4, 1946, p. 29; ibid., Aug. 9, 1946, p. 5; *PM*, Mar. 28, 1946, p. 2; June 2, 1946, p. 4; *NYT*, July 14, 1945, p. 3; *Daily Mirror*, Nov. 15, 1946; *New York Herald Tribune*, Nov. 15, 1946; *Daily News*, Nov. 15, 1946; Fohrenwald file, AH; Rabbi Alexander Rosenberg, "The Problem of Jailings of DPs," Mar. 7, 1946, Shearit Hapletah–Germany, YIVO, file 170; "Raids," n.d., AH; Henry Spector, "Military Police Raid in the Ulanen Kaserne, Bamberg," Nov. 25, 1946, AH; Abraham S. Hyman to Philip Bernstein, Dec. 5, 1946, AH.

4. Mintzer, "The Legal Situation of Jewish DPs in the American Zone, Germany," Sept. 23, 1946, Shearit Hapletah–Germany, file 170.

5. Ibid.

6. *NYT*, Mar. 20 and Mar. 31, 1946; *New York Herald Tribune*, Mar. 20, 31, and Apr. 5, 1946; *JE*, Apr. 5, 1946, p. 2; *JTA*, Mar. 20, 1946, p. 1; ibid., Apr. 1, 1946, pp. 1–2; ibid., Apr. 5, 1946, p. 1; Simon Rifkind, address Apr. 2, 1946, PM; *Indiana Jewish Chronicle*, Apr. 5, 1946, p. 1; *JA*, Apr. 4, 1946, p. 10; Central Committee of the Liberated Jews in the American Occupied Zone, "What Happened in Stuttgart on March 29, 1946?" Shearit Hapletah–Germany, YIVO, file 170; Simon Rifkind, Mar. 21, 1946, WJC–NY, file 59, drawer 272; Abraham Klausner to WJC, WJC–NY, file 74, drawer 272; Henry Monsky to James

F. Byrnes, Apr. 5, 1946, Shearit Hapletah–Germany, YIVO, file 159; Zalman Grinberg to American Jewish Conference, Apr. 26, 1946, Shearit Hapletah–Germany, YIVO, file 159.

7. Philip Bernstein to WJC, AJC, JDC, American Jewish Conference, and Jewish Agency for Palestine, prob. after May 1947, AH; Jean Greenwald to Celia Weinberg, July 31, 1947, Shearit Hapletah–Germany, YIVO, file 249; William Haber, notes on session with General Lucius Clay in Frankfurt, Jan. 15, 1948, AH; D.B.Pearl to Abraham Hyman, Jan. 28, 1948, AH; "The Franz Joseph Camp Incidents," AH; Zachariah Shuster and David Bernstein to John Slawson, May 10, 1946, AH; Kalman Stein to Leon Kubowitzki, Sept. 23, 1946, WJC–NY, file 81, drawer 272; *JTA*, Jan. 6, 1947; ibid., Apr. 20, 1947, p. 5; ibid., June 9, 1947, p. 1; ibid., Aug. 5, 1947, p. 4; ibid., Aug. 10, 1946, p. 4; ibid., Sept. 9, 1946, p. 7; *NYT*, Feb. 23, 1947.

8. "The Jewish Problem of the American Administration in Germany," *JTA*, Feb. 15, 1947, also in AH.

9. Zalman Grinberg to American Jewish Conference, Apr. 26, 1946, Shearit Hapletah–Germany, YIVO, file 159.

10. Philip Bernstein, final report, Oct. 20, 1947, Shearit Hapletah–Germany, YIVO, file 124; Philip Bernstein, report to WJC, AJC, JDC, American Jewish Conference, and Jewish Agency, late 1947, AH; interview with Philip Bernstein, OH.

11. Haber, notes on session with General Lucius Clay in Frankfurt, Jan. 14 and 15, 1948, AH.

12. Interview with Herbert Friedman, OH; Herbert L. Friedman file, AJA.

13. Interview with Emanuel Rackman, OH; telephone interview with Philip Bernstein; Schwarz, *Redeemers*, pp. 148–56.

14. Interview with Herbert Friedman, OH; Herbert Friedman file, AJA.

15. Herbert Friedman to General Mickelson, May 5, 1946, AJA; Alvin Rockwell to chief of staff, June 28, 1946, AH; Abraham Hyman, notes on Colonel Sage's report, July 31, 1946, AH; idem, comments on recommendations of Alvin J. Rockwell to deputy military governor, n.d., AH; idem to Walter I. Korn, Aug. 15, 1946, AH; Abraham Klausner to WJC, Apr. 1946, WJC–NY, file 74, drawer 272; *New York Herald Tribune*, Apr. 30, 1946; *JTA*, Apr. 30, 1946, p. 1; ibid., May 2, 1946, p. 9; ibid., May 3, 1946, pp. 3–4; ibid., May 5, 1946, p. 6; ibid., May 6, 1946, p. 3; ibid., May 13, 1946, p. 2; ibid., May 14, 1946, p. 3; ibid., May 17, 1946, p. 5; ibid., May 19, 1946, p. 2; ibid., May 21, 1946, p. 4; ibid., May 23, 1946, p. 1; ibid., Aug. 6, 1946, p. 3; *American Jewish Conference Bulletin*, May 3, 1946, p. 3; Joseph Glatzer to General McNarney, July 18, 1946, AH.

16. Interview with Abraham S. Hyman, OH; Herbert L. Friedman monthly report, May 1946, Herbert L. Friedman file, AJA; interview with Abraham Klausner, OH.

17. Leo Schwarz to Joseph Schwarz, Jan. 13, 1947, Shearit Hapletah–Germany, YIVO, file 9; "Maintenance of Law and Order Among United Nations Displaced Persons—Supplement No. 1," Dec. 27, 1946, AH.

18. "Maintenance of Law and Order Among United Nations Displaced Persons—Supplement No. 1," Dec. 27, 1946, AH.

19. John Marlowe, *The Seat of Pilate* (London: Cresset, 1959), pp. 206–10; Bauer, *Flight and Rescue*, pp. 242–43.

20. Bartley Crum, *Behind the Silken Curtain* (Port Washington, N.Y.: Kennikat, 1969), pp. 89–90. See also Richard Crossman, *Palestine Mission: A Per-*

sonal Record (New York: Harper and Brothers, 1947); J. H. Whiting to UNRRA team directors, Jan. 29, 1946, AH; *JTA*, Feb. 12, 1946, pp. 1–2; ibid., Feb. 24, 1946, p. 6; Simon Rifkind to Stephen S. Wise, Feb. 23, 1946, WJC–NY, file 59, drawer 272.

21. Marlowe, *Seat of Pilate*, pp. 206–10.
22. Bauer, *Jewish Emergence*, p. 74.
23. Marlowe, *Seat of Pilate*, pp. 206–10.
24. Mark Wischnitzer, *Visas to Freedom: The History of HIAS* (Cleveland: World Publishing, 1956), pp. 207–8, 212–13; *JTA*, May 8, 1946, p. 4; S. R. Mickelson to Joint Anglo–American Committee of Inquiry, n.d., AH; Irwin Rosen to Philip Rosen, Dec. 30, 1946, AH; *NYT*, Dec. 23, 1945, p. 1. For an analysis of why the immigration program did not succeed, see *JTA*, Mar. 3, 1946, p. 3; ibid., Oct. 8, 1946, p. 5; Newman, "Earl G. Harrison," pp. 254–58; Irwin Rosen to Philip Bernstein, Dec. 27, 1946, AH; Philip Bernstein to I. L. Kenen, Jan. 20, 1947, CAH; Dinnerstein, *America and the Survivors*, pp. 113–16.
25. Bauer, *Jewish Emergence*, p. 65.
26. Bauer, *History of the Holocaust*, pp. 341–42.
27. Philip Bernstein to I. L. Kenen, June 28, 1946, WJC–NY, file 80, drawer 272; Philip Bernstein to Kalman Stein, July 3, 1946, WJC–NY, file 80, drawer 272; *JTA*, June 27, 1946, p. 3.
28. *JTA*, Jan. 3, 1946, p. 3; ibid., Jan. 4, 1946, p. 2; ibid., Jan. 7, 1946, pp. 3–4; ibid., Jan. 10, 1946, p. 8; ibid., Feb. 1, 1946, p. 5; *Time*, Jan. 14, 1946, p. 23; *JF*, Feb. 1946, p. 24; *Congress Weekly*, Jan. 11, 1946, pp. 4, 16; ibid., Feb. 8, 1946, pp. 3–4; *Jewish Spectator*, Feb. 4, 1946, p. 4; *Indiana Jewish Chronicle*, Feb. 8, 1946, p. 2; *Chicago Tribune*, Jan. 6, 1946; Jacob Trobe to Joseph Schwartz, Jan. 4, 1946, Shearit Hapletah–Germany, YIVO, file 65; interview with Jacob Trobe, OH.
29. Philip Bernstein, final report, Oct. 20, 1947, Shearit Hapletah–Germany, YIVO, file 124; Philip Bernstein to WJC, JDC, AJC, American Jewish Conference, and Jewish Agency, late 1947, AH; interview with Philip Bernstein, OH.
30. Philip Bernstein to Kalman Stein, July 3, 1946, WJC–NY, file 80, drawer 272; *NYT*, June 27, 1946.
31. Philip Bernstein to I. L. Kenen, June 28, 1946, WJC–NY, file 80, drawer 272.
32. "Notes on Meeting of Representatives of the American Jewish Committee, American Jewish Conference, Jewish Agency, Joint Distribution Committee," July 8, 1946, WJC–NY, file 80, drawer 272.
33. Bauer, *Flight and Rescue*, pp. 243–44.
34. These sources included a correspondent for the *Jewish Morning Journal* and the Central Committee of Polish Jews, as well as U. S. ambassador Arthur Bliss Lane and William Bein, director of the JDC in Poland.
35. Philip Bernstein to Joseph T. McNarney ("Report on Poland"), Aug. 2, 1946, AJA; *JTA*, Aug. 2, 1946, p. 9; ibid., Aug. 5, 1946, p. 5.
36. C. Irving Dwork to Leon Kubowitzki, July 22, 1946, WJC–NY, file 16, drawer 274; I. Schwartzbart to WJC Officer Committee, July 25, 1946, WJC–NY, file 16, drawer 274. See also Joseph McNarney to War Department, July 7, 1946, AH; *JTA*, Apr. 26, 1946, p. 5.
37. C. Irving Dwork to Leon Kubowitzki, July 22, 1946, WJC–NY, file 16, drawer 274; I. Schwartzbart to WJC Officer Committee, July 25, 1946, WJC–NY, file 16, drawer 274.
38. David Wahl to Meir Grossman, July 23, 1946, WJC–NY, file 16, drawer 274.

Notes to Chapter 6

39. Ibid.
40. Ibid.
41. *JTA*, Aug. 11, 1946, pp. 1–2; ibid., Aug. 13, 1946, p. 7; ibid., Aug. 22, 1946, p. 4; ibid., Aug. 25, 1946, p. 2.
42. David Wahl to Meir Grossman, Aug. 19, 1946, WJC–NY, file 16, drawer 274.
43. Mark Clark to assistant secretary of war, June 30, 1946, AH; *JTA*, Feb. 12, 1946, p. 5; ibid., Aug. 29, 1946, p. 4; Nov. 22, 1946, p.4. See also Mark Clark's efforts to rectify the situation, Mark Clark to Philip Bernstein, Nov. 29, 1946, Shearit Hapletah–Germany, YIVO, file 124.
44. Bauer, *Flight and Rescue*, pp. 250–51. The Jewish Telegraphic Agency reported that "twelve thousand Jews from Poland" arrived in Vienna in the first seven days of August *JTA*, Aug. 9, 1946, p. 5. This number was given to the agency by Joseph Silver, a Cleveland attorney who headed the JDC operations in Vienna. See also *JTA*, May 10, 1946, p. 3.
45. Philip Bernstein to Joseph C. Hyman, Sept. 8, 1946, CAH.
46. Ibid.
47. Ibid.
48. Ibid., *JTA*, Sept. 10, 1946, p. 4; ibid., Oct. 16, 1946, p. 2; C. Irving Dwork to Arieh Tartakower, WJC–NY, file 16, drawer 274; M. W. Beckelman to Philip Bernstein, Dec. 11, 1946, AH.
49. JDC Italy file, Sept.–Dec. 1946; Philip S. Bernstein to M. A. Leavitt, Sept. 8, 1946; M. A. Leavitt to Joseph Schwartz, Sept. 20, 1946; Joseph Schwartz to M. A. Leavitt, Sept. 30, 1946.
50. *Congress Weekly*, Oct. 27, 1958, pp. 7–9.
51. "Conference with President Truman in the White House Executive Office," Oct. 11, 1946, AH.
52. Ibid.
53. Ibid.
54. Bauer, *Flight and Rescue*, pp. 261–70.
55. "Jewish Chaplains Accompany Trains," n.d. CJC, box 3, file B.
56. Yosef Miller, "Report to the Office of Rabbi Bernstein on the Escorting of DP Train from Salzburg, Austria to Heilbronn, Germany," Sept. 4, 1946, OH, p. 5.
57. Ibid., p. 6.
58. Albert A. Troy, report, Aug. 1946, AH. See also Bert A. Klein, "Report of 29 August 1946 Covering Activities on TDY," CJC, box 33, file 3; Herman Dicker to commanding general, Third U.S. Army, Sept. 12, 1946, AH; Yosef Miller, "The Misplaced Persons," May 10, 1971, OH; interview with Herman Dicker, OH.
59. Yosef Miller, "Report to the Office of Rabbi Bernstein on the Escorting of DP Train from Salzburg, Austria to Heilbronn, Germany," Sept. 4, 1946, OH, p. 7.
60. Ibid.
61. Herbert Friedman to Philip Bernstein, Sept. 21, 1946, AH; Leon Retter to Colonel Mickelsen, Sept. 15, 1946, AH.
62. Herbert Friedman to Philip Bernstein ("Report on Babenhausen"), Oct. 4, 1946, AH; interviews with Herbert Friedman and Herman Dicker, OH; Herbert Friedman file, AJA.
63. Interviews with Herbert Friedman, Yosef Miller, and Abe Loskove, OH; Herbert Friedman to Philip Bernstein, Sept. 21, 1946, AH.

64. Herbert Friedman to Philip Bernstein, Sept. 21, 1946, AH.
65. Philip Bernstein to G–5, Dec. 19, 1946, AH.
66. Bauer, *Flight and Rescue*, pp. 130–36.
67. John J. Maginnis Papers: Military Government and Journal, Jan. 7, 1946, DA.
68. Bauer, *Flight and Rescue*, pp. 135–41.
69. Interview with Max Helvarg, Eli Rock, and Henry Levy, OH.
70. Interviews with Saul Loeb, Ruth Kluger, and Herbert Friedman, OH.
71. Joseph Shubow to Temple B'nai Moshe, Board of Directors, Boston, PM; *JA*, Aug. 28, 1969, p. 6; ibid., Apr. 8, 1947, p. 14; ibid., Dec. 6, 1945, p. 6; interview with Saul Loeb (Shubow's assistant), OH.
72. Interview with Herbert Friedman, OH; Herbert Friedman to Aryeh Lev, Apr. 19, 1946, JWB, box 204.
73. Interview with Meyer Abramowitz, OH.
74. Interviews with Max Braude, Eugene Cohen, Samuel Burstein, Yosef Miller, and Abraham Klausner, OH; Dekel, *B'riha*, p. 88.
75. Interview with Milton Elefant, OH.
76. Bauer, *Flight and Rescue*, pp. 302–4; Aba Gefen, *Unholy Alliance* (Jerusalem: Yuval Tal, 1973), pp. 114–35.
77. Chaplain Abraham J. Klausner, report Mar. 20, 1947, CAH.
78. *JTA*, Aug. 6, 1946, p. 3.
79. Leo Srole, "Why the DPs Can't Wait," *Commentary*, Jan. 1947, p. 22.
80. Interview with Jacob Kraft, OH; Jacob Kraft file, DJHS.
81. Nathan Shapell, *Witness to the Truth* (New York: David McKay, 1974), pp. 265, 285–87; John H. Sampson, Jr., to Abraham Spiro, Oct. 11, 1946, NA–SM, file 247.
82. Interview with Morris Dembowitz, OH.
83. Interview with Meyer Abramowitz, OH.
84. Philip Bernstein, "Confidential Report on the Situation of Jewish DPs," Dec. 6, 1946, Shearit Hapletah–Germany, YIVO, file 124.
85. Srole, "Why the DPs," p. 16.
86. Interview with Meyer Abramowitz, OH.
87. Interviews with Meyer Abramowitz and Dixie Heim, OH; invitation to opening of children's summer camp, PM.
88. Interview with Max Meletzer, Hava Frank, and Gunther Meyer (survivors who knew Abramowitz in Berlin), OH.
89. Abraham S. Hyman, letter directed "To Whom It May Concern," Feb. 23, 1948, AH. See also interviews with Henry Levy, Abraham Loskove, and Harold Fishbein, OH.
90. Interviews with Yosef Miller, Atara Miller, Johnny Low, David Bar-El, Milton Marcus, and Melvin Greenbaum, OH; *Liberated*, 1, no. 1, published under the auspices of the Chaplain Section, Headquarters Command USFET by the Frankfurt Jewish GI Council, PM; Alex Grobman, "Encounters with Holocaust Survivors," *Jewish Spectator*, spring 1978, p. 50.
91. Interviews with Saul Loeb, Max Helvarg, Henry Levy, Harold Fishbein, and Herbert Friedman, OH; *JA*, May 30, 1946, pp. 1, 16; Joseph Shubow to Stephen Wise, Jan. 11, 1946, WJC–NY, file 56, drawer 272.
92. Interview with Leo Ginsburg, OH.
93. Nathan Barack to author, n.d., PM; *Palestine Post*, [1946], PM; J. A. Kellet to Nathan Barack, July 22, 1946, PM; Nathan Barack to commanding general, Eighty-Eighth Division, July 13, 1946, PM.

Chapter 7

1. Bauer, *Flight and Rescue*, p. 291.
2. Idem, *History of the Holocaust*, pp. 343–44.
3. Howard M. Sachar, *A History of Israel* (New York: Alfred A. Knopf, 1976), p. 247; Bauer, *Jewish Emergence*, p. 72.
4. Sachar, *History of Israel*, p. 257; Bauer, *Jewish Emergence*, p. 73.
5. Sachar, *History of Israel*, p. 265.
6. Bauer, *Jewish Emergence*, p. 73; Bauer, *History of the Holocaust*, p. 346.
7. Dinnerstein, *America and the Survivors*, p. 101; Zvi Ganin, *Truman, American Jewry and Israel, 1945–1948* (New York: Holmes and Meir, 1979), p. 65.
8. Ganin, *Truman, American Jewry*; p. 67.
9. Ibid., p. 65.
10. Dinnerstein, *America and the Survivors*, pp. 102, 114.
11. Ibid., p. 115.
12. Ibid., p. 117.
13. Ibid., p. 255.
14. Ibid., p. 251.
15. Ibid., pp. 217–53.
16. Sachar, *History of Israel*, pp. 270–71; Ganin, *Truman, American Jewry*, p. 77.
17. Ganin, *Truman, American Jewry*, pp. 79, 85, 93.
18. Ibid., p. 85.
19. Ibid., p. 93.
20. Ibid., pp. 104, 107.
21. Ibid., pp. 118–19.
22. Cohen, *Palestine*, pp. 190–91.
23. Peterson, *American Occupation*, p. 91.
24. Srole, "Why the DPs," p. 18.
25. Interviews with Max Wall and Aryeh Lev, OH.
26. Paul Gorin to chaplains of the Third Army, Feb. 1, 1946, PM.
27. Interviews with Yosef and Atara Miller, David Bar-El, and Bertram Levine, OH. Levine was the JWB director in Frankfurt and Heidelberg.
28. David Marcus to American Jewish organizations, Feb. 7, 1947, WJC–NY, file 69, drawer 272.
29. Interviews with Yosef Miller, Johnny Low (Yehuda Lev), and Rosamund Low, OH; Alex Grobman, "Encounter with Holocaust Survivors," p. 50.
30. David Marcus to American Jewish organizations, Feb. 7, 1947; interviews with Eliezer Dembitz and David Bar-El OH; Yosef Miller, "The Misplaced Person," OH.
31. Interviews with David Lippert, Milton Marcus, Melvin Greenbaum, David Marcus, Johnny Low, and Yosef and Atara Miller, OH; *Liberated* 1 and 2, CAH.
32. Courtney N. Burnap to Zalman Grinberg, Feb. 15, 1946, CAH.
33. Interview with Abraham Klausner, OH; Abraham Klausner to American Jewish Conference, Mar. 16, 1946, Shearit Hapletah–Germany, YIVO, file 672; Abraham Klausner to Maurice Ullman, cable, n.d., CAH; Abraham Klausner to J. Press, cable, n.d., CAH.
34. I.L. Kenen to Abraham Klausner, Mar. 29, 1946, Shearit Hapletah–Germany, YIVO, file 159.
35. *JE*, Apr. 5, 1946, p. 6.

36. Abraham Klausner to I. Rozkovsky, Mar. 19, 1946, Shearit Hapletah–Germany, YIVO, file 672.
37. *Record,* Mar. 1946, pp. 14–19; *JE,* Apr. 5, 1946, p. 6.
38. Interview with Abraham Klausner, OH.
39. Interview with Marvin Linick, OH.
40. Interview with Ann Liepah (Borden), OH.
41. Interviews with Ann Liepah (Borden), Abraham Klausner, and Marvin Linick, OH; Central Committee of Liberated Jews in Bavaria to JDC, n.d., CAH.
42. Leo Schwarz to Jack Whiting, July 17, 1946, Shearit Hapletah–Germany, YIVO, file 161.
43. Yehuda Bauer's interview with Abraham Klausner, OH; Abraham Klausner to Philip Bernstein, Dec. 6, 1946, AH; Philip Bernstein to I. L. Kenen, Jan. 6, 1947, AH.
44. Central Committee of Liberated Jews in Bavaria to Friends of the Shearit Hapletah, Nov. 7, 1946, PM; M. E. Schwartz to A. J. Klausner, Dec. 15, 1947, PM. M. E. Schwartz, area director for the Preparatory Commission for the International Refugee Organization (PCIRO) area team in Kassel, Germany, wrote Klausner as follows:

> On the eve of my departure from this area, permit me to extend to you my most heartfelt thanks on behalf of the team, the tens of thousands of displaced persons whom we were privileged to serve and myself for the understanding, unselfish and devoted job that you have done here for the past year.
>
> I doubt very much if there are any more people who know more than I of the service that you have rendered your God and people. In your accomplishments for suffering mankind you are one of the outstanding ministers. Your kind of ministering has not been limited to preaching dry sermons which the people normally forget after they have left their respective house of God. Yours has been the ministry of service, the ministry of help to the needy, and the alleviation of suffering of those in pain. You have been fearless and outspoken, always speaking your mind and honestly and truly without any mental reservations or double meanings.
>
> I know that you hate praise, but I would feel extremely bad if I had left here without expressing to you the sentiments of the people you came in contact with and myself. Praised [sic] be to you to whom praise is due. (M. E. Schwartz to A. J. Klausner, Dec. 15, 1947, PM)

45. Abraham Klausner, monthly chaplains report, NA–SM, file 201.
46. Interview with Abraham Klausner, OH; Abraham Klausner to Leo Schwarz, Oct. 7, 1946, Shearit Hapletah–Germany, YIVO, file 165.
47. *Fun Letzten Churben,* Aug. 1946, Munich, PM.
48. Beatrice Cuntz to Abraham Klausner, Nov. 25, 1946, CAH.
49. Beatrice Cuntz to Abraham Klausner, Oct. 9, 1946, PM; Abraham Klausner to Beatrice Cuntz, Nov. 4, 1946, PM; Helen Witkin to Abraham Klausner, Nov. 6, 1946, PM; David R. Wahl to Abraham Klausner, Dec. 13, 1946, CAH; Abraham Klausner to Vaad Hatzala, Dec. 27, 1946, CAH.
50. Interviews with Herbert Friedman, OH; *Stars and Stripes,* Dec. 9, 1947; Abraham Hyman, manuscript chapter on the American chaplains, PM.
51. Charles I. Carpenter to Philip S. Bernstein, Feb. 19, 1946, CJC, box 33, file 3.
52. Philip Bernstein to Charles I. Carpenter, Feb. 27, 1946, CJC, box 33, file 3; Charles I. Carpenter to Philip Bernstein, Mar. 4, 1946, CJC, box 33, file 3.

53. Philip Bernstein to Charles I. Carpenter, Feb. 27, 1946, CJC, box 33, file 3.
54. Philip Bernstein to Aryeh Lev, Nov. 18, 1946, CJC, box 3, file B.
55. Philip Bernstein to Luther D. Miller, Aug. 27, 1946, CJC, box 3, file B.
56. Ibid.
57. Luther D. Miller to David de Sola Pool, Oct. 3, 1946, CJC, box 2, file B; Luther D. Miller to David de Sola Pool, Oct. 16, 1946, CJC, box 3, file B.
58. Philip Bernstein to David de Sola Pool, Mar. 6, 1947, AH.
59. Philip Bernstein to David de Sola Pool, Mar. 6, 1947, AH; David M. Eichhorn to Philip Bernstein, Aug. 15, 1946, CJC, box 3, file B.
60. Philip Bernstein to Leon Adler, Dec. 26, 1946, CJC, box 3, file 9; Aryeh Lev to Philip Bernstein, Dec. 3, 1946, CJC, box 3, file B.
61. Telephone interviews with Philip Bernstein, Abraham Klausner, and Eugene Lipman.
62. Philip Bernstein to WJC, AJC, JDC, American Jewish Conference, and Jewish Agency, late 1947, AH.
63. Abraham Klausner to Fred Cramer, Jan. 7, 1947, PM; Robert A. Taft to Fred B. Cramer, Jan. 17, 1947, PM; Aryeh Lev to Luther D. Miller, Nov. 29, 1946, PM; interview with Abraham Klausner, OH; Yehuda Bauer's interview with Abraham Klausner, OH; Abraham Klausner, monthly reports, NA–SM, file 201. Before leaving, Klausner asked Ira Hirshmann, a prominent Jewish businessman who had once served as special representative for the WRB (1944) and special inspector general for UNRRA (1946), to write a letter introducing him to the directors of the UNRRA program for Germany and Bavaria. Hirschmann wrote back that Klausner's returning to Germany was the "best news" he had heard "in a long time." Furthermore, he sent a letter to these men, praising Klausner for his outstanding achievements. In one letter Hirschmann noted:

> The story of Chaplain Klausner is a saga in itself. When I was in Germany last year I found that he was one of the few individuals who ignored red tape, broke through and got things done. By that I mean he saved lives contrary to rules, etc. The work he did was nothing short of heroic. In the course of it he ran into some difficulties with routine agencies. His results in the face of their passivity constituted a reproach to them; if ever there was a constructive irritant he was it.
> Klausner should be of unquestionable value to you in your work and I commend him to you with all my heart and soul.

See Ira A. Hirschmann to Paul Edwards, Jan. 27, 1947, PM; Ira Hirschmann to Meyer Cohen, Jan. 24, 1947, PM; Abraham Klausner to Ira Hirschmann, Jan. 23, 1946, PM; Ira Hirschmann to Abraham Klausner, Jan. 27, 1947, PM.
64. I. L. Kenen to Philip Bernstein, Dec. 4, 1946, AH; Philip Bernstein to Abraham Klausner, Dec. 6, 1946, AH; Philip Bernstein to I.L. Kenen, Jan. 6, 1947, AH.
65. Interview with Abraham Klausner, OH.
66. Abraham Klausner to American Jewish Conference, May 2, 1948, AJA.
67. Abraham Klausner to Jankel Levin, July 5, 1947, CAH.
68. Abraham Klausner to American Jewish Conference, May 2, 1948., AJA.
69. Abraham Klausner to American Jewish Conference Executive Committee, Mar. 20, 1947, AH.
70. Abraham Klausner to American Jewish Conference, May 2, 1948, AJA.
71. Ibid.

72. Ibid.
73. "Report from Abraham J. Klausner," Mar. 20, 1947, AH.
74. Ibid.
75. Abraham Klausner to American Jewish Conference, May 2, 1948, AJA.
76. "Report from Abraham J. Klausner," Mar. 20, 1947, AH.
77. Ibid.
78. Ibid.
79. Leo Schwarz to Joseph Schwartz, Nov. 15, 1946, Shearit Hapletah–Germany, YIVO, file 162.
80. Ibid.
81. "Report from Abraham J. Klausner," Mar. 20, 1947, AH.
82. "An Evaluation of the American Joint Distribution Committee Program in the American Occupied Zone of Germany, from Its Inception to January 1947," Jan. 28, 1947, CAH.
83. Ibid.
84. "Report from Abraham J. Klausner," Mar. 20, 1947, AH.
85. Abraham Klausner to Philip Bernstein, Oct. 10, 1947, CAH.
86. Abraham Klausner to Philip Bernstein, Nov. 10, 1947, CAH.
87. William Haber to Meir Grossman, May 26, 1948, Shearit Hapletah–Germany, YIVO, file 65; Abraham Klausner to Abraham Hyman, Apr. 20, 1948, AH.
88. "Meeting of the Jewish Cooperating Organizations on Rabbi Klausner's Suggestions Respecting the DP Situation," May 4, 1948, AH.
89. Samuel Steinberg to Abraham Klausner, May 9, 1948, CAH.
90. Ibid.
91. Abraham Hyman to Abraham Klausner, June 22, 1948, AH.
92. Ibid.
93. Bauer, *Jewish Emergence,* pp. 77–78.
94. Joseph M. Hochstein and Murray Greenfield, *Jews' Secret Fleet* (New York: Gefen Books, 1987), pp. 125–31; Schwarz, *Redeemers,* pp. 240–63; Walter Laqueur, ed., *The Israel/Arab Reader* (London: Weidenfeld and Nicolson, 1969), pp. 109–12; *JTA,* Aug. 10, 1947, p. 4; ibid., Aug. 25, 1947, p. 3; ibid., Sept. 8, 1947, p. 2.
95. K. Sabbethai, "Exodus: In the Wilderness," *JF,* Nov. 1947, pp. 15–16.
96. Abraham Klausner to author, Sept. 19, 1989, PM; *JTA,* Oct. 24, 1947, p. 4; ibid., Oct. 28, 1947, p. 4.
97. Bauer, *Flight and Rescue,* p. 317; Laqueur, *Israel/Arab Reader,* pp. 113–22.
98. William Haber, final report, Dec. 20, 1948, AH.
99. Ibid.
100. Ibid.
101. Random notes on chaplains' conference, Jan. 17, 1948.
102. William Haber to AJC, JDC, WJC, Jewish Agency for Palestine, and American Jewish Conference, June 10, 1948, AH.
103. William Haber to Aryeh Lev, May 10, 1948, AH.
104. William Haber to David de Sola Pool, Sept. 8, 1948, JWB, box 218.
105. William Haber to Aryeh Lev, May 10, 1948, AH; William Haber to General Harold, Apr. 16, 1948, AH; William Haber to AJC, JDC, WJC, Jewish Agency for Palestine, and American Jewish Conference, June 10, 1948, AH; Abraham S. Hyman to Philip Bernstein, Oct. 22, 1948, AH; David de Sola Pool to William Haber, Aug. 29, 1948, JWB, box 218.

106. William Haber to AJC, JDC, WJC, Jewish Agency for Palestine, and American Jewish Conference, June 10, 1948, AH.

107. Bauer, *History of the Holocaust*, p. 348.

108. Shmuel Ettinger, "The Struggle for Independence and the Establishment of the State of Israel," in *A History of the Jewish People*, ed. Hillel Ben-Sasson (Cambridge: Harvard University Press, 1976), p. 1049.

109. Bauer, *Jewish Emergence*, p. 76.

110. Edward M. M. Warburg to Frank L. Weil, Feb. 26, 1946, CJC, box 3, folder 2.

111. *JA*, Aug. 28, 1969, p. 6. Although this was said about Chaplain Joseph Shubow, it was typical of the survivors' response to many of the chaplains.

Bibliography

Books and Monographs

Abella, Irving, and Harold Troper. *None Is Too Many: Canada and the Jews of Europe, 1933–1948.* Toronto: Dennys, 1982.

Abzug, Robert H. *Inside the Vicious Heart: Americans and the Liberation of Nazi Concentration Camps.* New York: Oxford University Press, 1985.

Acheson, Dean. *Present at the Creation.* New York: W. W. Norton, 1969.

Adams, Henry H. *Harry Hopkins: A Biography.* New York: G. P. Putnam's Sons, 1977.

Agar, Herbert. *The Saving Remnant.* London: Rupert Hart–Davis, 1960.

Allen, Colonel Robert S. *Lucky Forward: A True History of General George Pattons's Third Army.* New York: McFadden Bartell, 1965.

Allied Forces. Twelfth Army Group. *Report of Operations (Final After Action Report).* G–5 Section, vol. 7. Twelfth Army Group, [1948].

Ambrose, Stephen E. *Eisenhower: Soldier, General of the Army, President Elect, 1890–1952.* New York: Simon and Schuster, 1983.

American Jewry During the Holocaust. New York: Bunche Institute on the United Nations, 1984.

Anglo–American Committee of Inquiry. *Hearings before the Anglo–American Committee of Inquiry.* Washington: Ward and Paul, 1946.

Avriel, Ehud. *Open the Gates.* New York: Atheneum, 1975.

Bach, Julian, Jr. *America's Germany.* New York: Random House, 1946.

Balabkins, Nicholas. *Germany Under Direct Controls: Economic Aspects of Industrial Disarmament 1945–1948.* New Brunswick: Rutgers University Press, 1964.

Bar-Zohar, Michael. *The Avengers.* London: Arthur Barker, 1968.

Barish, Louis, ed. *Rabbis in Uniform.* New York: Random House, 1970.

Bauer, Yehuda. *A History of the Holocaust.* New York: Franklin Watts, 1982.
———. *American Jewry and the Holocaust.* Detroit: Wayne State University Press, 1981.
———. *Flight and Rescue: Brichah.* New York: Random House, 1970.
———. *From Diplomacy to Resistance.* Philadelphia: Jewish Publication Society of America, 1970.
———. *The Holocaust in Historical Perspective.* Seattle: University of Washington Press, 1978.
———. *The Jewish Emergence from Powerlessness.* Toronto: University of Toronto Press, 1979.
———. *My Brother's Keeper: A History of the American Jewish Joint Distribution Committee 1929–1939.* Philadelphia: Jewish Publication Society of America, 1974.
———. *Out of the Ashes: The Impact of American Jews on Post-Holocaust European Jewry.* New York: Pergamon, 1989.
Belsen. Irgun Sheerit Hapleita Me'haezor Habriti. Tel Aviv, 1957.
Ben-Sasson, H.H., ed. *A History of the Jewish People.* Cambridge, Massachusetts: Harvard University Press, 1976.
Bentwich, Norman. *They Found Refuge.* London: Cresset, 1956.
Berben, Paul. *Dachau.* London: Norfolk, 1975.
Bernstein, Philip S. *Rabbis at War.* Waltham, Mass.: American Jewish Historical Society, 1971.
Biale, David. *Power and Powerlessness in Jewish History.* New York: Shocken Books, 1988.
Blum, John Morton. *From the Morgenthau Diaries: Years of War 1941–1945.* Boston: Houghton–Mifflin, 1967.
Blumenson, Martin, ed. *The Patton Papers: 1940–1945.* Boston: Houghton–Mifflin, 1974.
Burstein, Samuel. *Rabbi with Wings: Story of a Pilot.* New York: Herzl, 1965.
Chandler, Alfred D., and Louis Galambos, eds. *The Papers of Dwight Eisenhower.* Vol. 6, *Occupation, 1945.* Baltimore: Johns Hopkins University Press, 1978.
Clark, Mark W. *Calculated Risk.* New York: Harper and Brothers, 1950.
Clay, Lucius D. *Decision in Germany.* New York: Doubleday, 1950.
Cohen, Naomi. *Not Free To Desist.* Philadelphia: Jewish Publication Society of America, 1972.
Coles, Harry L., and Albert K. Weinberg. *Civil Affairs: Soldiers Become Governors.* Washington: Department of the Army, 1964.
———. *United States Army in World War II.* Washington: Department of the Army, 1964.
Crossman, Richard. *Palestine Mission: A Personal Record.* New York: Harper and Brothers, 1947.
Crum, Bartley C. *Behind the Silken Curtain.* Port Washington, N.Y.: Kennikat 1947; 1949.
Dallek, Robert. *Franklin D. Roosevelt and American Foreign Policy 1932–1945.* New York: Oxford University Press, 1979.

Davidowicz, Lucy. *The War Against the Jews*. Philadelphia: Jewish Publication Society of America, 1975.

Deane, John R. *The Strange Alliance*. New York: Viking, 1947.

Dekel, Ephraim. *B'riha: Flight to the Homeland*. New York: Herzl, n.d.

Dinnerstein, Leonard. *America and the Survivors of the Holocaust*. New York: Columbia University Press, 1982.

Divine, Robert A. *American Immigration Policy, 1924–1952*. New Haven: Yale University Press, 1957.

Donnison, F. S. V. *Civil Affairs and Military Government: North West Europe 1944–1946*. London: HMSO, 1961.

The D.P. Story: The Final Report of the Displaced Persons Commission. Washington: GPO, 1952.

DPs Are People! New York: Church World Service, n.d.

Druks, Herbert. *The Failure To Rescue*. New York: Robert Speller and Sons, 1977.

Eisenhower, Dwight. *Crusade in Europe*. Garden City, N.Y.: Doubleday, 1948.

Elazar, Daniel J. *Community and Polity: The Organizational Dynamics of American Jewry*. Philadelphia: Jewish Publication Society of America, 1976.

Eliach, Yaffa and Brana Gurewitsch, eds. *The Liberators: Eyewitness Accounts of the Liberation of Concentration Camps*. Vol. 1 New York: Center for Holocaust Studies Documentation and Research, 1981.

Epstein, Julius. *Operation Keelhaul: The Story of Forced Repatriation from 1944 to the Present*. Old Greenwich, Conn.: Devin–Adair, 1973.

Fein, Helen. *Accounting for Genocide*. New York: Macmillan/The Free Press, 1979.

Feingold, Henry. *The Politics of Rescue: The Roosevelt Administration and the Holocaust, 1938–1945*. New Brunswick: Rutgers University Press, 1970.

Fitzgibbon, Constantine. *Denazification*. New York: W. W. Norton, 1969.

Fredricksen, Oliver J. *The American Military Occupation of Germany, 1945–1953*. U.S. Army Research, 1953.

Friedman, Saul. *No Haven for the Oppressed: United States Policy Towards Jewish Refugees, 1938–1945*. Detroit: Wayne State University Press, 1973.

Fun Letzen Churben. Munich, 1946.

Ganin, Zvi. *Truman, American Jewry, and Israel, 1945–1948*. New York: Holmes and Meier, 1979.

Gefen, Aba. *Unholy Alliance*. Jerusalem: Yuval Tal, 1973.

Gil, Yaakov. *Sefer HaBrigadah HaYehudit*. Tel Aviv: Tarbut, 1950.

Gilbert, Martin. *Auschwitz and the Allies*. New York: Holt, Rinehart, and Winston, 1981.

———. *Exile and Return: The Struggle for a Jewish Homeland*. Philadelphia: J. B. Lippincott, 1978.

Gimbel, John. *The American Occupation of Germany: Politics and the Military, 1945–1949*. Palo Alto: Stanford University Press, 1968.

———. *A German Community Under Nazi Occupation*. Palo Alto: Stanford University Press, 1961.

Goldmann, Nahum. *The Autobiography of Nahum Goldmann*. New York: Holt, Rinehart and Winston, 1969.

Goodwin, James. "Repatriation of Prisoners of War—Forcible and Non-Forcible." Army War College, 1960. Typescript.

Grinberg, Zalman. *Schuchrarnu MeDachau.* Herzilya: Massada, 1948.
Grobman, Alex, and Daniel Landes, eds. *Genocide: Critical Issues of the Holocaust.* Los Angeles and Chappaqua, N.Y.: Simon Wiesenthal Center and Rossel Books, 1983.
Grossmann, Kurt R. *The Jewish D.P. Problem, Its Origins, and Liquidation.* New York: Institute of Jewish Affairs, 1961.
Grosser, Alfred. *Germany in Our Time.* New York: Praeger, 1971.
Gun, Nerin E. *The Day of the Americans.* New York: Fleet, 1966.
Harold, John E. *An Annotated Bibliography: The American Military Occupation of Germany, 1945–1949.* Carlisle Barracks, Penns.: Military Research Collection, 1971.
Hart, B. H. Liddell. *History of the Second World War.* London: Cassell, 1970.
Hartmann, Susan M. *Truman and the 80th Congress.* Columbia: University of Missouri Press, 1971.
Hartrich, Edwin. *The Fourth and Richest Reich.* New York: Macmillan, 1980.
Hemmendringer, Judith. *Survivors: Children of the Holocaust.* New York: National, 1986.
Hirschmann, Ira A. *The Embers Still Burn.* New York: Simon and Schuster, 1949.
Hochstein, Joseph M., and Murray Greenfield. *Jews' Secret Fleet.* New York: Gefen Books, 1987.
Holborn, Louise W. *The International Refugee Organization.* London: Oxford University Press, 1956.
Honeywell, Roy J. *Chaplains of the U.S. Army.* Washington: Office of the Chief of Chaplains, 1958.
Hull, Cordell. *The Memoirs of Cordell Hull.* Vol. 2. New York: Macmillan, 1948.
Janowsky, Oscar. *The JWB Survey.* New York: Dial, 1948.
Jewish Agency for Palestine. *The Jewish Case Before the Anglo–American Committee of Inquiry.* Jerusalem: Jewish Agency for Palestine, 1947.
———. *Report of Activities, 1947/1948: U.S. Zone Germany.* Munich: Jewish Agency for Palestine, 1949.
Kaplan, Louis, L. and Theodore Schuchat. *Justice—Not Charity: A Biography of Harry Greenstein.* New York: Crown, 1967.
Karski, Jan. *Story of a Secret State.* Boston: Houghton, Mifflin, 1944.
Kempner, Harold, ed. *Operations in U.S. Zone Germany, 1948.* Munich, 1948.
Kertzer, Morris N. *With an H on My Dog Tag.* New York: Behrman House, 1947.
Kimche, Jon, and David Kimche. *The Secret Roads.* New York: Farrar, Straus, and Cudahy, 1955.
Klein, Isaac. *The Anguish and the Ecstasy of a Jewish Chaplain.* New York: Vantage, 1974.
Kohanski, Alexander S., ed. *Proceedings of the Second Session, December 3–5, 1944.* New York: American Jewish Conference, 1945.
———. *The American Jewish Conference, Its Organization and Proceedings of the First Session, August 29 to September 2, 1943.* New York: American Jewish Conference, 1944.
Kolko, Gabriel. *The Politics of War.* New York: Random House, 1968.
Kolko, Joyce, and Gabriel Kolko. *The Limits of Power: The World and United States Foreign Policy, 1945–1954.* New York: Harper and Row, 1972.

Kranzler, David. *Thy Brother's Blood: The Orthodox Jewish Response During the Holocaust.* Brooklyn: Mesorah, 1987.

Kubowitzki, A. Leon. *Unity in Dispersion: A History of the World Jewish Congress.* New York: World Jewish Congress, 1948.

Kuklick, Bruce. *American Policy and the Division of Germany.* Ithaca: Cornell University Press, 1972.

Landman, Isaac, ed. *Sefer Hahitnadvot.* Jerusalem: Bialik Foundation, 1949.

Laqueur, Walter. *The Terrible Secret: Suppression of the Truth About Hitler's "Final Solution."* Boston: Little, Brown, 1980.

Laqueur, Walter, and Richard Breitman. *Breaking the Silence.* New York: Simon and Shuster, 1986.

Le Chene, Evelyn. *Mauthausen.* London: Methuen, 1971.

Levin, Meyer. *In Search.* New York: Horizon, 1960.

Levinger, Lee. *Chaplains to the Rescue.* New York: Jewish Welfare Board, 1946.

Lipsky, Louis. *Memoirs in Profile.* Philadelphia: Jewish Publication Society of America, 1975.

Lipstadt, Deborah E. *Beyond Belief.* New York: Free Press, 1986.

Livazer, N. H. *Berchato Shel Harabi.* Jerusalem: Boys Town, 1977.

The Living Brigade: The Meeting of the Volunteers from Eretz Israel with the Holocaust Survivors. Tel Aviv: Beth Hatefutsoth, 1983.

Lookstein, Haskel. *Were We Our Brother's Keepers? The Public Response of American Jews to the Holocaust, 1938–1944.* New York: Hartmore House, 1985.

Lowenheim, Francis L., Harold D. Langley, and Manfred Jones, eds. *Roosevelt and Churchill: Wartime Correspondence.* New York: Saturday Review, 1975.

McNeill, William Hardy. *Survey of International Affairs, 1939–1946.* New York: Oxford University Press, 1943.

Maginnis, John J. *Military Government Journal: Normandy to Berlin.* Amherst: University of Massachusetts Press, 1971.

Manuel, Frank E. *The Realities of American–Palestine Relations.* Washington: Public Affairs Press, 1949.

Marcus, Jacob Rader, and Abraham J. Peck, eds. *Among the Survivors of the Holocaust—1945: The Landsberg DP Camp Letters of Mayor Irving Heymont, United States Army.* Cincinnati: American Jewish Archives, 1982.

Marlowe, John. *The Seat of Pilate.* London: Cresset, 1959.

Medoff, Rafael. *The Deafening Silence: American Jewish Leaders.* New York: Shapolsky, 1988.

Meritt, Anna J., and Richard L. Meritt, eds. *Public Opinion in Occupied Germany.* Chicago: University of Illinois Press, 1970.

Michel, Henri. *The Second World War.* New York: Praeger, 1975.

Mills, Walter, ed. *The Forrestal Diaries.* New York: Viking, 1951.

Morse, Arthur D. *While Six Million Died: A Chronicle of American Apathy.* New York: Random House, 1967.

Nadich, Judah. *Eisenhower and the Jews.* New York: Twayne, 1953.

Oif der Frei. Stuttgart, 1946.

Patton, George. *The Patton Diaries, 1940–1945.* Boston: Houghton Mifflin, 1974.

Penkower, Monty Noam. *The Jews Were Expendable: Free World Diplomacy and the Holocaust*. Urbana: University of Illinois Press, 1983.

Peterson, Edward N. *The American Occupation of Germany: Retreat to Victory*. Detroit: Wayne State University Press, 1977.

Polier, Justin Wise, and Jonas Waterman Wise, eds. *The Personal Letters of Stephen Wise*. Boston: Beacon, 1956.

Proceedings of Conference of Scholars on the Administration of Occupied Areas 1943–1955. Independence, Mo.: Harry S. Truman Library, 1970.

Proudfoot, Malcolm J. *European Refugees*. London: Faber and Faber, 1957.

Rabinowitz, Dorothy. *New Lives*. New York: Alfred A. Knopf, 1976.

Rabinowitz, Louis. *Soldiers from Judea. Palestinian Jewish Units in the Middle East, 1941–1943*. New York: American Zionist Emergency Council, 1945.

Reiss, Anselm. *Report of Activities in the United States Zone of Occupation for the Year 1947. Zone Headquarters*. Munich: 1948.

Rontch, Isaac, ed. *Jewish Youth at War: Letters from American Soldiers*. New York: Marstin, 1945.

Ross, Robert W. *So It Was True: The American Protestant Press and the Nazi Persecution of the Jews*. Minneapolis: University of Minnesota Press, 1980.

Rothchild, Sylvia. *Voices from the Holocaust*. New York: New American Library, 1981.

Sachar, Abraham L. *The Redemption of the Unwanted*. New York: St. Martin's/Marek, 1983.

Sanders, Ronald. *Shores of Refuge*. New York: Henry Holt, 1988.

Schachner, Nathan. *The Price of Liberty: A History of the American Jewish Committee*. New York: American Jewish Committee, 1948.

Schechtman, Joseph B. *The United States and the Jewish State Movement: The Crucial Decade 1939–1949*. South Brunswick, N.J.: Thomas Yoseloff, 1956.

Schwarz, Leo W. *The Redeemers*. New York: Farrar, Strauss, and Young, 1953.

———. *The Root and the Bough*. New York: Rinehart, 1949.

Schwarzbart, Isaac I. *Twenty-Five Years in the Service of the Jewish People: A Chronicle of Activities of the World Jewish Congress, August 1932–February 1957*. New York, 1957.

Sefer, Doldot. *Hahagana*. 3 vols. Tel Aviv: Am Oved, 1971–72.

Selzer, Michael. *Deliverance Day: The Last Hours at Dachau*. Philadelphia: J. P. Lippincott, 1978.

Semmes, Harry H. *Portrait of Patton*. New York: Paperback Library, 1964.

Sherwood, Robert E. *Roosevelt and Hopkins*. New York: Harper and Brothers, 1948.

Shneiderman, S. L. *Between Fear and Hope*. New York: Arco, 1947.

Sington, Derrick. *Belsen Uncovered*. London: Duckworth, 1946.

Slater, Leonard. *The Pledge*. New York: Simon and Schuster, 1970.

Smith, Marcus J. *The Harrowing of Hell: Dachau*. Albuquerque: University of New Mexico Press, 1972.

Snetsinger, John. *Truman, the Jewish Vote, and the Creation of Israel*. Stanford: Hoover Institution Press, 1974.

Sowden, J. K. *The German Question: 1945–1973*. New York: St. Martin's, 1975.

Stone, I. F. *Underground to Palestine.* New York: Boni and Gaer, 1946.
Supreme Headquarters, Allied Expeditionary Force. *Handbook For Unit Commanders (Germany).* Rev. ed. SHAEF, 1945.
Supreme Headquarters, Allied Expeditionary Force. *Military Government of Germany Technical Manual for Public Health Officers.* SHAEF, n.d.
Supreme Headquarters, Allied Expeditionary Force. *Military Government in Germany Technical Manual: Public Safety.* SHAEF, 1945.
Sykes, Christopher. *Crossroads to Israel 1917–1948.* Bloomington: Indiana University Press, 1973.
Syrkin, Marie. *The State of the Jews.* Washington: New Republic Books, 1980.
Tartakower, Arieh, and Kurt R. Grossman. *The Jewish Refugee.* New York: Institute of Jewish Affairs, 1944.
Terkel, Studs. *The Good War.* New York: Pantheon Books, 1984.
Truman, Harry S. *Memoirs: Years of Decision.* New York: Doubleday, 1955.
Tsamriyon, Tsemah. *Haetoenoot Shel Shearit Hapletah BeGermania Kebetooyeh LeBayoteha.* Tel Aviv: Organization of Holocaust Survivors from the British Zone, 1970.
U.S. Army. Third Army. *Mission Accomplished: Third United States Army Occupation of Germany, 9 May 1945–February 1947,* Third Army, 1947.
U.S. Department of State. *Foreign Relations of the United States Diplomatic Papers: The Conferences at Malta and Yalta, 1945.* Washington: GPO, 1955.
———. *Germany 1947–1949: The Story in Documents.* Washington: Office of Public Affairs, 1950.
U.S. Department of the Army. *Fraternization with the Germans in World War II.* Frankfurt am Main: Department of the Army, 1947.
U.S. European Command. *Historical Division: Displaced Persons.* Frankfurt am Main: USEC, 1947.
U.S. Forces, European Theater. *Occupation.* USFET, n.d.
U.S. Military Governor of Germany. *Military Government Under Allied Occupation: U.S. Zone.* Monthly report. Office of Military Government for Germany (U.S.), 1946–48.
U.S. President's Committee on Religion and Welfare in the Armed Forces. *The Military Chaplaincy.* Washington: GPO, 1950.
U.S. Sector Military Government of Berlin. "Military Government Under Allied Occupation: Berlin, U.S. Sector." Office of Military Government (Berlin District), 1945–1946. Mimeo.
U.S. War Department. *The Chaplain.* Technical manual TM16–205. Washington: GPO, 1944 and 1947.
———. *Military Education: The Chaplains' School.* Washington: War Department, 1926.
Vida, George. *From Doom to Dawn: A Jewish Chaplain's Story of Displaced Persons.* New York: Jonathan David, 1967.
Vrba, Rudolph. *I Cannot Forgive.* New York: Grove, 1964.
Warhaftig, Zorach. *Relief and Rehabilitation: Implications of the UNRRA Program for Jewish Needs.* New York: Institute of Jewish Affairs, 1944.
———. *Uprooted: Jewish Refugees and Displaced Persons After Liberation.* New York: Institute of Jewish Affairs, 1946.

Warren, Helen. *The Buried Are Screaming.* New York: A. S. Barnes, 1960.

Wasserstein, Bernard. *Britain and the Jews of Europe, 1939–1945.* London: Oxford University Press, 1979.

Wiesel, Elie. *A Jew Today.* New York: Random House, 1978.

Wilder-Okladek, F. *The Return Movement of Jews to Austria After the Second World War.* The Hague: Martinus Nijhoff, 1969.

William, Francis, ed. *Twilight of Empire: Memoirs of Prime Minister Clement Atlee.* New York: A. S. Barnes, 1960.

Wischnitzer, Mark. *Visas to Freedom: The History of HIAS.* New York: World, 1956.

Woodbridge, George. *UNRRA.* 3 vols. New York: Columbia University Press, 1950.

Wyman, David S. *The Abandonment of the Jews: America and the Holocaust 1941–1945.* New York: Pantheon Books, 1984.

———. *Paper Walls: America and the Refugee Crisis, 1938–1941.* Amherst: University of Massachusetts Press, 1968.

Zaar, Isaac. *Rescue and Liberation.* New York: Bloch, 1954.

Ziemke, Earl F. *The U.S. Army in the Occupation of Germany.* Washington: Center of Military History, 1975.

Zink, Harold. *American Military Government in Germany.* New York: Macmillan, 1947.

Articles

Adelman, Ken. "Seeing Too Much." *Washingtonian,* July 1988.

Adler-Rudel, S. "Jewish Literature in the DP Camps." *Jewish Spectator,* September 1947.

Adlerstein, F. R. "American Jewish Conference Team Reports on Camps in Germany." *American Jewish Conference Record,* January 1946.

———. "America's DP Record Is Far from Perfect." *Saturday Evening Post,* August 2 1947.

———. "Among Ourselves: Congress Passes Measure Admitting up to 205,000 Displaced Persons." *Survey Graphic,* July 1948.

———. "How Europe's Lost Are Found." *American Mercury,* October 1945.

Apenszlak, Jacob. "The Reconstruction of Polish Jewry." *Jewish Forum,* August 1944.

Asofsky, Isaac L. "HIAS Executive Director Reports on Ten-Week Survey of Emigration Needs in Europe." *Rescue,* January 1947.

Aufricht, Hans. "Some Prerequisites of Jewish Post-War Adjustment." *Jewish Forum,* April 1943.

Baird, Alexander. "The Future of the Jews in Eastern Europe." *Contemporary Jewish Record,* February 1945.

Baron, Salo. "The Spiritual Reconstruction of European Jewry." *Commentary,* November 1945.

Bauer, Yehuda. "The Goldberg Report." *Midstream,* February 1985.

———. "The Holocaust and the Struggle of the Yishuv as Factors in the Establishment of the State of Israel." In *The Catastrophe of European Jewry,* ed. Yisrael Gutman and Livia Rothkirchen. Jerusalem: Yad Vashem, 1976.

———. "The Initial Organization of the Holocaust Survivors in Bavaria." *Yad Vashem Studies* (Jerusalem) 8(1970).

———. "What Did They Know?" *Midstream,* April 1968.

Benedict, Libby. "After Germany Is Liberated." *Congress Weekly,* November 1941.

Bentwich, Norman. "New Generation in Post-War France." *National Jewish Monthly,* November 1947.

Bernard, William S. and Abraham G. Duker. "Refugee Asylum in the United States: How the Law Was Changed To Admit Displaced Persons." *International Migration,* 13, no. 112 (1975).

———. "Who Killed Cock Robin?—The DP Act Discussed." *Day* (New York), August 29, 1948.

Bernstein, David. "Europe's Jews, Summer 1947: A Firsthand Report by an American Observer." *Commentary,* August 1947.

Bernstein, Philip S. "An Audience with Pope Pius." *Congress Weekly,* October 27, 1958.

———. "Displaced Persons." *American Jewish Year Book,* 49(1947/48).

———. "The DPs and America." *Congress Weekly,* April 23, 1948.

———. "Fifteen Months as Jewish Adviser." *Record of the American Jewish Conference,* October 1947.

———. "Status of Jewish Displaced Persons." *U.S. Department of State Bulletin,* June 29, 1947.

Blondheim, S. Hillel. "New Year in France, 5705: A Letter from Abroad (Somewhere in France)." *Menorah,* Autumn 1944.

Cohen, Henry. "Crisis and Reaction." *American Jewish Archives* (Cincinnati) June 1953.

———. "Life in a DP Camp." *Congress Weekly,* January 3, 1947.

———. "The 'Jewish' Displaced Persons." *Jewish Frontier,* March 1947.

———. "The International Refugee Organization." *Jewish Frontier,* May 1947.

Cohen, Morris R. "Conference of Christians and Jews Favors Return of War Orphans to Original Community." *JTA Daily News Bulletin,* August 7, 1946.

———. "Congress Passes Narrow DP Bill; Designed to Exclude Jews." *Law and Social Action,* May 1948.

———. "Congress Points to Special Jewish Relief Problems. Asks United Nations Agency To Recognize a Jewish Body as Part of Relief and Rehabilitation Machinery." *Congress Weekly,* November 19, 1943.

———. "Jewish Studies of Peace and Post-War Problems." *Contemporary Jewish Record,* April 1941.

Cousins, Norman. "An Apology for Living." *Saturday Review of Literature,* October 9, 1948.

———. "Crimson Faces at the Pier; Displaced Persons Act of 1948." *Commonweal,* September 10, 1948.

Dawidowicz, Lucy. "American Jewry and Holocaust." *New York Times Magazine,* April 18, 1982.

Diamond, Jack. "Jewish Overseas Relief Organizations." *Jewish Frontier,* August 1945.

Dicker, Herman. "The U.S. Army and Jewish Displaced Persons." *Chicago Jewish Forum,* Summer 1961.

Dijour, Ilja M. "Jewish Migration—Past and Post-War." *Jewish Social Service Quarterly,* September 1943.

Dinnerstein, Leonard. "Anti-Semitism Exposed and Attacked 1945–1950." *American Jewish History*, September 1981.

———. "Anti-Semitism in the Eightieth Congress: The Displaced Persons Act of 1948." *Capitol Studies*, 6, no. 2 (Fall 1978).

———. "Displaced Persons." *Commonweal*, March 1, 1946.

———. "Displaced Persons Still Seek Places and Food." *Christian Century*, February 12, 1947.

———. "DP Camps Harbor Some Useful People." *Saturday Evening Post*, April 25, 1947.

———. "DP's Whose Responsibility?" *Saturday Evening Post*, February 1, 1947.

———. "The United States and the Jews: Policies Toward the Displaced Persons After World War II." *American Jewish History*, March 1979.

Drutman, D. "Displaced Jewry in the American Zone of Germany." *Journal of Jewish Sociology*, December 1961.

Duker, Abraham G. "Admitting Pogromists and Excluding Their Victims." *Reconstructionist*, October 1, 1948.

———. "The DP Scandal Reviewed." *Day*, July 25, 1948.

———. "Political and Cultural Aspects of Jewish Post-War Problems." *Jewish Social Service Quarterly*, September 1942.

Dunner, Joseph. "The Jews That Remain." *Nation*, July 6, 1946.

Dushkin, Alexander M. "The Educational Activities of the JDC in European Countries." *Jewish Social Service Quarterly*, June 1949.

Emerson, Herbert. "The Post-War Problems of Refugees." *Foreign Affairs*, January 1943.

Fay, Sidney B. "Displaced Persons in Europe." *Current History*, March 1946.

Feingold, Henry L. "Who Shall Bear Guilt for the Holocaust: The Human Dilemma." *American Jewish History*, March 1979.

Flowerman, Samuel H., and Marie Jahoda. "Polls on Anti-Semitism." *Commentary*, April 1946.

Fishman, Joel S. "The Annelce Beekman Affair and the Dutch News Media." *Jewish Social Studies* 40(Winter 1970).

———. "Jewish War Orphans in the Netherlands: The Guardianship Issue 1945–1950." *Wiener Library Bulletin* 26(1973–74).

———. "The Reconstruction of the Dutch Jewish Community and its Implications for the Writing of Contemporary Jewish History." *Proceedings of the American Academy for Jewish Research* 45(1978).

Frank, Murray. "Freedom to move." *Life*, August 30, 1948.

———. "UNRRA—and Jewish Reconstruction." *Chicago Jewish Forum*, Spring 1945.

Friedman, Paul. "The Road Back for the DPs." *Commentary*, December 1948.

Friesel, Evyatar. "From a Soldier's Letters." *Congress Weekly*, October 19, 1945.

———. "The Holocaust and the Birth of Israel." *Wiener Library Bulletin*, n.s. 32 (1979).

Gelber, Joav. "Germany." *Commonweal*, March 14, 1947.

———. "Haaspectim Hapolitim Lehakamat Hakoach Haolom Beyishuv Haaretzyisraeli Betkufat Melchemet Haolom Hashneya." *Yalkut Moreshet*, November 1974.

Genizi, Haim. "Philip Bernstein, Advisor on Jewish Affairs, May 1946–August 1947." *Simon Wiesenthal Center Annual* 3(1986).

Glassgold, A. C. "Self-Help Is the Slogan of Jewish DP's." *American Jewish Conference Record,* August 1946.

Goldmann, Nahum. "Post-War Problems." *Congress Weekly,* November 28, 1941.

Goldstein, Israel. "Recollections of a Visit to Liberated Germany." *New Palestine,* October 12, 1945.

Graeber, Isaque. "Europe's Jews After the War." *National Jewish Monthly,* January 1945.

Greenberg, Hayim. "Bankrupt." *Yiddisher Kemfer,* February 12, 1943. Also in *Midstream,* March 1964.

———. "Migration in the Post-War World." *Jewish Frontier,* September 1943.

———. "The Plan for Destruction." *Jewish Frontier,* November 1942.

———. "Proposed Homes for Jews." *Jewish Frontier,* April 1942.

Grinberg, Zalman. "Despair of Jewish Survivors." *Congress Weekly,* November 2, 1945.

———. "Ort's Great Task in the DP Camps." *Ort Economic Review,* March 1946.

Gringauz, Samuel. "Jewish Destiny as the DPs See It." *Commentary,* December 1974.

———. "Our New German Policy and the DP's; Why Immediate Resettlement Is Imperative." *Commentary,* June 1948.

Grobman, Alex. "American Jewish Chaplains and the *Shearit Hapletah:* April–June 1945." *Simon Wiesenthal Center Annual* (1984).

———. "From the Holocaust to the Establishment of the State of Israel." In *Genocide,* ed. Alex Grobman and Daniel Landes. Los Angeles and Chappaqua, New York: Simon Wiesenthal Center and Rossel Books 1983.

———. "Jewish GI's and Holocaust Survivors." *Jewish Spectator,* Spring 1978.

———. "The Warsaw Ghetto Uprising in the American Jewish Press." *Wiener Library Bulletin,* n.s. 37/38 (1976).

———. "What Did They Know? The American Jewish Press and the Holocaust." *American Jewish History,* March 1979.

Grossmann, Kurt R. "Relief and Rehabilitation and the Jews." *Jewish Frontier,* January 1944.

———. "Report on the Displaced Persons." *Congress Weekly,* February 13, 1948.

———. "Rescue and Relief Work of the WJC." *Jewish Social Service Quarterly,* September 1946.

———. "The UNRRA Crisis." *Congress Weekly,* September 20, 1946.

Grossman, Meir. "Viewing the Brighter Side." *Congress Weekly,* January 19, 1945.

Gruss, Emanuel. "In a Camp of Displaced Jews." *Congress Weekly,* June 29, 1945.

Harrison, Earl G. "Hospitality with Limits; Displaced Persons Act of 1948." *Survey Graphics,* November 1948.

Herschaft, Jean R. "A Talk with Ira Hirschmann." *National Jewish Monthly,* July–August 1963.

Hurwitz, Maximilian. "The Jewish DP Papers in Germany." *Congress Weekly,* February 8 1945.

Hyman, Abraham S. "Displaced Persons." *American Jewish Year Book* 50(1948/49).
———. "Italy." *Congress Weekly*, February 7, 1947.
———. "Victory After Liberation." *Congress Weekly*, April 18, 1955.
Itzhaki, Solomon. "Whither Surviving Jews?" *Congress Weekly*, May 25, 1945.
Jacob, Ernest I. "The Refugee's Won't Go Home." *National Jewish Monthly*, October 1944.
Jacoby, Gerhard. "Jewish DPs and the Jewish Brigade." *Congress Weekly*, February 7, 1947.
———. "Jewish State—Thanks to the Remnant." *Yiddisher Kemfer*, January 23, 1948.
———. "Jews in a World of Chaos: A Symposium." *Congress Weekly*, April 23, 1948.
———. "The Story of the Jewish DP." *Jewish Affairs* 2, no. 6 (November 15, 1948).
Karbach, Oscar. "Inquiries After V-E Day." *Congress Weekly*, June 1, 1945.
———. "Jews in a Changing World." *Congress Weekly*, July 20, 1945.
———. "Problem of the 'Living Corpses'." *Congress Weekly*, July 14, 1944.
Katz, Shlomo. "The Jewish Displaced Persons: A Survey." *Jewish Frontier*, July 1946.
———. "No Hope Except Exodus." *Commentary*, April 1946.
Kaufman, Menachem. "Atidah Shel Shearit Hapletah Ushealat Eretz Yisrael Beanei Hairgunim Halo-Zionim BeArzot Habrit BeShnot 1945." *Yalkut Moreshet*, June 1976.
Kilgsberg, Moses. "American Soldiers on Jews and Judaism." *YIVO Annual*, 5 (1950).
Kimche, Jon. "British Labor's Turnabout on Zionism." *Commentary*, December 1947.
Klerr [Kleinlerer], Edward D. "What Next for DPs in Italy?" *National Jewish Monthly*, September 1947.
Kubowitski, Leon. "Jews in Western Europe." *Congress Weekly*, June 8, 1945.
Lamm, Hans. "The Challenge of Post-War Anti-Semitism." *Jewish Forum*, April 1943.
Laqueur, Walter. "Jewish Denial and the Holocaust." *Commentary*, December 1979.
———. "The Mysterious Messenger and the Final Solution." *Commentary*, March 1980.
Lehman, Herbert H. "It Is Within Our Power." *National Jewish Monthly*, April 1946.
Lestchinsky, Jacob. "New Conditions of Jewish Survival." *Jewish Frontier*, April 1947.
Levy, Henry. "Anglo–American Committee on Inquiry." *American Jewish Year Book* 48(1946/47).
Lorge, Ernst M. "A Tragic Object Lesson." *Jewish Frontier*, August 1945.
McNarney, Joseph T. "The Only Solution." *Congress Weekly*, April 23, 1948.
Mangan, Sherry. "The Outlook for France's Jews: The National Crisis Threatens Their Security." *Commentary*, November 1947.

Marcus, Robert S. "A Chaplain in Germany." *Congress Weekly*, April 20, 1945.
———. "A Conference of Survivors." *Congress Weekly*, August 17, 1945.
———. "535 Children Leave Buchenwald." *Congress Weekly*, June 29, 1945.
———. "From a Chaplain's Notebook." *Congress Weekly*, March 8, 22, 29; May 3, 10; and November 1, 1946.
———. "From Buchenwald to Palestine." *Congress Weekly*, October 6, 1945.
———. "Jews in Belgium." *Congress Weekly*, March 29, 1946.
———. "Postwar Political Problems." *Congress Weekly*, February 13, 1948.
———. "The Story of Frankfurt Under the Nazis." *Congress Weekly*, June 15, 1945.
———. "The Thousands Who Were Saved: Report from a German Concentration Camp." *Congress Weekly*, May 11, 1945.
———. "Voice of the Survivors." *Congress Weekly*, February 15, 1946.
Massing, Paul W., and Maxwell Miller. "Should Jews Return to Germany?" *Atlantic Monthly*, July 1945.
Marion, Zyd. "Paris Jewry Revisited." *Jewish Spectator*, June 1945.
Moskowitz, Moses. "The Germans and the Jews: Postwar Report." *Commentary*, July 1946.
"Nauseated by the Sights and Odors." *American Jewish Archives*, 31, no. 1 (April 1979).
Ott, Jacob M. "Our New German Policy and the DP's; Why Immediate Resettlement is Imperative." *Commentary*, June 1948.
———. "Our Own Open Door." *Commonweal*, August 30, 1946.
———. "The Polish Pogroms and Press Suppression." *Jewish Forum*, January 1946.
———. "The Return to Luxemburg." *Congress Weekly*, March 16, 1945.
Papanek, E. "Pass the Stratton Bill." *Nation*, June 7, 1947.
———. "American Jewish Committee Active in Consideration of Peace and Post-War Problems." *American Jewish Year Book*, 43, 45, 47 (1941–46).
———. "They Are Not Expendable: The Homeless and Refugee Children in Germany." *Social Service Review*, September 1946.
Penkower, Monty Noam. "In Dramatic Dissent: The Bergson Boys." *American Jewish History*, March 1981.
Pinsky, Edward. "American Jewish Unity During the Holocaust—the Joint Emergency Committee 1943." *American Jewish History*, June 1983.
Pinson, Koppel S. "Jewish Life in Liberated Germany." *Jewish Social Studies* 9, no. 1 (January 1947).
———. "Political Aspects of Relief." *Congress Weekly*, December 29, 1944.
Prager, Moshe. "Problems of Displaced Jews." *Congress Weekly*, May 19, 1944.
———. "Problems of Liberation." *Congress Weekly*, June 23, 1944.
———. "Sketches of a Heroic Era." *Jewish Frontier*, December 1948.
Proudfoot, M. J. "Anglo–American Displaced Persons Program for Germany and Austria." *American Journal of Economics and Sociology*, October 1946.
Reich, Nathan. "Post-War Reconstruction of the Jews in Europe." *Jewish Social Service Quarterly*, September 1944.
Reiss, Anselm. "Relief and Rehabilitation." *Congress Weekly*, November 19, 1943.

Bibliography 245

———. "Relief and Rehabilitation of European Jewry: Memorandum submitted to the Council of the United Nations Relief and Rehabilitation Administration by the World Jewish Congress." *Congress Weekly*, November 26, 1943.

———. "The Situation in Poland." *Congress Weekly*, March 7, 1947.

———. "Rescue and Retribution." *Congress Weekly*, April 7, 1944.

Ribalow, Harold U. "Those Jews Who Survived." *Congress Weekly*, September 20, 1946.

Rifkind, Simon H. "Disinherited Jews of Europe Must Be Saved." *American Jewish Conference Record*, April 11, 1946.

———. "I Lived with The Jewish DPs." *Congress Weekly*, April 12, 1946.

Roberts, J. Stephen. "They Find No Peace." *Congress Weekly*, October 1 1948.

Robinson, Jacob. "Postwar Jewish Problems." *Congress Weekly*, May 29, 1942.

———. "Preparing for Peace." *Congress Weekly*, February 21, 1941.

Rock, Eli. "The Incomparable Dr. Schwartz." *Jewish Exponent*, October 29, 1971.

Rothschild, Guy de. "European Jewry Speaks." *New Palestine*, October 12 1945.

Sage, Lt. Colonel Jerry M. "Future of Displaced Persons in Europe." Statement in *U.S. Department of State Bulletin*, July 13, 1947. Also in *Interpreter Releases*, August 12, 1947.

Sagi, Nana. "'Illegal' Immigration—1945–1948: The Epic of Aliya Bet." *Midstream*, March 1971.

Schirn, Otto. "Problems of French Jews." *Congress Weekly*, June 30, 1944.

Schlossberg, Joseph. "The Jews After the War." *Congress Weekly*, January 9, 1942.

Schwarz, Joseph J. "Jewish Relief Picture in Central and Western Europe." *Jewish Social Service Quarterly*, September 1941.

———. "The Joint Distribution Committee in War Time." *Jewish Social Service Quarterly*, December 1943.

Schwarz, Leo W. "Summary Analysis of AJDC Program in the U.S. Zone of Occupation, Germany." *Menorah*, Spring 1947.

———. "When Liberation Came." *Congress Weekly*, May 24, 1965.

Segal, Louis. "Apologists for the JDC" *Congress Weekly*, October 6, 1945.

Segalman, Ralph. "The Psychology of Jewish Displaced Persons." *Jewish Social Service Quarterly*, June 1947.

Shneiderman, S. L. "I Saw Kielce: The Worst Pogrom." *National Jewish Monthly*, December 1946.

Shuster, Zachariah. "Between the Milestones in Poland: The Story Behind the Mass Flight of Polish Jewry." *Commentary*, August 1946.

———. "Must the Jews Quit Europe?" *Commentary*, December 1945.

Smelansky, Moshe. "The Anglo–American Report Points the Way." *Commentary*, July 1946.

Spizman, L. "Death and Resurrection: In the Concentration Camps." *Jewish Frontier*, August 1945.

Srole, Leo. "Landsberg: A Vibrant Community Emerges from Rubble." *Hadassah Magazine*, December 1946.

———. "Why the DP's Can't Wait." *Commentary*, January 1947.

Stein, Kalman. "Jews in Europe of Tomorrow." *Congress Weekly*, April 27, 1945.

Stigliani, Nicholas A. and Antoinette Marzotto. "Fascist Anti-Semitism and the Italian Jews." *Wiener Library Bulletin* 28(1975).

Syrkin, Marie. "DP Schools." *Jewish Frontier*, March 19, 1948.

———. "I Met a Black Marketeer." *Jewish Frontier*, August 1947.

———. "My DP Students." *Jewish Frontier*, June 1965.

———. "Reaction to News of the Holocaust." *Midstream*, May 1968.

———. "Two DP Children." *Pioneer Woman*, October 1947.

———. "What American Jews Did During the Holocaust." *Midstream*, October 1982.

Szajkowski, Z. "Letter from Europe." *Jewish Frontier*, October 1945.

Tartakower, Aryeh. "The Critical Task Ahead." *Congress Weekly*, June 30, 1944.

———. "The Displaced and Destitute." *Jewish Frontier*, January 1946.

———. "The Future of the Jew in Europe." *Congress Weekly*, December 29, 1944.

———. "Jews in 'New Europe'." *Jewish Frontier*, July 1945.

———. "The Less-Than-DPs." *Jewish Frontier*, August 1947.

———. "The Stratton Bill." *Jewish Frontier*, August 1947.

———. "UNRRA—and the Jewish Case." *Jewish Frontier*, December 1943.

———. "The UNRRA Program and Jewish Needs." *Congress Weekly*, September 15, 1944.

Tuck, W. H. "UNRRA Polls Displaced Jews on Migration Plans; First Vote Shows Palestine Is Favored." *JTA Daily News Bulletin*, February 3 1946.

———. "Year of decision of the DP's." *Rescue*, January 1948.

Unsdorfor, S. B. "Vignettes from the DP Camps." *Congress Weekly*, October 25, 1946.

———. "The Yellow Star," in *Anthology of Holocaust Literature*, ed. Jacob Glatstein, Israel Knox, and Samuel Margoshes. Philadelphia: Jewish Publication Society 1969.

Waren, Helen. "'Jottings' from Germany." *Jewish Frontier*, November 1945, March 1946, April 1946.

Wasserstein, Bernard. "The JDC During the Holocaust." *Midstream*, February 1985.

———. "The Myth of 'Jewish Silence'." *Midstream*, August–September 1980.

Wechsberg, J. "Hell's Orphans." *Saturday Evening Post*, October 23, 1948.

Werner, Alfred. "Defeat by Anti-Semitism." *Congress Weekly*, October 8, 1943.

———. "When Will the DP's Be Admitted?" *Commonweal*, February 6, 1948.

Wise, Jonah B., and James G. Heller. "One Million Jews." *National Jewish Monthly*, June 1945.

Wyman, David. "Letters to the Editor." *New York Times Magazine*, May 23, 1982.

"Yoman Exodus." *Yalkut Moreshet*, March 1968.

Ziv-Av, Yitchak. "The JDC Must Explain." *Congress Weekly*, November 23, 1945.

Manuscript Sources

Advisor on Jewish Affairs. "Reports of the Advisors on Jewish Affairs to the United States Command in Germany and Austria, 1947–1950." Abraham Hyman Archives, Jerusalem.

Eichhorn, David M. "Autobiography." American Jewish Archives, New York.

Fleishman, Alfred. "I Saw the Remnant of Israel," N.d..

Ganin, Zvi. "The Diplomacy of the Weak: American Zionist Leadership During the Truman Era, 1945–1948." Ph.D. diss., Brandeis University, 1975.

Goldman, Meyer. "Memorandum." N.d. Center for Holocaust Studies, New York.

Gorin, Rabbi Paul. "Saving Jewish Lives: A Rabbi's Reminiscences." February 21, 1975. Central Archives for the History of the Jewish People, Jerusalem.

Keren, Nili. "Hazalat Yeladim Betsarfat Bitkufat Hakibush Hagermani 1940–1944 Al-Yedeh Eargunim Yedudim." Master's thesis, Institute of Contemporary Jewry, Hebrew University, Jerusalem, 1975.

Klausner, Abraham. "A Detailed Report on the Liberated Jew as He Now Suffers His Period of Liberation under the Discipline of the Armed Forces of the United States." June 24, 1945. Central Archives for the History of the Jewish People, Jerusalem.

Levinger, Lee. "The Jewish Chaplains and CANRA." 1974. Jewish Welfare Board Archives, New York.

Liebschutz, Thomas Philip. "Rabbi Philip S. Bernstein and the Jewish Displaced Persons." Master's thesis, Hebrew Union College-Jewish Institute of Religion, 1965.

Lipman, Eugene. "Summary of War Experiences." N.d. American Jewish Archives, Cincinnati.

Lorimer, M. Madeline. "America's Response to Europe's Displaced Persons, 1948–1952: A Preliminary Report." Ph.D. diss., St. Louis University, 1964.

Miller, Yosef. "The Misplaced Persons." May 10, 1971. Institute of Contemporary Jewry, Hebrew University, Jerusalem.

Moscovitz, Shlomo. "The United States Recognition of Israel in the Context of the Cold War, 1945–1948." Ph.D. diss., Kent State University, 1976.

Neustadt-Noy, Isaac. "The Unending Task: Efforts to Unite American Jewry from the American Jewish Congress to the American Jewish Conference." Ph.D. diss., Brandeis University, 1976.

Newman, Gemma Mae. "Earl G. Harrison and the Displaced Persons Controversy: A Case Study in Social Action." Ph.D. diss., Temple University, 1973.

Sachar, David B. "David K. Niles and United States Policy Toward Palestine: A Case Study in American Foreign Policy." Harvard University, 1959.

Sage, Jerry M. "The Evolution of U.S. Policy Toward Europe's Displaced Persons: World War II to June 25, 1948." Master's thesis, Columbia University, 1952.

Tripp, Eleanor Baldwin. "Displaced Persons: The Legislative Controversy in the United States, 1945–1950." Master's thesis, Columbia University, 1966.

Index

Abramowitz, Mayer: involvement with the Berihah, 154–56; and with the Jews in Germany, 158–60
Acheson, Dean, 115, 145, 168
Adler, Cyrus, 6
Adler, Leon, 190
Advisor on Jewish Affairs: definition of role, 3; impact of Harrison Report, 85–86; Judge Rifkind appointment, 95; importance of position, 132; William Haber, 185
Agudat Yisrael, 48, 115
Ainring, 96
Allach, 38, 46, 55, 60
Am Stau, 188
American Federation of Lithuanian Jews, 100
American Jewish Committee (AJC), 114, 144–45, 168, 186
American Jewish Conference: and the U.S. Congress, 70–71; and the Feldafing displaced persons camp, 82; and the Harrison Report, 85; and its mission to displaced persons in the American Zone, 87; and its report on conditions in Europe, 95; and Judah Nadich, 127; and Philip Bernstein, 128, 144; and Howard C. Peterson, 136; and Dean Acheson, Robert Patterson and John Hilldring, 147–47; and Zalman Grinberg, 172; and Abraham Klausner, 181, 185–86
American Jewish Congress, 52, 84, 87
American Jewish Joint Distribution Committee (JDC): definition of, 2; and the chaplains in Italy, 13, 19, 21, 22, 131; and CANRA, 13–14, 63; and the Jewish Brigade, 17–18; and the chaplains, 20, 26–27, 64; and Judah Nadich, 23, 87; and the OSE, 24; and the chaplains in France, 32; and its effort to get into Europe, 44, 54; and the Jewish soldiers, 46; and Isaac Klein, 61; and Abraham Klausner, 66, 99–100, 175, 181, 183–86, 189; and the visit by Earl G. Harrison, 72; and the displaced persons camp, 76; and the advisor on Jewish Affairs, 77–78; and the decline of the morale of the displaced persons, 84–85; and the Landsberg displaced persons camp, 94; and the problems in

249

Linz, Austria, 98; and Zalman Grinberg, 99, 172; and the mail service, 102; and the package program, 104, 170–71; and the displaced persons schools, 111; and *Unzer Weg*, 122; and the chaplains' criticism, 123–29, 133; and the legal issues, 134; and the assistants to the advisors on Jewish Affairs, 137; and Philip Bernstein, 144–45, 148; and David R. Wahl, 146; and the supplies for transports, 151; and Mayer Abramowitz, 159; and Nathan Barack, 162; and Herbert Friedman, 176; and the displaced persons chaplains, 179–80; and the contribution of the chaplains, 191; and author's conclusions, 193–94, 195–96
Anders, Wladyslaw, 12
Anglo-American Commission, 145
Anglo-American Commission on Palestine, 166
Anglo-American Committee of Inquiry, 88
Ansbach, 125
Anzio, 56
Appelbaum, S., 24
Arnold, William R., 6, 8, 70
Aschaffenburg, 152
Aschau, 125
Attlee, Clement R., 88
Avigur, Shaul, 164

Babenhausen, 16, 152
Bad Aibling, 152
Bad Gastein, 98, 102
Bad Hamburg, 158
Bad Neustadt, 93
Bad Wildugen, 158
Bamberg, 93, 96, 125
Bar-El David, 170
Barack, Nathan, 120, 162–63
Barish, Louis, 190
Barker, R. W., 161
Bayreuth, 90–91
Becker, Lavy, 125, 132
Begin, Menachem, 165
Bein, William, 144
Ben Gurion, David, 116, 130
Bencowitz, Isaac, 176

Bensheim, 47, 160
Bergen-Belsen, 40, 51, 62, 67, 108–10, 120, 132, 157
Berihah: formation of, 111; and Eugene Lipman, 112–14; and the American military, 116; and Herbert Eskin, 117; and Abraham Haselkorn, 118; and Max Braude, 120; and the chaplains, 133, 195; and increased immigration, 141–42; and UNRRA, 143; and Joseph Shubow, Herbert Friedman and Mayer Abramowitz, 154–55; and Eugene Cohen, Max Braude, Eugene Lipman, Samuel Burstein, Yosef Miller, Milton Elefant, Mayer Abramowitz, Herbert Friedman, and Abraham Klausner, 156–57; and the Haganah, 164; and Abraham Klausner, 189
Berkowitz, Sidney (Burke), 60
Bernstein, Philip S.: as Executive Director of CANRA, 7; and Chaplains' School, 11; and Earl Stone, 12; and Louis Kraft, 13; and Samuel Teitelbaum, 19; and package program, 23; and chaplains' involvement with displaced persons, 23–24; and Abraham Haselkorn, 26–27; and Abraham Klausner report of June 1945, 65–66, 69; and Max Braude, 121; and Eli Bohren tribute to Klausner, 130–31; on becoming advisor on Jewish affairs, 136–37; and Herbert Friedman, 138, 152, 156, 176; and Abraham Hyman, 139; visit to Poland, 144–45; and American military, 147; criticism of JDC, 148–49; meeting with Pope Pius XII and President Truman, 149–50; and Abraham Klausner's leaving Germany in 1947, 185; and American Jewish Conference Meeting, 186
Bevin, Ernest, 88, 166
Bindermichl, 98
Black Sabbath, 165
Board of Jewish Deputies of British Jews, 71

Index 251

Bogenhausen, 173
Bohnen, Eli A.: at Dachau, 38; visits to displaced persons camps, 97; and the establishment of displaced persons camps at Bindermichl and Bad Gastein, 98–99; and the package program, 102; tribute to Abraham Klausner, 130–31
Bokser, Ben Zion, 170
Brann, 98
Braude, Max: at Dachau, 38; establishment of relief effort, 39; prevention of Klausner court-martial, 56; provision of food for Jews at Feldafing, 59; response to Klausner report, 69–70; at Feldafing Conference, 107; reluctance to discuss his activities, 120–21; involvement in Berihah, 156
Bremen, 92, 188
Breslau, Isadore, 92
Bretkopf, Jack, 55
Brickner, Barnett R., 7, 13
Brit Chabuzim Dateyim (BACHAD), 61
British White Paper of 1939, 74
Buchberg, 42, 93
Buchenwald, 37, 39, 40, 45, 47, 48, 50–51, 53, 55, 64, 77
Burris, Walter, 90–91
Burstein, Samuel, 156, 190

Caller, Cy, 106, 118–20, 131
Camp Kilmer, 176
Carpenter, Charles I., 178
Celler, Emanuel, 70–71
Central Committee of Liberated Jews in Bavaria, 60, 107, 109, 174, 184–85, 195
Central Committee for Northern Bavaria, 92
Central Conference of American Rabbis (CCAR), 3, 6, 8
Chalon, 32
Chaplains' School, 9, 11, 13
Chartres, 30
Chateau Mehancourt, 26–30
Children's Summer Camp, 160
Ciechanowski, Jan, 15
Clark, Mark, 97–98, 137, 147, 149

Clay, Lucius B., 53–54, 79, 137, 176
Cohen, Eugene, 152, 156
Collins, Harry J., 97–98, 103
Combined DPX, 77–78
Commission on Jewish Chaplaincy (CJC), 3
Committee for the War Stricken Jewish Population, 53
Committee on Army Navy Religious Activities (CANRA): definition of, 3; structure of, 7; and the Rabbinical Assembly of America, 8; and Aryeh Lev, 9; and Philip Bernstein, 11–12, 137, 178; and Barnett R. Brickner, 13; and the JDC, 14, 22–23, 127–28; and chaplains before leaving for Europe, 15; and discretionary funds, 19; and Abraham Haselkorn, 26; and communications from chaplains, 32; and chaplains work with displaced persons, 35, 65, 70, 194, 196; and Dwight D. Eisenhower, 87; and package program, 104; and Max Braude, 121; and Max Wall, 130
Congress Weekly, 34, 40, 84
Crum, Bartley, 141–42
Cultural Reconstruction Corporation, 176
Cyprus, 166, 182, 187, 189

Dachau, 38–39, 42–43, 46, 50, 55–56, 60–61, 85
Davis, Morris, 32
Dawson, William W., 91
de Sola Pool, David, 7, 9
Decter, Aaron, 32
Degerloch, 50
Deggendorf, 83, 125
Dembitz, Eliezer, 170
Dembowitz, Morris, 31, 92, 131, 158, 175
Der Tog, 5, 28
Deutsches Museum, 60, 107
Dicker, Herman, 31, 93, 103–4, 152
Dickstein, Samuel, 70
Dieburg, 160
Displaced Persons (DPs): and the chaplains, 2, 4, 124, 133, 192–95; and the advisor on Jewish Affairs, 3; and the Chaplains'

School, 13; and the World Jewish Congress, 20–21; and the American military, 37, 44, 61, 69–70, 157; and the Allies, 41–42; and Abraham Klausner, 46, 47, 58, 126, 175, 185, 196; and Ernst Lorge, 48; and the Harrison Report, 70, 90; and Henry W. Morgenthau, Jr., 72; and Dwight Eisenhower, 79; and George Patton, 81; and the Landsberg Camp, 94; and Eli Bohnen, 98; and Haskell Hollander, 105; and Eugene Lipman, 113–14; and David Ben Gurion, 130; morale of, 134, 142, 157; and Mayer Abramowitz, 158; and Nathan Barack and George Frederick, 163; and President Truman, 166; and the black market, 169; and Yosef Miller, 170; and Meyer Goldman, 178; and Samuel Steinberg, 186
Displaced Persons Act of 1948, 143, 167
Displaced Persons Act of 1950, 167
Displaced Persons Executive (DPX), 37, 42
Dissen, 138
Dobkin, Eliyahu, 108, 110
Dora, 46
Dos Fraje Wort, 121
Dunn, Andrew Carnegie, 113

Eggendorf, 48
Eichhorn, Max David, 24, 31, 38–39, 128
Eisendrath, Maurice, 66
Eisenhower, Dwight D.: and Lucius B. Clay, 53; and Harrison report summary, 76; and Truman letter of August 31, 1945, 78, 79–80; response to General Patton, 81; response to the Harrison Report, 82; and the impact of the Harrison Report, 85–86; response to criticism, 115; and assistance to Berihah, 116; as advisor on Jewish affairs, 132
Elefant, Milton, 156
Elgart, Saul, 92

Elkins, 61
Ellenbogen, Edward, 12
Englisch für Jedermann, 98
Epes, 98
Epstein, Judith, 103
Eskin, Herbert: and the French Jewish community, 31; and the Jewish community of Stuttgart, 49–50; and CANRA, 63; reprimand from the military, 91–92; and collecting arms for Palestine, 117; replaced by Leo Ginsburg, 161

Fahrenwald, 94
Father Devaux, 24–26, 28
Fay, Patrick, 106, 132
Federal Bureau of Investigation (FBI), 172
Federation of Temple Sisterhoods, 172
Feldafing, 59, 60, 79–83, 107, 121
Fierst, Joseph, 115
Fighters for the Freedom of Israel (Lechi), 165
Fine, Alvin, 101
Fischer, 71
Fishman, Irving, 19
Flak-Kaserne, 60
Fleishman, Alfred, 87
Florence, 119–120
Frankfurt, 125
Frankfurt Jewish G.I. Council, 170–71
Frankfurter, Felix, 15
Frederick, George, 163
Friedman, Herbert L.: as troubleshooter for Philip Bernstein, 138; at the Landsberg trial, 139; visit to Poland, 144; at Babenhausen, 152; involvement with Berihah, 154–56; under military investigation, 171; and the I. G. Farben warehouse in Offenbach, 175–76
Friedman, Leo, 33
Fulda, 77, 158
Fun Letzen Churben, 175, 195
Fürstenfeldbruck, 93
Fürth, 90, 125

Gafan, Jean, 93

Ganz, Irving, 93
Gauting, 58, 60
Gerhardt, Charles H., 92
Geringshof, 48
Gibson Harvey D., 76, 83
Ginsburg, Leo, 161
Goldfarb, Harold, 120
Goldman, Meyer: and the Jewish children in Maastricht, Holland, 33; and the Jewish community in Fürstenfeldbruck, 93; with the children of Namur, 122–23; under military investigation, 171; confrontation with the military, 178
Goldmann, Nahum: appreciation of chaplains, 54; and Robert Marcus to visit Bergen-Belsen, 62, 67; contact with George Warren, 72; letter from Simon Rifkind, 95; argument in favor of partition, 167–68
Goldstein, Israel, 82, 86
Goppingen, 83
Gorin, Paul, 102, 106, 169
Gorrelick, Benjamin, 103, 105, 131
Grady, Henry F., 160
Grady Commission, 166
Graham, Fred, 32
Green, Fay, 113
Greenleigh, Arthur, 21
Grew, Joseph, 72, 76
Grimma, 48–49
Grinberg, Zalman: at St. Ottilien, 58–59; appeal to the United Nations, 84; observation of postwar, 89; protest letter to American Jewry, 99; at the Feldafing Conference, 107; attempt to attend UJA meeting in U.S., 132; cable to American Jewish Conference, 136; trip to U.S., 171–73
Grossman, Meir, 144
Guttman, Meyer, 47

Haber, William, 185–86, 189, 190–91
Hadassah, 52, 103, 172
Haganah, 111, 113, 164–65, 182
Haifa, 187
Hamburg, 188

Hardman, L. H., 62
Harrison, Earl G., 72
Harrison Report, 73–75; and the reaction of Dwight Eisenhower, 82; impact of, 85–86, 88–89, 93, 98, 115–16, 155, 195
Haselkorn, Abraham: and the Jewish children in LeMans, 24–28; and the survivors in Mannheim, 46–47; and the package program, 103; and the use of Yom Kippur rations, 105–6; work with Berihah, 118–20; survivor tribute to, 129
Haselkorn, Mrs., 103
Hashomer Hazair, 48
Hebrew University, 176
Hechalutz World Organization, 53
Heidelberg, 158
Heidenheim, 92
Heilbronn, 50, 151
Heilbrun, Edward, 114
Heimberg, Eli, 38, 97–98, 131
Helvarg, Max, 155
Hertz, 102
Hesslingen, 155
Heubner, Clarence, 114
Heymont, Irving, 94
Hilldring, John H.: and the role of CAD and chaplains, 20–21; and Pilsen incident, 114–15; meeting with major Jewish organizations, 145–47; meeting with Zalman Grinberg, 172
Hillersleben, 51
Hochman, Jacob, 34
Hollander, Haskell, 105
Hoter-Yishai, 108
Howley, 161
Hume, 98
Hutler, Albert A., 47
Hyman, Abraham S., 138, 139, 186
Hyman, Irwin, 71
Hyman, Joseph C., 22

Indiana Jewish Chronicle, 85
Intergovernmental Committee on Refugees, 18, 72
International Refugee Organization (IRO), 183
Irgun Zvai Leumi (IZL), 165

Jarblum, Mark, 71
Jewish Advocate, 28
Jewish Agency for Palestine: and the British Army, 17; and Sylvia Neulander, 52; and Earl G. Harrison, 75; and Judah Nadich, 87; and the Conference at Feldafing, 108; and Dwight Eisenhower and W. Bedell Smith, 116; and Eugene Lipman, 117; and Abraham Haselkorn, 118, 174, 182; and the assistants to the advisor on Jewish Affairs, 137; and increased immigration, 141; and Philip Bernstein, 144–45; and Black Sabbath, 165; and the response to the Morrison-Grady Committee report, 167
Jewish Brigade: and Edward Ellenbogen, Earl Stone, and Samuel Teitelbaum, 12; definition of, 17; and the survivors, 44, 60; and St. Ottilien, 107–8; and the Jewish youth, 110; and Berihah, 111; and Sylvia Neulander, 112; and Herbert Eskin, 117; and Abraham Haselkorn and Cy Caller, 117–19; and Max Braude, 120
Jewish Chaplain, 5, 11, 131
Jewish Chronicle, 63
Jewish Exponent, 85–86
Jewish Frontier, 16
Jewish Institute of Religion (JIR), 172
Jewish Publication Society, 34
Jewish Spectator, 54, 68
Jewish Telegraphic Agency, 5, 28, 40, 96, 114, 136
Jewish Theological Seminary, 6
Jewish Welfare Board (JWB) Committee on Chaplains, 6

Kabbalah, 176
Kaplan, Eliezer, 117
Kaplan, Israel, 175
Karski, Jan, 15
Kassel, 80, 158, 180, 188–89
Katzki, Herbert, 72
Kaufman, Samuel, 119–20
Keating, Frank H., 91
Kellet, J. A., 162

Kenen, I. L., 172
Kenner, Albert, 94–95
Kertzer, Morris, 17
Keyes, Geoffrey S., 152
Kibbutz Buchenwald, 48, 158
Kibbutz Geulim, 91
Kielce, 143–44, 149
King David Hotel, 165
Klausner, Abraham J.: as volunteer for service in Far East, 15; arrival at Dachau, 39; survey of seventeen displaced persons camps, 42–43; approach to the military regarding displaced persons, 46; and *Shearit Hapletah* volume 57–58; and transfer of Jews from Dachau, 60–61; June 1945 report to American Jewry, 65–67; impact on Harrison Report, 72–77; second phase of liberation, 89; and Leo Srole resignation at Landsberg, 93–94; and package program, 99; "Kol Nidrei" sermon, 100; response to package program, 100–101; establishment of the Central Committee, 106–8; establishment of *Unzer Weg*, 121; and the JDC, 124, 125–26; and the survivors, 129–30; tributes to Klausner from other chaplains, 130–31; cable to American Jewish Conference, 136; as advisor at Landsberg trial, 139; involvement in Berihah, 156; *Shearit Hapletah* volume, 157; under investigation from military, 171–74; forced to leave the military, 174–75; return to the military, 180; suggestions on how to deal with the survivors, 182–83; criticism of the JDC, 183–85; frustration with the displaced persons and his solution, 185–87; involvement with the *Exodus*, 187–89
Klein, Isaac: and the Jews of Rheims, 30; and the Jews of Chartres, 30–31, 33; and the Jews of Belgium, 61–62, 123; criticism of JDC, 124; deserving recognition, 131

Kluger (Aliav), Ruth: and Judah Nadich, 71; and Sylvia Neulander, 112; and Eugene Lipman, 116–17; and Herbert Friedman, 155
Koppelman, Herbert P., 70
Kraft, Jacob, 106, 157
Kraft, Louis, 13, 22, 34, 104
Kubowitski, Leon: plan to exterminate Jews of Europe, 16; and Robert Marcus, 33–34; and Abraham Klausner, 132–33

Lamm, Hans, 87
Lampertheim, 125, 160
Lane, Arthur Bliss, 144
Landsberg, 56, 59, 93–96, 121, 132, 138
Landsberger Lager Cajtung, 121
Langenzell Castle, 91
Le Mans, 24, 26, 27, 46
Leavitt, Moses A., 115, 124
Lefkowitz, David, Jr., 93
Lefkowitz, Sidney M., 55
Lehman, Herbert S., 71, 172
Leipheim, 125
Lesves, 61
Lev, Aryeh: and the Chaplains' School, 9, 11; and British Jewish chaplains, 63; report on trip to Europe, 63–64, 70; and package program, 104
Leventhal, Louis E., 137, 185–86
Levin, Carl, 52
Levin, Meyer, 28, 32
Levine, Joseph, 92, 125
Levitsky, Louis, 7
Levy, Henry, 155
Levy, Issac, 63
Liepah, Ann, 91, 125, 174
Lindenfels, 160
Linick, Marvin, 174
Linz, 98, 150–51
Lipman, Eugene J.: and the possibility of meeting survivors in Europe, 11; with displaced persons in Cologne, 50; in Niederbayern and Oberpfalz, 92; and package and mail service program, 101–2; involvement with Berihah, 112–14, 156; becoming a liaison officer with Jewish Agency, 116–17; deserving of recognition, 131, 156
Livazer, Herschel, 30, 103, 190
Loeb, Saul, 155
Lorge, Ernst, 48–49, 53, 158
Loskove, Abe, 125
Low, Johnny (Yehuda Lev), 170
Low, Rosamund, 170
Ludwigshohe, 83

McCarran, Patrick, 167
McCormack, John W., 146
McDonald, 60
McNarney, Joseph T.: as replacement for Dwight D. Eisenhower, 135; and the advisor on Jewish Affairs, 136; and Philip Bernstein, 144; and the report on monthly costs of displaced persons, 145; report from Secretary Patterson and response, 146–47; praise from Philip Bernstein, 149; package program, 169; and displaced persons chaplains, 179
Maier, Erich, 100
Malin, Patrick, 20, 72
Marburg, 90, 158
Marcus, Colonel, 106
Marcus, David, 171
Marcus, Robert: and package program, 22; and the Jews of Maastricht, 33; and letter from Leon Kubowitzki, 33–34; at Buchenwald, 40; and the children of Kibbutz Buchenwald, 48, 51–52; contact with British Jewish chaplains, 62; report from Bergen-Belsen, 67–68; cable to Stephen S. Wise, 76–77; criticism of the American military, 84; at first Conference of the Central Committee, 108; accompanied children to Palestine, 120; criticism of JDC, 124, 128; deserving of recognition, 131
Marseilles, 105–6, 118–19
Marshall, George C., 21, 76
Mauthausen, 108
Merkaz Lagolah, 18
Micklesen, Stanley M., 78, 117
Milgrom, Louis, 102
Miller, Luther D., 179

Miller, Yosef, 150–52, 156, 160, 170–71
Mintzer, Oscar A., 134–35
Morgan, Frederick E., 143–44
Morgenstern, Julius, 66
Morgenthau, Henry, Jr., 72, 76, 176
Morrison, Herbert, 166
Morrison-Grady Committee, 167–68
Mossad, 164
Muhldorf, 59
Munich Writer's Union, 175

Nadich, Judah: and Philip Bernstein, 23; and Father Devaux, 26; and foreign correspondents, 32; and British Jewish chaplains, 63; and the JDC, 64, 124–27, 193; and Max Braude, 69; replaced by Irwin Hyman, 71; and Jacob Trobe, 78; and visit to displaced persons camps, 78–79; and Walter Bedell Smith, 79; and criticism of Eisenhower policy, 80; and role as advisor on Jewish Affairs, 86–87; and *Unzer Weg*, 121
Namur, 61–62, 121, 123
National Jewish Welfare Board (JWB): and the chaplains and the Jewish military personnel, 6–7, 9; and Jewish survivors, 12–13, 23–24; and the letter program, 57; and Max Braude, 69–70; and Robert Marcus, 84; and Herman Dicker, 104; and Abraham Klausner, 125
Neufeld, Maurice, 18
New Palestine, 98, 102
Niederbayern, 92
Nonsectarian Committee of the Resistance, 52
Nordhausen, 46, 55
Notre Dame de Sion, 24
Nuremberg, 90, 94

Oberfalz, 92
Oeuvre de Secours aux Enfants (OSE), 24, 51–53
Offenbach, 137, 175
Organization for Rehabilitation through Training (ORT), 137, 181

Palermo, 12
Palmach, 164
Paperman, Aaron, 17
Patton, George, 12, 79, 81, 86, 114
Pava, Simon, 92, 101, 131
Pensing, 42
Pesachowitz, 173–74
Peterson, Howard C., 136
Pilsen, 50, 112–15
Pinson, Kopel S., 176
Plaut, W. Gunther, 34
Plessner, Cal, 47
Pocking, 96, 125
Poeletti, Charles, 18
Poliakoff, Manuel, 34, 92
Pope Pius XII, 149
Poppendorf, 188
Port de Bouc, 188
Potsdam, 78
Pottenstein, 90
Prague, 112–14
Price, Byron, 76, 83

Rabbinical Assembly of America (RAA), 3, 6, 8
Rabbinical Council of America (RCA), 3, 6, 8
Rabkin, Benjamin J., 70
Rackman, Emanuel, 137–38, 175
Radom, 46
Rayfial, Leo, 70
Raymond, Otto B., 58
Red Cross, 42, 51, 59, 66, 99, 107
Regensburg, 91, 106, 131, 138
Reilly, C. J., 91
Reinhart, Emil F., 48
Rheims, 30, 103
Ribner, Herbert, 119–20, 131
Rice, James P., 98
Richmond, Milton, 60, 72
Rifkind, Simon: as replacement for Judah Nadich, 87; and the Landsberg Camp, 94–95; and Ruth Kluger, 116–17; and Abraham Klausner, 126, 172, 185; and Zalman Grinberg, 132; and reports to WJC, 133; and departure from Germany, 136; and Senator Wagner, 146
Rinehart, 98
Rock, Eli, 155
Rosen, Samuel, 27

Rosenberg, Anna M., 71–72
Rosensaft, Yossel, 132
Rubin, David I., 11–12
Ruslander, Selwyn, 18

St. Ottilien, 58, 60
St. Ottilien Conference, 109
Salzburg, 97–98, 102, 107–8, 112–14, 143
Sandhaus, Morris, 33
Sandrow, Edward, 104–5
Saperstein, Harold: meeting with Lucius B. Clay, 53–54; and Vicar André, 122–23, 131
Sar, Samuel L., 87
Schacter, Herschel, 11, 39–40, 48, 53, 55, 64
Schlactensee, 158–59
Schloss Brunninglinden Kladow, 160
Schloss Langezell, 47
Schnek, Emanuel, 21
Scholem, Gershon, 176
Schongau, 96
Schottland, Charles I., 77
Schreiber, 38
Schwabach, 90
Schwabenhausen, 58
Schwandorf, 96
Schwartz, Joseph: and the French Jewish community, 22; and Philip Bernstein, 26, 149; and Earl G. Harrison, 72; and Judah Nadich, 78; and John Hilldring, 115; and Abraham Klausner, 124; and Leo Schwarz, 183–84
Schwartzenborn, 160
Segal, Alfred, 173
Segal, Jacob, 32
Shalit, Levi, 121, 130
Shaltiel, David, 71
Shanghai, 101
Shanok, Morton, 28
Shearit Hapletah (volumes 57, 107, and 157): definition of, x, 121, 129, 130, 160, 175, 191, 197
Shubow, Joseph: and Arieh Tartakower, 54; and L. H. Hardman, 62; and Stephen S. Wise, 67–68; and representatives from Bergen-Belsen, 110; and Leon Kubowitzki, 115; and deserving recognition, 131; and involvement in Berihah, 154–55; and UNRRA camp in Berlin, 160–61
Silver, Abba Hillel, 66
Skorneck, Philip S., 155
Smith, Irving J., 59–60, 107
Smith, Walter Bedell: meeting with Judah Nadich, 78–79; visit to Feldafing, 82; visit to Landsberg, 94–96; meeting with David Ben Gurion, 116
Sobel, Louis H., 127
Spiro, Abraham, 56, 90–91, 131, 157
Srole, Leo, 93–96, 132, 157, 159, 169
Stars and Stripes, 91
Steinberg, Samuel, 186
Stern, Abraham, 165
Stern Gang, 161
Stettin, 154–55
Stevens, George, 38
Stimson, Henry L., 21, 76
Stone, Earl, 12, 13
Struth, 125
Stuttgart, 46, 49, 79–80, 83, 91–92, 125, 135, 161, 190
Supreme Headquarters, Allied Expeditionary Forces (SHAEF), 36–37, 50–53
Syrkin, Marie, 15–16

Taft, Robert A., 180
Tartakower, Arieh, 54–55, 114–15, 132
Techeyat Hamaytim, 121
Teheran, 1, 12
Teicher, Milton, 24
Teitelbaum, Samuel, 12, 19, 20, 124
Tempelhof, 159
Tempio Israelita, 17
Teuchenreuth, 96
Theresienstadt, 50, 112
Thionville, 51, 53
Tnuat Hameri, 165
Toifeld, Aaron J., 32
Torgau, 48
Toulon, 118
Trachtenberg, 24–27
Trieste, 156, 162
Trobe, Jacob, 77, 83, 126, 132, 172
Troy, Albert, 151

Truman, Harry S.: and Anna M. Rosenberg, 71–72; and Earl G. Harrison, 72–73, 76, 195; and Dwight Eisenhower, 78–79, 98; and Byron Price, 83; and the British government, 87–88, 166; and the issue of infiltration, 115–16, 146; and the attempt to admit Jews to the U.S., 142, 164, 167; and Philip Bernstein, 149–50; and Nahum Goldmann, 168
Truscott, Lucian K., 94
Turkheim, 42
Tutzing, 59

Udine, 120, 162–63
Ulio, J. A., 71
Union of American Hebrew Congregations, 172
United Jewish Appeal (UJA), 132, 176
United Nations Relief and Rehabilitation Agency (UNRRA): definition of, 2–3; and the Jewish Brigade, 18; and its limitations, 44, 83; and the Vaihingen concentration camp, 47; and the *Shearit Hapletah* volumes, 57; and Abraham Klausner, 42, 65–66, 99, 181, 183, 185; and the American Jewish Conference, 71; and the Harrison Report, 72; and Dwight Eisenhower, 82; and representatives of the American Jewish Conference, 87; and Leo Srole at the Landsberg camp, 93–95, 97; and the JDC, 123; and the World Jewish Congress, 132; and the assistants to the advisor on Jewish Affairs, 137; and Philip Bernstein, 148; and Joseph Shubow, 160–61; and Zalman Grinberg, 172; and Jack Whiting, 174; and the displaced persons chaplains, 178–79
United Nations Special Committee on Palestine (UNSCOP), 187–88
United States Forces, European Theater (USFET), 36, 53, 77–78, 97, 148
University of Michigan, 185

Unzer Leben, 121
Unzer Weg, 121–22, 129–30, 175, 188, 195

Vaihingen, 46
Vatican, 187
Verviers, 15
Vicar André, 62, 122–23
Vida, George, 15, 93
Vilna Ghetto, 175

Wagner, Robert, 146
Wahl, David R., 146
Wald, 59
Wall, Max: encounter with Hungarian Jewish teenagers, 35; and the package program, 100, 169; praise of Abraham Klausner, 130; deserving recognition, 131
Wallace, Henry A., 146
Wallenberg, 96
War Department, 8–9, 20–21, 71, 114, 126, 136
War Refugee Board (WRB), 72
Warburg, Edward M. M., 125–26, 132, 191
Warren, George L., 72, 172
Warsaw Ghetto, 15
Waxman, Shammai, 129
Weinberg, Celia, 125
Weiss, Samuel A., 70
Wels, 109
Wetzlar, 156, 160
Whiting, Jack, 174
Wildflecken, 77, 84
Winning, Charles, 47
Wise, Stephen S.: and Sylvia Neulander, 52; and Harold Saperstein, 54; and Robert Marcus, 62; and Abraham Klausner, 66–67, 69; and Joseph Shubow and Robert Marcus, 67–68; and George Warren, 72; and Robert Marcus, 76, 77; and Simon Rifkind, 95
Wolfratshausen, 83, 93
World Jewish Congress (WJC): and the JDC, 3; and the chaplains in Italy, 19; and the Civil Affairs Department (CAD) of the War Department, 20–21, 114; and the chaplains in France, 32; and the need for the chaplains to

provide continuous information, 33–34; and Robert Marcus, 40, 62, 67–68, 77; and the survivors' complaints, 45; and Herschel Schacter, 53; appreciation for chaplain's help, 54; and Abraham Klausner, 66–67, 133, 186; and response to Joseph Shubow and Robert Marcus, 68; and Judah Nadich, 87; and Simon Rifkind, 95–96, 132; and Erich Maier, 100; and Philip Bernstein, 128; and Zalman Grinberg, 172

Wurzen, 48

Yahil, Haim, 141, 144, 154, 174
Yishuv, 3, 165

Zeilsheim, 78, 83, 93, 160
Ziskind, Bernard, 106